Chasing Methuselah

Chasing Methuselah

Theology, the Body, and Slowing Human Aging

TODD T. W. DALY

Foreword by Brent Waters

CASCADE *Books* · Eugene, Oregon

CHASING METHUSELAH
Theology, the Body, and Slowing Human Aging

Copyright © 2021 Todd T. W. Daly. All rights reserved. Except for brief quotations in critical publications or reviews, no part of this book may be reproduced in any manner without prior written permission from the publisher. Write: Permissions, Wipf and Stock Publishers, 199 W. 8th Ave., Suite 3, Eugene, OR 97401.

Cascade Books
An Imprint of Wipf and Stock Publishers
199 W. 8th Ave., Suite 3
Eugene, OR 97401

www.wipfandstock.com

PAPERBACK ISBN: 978-1-5326-9800-2
HARDCOVER ISBN: 978-1-5326-9801-9
EBOOK ISBN: 978-1-5326-9802-6

Cataloguing-in-Publication data:

Names: Daly, Todd T. W., author. Waters, Brent, foreword.

Title: Chasing Methuselah : theology, the body, and slowing human aging / Todd T. W. Daly.

Description: Eugene, OR: Cascade Books, 2021 | Includes bibliographical references and index.

Identifiers: ISBN 978-1-5326-9800-2 (paperback) | ISBN 978-1-5326-9801-9 (hardcover) | ISBN 978-1-5326-9802-6 (ebook)

Subjects: LCSH: Longevity—Moral and ethical aspects. | Longevity—Theology. | Medical technology—Moral and ethical aspects.

Classification: RA776.75 .D33 2021 (paperback) | RA776 (ebook)

02/05/21

In memory of, and gratitude for, Harriet, who endured very old age with grace, and her husband Warren, who didn't get a chance to.

Blessed is He who put on Adam
And by means of the Wood of the Cross
Made him leap back into Paradise.
—St Ephrem, *Hymns on the Fast*

Contents

Foreword by Brent Waters — ix
Preface — xi
Acknowledgments — xiii
Abbreviations — xv
Introduction — 1

Chapter 1   Gilgamesh, Gonads, and Gerontogenes: Life Extension Moves from Legend to Laboratory — 19

Chapter 2   Theology and the Development of Aging as a Medical Problem — 78

Chapter 3   Relief of Man's Estate: Francis Bacon and the Theological Origins of the Modern Quest to Slow Aging — 113

Chapter 4   Adam Again: *Theōsis* and the Ascetically Ageless Body — 156

Chapter 5   The Last Adam and Slowing Aging — 204

Conclusion — 255
Bibliography — 259
Subject Index — 295
Scripture Index — 305

Foreword

Todd Daly has written a timely book about aging (no pun intended). Among its many accomplishments, modern medicine has extended longevity. Many people are living longer and healthier lives. There is no reason to challenge or question the efficacy of this achievement. Yet medicine is now waging a war against aging, treating it as a disease, and the more Promethean transhumanists promise that it is only a matter of time before technology transforms us into immortal beings. Daly does not decry these efforts in any wholesale manner, but as a skillful theologian and bioethicist he reminds the reader that the issue is more complex than first meets the eye. He carefully deploys a Christian anthropology and teleology, insisting that the quest for greater longevity always poses the question why should we want to live longer, and reminds the transhumanists that even if our wildest dreams should come true, we will still remain mortal creatures.

Daly has also written an engaging book. He draws upon the Christian theological tradition and a number of contemporary theologians to trace the lineage of our current circumstances. He explains clearly how we got to where we are today, and that arrival is free of any unnecessary condemnation or commendation, as well as any unhelpful appeal to an imagined utopia or apocalypse lying just over the horizon. The combination of theology and ethics gently pushes the reader to consider who they are as embodied and thereby finite creatures who grow old over time. And that is no reason to despair, for that is what creatures are intended to do by their creator.

BRENT WATERS

Preface

In this book I examine, from a Christian perspective, contemporary attempts to lengthen the human lifespan by slowing human aging. Twenty years ago, longevity science was struggling for legitimacy, and hence the number of ethical treatments engaging the science were relatively sparse. While the field has grown considerably over the last two decades, Christian engagement with this issue—with a couple of notable exceptions—continues to lag behind. This book reflects one attempt to address this gap from within the Christian faith.

If the world of anti-aging medicine is strange, the discipline of Christian ethics is no less strange. Just as there are several promising pathways to longevity, the same might be said for methodologies in Christian ethics. There is rarely agreement on the nature, method, or even purpose of Christian ethics. In this Christian examination of longevity research, I consider the biomedical project of slowing aging in light of the knowledge of God as revealed in Jesus Christ as witnessed to in Scripture, and as proclaimed by those who have followed the creeds of the Christian faith throughout the centuries, a position that might very well be criticized along methodological lines, but will not be defended here. This means that this book is no less a work in theological ethics insofar as it brings a christological anthropology to bear on the scientific quest to attenuate aging by manipulating the body. Indeed, insofar as aging-attenuating science aims to remake the human body, we should expect Christology to have something to say on the matter. In rushing too quickly into these theological concerns, however, we run the risk of ignoring a fundamental, yet critical question of Christian (indeed all) ethics. The question "What is going on?," claimed H. Richard Niebuhr (1894–1962), is probably the most difficult, yet crucial, question to ask.

In the first three chapters of this book I attempt to answer this question. In surveying the long and eventful history of the search for that elusive *elixir vitae*, I consider how aging has come to be seen primarily as an enemy and how the quest to bring it under technological control shapes our understanding of the body. The expansive nature of this question required a jumping around with respect to chronology. While the first chapter follows a strict chronological order, chapters 2 and 3, for thematic reasons, do not. For during this study it became clear that theology had a role to play in these shifting attitudes on aging and death. I was surprised however to discover the origins of this modern biomedical project to slow aging were *theological*. Francis Bacon (1561–1626) argued for a new, practical science devoted to regaining a measure of control over nature in order to slow human aging, thereby regaining the benefits enjoyed by prelapsarian Adam and the biblical patriarchs, a project he framed as a return to the garden of Eden.

The last two chapters take up Bacon's ideas and critique them from two vantage points—the first and last Adam—both of which have something to say about the human body as it relates to aging and death. Drawing in particular upon Bacon's rhetoric of a scientific return to Eden, I consider the insights of Athanasius (251–356) and St. Antony (296–373), who also spoke of slowing aging as recapturing the life of prelapsarian Adam. However, their understanding of regaining longevity was situated in the moral task of character formation, which focused on fasting and prayer, understood as reordering one's body and soul. I use this vision to critique the Baconian, or modern biomedical project of aging-attenuation. To give however an explicitly Christian response to life extension, I conclude the work by reflecting on the implications of the *last* Adam, Jesus Christ. Here I draw on the insights of Karl Barth's (1886–1968) exposition of the real man Jesus—particularly the relationship between Jesus' body and soul. For the real man Jesus is determinative for both our understanding of what it means to have—and indeed be—an aging body, and the moral disorders that follow when the body and soul are "out of order." I conclude this study by drawing some tentative conclusions concerning both the promise and the dangers of aging-attenuation science.

Acknowledgments

The composition of this book is inevitably the result of more people than could possibly be named and thanked here. This includes several authors of books and articles who have taken time to write on things both mysterious and mundane, who are known to me only by what they have written, many of whom are no longer alive to clarify, elaborate, or defend what they have written. Without such authors it would not have been possible to conceive this project, much less complete it. There are also numerous teachers, classmates, and students who have blessed me with their wisdom, thoughtfulness, and friendship.

I'm particularly appreciative of those who have helped me to pursue and complete this particular project by offering words of encouragement and generous feedback, especially Nicholas Adams, James Herrick, Michael Northcott, and Robert Song. Nicholas Adams and Michael Northcott where particularly helpful in teaching me that the Church Fathers should be critical dialogue partners in Christian ethics. A very brief, but remarkably fruitful discussion with the late church historian and theologian David Wright (1937–2008), who suggested I investigate the Desert Fathers with regards to fasting, has influenced this book immensely. No single meeting or discussion has shaped this project more than the sixty minutes I spent soaking up his wisdom one summer morning in New College's Rainy Hall at the University of Edinburgh. But I'm no less grateful for the sustained support I've received from many others. I owe a special debt of gratitude to C. Ben Mitchell, whose constructive criticism, generous feedback, and words of encouragement in the early stages were instrumental to seeing this project reach its conclusion. It is a blessing to be called your friend. I'm also thankful for the relationships formed through a fellowship with the

Paul Ramsey Institute at the Center for Bioethics and Culture led by Jennifer Lahl, particularly Brian Green, Bill Hurlbut, Gilbert Meilaender, and Christopher White.

It has also been an honor and blessing to serve as a fellow at the Center for Bioethics and Human Dignity. This fellowship has afforded me ample opportunities for fruitful discussions and instructive comments on this project. I'm thankful for Paige Cunningham, Matthew Eppinette, Claretta Dupree, Michael Sleasman, and especially Brent Waters, for his insightful observations on this project. This book has also benefitted through interactions with my thoughtful colleagues at Urbana Theological Seminary: Andrew Blaski, Kenneth Cuffey, Melody Green, Michael McQueen, Peter Spychalla, and Joe Thomas. I have also benefitted greatly from Ronald Cole-Turner, Mark Galli, James Kushiner, Calvin Mercer, and Tracy Trothen, whose critical feedback improved my writing, even as they graciously afforded me opportunities to publish material related to this book. Others who are more deserving than mere acknowledgment include Scott Althaus, Demian Alvarez, Kay Avila, Hunter Bailey, Jeffrey Bishop, Randy Boltinghouse, Lee Bond, Heidi Campbell, Elaine Carovilla, Jay Chandra, Bill Cheshire, Cliff Christians, Bob Cranston, Jim Critchlow, Jason Curtis, Tom and Diane Daly, Terry Daly, Brent Dickman, Pearce Durst, Ginger Eppinette, David Fergusson, Christopher Fischer, Marcel and Miryung Fontijn, Fabrice Jotterand, Lauris Kaldjian, Chris Keith, Darren Kennedy, Sylvia Klauser, Irene Koshik, Bob Kuo, Robert Kurka, Dan Lahl, Callum MacKellar, Andrew McFarlane, Paul McNamara, Joylon Mitchell, Ryan Neal, Carey Newman, Paul Nimmo, David Norman, Ned O'Gorman, Donal O'Mathuna, S. Jay Olshanksy, Eric Ortlund, Suzanne Owen, Guy Richard, David Richards, Brian Sauder, Craig Sayle, Ash Scarborough, Patrick Smith, David Suryk, Paul Thomason, and Bruce Vojak.

Lastly, and most importantly, I'd like to thank my children, Skye and Grey, who daily remind me what really matters, and my wife, Ann, who always finds something redemptive in my writing, and whose encouragement constantly wards off the encroachment of destructive doubt. You are more than I deserve.

Abbreviations

ANF	*The Ante-Nicene Fathers: Translations of the Writings of the Fathers Down to AD 325*
CD	Karl Barth, *Church Dogmatics*
KD	Karl Barth, *Kirchliche Dogmatic*
NPNF1	*A Select Library of Nicene and Post-Nicene Fathers of the Christian Church, First Series*
NPNF2	*A Select Library of Nicene and Post-Nicene Fathers of the Christian Church, Second Series*
WFB	*The Works of Francis Bacon, Baron of Verulam, Viscount St. Alban, and Lord High Chancellor of England*
WNE	*The Works of Nathanael Emmons, D.D., Third Pastor of the Church in Franklin, Massachusetts*

Introduction

The idea is to die young as late as possible.

—Ashley Montagu

You can live to be a hundred if you give up all the things that make you want to live to be a hundred.

—Woody Allen

Remember also your Creator in the days of your youth, before the evil days come, and the years draw nigh, when you will say, "I have no pleasure in them."

—Eccl 12:1 RSV

A TALE OF TWO ENDINGS

"You're trying to get rid of me," protested Bill to his son. Now in his eighties, Bill had spent a significant portion of the last three years coping with an increasingly compromised body and declining mental skills, all while trying to care for his wife, who was suffering from several maladies of her own. Bill often felt belittled, patronized, and cajoled by those who thought they knew better, especially his own children. It wasn't always like this. Apart from a heart attack he suffered a few years prior, Bill maintained relatively good health until his retirement at age seventy-seven. Though he had clearly lost a step or two after the heart attack, he was still a very gifted leader with a quick wit, astonishing abilities of collaboration, and a reputation as someone who could get things accomplished. Bill especially enjoyed deep, enriching, and challenging conversations with his eldest son Cal, a neurologist. But shortly after Bill's retirement, his mental proclivities began to slip away. Cal noticed that their conversations had grown shorter; the range of subjects they discussed narrowed and became more focused on the past. Gone were the days where Bill could initiate and carry on nuanced, open-ended conversations on a wide array of current events. Over time discussions would dwindle to platitudes about the weather. Interaction became one-directional, typically in the form of concrete matters of expedience: "Are you taking your medication?" "Are you working with your physical therapist?" Having recently been treated for prostate cancer and proctitis—inflammation of the rectum and anus—Bill was now dealing with occasional bouts of bronchitis and delirium. Hospital stays were growing longer; life at the assisted living facility was becoming more difficult. The frequent hospitalization also made it harder for Bill to visit his wife Marjorie, who had been in a nursing home for some time. This hospitalization proved a mixed blessing for Bill, however, as he was often subjected to hours of verbal abuse from Marjorie, who was suffering from the collective effects of severe dementia, frequent urinary tract infections, arthritis, osteonecrosis, and a weak heart.

When Bill was strong enough to leave the hospital, Cal and his siblings were able to have him placed in a room adjacent to Marjorie at the nursing home, which enabled him to spend more time with his wife while allowing him the rest he needed. By this time Marjorie had become extremely confused, now mixing her days and nights. But at least Bill could get some sleep in his own room while nurses attended to Marjorie. This situation seemed relatively tolerable until Bill came down with yet another case of bronchitis and was readmitted to the hospital. It was clear that Bill's ability to continue the relentless battle against the physical, emotional, and psychological effects of aging was all but spent with his latest setback. He would never leave the hospital. Thankfully, Cal and the rest of Bill's children were able to read Scripture, sing hymns, and say goodbye, even though Bill was by this time too weak to respond verbally. Conversations were all one-way now, and eventually Bill began to tire of these as well. One afternoon he cut off his son Cal in mid-sentence, summoning the last bit of his energy to gesture with his index finger across his throat as if to say "enough." Bill died three days later at eighty-three years of age. Marjorie was moved to a facility nearer to family, where over the next year she would be hospitalized six different times for recurring bouts of pneumonia and several small strokes, recovering well enough each time to make it back to the nursing home, but a little weaker and more confused after each hospitalization. Though largely confined to the wheelchair or bed, Marjorie was still able to attend Cal's church adjacent to the home. While her periods of lucidity were becoming increasingly rare, she never forgot the lyrics to the church hymns she sang as a child. When Marjorie sang them, it was as if the fog of dementia momentarily lifted, transforming her into her "old self." The fog however always returned. Shortly after her last hospital stay, Marjorie returned again to the nursing home, where she died in her wheelchair as she was waiting to be taken to the Sunday evening church service.

A year before Alexander Graham Bell completed his invention of the telephone, Jeanne Louise Calment was born on February 21, 1875 in Arles, the small French village where she would spend her entire life. Madame Calment would die 122 years later as the longest-lived person in modern history. Born into a bourgeoisie family, Calment was never required to work, and spent a large portion of her life pursuing the leisurely activities of tennis, bicycling, piano, and opera. She became something of a celebrity in France thirteen years after her one-hundredth birthday, when the town of Arles celebrated the centenary of Vincent van Gogh's (1853–1890) visit. Calment had met van Gogh herself when she was thirteen, but would often say that she found him unkempt and generally unimpressive. Thereafter the village began to publicly recognize her birthday, celebrating what would become known as "Jeanne D'Arles." Madame Calment married her wealthy cousin and later had a daughter, but she would outlive them both, losing her daughter to pneumonia in 1936 and husband to food poisoning several years later. Her only grandson, whom she raised after the death of her daughter, tragically died in an auto accident in 1963. Calment remained active throughout the majority of her later life, taking up fencing at age eighty-five, and continued to bicycle into her early hundreds. From the age of ninety on, Madame Calment was supported by the income of Andre-Francois Raffray, who signed a contingency contract paying a lifetime annuity of 2,500 Francs per month in return for ownership of Calment's flat upon her death, a common practice in France. Though Madame Calment's parents were long-lived (her mother and father living to eighty-six and ninety-four respectively), Mr. Raffray could hardly have anticipated that Madame Calment would outlive them by nearly three decades. He died at age seventy-seven before ever taking ownership of her flat, his family continuing to cover the annuity until Calment's death.

In spite of these profound losses, Madame Calment largely retained an indefatigable spirit with considerable mental acuity for most of her life. Calment's story is all the more remarkable considering she took no special precautions to extend her life. She started smoking at age twenty-one—limiting herself to two cigarettes daily—and quit when she reached age 117, apparently because she didn't like asking for help to light them. Calment ate about two kilos of chocolate per week until her doctor was finally able to convince her to give it up at the age of 119. When asked, she attributed her longevity to port wine and olive oil. Though she appeared to be immune from many of the maladies that afflict the elderly, Calment eventually moved into a nursing home at 110, and was largely confined to a wheelchair when she fell and fractured her femur five years later. Even as her body continued to deteriorate, however—during her last few years she was nearly blind and deaf—Calment maintained a razor-sharp wit and a wry sense of humor. When one of the attendees of her one hundred twentieth birthday party bid her farewell until next year, she retorted, "Why not? You don't seem to be in such bad health."[1]

From a certain distance, these two endings speak of two disparate paths of old age, though all such paths eventually converge. Should we be fortunate enough to escape the diseases that often kill in the prime of life—cancer, diabetes, liver, kidney, and blood disorders to name a few—the chances are quite high that our own endings will follow a similar script. It is more likely however that the odds of experiencing Bill's or Marjorie's later years is significantly higher than Madame Calment's. Without trying to romanticize the afflictions that nearly always accompany aging, if given a choice, most of us would prefer Madam Calment's ending, though these stories attest, in their own ways, to the harsh realities of the inevitable decline that comes with aging. In fact, we would much rather live a long life and die "in the pink of health." Despite all of the advances in medicine over the last several decades, however, the current trends in longevity suggest that the great majority of us will not be so fortunate. Recent advances in aging research however may one day enable us to live for a century or more in a state of relatively good health. A quest is underway to extend the human life-span by slowing aging, bolstered by success in laboratory animals. Aging attenuation has moved from legend to the laboratory. The inevitability of aging and death is now being seriously questioned by the relatively young scientific disciplines of biogerontology, evolutionary biology, and pharmacogenetics.

The quest for longevity by slowing human aging may seem a strange one, given that life expectancies have steadily climbed over the last century. Those born in the most developed nations during the first decade of the new millennium can expect to reach seventy-five or eighty years or more, as increasing numbers are living into their eighties and even nineties, which reflects a near doubling of the life-span of those born at the turn of the twentieth century.[2] A 2010 report by the Federal Interagency Forum on Aging-

1. Allard et al., *Jeanne Calment*, 18.
2. Fukuyama, *Posthuman Future*, 57. See http://www.demog.berkeley.edu/~andrew/1918/figure2.html and http://www.cia.gov/cia/publications/factbook/geos/us.html. In the United States the life expectancy for babies born in 2000 was 79.6 and 73.5 years

Related Statistics flatly stated the obvious: "Americans are living longer than ever before."[3] These gains in longevity can largely be attributed to advances in medicine such as the reduction of infant mortality, and the effective immunization of tuberculosis, smallpox, and other diseases. Improved hygienic conditions have also contributed to our increased longevity. Despite these increases in longevity, however, there has been no substantial change in the *maximum* human life-span of approximately 120 years, highlighting the fact that we have not altered the rate of the human aging process itself. Though the last century has witnessed unprecedented increases in life expectancy, it is now widely acknowledged that we are approaching our biological limit to longevity, and with it the recognition that conventional approaches to medicine that seek to treat or cure individual diseases will continue to yield only marginal gains in the overall human longevity.[4]

These gains in life expectancy have however been accompanied by an increase in chronic illness and diseases associated with aging. Acute infectious diseases like tuberculosis, rheumatic fever, and smallpox have been replaced by chronic maladies associated with aging such as Parkinson's, Alzheimer's, arteriosclerosis, arthritis, adult onset diabetes, chronic obstructive pulmonary disease, and cancer.[5] Marginal gains in life expectancy mean that increasing numbers of individuals are likely to experience a prolonged state of decline before death. Though life may now be *longer*, it is not necessarily *healthier*. In 2005 the President's Council on Bioethics noted that "*the defining characteristic of our time seems to be that we are both younger longer and older longer.*"[6] Indeed, though life expectancies have been hovering around 78.7 years since 2014 for the total US population, life expectancies at ages sixty-five and eighty-five have continued to increase.[7]

---

for females and males respectively. There are of course other eras prior to the twentieth century where life expectancies exceeded those in 1900. For instance, it has been noted that in Stratford-upon-Avon that nearly one-third of men and one-fifth of women lived beyond sixty years of age between the period of 1570 and 1630. Moreover, the average age of appointment of the archbishops of Canterbury for the nine bishops spanning the seventeenth century was sixty, while the average age of death was seventy-three. See also Haycock, *Mortal Coil*, 9.

3. The Federal Interagency Forum on Aging-Related Statistics, *Older Americans 2010*, 24.

4. Olshansky, "Session 2." See also President's Council, *Beyond Therapy*, 166.

5. Fries, "Aging, Natural Death," 132.

6. President's Council, *Taking Care*, 6, 22.

7. Xu et al., "Mortality in the United States, 2018," 1. In 2018 life expectancy at birth increased by 0.1 year from 78.6 years in 2017, largely due to a decrease in mortality in cancer, unintentional injuries, chronic respiratory diseases, and heart disease. US life expectancy actually decreased 0.2 years between 2010 and 2014, and decreased 0.3

Under current mortality conditions, those who live to see sixty-five can expect to live on average about nineteen more years.[8] In 2010 there were approximately six million Americans aged eighty-five or older, a figure that is expected to nearly quadruple to twenty-one million by 2050.[9] Though we may experience a longer period of health and vitality than previous generations, we are also "far more likely to suffer protracted periods of age-related disability and dependence because we live to ages that few people reached in the past."[10] In 2005 the average duration of this decline was approximately two years, a figure that is only likely to increase.[11]

The American Heart Association (AHA) plans on taking aggressive action to address the growing trend of people living longer, but in a state of generally declining or poor health. In early 2020, the AHA released a massive 458-page report outlining several steps to heart health with the aim of increasing the healthspan—a somewhat amorphous and vague concept—by two years (from sixty-six years to sixty-eight years) worldwide by 2030.[12] Their approach to promoting heart health, called "Life's Simple 7," includes advice on keeping active and maintaining a healthy weight, becoming informed about good and bad cholesterol, learning about blood sugar and diabetes mellitus, abstaining from all forms of tobacco, pursuing a heart-healthy diet, and keeping blood pressure at healthy levels. While these goals seem laudable, accepting their calculation of sixty-six years on average for good health would mean that the last thirteen years of a person's life, on average, might be described as a state of suboptimal or declining health. The degree to which their hygienic regimen—though backed by sound science—will be adopted, is something enormously difficult to predict. There is also troubling data, for instance, showing that the marginal increases in pursing a healthy lifestyle (e.g., physical activity, proper diet, abstinence from tobacco) are being offset by rising obesity rates in children and adults, "abysmally low" rates of physical activity, uncontrolled high blood sugar rates, and the vaping epidemic among the young today.[13]

However one describes a relative state of health beyond one's late sixties, living through this later period of life increases the likelihood that our

---

years from 2014–2017. See Xu et al., "Mortality in the United States, 2018," 5.

8. Federal Interagency Forum on Aging-Related Statistics, *Older Americans 2016*, 26.
9. Alzheimer's Association, "2011 Alzheimer's Disease Facts and Figures," 12.
10. President's Council, *Taking Care*, 7, 11, 19–20.
11. President's Council, *Taking Care*, 12.
12. Verani et al., "Heart Disease and Stroke Statistics—2020 Update." For the concept of healthspan see Kaeberlein, "How Healthy is the Healthspan Concept?"
13. American Heart Association, "Living Longer is Important."

last two or three years will follow a script similar to that of Bill or Marjorie. The idea of a prolonged period of decline with a steadily, irrevocable diminishment in capacities is deeply abhorrent in a culture that celebrates youthfulness, productivity, and independence. We live in an age where the specter of death and the decline of old age is increasingly concealed from public view in hospital wards, intensive care units, and nursing homes. Death is also obscured in daily life and the seemingly innumerable demands placed upon our attention, driving thoughts of our own mortality far from our collective consciousness.[14] We hope for a sudden, unexpected death in one's sleep before the diseases, debilities, and frailty of old age are able to fully set in, before we are forced to navigate the progressive decline and painful betrayal of a body that is increasingly unable to accommodate the desires that outpace it. Despite the tremendous increases in longevity over the last century, death remains an affront to our scientific capabilities, a reminder of our limited ability to control nature. One could easily argue that the fear of death and decline is a key motivating factor of the modern biomedical project that seeks to delay death as long as possible. While technology has enabled us to conceal the death of others and avoid our own death by putting it off for several years, our fear of decline and death has not abated. For all of the advances in medicine over the last century, the likelihood of experiencing and ending like Bill or Marjorie increases with each new medical breakthrough.

AGING ATTENUATION COMES OF AGE

Over the last two decades however, scientists and researchers have made substantial progress in uncovering the biological processes of the human aging process, suggesting that aging may not be as intractable as once thought. Some have declared that "the belief that aging is an immutable process, programmed by evolution, is now known to be wrong."[15] We may no longer need homespun remedies like port wine and olive oil. The search for greatly extended lives has moved from the realms of myth, magic, and quackery to legitimate science. Advances in the relatively young field of biogerontology—the study of human aging—have offered promising insights

---

14. The literature here is immense. See May, "Sacral Power"; Anderson, *Theology, Death and Dying*; Ariès, *Hour Of Our Death*; Bauman, *Mortality, Immortality and Other Life Strategies*; Becker, *Denial of Death*; Choron, *Death and Western Thought*; Hauerwas, *Naming the Silences*; Kübler-Ross, *On Death and Dying*; Mitford, *American Way of Death*.

15. Olshansky et al., "Pursuit of the Longevity Dividend," 28.

into the prolongation of healthy life, leaving some scientists optimistic that human aging may soon become the latest process to yield to technological manipulative effort. Though not all not who study the human aging process are intent on slowing it down, several procedures have been devised for expressly this purpose. Techniques like selective breeding, caloric restriction, and genetic manipulation have not only demonstrated that the aging process can be slowed, but have also shown that doing so extends the health of these mammals and multicellular organisms—in some cases well beyond what was once thought possible. For instance, researchers have lengthened the life-span of the nematode worm *sevenfold* by altering a single gene.[16] The life-spans of laboratory mice have increased by 70 percent by utilizing a combination of genetic alteration and caloric restriction.[17] These successes suggest that aging attenuation is now garnering more mainstream medical support.[18] In 2019 the *MIT Technology Review* devoted an issue to the science and potential consequences of living longer. That scientists have been able to extend the period of *health* for these organisms gives researchers hope that similar techniques would work with humans, producing similar results, assuaging fear of a protracted physical and cognitive decline.[19] One year earlier *Time* magazine released an issue with the title "How to Live Longer," containing brief reviews on the science of longevity such as "Is an Anti-Aging Pill on the Horizon?"[20] Such questions are no longer far-fetched. In 2019 researchers were surprised to discover that human aging (as measured by four epigenetic clocks that measure cellular aging) had actually been *reversed* in patients who received a combination of drugs aimed at regenerating thymus tissue in adults.[21] Geneticist Steve Horvath, one of several designers of the study at the University of California Los Angeles, expressed his surprise: "I'd expected to see slowing down of the clock, but not a reversal."[22]

---

16. Partridge and Gems, "Mechanisms of Ageing," 165–75. The life-span was increased from thirty-one days to just under two hundred days.

17. Bartke et al., "Extending the Lifespan of Long-lived Mice," 412.

18. Several have noted the current battles for legitimacy and orthodoxy within the field of gerontology. See Juengst et al., "Biogerontology, 'Anti-aging Medicine.'"

19. Classic examples of such fear are presented in the story of Tithonus, who was kidnapped by Eos, Titan goddess of the dawn, in order to be her lover. She petitioned Zeus to grant Tithonus immortality, forgetting however to ask for his eternal youth. A more recent example is found in the Struldbruggs of Jonathan Swift's *Gulliver's Travels*, who aged without any hope of dying.

20. Sifferlin, "Is an Anti-Aging Pill on the Horizon?," 72.

21. Fahy et al., "Reversal of Epigenetic Aging," e13028.

22. Abbott, "Trial Hints at Age-Clock Reversal," 173.

These breakthroughs have captured the attention of aging baby boomers and venture capitalists alike, spawning new organizations like AgeX, Elysium, GenuCure, Juvenescence, the Methuselah Foundation, and Rejuvenate Bio, devoted to understanding aging in order to bring it under technological control.[23] Some of these companies have focused their efforts on creating pharmaceuticals that mimic the life-extending effects afforded by dietary restriction and genetic manipulation. Elixir Pharmaceuticals, for instance, was working on identifying "longevity genes" that will one day yield drugs to both slow aging and reduce the disease and disability that accompany it. Elixir obtained an exclusive license from the University of Connecticut to patent applications relating to Dr. Stephen L. Helfand's discovery of the INDY gene (I'm Not Dead Yet), which effectively doubles the life-span of fruit flies. Though Elixir was shut down in 2013, research on the INDY gene continues to show promise.[24]

It is clear that efforts to modulate human aging are driven in part by a desire to shorten the period of decline before death. There are however at least two general narratives of longevity within the field of aging research. One theory, known as the "compressed morbidity approach," seeks to expand the human *health* span within current biological limits.[25] It is hoped that slowing the aging process will "add life to one's years" by mitigating many of the diseases associated with aging, thereby reducing or compressing the period of decline preceding death. Those adopting this approach argue that the proper goal of attenuating aging "is for all of us to lead long lives free of chronic disease and disability, and then die rather quickly as we reach the limits of the human life span, 'worn out' from the fundamental processes of aging."[26] This approach seems largely uncontroversial and indeed warranted, given especially the pronouncement by President's Council on Bioethics that we are headed toward a "mass geriatric society."[27]

Compressing the period of morbidity garners further economic support given the increasing medical costs in caring for the elderly, where the

23. The Methuselah Foundation is a non-profit organization devoted to the purpose of significantly extending the healthy life-span through scientific research. Each year they award a cash prize, called M-Prize to the team of scientists who breaks the record for engineering the longest-lived mouse, in addition to a prize for the team able to "develop the most successful late onset rejuvenation." See http://www.mprize.org/.

24. Willmes, "Longevity Gene INDY."

25. Post and Binstock, "Introduction," 2. This term can be traced back to James F. Fries. See Fries, "Aging, Natural Death."

26. Juengst et al., "Biogerontology, 'Anti-aging Medicine,'" 25. See also Austad, "Adding Years to Life," where the author admits the desire to die "in the pink of health" as the ideal, though there is no known way to ensure this.

27. President's Council, *Taking Care*, xvii, 11.

most common age-associated diseases like cancer, heart disease, and stroke account for nearly 50 percent of the United States healthcare budget, and where, at the turn of the last century, 90 percent of healthcare expenditures are spent on extraordinary care often required in the last two to three years of life.[28] When one considers that the number of Americans with a single age-related malady like Alzheimer's Disease is expected to rise from 5.4 million in 2011 to nearly 16 million by 2050, with the accompanying economic toll rising from $183 billion (2011) to over $1 trillion annually by midcentury, it seems clear that the impact of Alzheimer's alone may prove catastrophic to our healthcare system.[29] Positively, slowing human aging would likely produce what some have called a "Longevity Dividend."[30] Economists are well aware of the 0.3 to 0.5 percent increase of income per capita for countries that have even a modest five-year life expectancy advantage over others.[31] This gain is significant when one considers that the average per capita income growth for all countries between 1965 and 1990 was approximately 2 percent per year. University of Chicago economists calculated that the gains in life expectancy from 1970 to 2000 "added about $3.2 trillion *per year* to national wealth."[32] Given the potential economic promise of even a moderate increase in average life-span, coupled with the more alarming economic indicators, the compressed morbidity scenario is indeed extremely attractive, even as proponents may not entirely rule out attaining life-spans that eventually exceed current biological limits.

The second narrative, which might be called the "adding years to life" approach, is more ambitious. These scientists and gerontologists believe that the current biological limit to human longevity is a temporary barrier that will one day be greatly surpassed, yielding healthy life-spans that potentially stretch to several hundred years. Their main hope is to delay the onset of age-associated pathologies as long as possible—in addition to compressing the period of morbidity—though it is not entirely clear that slowing the aging process itself would do anything more than push back the initial occurrence of a long physiological decline.[33] Though the first approach may

28. Klatz, "Anti-Aging Medicine," 61.

29. Alzheimer's Association, "2011 Alzheimer's Disease Facts and Figures," 12. The report also estimates that 5.2 million of the 5.4 million estimated sufferers were over sixty-five years of age.

30. Olshansky et al., "Longevity Dividend," 31. See also Olshansky, "Wrinkle in Time."

31. Bloom and Canning, "Health and Wealth," 1207-09.

32. Murphy and Topel, "Value of Health," 872.

33. There is a movement known as transhumanism or posthumanism that aspires towards earthly immortality, or life as long as one wants it. See Klein, ed., *Scientific Conquest of Death*.

be far less controversial, this latter approach, for obvious reasons, is more attractive.

Though conflicts will likely remain regarding the overall goal of longevity medicine, it is difficult to maintain the distinction between slowing aging for the compression of morbidity and slowing aging for an extended life. Common to both narratives however is the assumption that suffering in the form of aging is inimical to human flourishing, a doctrine that drives much of biomedicine. If indeed aging is construed primarily as suffering, then, as Eric Juengst has astutely observed, "delaying age-associated illnesses as long as possible before death is the obvious goal, whether within or beyond the historical life span."[34] A second commonality between these approaches to aging attenuation is their instrumental stance taken toward it. While in some way death may still be medicine's *ultimate* enemy, aging is now the more *immediate* enemy.[35] Though historically aging has not been considered a disease, it is increasingly considered as a disorder amenable to clinical therapy. Despite these internal conflicts, the idea of a significantly prolonged healthy life has captured the public's imagination, as demonstrated by an increased willingness to invest considerable resources in attempts to merely perpetuate the appearance of youth. Indeed, over one hundred million Americans already use some form of anti-aging regimen to mask its effects, in the form of pills, periodic fasting, or plastic surgery.

In a climate of both increased expectations concerning life expectancy and a growing awareness that our endings are likely to be drawn out affairs marked by deterioration and dependency, the possibility of slowing down the aging process has become increasingly attractive. A life that spans well beyond the biblical threescore and ten seems the perfect antidote for a culture increasingly obsessed with youth and morbidly fearful of death and decline. Even the more modest goal of maximizing health within current human biological limits of roughly 120 is significant; who at age seventy would *not* want an additional fifty years of relative health? If we were able to one day attenuate aging in accordance with our desires, it would seem that most would readily want to do so, supposing that the standard of living remains high. Indeed, the list of possibilities and interests always outstrips the span of human life, whether our desires are driven by hedonistic or humanist impulses.

To date, the ethics of aging attenuation contain assumptions that often go unchallenged, leaving fundamental questions unasked. Questions such

---

34. Juengst et al., "Biogerontology, 'Anti-aging Medicine,'" 26.

35. Olshansky, "Session 2." Olshansky asserts that "aging should be the enemy, not death. Going after the aging process itself, I think is fundamental."

as whether or not slowing down aging is a good thing, whether aging should be treated as a technological problem, or how living longer might impact our relationship with God, one another, nonhuman creation, and the environment often go unarticulated. Much of this has to do with the hegemonic influence of science on ethical discussions where a toxic confluence of manifest destiny and technological determinism proves inimical to ethical concerns beyond utility and consequences, though consequences certainly matter. For several in the scientific community, the pursuit of aging attenuation is a foregone conclusion. Indeed, the search for the means to produce youthful health has been described as "no less than a matter of national necessity."[36] One gets the sense that the deeper questions surrounding aging are either irrelevant or have already been settled. Since, for instance, biologist Tom Kirkwood sees slowing aging as an indisputable good, his concerns are primarily methodological—"whether we will use germ-line or somatic gene therapy, and what gene delivery system we might use."[37] Others admit that moral concerns mean little to the inevitable march of gaining new knowledge. Whether slowing aging is socially desirable or not, notes Steven Austad, "if science uncovers therapies that can do it, those therapies will be employed."[38] Whatever the potential anthropological, social, and cultural upheavals that might result from significant gains in life extension, we must simply "prepare for them as best we can."[39] Even skeptics admit that the technological imperative to control nature will likely continue on undeterred.[40] Those who dare question life extension are often accused of irrationally protecting a "cramped and limited vision of human nature."[41] There is also an underlying hubris at work in assuming that science will successfully mitigate any unforeseen technological problem with better technology.

This is not to deny that a longer, healthier life may be good. After all, if life is a good gift of God, it is not immediately clear why a longer life would *not* be better. Even here however, one would think that the means by

---

36. Perry, "Rise of the Gero-Techs," 57. Even those critical of the aging-attenuation project like Daniel Callahan agree with Perry's assessment, though Callanan sees "national necessity" as another way of saying "research imperative." See Callahan and Topinkova, "Is Aging a Preventable or Curable Disease?"; Callahan, *What Price Better Health?*, ch. 3.

37. Kirkwood, *Time of Our Lives*, 228.

38. Austad, *Why We Age*, 181. Others acknowledge that the coming of biomedical technologies to extend human life is inevitable. See Olshansky and Carnes, *Quest for Immortality*, 185.

39. de Grey et al., "Time to Talk SENS," 453, 460.

40. Medvedev, "Structural Basis of Aging," 16.

41. Bailey, "Forever Young."

which this might be achieved matters greatly. Yet, the means are too readily overlooked or ignored in much of the contemporary ethical discussion surrounding aging-attenuation, bearing witness to the domination of consequentialist thought, roughly translated as "the end justifies the means." A consequentialist framework however is blind to moral traditions and resists questions concerning one's character and the ordering of one's values in favor of calculating the likely outcomes as the sole determinant of rightness.[42] Whether one argues for or against slowing aging along consequentialist lines, the arguments and counterarguments are often plagued by interminability, a key feature of contemporary moral debates.[43] Moreover, the future often proves unkind to predictive calculations, as unforeseen outcomes inevitably mock what was once thought to be comprehensive preparedness. Certainly, the potential consequences of a particular action or practice ought to play some role in moral reflection, but to focus solely on likely or desired outcomes obscures more fundamental moral questions, questions like those posed above.

Dorothy Sayers (1893–1957), genius of the detective novel, was acutely aware of the genre's inherent shortcomings (and hence its attractiveness) insofar as these novels deliberately define everything as a finite problem capable of being solved "without remainder." She observed how we tend to look upon all phenomena and even life itself in this way. But in order to persuade ourselves that we can solve life too, says Sayers, we define life in ways that admit of a solution, ways that will always prove unacceptably reductive. She points out that approaching all phenomena as problems is almost absurd. "Can one solve a rose?" she asks. The question is nearly meaningless, unless one reduces the rose to its chemical composition or a complex geometrical description, or perhaps if one wanted to create a lime green rose with bright orange polka dots. However, even if a chemist were to fully describe its composition, observes Sayers, the rose is no less "solved," nor is its chemical makeup of any use to the woman who wants to put one in a vase.[44] In a similar way, viewing aging and death *only* as problems for solving is to define them in ways that foreclose other deeper considerations that are rooted in the inevitability of such phenomena. That those who question

---

42. See for instance Davis, *New Methuselahs*.

43. MacIntyre, *After Virtue*, 6. While MacIntyre argues that these debates involve systematic disagreement and conflict over ends—a key feature of liberal societies lacking agreement on ends in the absence of a common overarching narrative in which to situate the good(s) necessary to flourish—the life extension debate between consequentialists illustrates too that the interminable character of such debates need not stem solely from the conceptual incommensurability of moral presuppositions.

44. Sayers, *Letters*, 270.

whether or not we should be trying to solve aging and death are routinely labeled bio-Luddites or "lovers of mortality" suggests that life and aging may have already been reframed in a detective novel kind of way. Such thin interpretations of aging see life itself as a consuming technological struggle against the greatest enemy, death, finding it nearly incomprehensible that our collective *modus operandi* should be anything but an all-out technological war against it. For as Sayers notes, "from very early days, alchemists have sought for the elixir of life, so reluctant is man to concede that there can be any problem incapable of solution."[45] The tremendous energy spent on trying to solve aging may leave one bereft of resources for considering the inevitability of aging.

Once again, this is not to argue against attempts to intervene in the human aging process, but is rather an objection against seeing aging and death *only* as a technological problem with a dose of consequentialism thrown in to account for things that ultimately cannot be accounted for. Beyond the causes and mechanisms associated with human aging, however, lie deeper religious and ethical questions that are suppressed by considering aging only as a problem to be solved, as though living well could be understood merely as living a long time. This is not to deny that religious or theologically informed ethical approaches to life extension are without their own challenges. Indeed, formulating a theological response to life extension by slowing aging will likely prove more difficult than other ethical approaches that considerably limit, if not forbid, any appeals to the transcendent. Yet, as the science marches on, religious responses to aging attenuation have for the most part been lacking in both number and depth. Ethical discussion of aging attenuation by those in the scientific community continues to outpace the moral reflection from philosophers, ethicists, and especially Christian theologians.[46] This is significant, for if our use and even promotion of anti-aging products already on the market serves as any indication of our receptivity to living longer by such means, it would seem that Christians generally exercise little to no discernment here.[47] If, or perhaps when,

---

45. Sayers, *Letters*, 255. She goes on to note: "And of late we note a growing exasperation in the face of death. We do not so much fear the pains of dying, as feel affronted by the notion that anything in this world should be inevitable," save perhaps the inevitability of progress.

46. Carole Bailey Stoneking notes that even theologians who have recently looked at aging have failed in this regard, treating aging merely as a matter of "social policy: unemployment, poverty, disease, health care, retirement, and pensions." See Stoneking, "Modernity," 73.

47. There is ample evidence to suggest that Christians too are not immune to the cult of youth. Pat Robertson's Christian Broadcasting Network (CBN) recently published an article entitled "Anti-Aging 'Secrets' Revealed," featuring Harry Lodge's best

aging-attenuation becomes widely available—admittedly a questionable assumption in its own right—there is little reason to expect that we will have the theological resources necessary to think through such things. As will become clear, the challenges posed by the enigma of aging itself and attempts to slow it are by no means easily addressed by the Christian narrative of creation, reconciliation, and redemption of humankind, and the person upon whom our redemption rests.

This book attempts to address this gap by offering a theological analysis of life extension by slowing aging from a Christian perspective. As a *Christian* examination of longevity research, I consider the biomedical project of slowing aging in light of the knowledge of the Word of God, Jesus Christ, as witnessed to in Scripture, and as proclaimed by those who have followed the creeds of the Christian faith throughout the centuries. In particular, this book deals with theological ethics insofar as it brings a christological anthropology to bear on the scientific quest to attenuate aging by manipulating the body. Indeed, insofar as aging-attenuating science aims to remake the human body, we should expect Christology to have something to say on the matter. It begins however by asking a critical, yet often overlooked question; namely, "What is going on?"[48] In particular, we consider how aging has come to be construed as a problem largely for science and medicine, an investigation which will include—somewhat surprisingly—contributions from theology. In the first half of the book, then, I trace the relationship between aging attenuation and theology in the modern era, particularly how aging is interpreted as a problem primarily for modern medicine. After a historical survey of the various quests for longevity from *Gilgamesh* to modern genetics, I explore how attitudes toward aging and death in early America shifted from passive acceptance to empowered hostility, noting the subtle changes in the relationship between aging and morality. With the aid of Thomas R. Cole, this narrative illustrates how the development of science

---

seller *Younger Next Year*, which discusses how certain lifestyle choices promote cellular growth. http://www.cbn.com/cbnnews/healthscience/2009/August/Anti-Aging-Secrets-Revealed/. A more recent article on the same site discusses how Christians can "beat the clock" without needles, surgery, or spending too much money, getting tips from "one of America's top beauty doctors," Dr. Doris J. Day, physician of the Hollywood stars.

48. H. Richard Niebuhr considered the question "What's going on?" as of fundamental importance, preceding the second question, "What should I do?" See Niebuhr, *Responsible Self*, 60. As Oliver O'Donovan has noted, determining what a particular situation means is often more difficult than determining what Scripture means. See O'Donovan, *Church in Crisis*, 59. Indeed, more recently O'Donovan notes that a primary intellectual challenge for Christian ethicists involves being alert to the world and interpreting the times. See *Self, World, and Time*, x–xi.

and medicine influenced long-held theological beliefs concerning God's sovereignty vis-à-vis the length of one's life. More specifically, I show how theology provided the foundation for a new instrumental science devoted to "relieving man's estate" in the figure of Francis Bacon (1561–1626), who drew on the biblical imagery of prelapsarian Eden in arguing for an instrumental science devoted to slowing human aging. Throughout this account I illustrate how developments in science and medicine foster an increasingly hostile stance toward the aging body that considerably mitigates its moral significance.

The opening chapter traces the development of prolongevity efforts and related theories of aging from folk stories to contemporary science, giving particular attention to shifts in attitudes toward the aging body. I argue that the conceptual distance between disease and aging has continued to shrink as theories of human aging become more complex and the modes of bodily intervention more invasive. Moreover, as aging is more likely to be interpreted as a disease, the human body tends to be increasingly construed as an adversary or obstacle to the human will. Chapter 2 explores how shifting theological interpretations of death and aging have shaped Christian attitudes toward aging and long life. By drawing on the work of cultural historian Thomas R. Cole, I show how aging, which was once seen as a natural part of human existence, was gradually reinterpreted as a problem for medicine. If the Calvinist understanding of aging and death afforded Christians a degree of existential integrity vis-à-vis one's own body, the demise of this same perspective spawned a melioristic attitude toward aging suffused with moral overtones, enjoining Christians to engage in behaviors and bodily practices that would promise long life. However, the eventual failure of such practices helped foster a decidedly negative attitude toward the aging body, leaving it as a problem ripe for medical intervention, particularly the new science envisioned earlier by Francis Bacon (1561–1626), who called for a new, practically oriented science devoted to improving the lot of humankind primarily by considerably slowing the aging process.

In chapter 3 I look more closely at the program of Francis Bacon, whose call for research into the causes of human aging was a core feature of a new scientific methodology that focused on human instrumentality in reordering nature. Bacon's project of investigating aging in order to significantly extend the human life-span was inscribed within the Christian drama of creation, fall, and resurrection as recorded in Scripture. Particularly, his call for an inductive science was fundamentally devoted to relieving the afflictions of human existence and restoring the power and longevity that Adam had enjoyed in the garden of Eden before the fall. In this theologico-scientific narrative of redemption however, the aging body is largely presented as a problem for medicine to the exclusion of richer, christological accounts of human beings as embodied, finite creatures.

In the second half of the book I draw on resources of the Christian theological tradition that call attention to issues overlooked in the biomedical attempt to slow human aging, namely, the formative role of the aging, finite body. In moving toward a reparative reading of Bacon's theologico-scientific account of slowing human aging, I use Athanasius's (296–373) understanding of fasting—particularly the relationship between formation and longevity—to critique Bacon's account of aging attenuation as a return to prelapsarian Eden. I argue that Athanasius's account of longevity is rooted in a more theologically robust understanding of human embodiment, drawing attention to potential risks in pursuing aging attenuation through technology alone. Though the Athanasian counter-narrative offers a different interpretation of regaining a portion of the *first* Adam, I argue that any Christian theological response to aging attenuation must be interpreted in reference to God's activity in and through Jesus Christ, the *last* Adam. Here I draw upon the Christology of Karl Barth (1886–1968) and his explication of the real man Jesus vis-à-vis human finitude, offering particular christological implications for aging-attenuation through technology.

In chapter 4 I explore the constellation of beliefs surrounding asceticism with particular emphasis on fasting by examining the theological anthropology of Athanasius in his works *On the Incarnation*, the *Life of St. Antony*, and St. Antony's letters. Fasting was construed as a primary means by which one could "reorder" one's body and soul and thus regain the prelapsarian life of Adam in Eden, where the Christian's soul might once again be subservient to God, and the body obedient to one's soul. Both Athanasius and Antony asserted however that a heightened longevity by slowing the body down was a by-product of this moral enterprise, serving as evidence that the Christian was indeed engaged in the process of becoming like God (*theōsis*). Chapter 5 builds on Athanasius's account of longevity with reference to the last Adam, Jesus Christ, as articulated by Karl Barth. Barth's christological anthropology as revealed in the real man Jesus not only underscores the appropriateness of human aging and finitude, but provides the divine vantage point from which all disorders of body and soul gain their intelligibility, particularly the disorders of "sloth" and "care," taking the form of anxious activity and dissatisfaction with one's temporal existence, the very afflictions Antony's fasting regimen was meant to address. In light of Barth's christological account of the human creature, I interpret the modern biomedical project of aging-attenuation as one of anxious activity and fear—sloth and care—understood as the disorder of one's body and soul. Moreover, insofar as the body is treated primarily as an object of manipulation, this aging-attenuation project forecloses thicker understandings of embodiment that recognize the body's role in the moral formation of the individual. The attempt to engineer a pill to mimic the effects of caloric restriction is perhaps the clearest indicator of this.

I conclude that fasting, though not immune to abuse, can be practiced as an integral discipline for the development of character within the context of a community constituted by the practices of baptism and the eucharist, thereby addressing the disorder of body and soul that engenders fear over one's finitude, while also allowing for the possibility of attenuating the aging process. This is not to argue that fasting is somehow more "natural," much less morally superior to other, technological forms of aging-attenuation. It is only to highlight the potential dangers of aging-attenuating technology. Indeed, we need not reject Bacon's more melioristic program entirely—notwithstanding its shortcomings with respect to the moral significance of the body that were raised by Athanasius's account of a return to Eden. For both Athanasius's and Barth's theological understanding of human aging can accommodate what we might call a "radical" extension of life. Indeed, the deep ethical ambiguities surrounding human aging have hardly been "solved" in this work. Rather, I have attempted to provide some theological lenses through which Christians might view aging, lenses that highlight issues of the human body and its role in the cultivation of virtue, thereby offering a perspective on aging-attenuation to which the modern biomedical project is blind, a perspective, it is hoped, faithful to the tension expressed in Paul's exclamation, "To live is Christ, to die is gain" (Phil 1:21 RSV).

Chapter 1

Gilgamesh, Gonads, and Gerontogenes

Life Extension Moves from Legend to Laboratory

> Oh that there were a medicine curing age . . .
> —Regimen of Health of Salerno

> The rapid progress true science now makes, occasions my regretting sometimes that I was born so soon. It is impossible to imagine the height to which may be carried, in a thousand years, the power of man over matter. . . . all diseases may by sure means be prevented or cured, not excepting even that of old age, and our lives lengthened at pleasure even beyond the antediluvian standard.
> —Benjamin Franklin

> These bodies which we now wear belong to the lower animals; our minds have already outgrown them; already we look upon them with contempt. A time will come when Science will transform them by means which we cannot conjecture . . . Disease will be extirpated; the causes of decay will be removed; immortality will be invented.
> —William Winwood Reade

Long life was once associated with a particular place. Eating a rare rejuvenating plant or bathing in a fountain of youth involved the conquering of distance that usually involved a perilous journey navigating inhospitable or forbidden terrain. So goes one of the oldest of such stories, the Sumerian *Epic of Gilgamesh*.[1] It may not be surprising that the world's first hero, the semi-divine warrior-king Gilgamesh, is taking a journey to the remote region of Dilmun in search of Utnapishtim the Faraway, who survived the great flood and had been granted eternal life by the gods. Driven by anguish and a new fear of death after the gods had destroyed his closest friend Enkidu, Gilgamesh crosses "the waters of death" in order to reach Utnapishtim and learn his secret of earthly immortality. He learns of a thorny plant at the bottom of the sea that will wound his hands but also restore his lost youth should he be able to grasp hold and take it. Elated at the prospect of rejuvenation for both himself and the old men of his beloved city Uruk, Gilgamesh declares the plant's name "The Old Men Are Young Again."[2] However, shortly after his attaining the plant, it was stolen by the serpent when Gilgamesh set it aside to bathe. He wept bitterly when he discovered the plant was gone, and returned to Uruk empty handed, having failed in his quest.

Gilgamesh's hope in the possibility of forestalling or even reversing the effects of aging is as old as humanity itself. His quest reflects a deep human yearning for existence to continue on by whatever means necessary, to ward off the encroaching signs of diminishment and keep old age at bay for as long as possible before the evil days come, the body is bent over, the hands tremble, the eye grows weak, frailty of frame shrinks the world, and fear outlives desire (Eccl 12:1–7). Though the means and methods by which prolongevity might be achieved have continually changed throughout history, the desire for longer, healthier life is nearly universal.

The quest for longevity has progressed from Gilgamesh to the genome. What was once measured in nautical miles is now measured in nanometers, as legendary narratives are now being rewritten in the laboratory as history. This chapter briefly traces the progression of prolongevity attempts and related theories of aging throughout history, from legend to laboratory, focusing particular attention on the implicit attitudes towards the body along the way. Though such quests are embedded in different systems of thought and cultures, a gradual shift in attitudes toward the human body can be discerned as legend and myth have given way to discoveries into the inner workings of the human body at the molecular and genetic levels and the

---

1. Sandars, trans., *Epic of Gilgamesh*.
2. Sandars, trans., *Epic of Gilgamesh*, 116.

scientific narratives that make the human body intelligible. Over time the human body has been perceived with increasing suspicion; once an ally, it is now more commonly viewed as an advancing enemy. With each new technological breakthrough, the conceptual distance between aging and disease continues to shrink.

The erosion of the distinction between aging and death is significant, as it provides a way of determining the kinds of bodily intervention that are warranted from those that might be more questionable. Christians have long applauded the developments of traditional medicine that have either cured or mitigated disease. Indeed, theological warrants supporting the battle against diseases are well-established. Treating aging as a disease however is more controversial, for the scientific quest to slow aging may suggest a fundamental dissatisfaction with human nature itself, a perspective that entails a somewhat hostile stance toward the human body. A blurring of the normal and pathological also challenges a Christian understanding of embodiment by potentially undermining the body's relevance for discipleship and the formation of character. Hence, providing an inductive sketch of the shifting attitudes concerning embodiment—with some attention to the larger narratives in which such attitudes are situated—will be important in illustrating the subtle and not-so-subtle ways in which the quest for longevity might shape our being in ways contrary to the Christian metanarrative, in particular the gospel of Jesus Christ and the way of discipleship.

LONGEVITY LEGENDS, AND THE LEGENDS OF LONGEVITY

According to historian Gerald J. Gruman, the earliest quests for longevity, known as "Hyperborean legends" (i.e. "beyond the north wind"), attached immortal life to a remote place containing a special stream, river, fountain, or vegetation. The *Epic of Gilgamesh* may be the archetypal tale behind all such legends.[3] These legends reflect a basic theme in the world of folklore known as the Abode of the Blest, various remote regions where the supernatural and natural mingled, whose vegetation or environmental conditions like the air or water promoted longer life and heightened immunity from the ravages of aging and disease. These sacred places have ranged from Mount Tmolus in Asia Minor to the set of islands in Western Europe known as *Tír na nÓg* (the Land of Youth). Inhabitants of this land were believed to have been immune from aging and death by eating enchanted mushrooms

---

3. Gruman, "History of Ideas," 22.

or food cooked in a magic cauldron.[4] A Persian legend taught that those allowed to enter the Land of Yima could expect to live three centuries or more without experiencing hunger, thirst, heat, cold, senility, or hatred.[5] The book of Genesis also links geography with longevity, where an indefinite extension of earthly life was possible through eating the fruit from the tree of life in the garden of Eden situated at the mouth of rivers Tigris and Euphrates, though this biblical book of beginnings contains distinctive theological elements distinguishing it from other literature of the Ancient Near East. In defending the antediluvian life-spans of the ancients, Augustine (354–430) drew on Pliny the Elder's report of a nation where longevity far outstripped his own North Africa. "Thus, if we believe that places unknown to us now furnish examples of a length of human life lying outside our experience, why should we not believe the same of times unknown to us?"[6]

Such stories have largely been demythologized with continued exploration and mapping of the world, though some hyperborean tales persist today. Javier Pereira, a Zenú Indian from Columbia, was dubbed a "modern-day Methuselah" upon his arrival in Washington, DC in 1956. Pereira claimed he was 167 years old, though experts at Cornell Medical Center scaled back the estimate to 150 years after examining him, attributing his longevity to the low-fat diet of that region.[7] Somewhat analogous to the hyperborean legends are the so-called blue zones of Okinawa, Japan; Sardinia, Italy; and Loma Linda, California. These residents are known to be exceptionally long lived today, which can be attributed to diet (Okinawa), genes (Sardinia), and hygienic practices common to Seventh-day Adventists (Loma Linda).[8]

It might be said that the deep yearning to transcend our limitations and the frustrations of finitude are a core part of what makes us human. One might also assert however that the human response to this desire to continue on is in some sense constitutive of our creaturehood. These accounts of the search for longevity, from the earliest mythological accounts in literature to historical accounts of voyages over land and sea, bear witness to this universal desire. The vast majority of hyperborean stories reflect the view that a longer, healthier life is a laudatory aim, one worth seeking despite tremendous personal risks. It is interesting to note however that the earliest known

---

4. Gruman, "History of Ideas," 22–23.

5. Gruman, "History of Ideas," 23.

6. Augustine, *City of God*, 651. Pliny claimed a nation whose inhabitants routinely lived 200 years.

7. James, "167 or Not," 29.

8. Aronson, *Elderhood*, 263.

record of such a quest, the *Epic of Gilgamesh*, reads as a cautionary tale in this regard. In the *Epic*, Siduri, the divine wine-maker, reminds Gilgamesh that any quest for earthly immortality is "wandering over pastures in search of the wind," for only the gods retain life and death for their own keeping.[9] Better, says Siduri, to "fill your belly with good things; day and night, night and day, dance and be merry, feast and rejoice ... cherish the little child that holds your hand, and make your wife happy in your embrace; for this too is the lot of man."[10] Only after Gilgamesh accepts his divinely ordained finitude is he declared wise.[11] This theme is also found in early Greek literature, such as Hesiod's *Prometheus* and the writing of Sophocles. In *Oedipus of Colosus*, Sophocles chides the one "who craves excess of days, scorning the common span," as "a giddy wight who walks in folly's ways."[12] In a similar vein, Genesis implies that Adam and Eve might have lived indefinitely had they obeyed God, which they forfeited by eating from the forbidden tree of the knowledge of good and evil. Afterwards God drove them out of Eden, stationing cherubim and a flaming sword to guard the entrance, lest Adam "put forth his hand and take also of the tree of life, and eat, and live forever," (Gen 3:22b RSV), sparing the first couple an indefinite life-span in a state of moral corruption.[13] Appeals to Genesis would continue well into the modern era, and will certainly be an integral component of the Christian narrative in which human aging must be situated.

The earliest systematic attempts to slowing aging occurred in the Chinese philosophico-religious system developed between 350 and 250 BCE known as Taoism. Taoists fashioned magic and folklore into a rationalized and disciplined system known as "the way" (*tao*).[14] Taoist practice was informed by a monistic view of nature and pantheistic cosmology that linked human breath with the divine.[15] As an admixture of earth and air, the impure and

9. Sandars, trans., *Epic of Gilgamesh*, 101–2.

10. Sandars, trans., *Epic of Gilgamesh*, 102.

11. Sandars, trans., *Epic of Gilgamesh*, 117.

12. Sophocles, *Oedipus*, 261.

13. While the genre of the first several chapters of Genesis remains a point of contention among scholars, Christians generally regard this narrative as portraying an account of events that took place in history, a perspective capable of accommodating a more "literal" interpretation on the one hand, or a more "mythological," "symbolic" account on the other, reflecting the language and imagery common to the Ancient Near East.

14. Gruman, "History of Ideas," 30, 39.

15. Gruman, "History of Ideas," 39. According to Gruman, Taoist philosophical principles of pantheism, mysticism, quietism, and primitivism all lent themselves nicely to the possibility of greatly extending life. Their naturalistic pantheism endowed man with the spark of the divine, mysticism offered communication with the vivifying force of the *tao*, quietism enabled one to conserve one's forces, avoiding the stress that

the divine, Taoists thought it possible for human creatures to experience a transformation from a physical body to an immortal being, or *hsein*, through respiratory practices that mirrored the cosmic breathing of nature itself.[16] By pursuing a complex set of exercises known as embryonic respiration, an adept could hope to "overcome old age" by mimicking the breathing of a fetus and perfect the bodily harmony enjoyed before birth. Embryonic respiration also reduced the need for foods thought to be harmful to the body while cultivating the ability to derive nourishment from the air. Taoist immortality was construed as a gradual internal transformation of the body, punctuated by a final apotheosis known as the "deliverance of the corpse" that involved the *apparent* death and burial of the individual. This supposed corpse represented only a sword or piece of bamboo that the successful adept had caused to assume the form of a human, effectively masking his having attained *hsein*-ship. Stories circulated of *hsein* reappearing after "death" and burial, or exhumed graves of *hsein* containing a stick of bamboo, or being found empty.[17] Though *hsein* might travel to a remote terrestrial paradise or even travel to the heavens, it was not uncommon for some to remain on earth. Po Shih Sheng, for instance, chose to remain on earth even after two millennia of living in a youthful state.

In addition to the numerous methods that contributed to an adept's gradual progression into *hsein*, Taoism incorporated a decidedly moral component to this transformation as well. Longer life without virtue was not possible; the one who aspired to immortality was expected to grow in loyalty, fidelity, obedience, and goodness.[18] So the ancient sage Ko Hung (fourth century BCE): "If one does not lead a virtuous life but exercises himself only in magical tricks, he can by no means attain long life."[19] Once again, their monistic, yet pantheistic cosmology stressing the unity of all things and the theological anthropology that focused on breathing over the more earthly needs of the body engendered religious practices that centered around prayer to the myriad of divinities that were both internal and external to the body, as well as meditation with the aim of achieving mystical union with the *tao*. Internal deities local to particular organs were implored to

---

harms the body, and primitivism taught that one could return to the way of life of the ancients to attain prolongevity. "History of Ideas," 31.

16. Gruman, "History of Ideas," 38–39.

17. Gruman, "History of Ideas," 38–39.

18. Gruman, "History of Ideas," 33. He summarizes: "All through the literature of Taoist prolongevitism there are warnings that physical methods alone are not sufficient for the attainment of immortality; that ethical and religious considerations must also enter into account."

19. Feifel, "Pao-p'u tzu nei-p'ien," 209–10.

remain, while external deities like the Director of Destiny, who had power to lengthen or shorten life according to one's merits, were appeased through prayer and good deeds.[20]

Even a system so fundamentally committed to the promulgation of longer life was not however devoid of criticism from within. The sage Chuang Tzu ridiculed the respiratory and dietary techniques used to achieve a longer life, extolling instead a vision of life more akin to Stoic ideals: "the Superior man . . . rejoices not in long life, and grieves not for early death."[21] In the main, however, Taoist prolongevity generally held longer life was attainable through systematic practices designed to optimize the body's functioning. Indeed, Gruman has dubbed Taoism a "proto-science" given its emphases on naturalism, empiricism, and cult of skill.[22] Even so, this system of longevity was embedded in a cosmology that resisted any sharp distinction between the material and the spiritual, the mundane and the mystical. Though generalizations about such a complex system can only be made tenuously, it might be said that Taoist prolongevity tended to view the body as an ally in the quest to slow down aging, even as the state of *hsein*-ship challenged the goodness of the material body. The body's innate powers could be harnessed and aligned with the cosmos through the use of proper techniques, thereby slowing down the body's aging processes, and, in extreme cases, achieving immortality. Though Taoist longevity would gradually perish, remnants of their system would survive in the form of alchemy, spreading to the West through the texts of Islamist scholars in Spain and North Africa and finally Europe.

Alchemy takes its name from Greek term referring to the transmuting of metals to distill an elixir that could be used to cure disease and extend life. The belief that gold and other elements could be transformed into potable form would span from early Taoist alchemy through late Latin alchemy in the figure of Paracelsus (1493–1541). By the time alchemy had reached Europe in the twelfth century, however, it had been stripped of its more fantastic elements and, as Gruman observes, represented the first systematic attempt in the West to extend health and youth by altering the aging process. Though today alchemy is commonly viewed as a pseudoscience, the notion that life could be extended by hundreds of

20. Gruman, "History of Ideas," 47–48.

21. Gruman, "History of Ideas," 33. Gruman also notes that the ancient Chinese scripts were ambiguous and laconic, and readily capable of competing interpretations.

22. Gruman, "History of Ideas," 35–36, 48.

years through creative chemistry would occupy the minds of Robert Boyle (1627–1691) and Isaac Newton (1643–1727).[23]

Roger Bacon (1214–1292), an early apologist for slowing aging, offered one of the first alchemical arguments for slowing aging, seeking to reconcile longevity with his Christian faith. He framed his project as a return to antediluvian life-spans as recorded in Scripture. Though the doctrine of original sin, which effectively imposed a "limit in Nature" after the fall from grace, prevented Bacon from speculating about an earthly immortality, he believed that life-spans could be lengthened to at least 150 years, nearly three times the average life span of his day.[24] Bacon saw no reason why life-spans might not once again approach those of Methuselah.[25] For he also attributed the curtailment in human longevity to poor hygienic practices and a general ignorance of the medicines that might be developed through alchemy. Bacon included an extensive discussion of the subject in his *Opus tertium* (1267), and later wrote a lengthy treatise entitled *The Cure of Old Age, and Preservation of Youth* in which he recommended making medicines derived from animals thought to be immune from aging, and thus capable of repairing human faculties and restoring bodily strength.[26] None proved successful.

Though alchemy's influence would slowly wane over the coming centuries, it did enjoy a brief period of revival during the Renaissance through the work of the Swiss physician Philippus Aureolus Theophrastus Bombastus von Hohenheim, later known as Paracelsus (1493–1591). Referred to as the "Martin Luther" of medicine by his contemporaries, Paracelsus updated the alchemy of the Middle Ages. He reasoned that if a corpse could be preserved from decay through embalming, a living body could then be preserved through alchemy. Like his predecessor Roger Bacon, Paracelsus believed that God had created such medicines for prolonging life—medicines derived from the earth that "not onely can cure our diseases, but also can preserve our life and health."[27] The problem of aging then was one of human ignorance. Adam, being the wisest of all men, had perfect knowledge of such medicines in the garden of Eden. Paracelsus was intrigued by what Adam might have accomplished had he continual access to the tree of life. This tree, he thought, was both natural and supernatural, and therefore "hath its place in Medicine, as well as in Divinity . . ."[28]

23. Haycock, *Mortal Coil*, 48.
24. Bacon, *Letter Concerning Marvelous Power*, 35.
25. Bacon, *Letter Concerning Marvelous Power*, 35, 37.
26. Gruman, "History of Ideas," 64, 65. These included snakes, the eagle, and stags.
27. Paracelsus, *Treatise Concerning Long Life*, 382.
28. Paracelsus, *Treatise Concerning Long Life*, 383.

Paracelsus saw medicine as preserving the "Life" or "Spirit" that both animates the body and somehow arises from the body. Just as striking steel against flint produces a fire, though neither flint nor steel possess "a fiery nature," so too "Life" comes from that which is not alive. Though an impenetrable mystery, Paracelsus believed that life could be lengthened precisely because it was incorporeal: if life is like a fire, medicine is the wood. "So life, the more it hath of the humour of life, so much the more the Spirit of life abounds."[29] Drawing on Aristotle's theory of the fifth element or quintessence (*quinta essentia*) by which things are made immortal, Paracelsus thought it possible to extract or distill the quintessence of the four earthly elements into an *aqua vitae*, thereby bringing heaven to earth. Earlier Roger Bacon had likened the alchemic quintessence to the fruit dangling from the tree of life in the garden of Eden.[30] Alchemy could bring heaven to earth, leading humankind, as it were, back to the gates of Eden. However, Paracelsus asserted that Eden's gates should remain barred as taking the *quinta essentia* was not only against nature and its predetermined limits, but unchristian.[31] Paracelsus had already identified several herbs and *quintae essentiae* that might extend life for up to forty years.[32] He also recognized that hygiene, locality, and diet influenced longevity. Indeed, "The intemperance of great men is most often the cause of their short lives; and this they have a part of the reward of their wickedness."[33] Indeed, if meat and wine were consumed in moderation, one could hope for a longer life. The impact of hygiene on longevity however did not possess the power of those medicines provided by God, yet to be discovered.

By the early seventeenth century it was becoming increasingly clear that alchemy had come to the end of the road with Paracelsus, who did not live to see fifty.[34] Though promulgated by legitimate philosophers and scientists, it could never overcome the tinge of charlatanism that so often accompanied it, and was doomed to fail as the few supposed success stories were heavily outweighed by its failures. Alchemy's critics included Francis Bacon (1561–1626), who would later lay the groundwork for the modern scientific methodology that includes current attempts to forestall aging.[35]

29. Paracelsus, *Treatise Concerning Long Life*, 381.
30. Bacon, *Opus Majus*, 2:624–25. For Bacon, "this fruit is thought to have elements approaching equality."
31. Minois, *History of Old Age*, 271. Minois notes that Paracelsus believed that life has a natural and predetermined limit that ought not to be artificially extended.
32. Paracelsus, *Treatise Concerning Long Life*, 397.
33. Paracelsus, *Treatise Concerning Long Life*, 375.
34. Gruman, "History of Ideas," 67.
35. There is no known family relation between Roger Bacon and Francis Bacon.

Though Bacon himself believed that extending the human life-span should be the highest goal of medicine, he heaped scorn on the notion of achieving earthly immortality through alchemy, expressing bewilderment that "men should be so demented."[36] Rather, the prolongation of life required a thorough understanding of the body's processes and the effects of diets, baths, ointments, and "proper Medicines." Alchemy came to be rejected on other grounds as well. In 1684 Thomas Burnet (1635–1715) argued in *Sacred Theory of the Earth* that the biblical flood had irrevocably rendered the world less fertile, thereby preventing a return to Methuselah-like life-spans. The vegetation that contributed to stamina of the biblical patriarchs was destroyed in the deluge.[37]

If alchemy was not the answer to the renewal of youth, part of its solution—namely hygiene and diet—was nevertheless considered effective in enhancing one's chances to at least retain youth, even if such gains were comparably small to the prognostications put forward by alchemists. In short, the notion that proper diet and exercise could reduce the incidences of diseases that cause death and actually allow one to age "naturally" was promulgated in the eighteenth and nineteenth centuries. While traces of this line of thinking were identifiable in Taoism, the resurgence of longevity through hygiene owes much to the "Apostle of Senescence," the Venetian nobleman Luigi Cornaro (1467–1566) and his work entitled *Discorsi della vita sobria* (*Discourses on the Temperate Life*).[38] By his own account, Cornaro had nearly ruined his health by his mid-forties, having lived a life of dissipation and overindulgence. When warned by his physician that death was imminent, he adopted a sober form of life like the ancient hermits and patriarchs of old, significantly curtailing his diet, giving up rich foods, abandoning destructive habits of excess, avoiding overly strenuous exercise, exposure to extreme weather, the keeping of "ill-Hours," negative thoughts, and even women.[39] Cornaro devoted most of attention and energy to honing his diet, following a prudential calculus informed by the dictum that one who eats little, over time, eats much (by having lived much longer). His diet consisted of some twelve ounces of bread, soup, egg yolks, and meat, with scant allowance for wine.[40] The results were

---

36. Bacon, *History of Life and Death*, in *WFB*, 5:266, 289. Bacon did not entirely reject the notion that gold, pearls, and certain gems could be developed into a potable form for greater longevity, but rather the fantastic notions surrounding alchemy.

37. Haycock, *Mortal Coil*, 77.

38. This work was first translated into English in 1634. The fourth edition assumed the title *Sure and Certain Methods of Attaining a Long and Healthful Life* (1727).

39. Cornaro, *Sure and Certain Methods*, 6, 45–46.

40. Cornaro, *Sure and Certain Methods*, 9.

dramatic, and Cornaro likened his recovery to a "Sort of Resurrection."[41] Where alchemy had failed, temperance triumphed. Not only could a man preserve his health for a hundred or more years, but also spare himself "the Pain of a violent Death."[42] Drawing on the humoral theory of Aristotle and Galen, he held that a proper regimen preserved one's own natural supply of "Radical Moisture," containing "all the Properties that are fancied to be in *Aurum Potabile* [potable gold], and the *Elixir* which a great many Persons have sought after in vain."[43] Though he expressed a feeling of being "immortalized," and "born again" by the large number of his children and grandchildren, Cornaro rejected any project of immortality as humans have a limited supply of radical moisture. Nevertheless, a proper regimen would secure a very long life, and an easy, "natural" death, to which all must finally and gracefully submit.

Cornaro's regimen however was more than just sound hygienic advice. It was suffused with the belief that God has ordained "that everyone should attain the extreme limit" of age, so the old might enjoy the fruits of increased wisdom "wholly freed from the bitter fruits of sensuality."[44] Cornaro described this regimen as a "Divine Sobriety" and a "Sovereign Antidote," pleasing to both God and Nature.[45] Sobriety was the sister of all other virtues and the root of health; she was "the faithful guardian of the Life of Man, whether he be rich or poor, young or old."[46] Cornaro's gospel, it seemed, was good news for everyone, though it was a salvation by works. He was convinced that if man would only become his own physician, there would be little need for another.[47] Indeed, Cornaro's friends were so impressed with his dramatic recovery that they encouraged him to write a manual of sorts for others. *Discourses on the Temperate Life* proved especially popular in England, where it underwent fifty revisions in the eighteenth and nineteenth centuries.[48] Subsequent revisions took on an added gravitas and

---

41. Cornaro, *Sure and Certain Methods*, 6.

42. Cornaro, *Sure and Certain Methods*, 12, 24. Later in this same work he asserts that those who model their lives after the hermits and saints of old "might very probably attain . . . the age of Sixscore" (45).

43. Cornaro, *Sure and Certain Methods*, 12. The theory that aging results from a loss of bodily moisture put forward by Aristotle and Galen still held sway in the fifteenth century.

44. Cornaro, *Discourses on the Temperate Life*, 98. See also Gruman, "History of Ideas," 69.

45. Cornaro, *Sure and Certain Methods*, 11, 22–23.

46. Cornaro, *Sure and Certain Methods*, 23.

47. Cornaro, *Sure and Certain Methods*, 11.

48. Gruman, "History of Ideas," 71.

legitimacy given that he was able to revise the work several times before his death at the age of ninety-eight. Cornaro's work is credited for popularizing the idea that a few elementary hygienic practices—especially dietary ones—will enable most to extend their life-spans significantly and usher in a gentle, natural death in old age.

Similar works would soon follow, authored by Sir William Temple ("Of Health and Long Life" [1770]) and the illustrious German physician Christopher Hufeland (1762–1836), who set the maximum human life-span at 200 years.[49] However, when Cornaro's regimen failed to produce similar results in others, hygiene was seriously challenged as a legitimate path toward longer life. Hygienic methods were thrown into further disrepute by the continual expansion of medicine, which had developed effective weapons against disease through the rise of bacteriology, the development of vaccines, antisepsis, anesthesia, surgery, and complex techniques of epidemiology.[50] The older stories of super-centenarians that animated hygienic longevity were dismissed in the face of increasingly rigorous methods of historical criticism, not the least of which involved the development of better record keeping. By the late nineteenth century it was nearly impossible to believe, for instance, that the famous English farmer's servant Thomas Parr (1483–1635), buried in Westminster Abbey, had lived 152 years. In 1873 William J. Thomas, a librarian at the House of Lords, wrote a book entitled *Human Longevity, its Facts and its Fictions*, where he convincingly demonstrated that Parr's claims, among others, were the product of what he called folklore.[51] Parr's case has served as a reminder of our misguided zeal, revealing "how desperately gullible we humans are about things we fervently wish to believe."[52] By the nineteenth century it had become clear that, contrary to both Roger Bacon and Cornaro, God and nature would only get one so far towards a longer life. Though one might live longer through the pursuit of personal discipline, the real promise for longer life would come from the continued development of science and medicine.

It is worth pausing at this juncture in order to briefly consider the attitudes towards the body inherent in these schemes for securing longer life, tenuous as such claims might be. For it could be argued that after the recognized failure of hygienic methods, there is a discernible shift in perception regarding the phenomenon of aging, and accompanying changes in attitude towards the human body. Though both alchemy and hygienic

---

49. Gruman, "History of Ideas," 73.
50. Gruman, "History of Ideas," 74.
51. Gruman, "History of Ideas," 74.
52. Austad, *Why We Age*, 1.

methods treated aging as a problem, and foreshadow our scientific climate today, they considered the ultimate solution to aging as external to the body, whether a potable quintessence or the disciplined consumption of foods thought to enhance bodily preservation. The guiding principle for alchemists was discovering the vital principal distilled from elements external to the body that would augment the human body, while hygienists worked under the assumption that the right kind and quantity of food, coupled with other hygienic practices, was itself a kind of medicine for the body.[53] There are of course differences between these two schools of thought. The hygienic regimen generally assumed that a healthy body was a matter of cultivating dietary discipline in order that one might help one's body reach the far shore of old age in accordance with God and nature. Latin alchemy on the other hand seemed to regard the body as in need of greater augmentation or assistance. Nevertheless, most hygienists and alchemists managed to situate their longevity programs within a largely Christian framework that recognized a limit to human longevity, making peace in one way or another with the opening chapters of Genesis.

Even with their different methodologies however, both Latin alchemy and the hygienic methods seem to share on some basic level an attitude that perceives one's own body as an ally in seeking longer life. Alchemic and hygienic methods of prolonging life were seen to work *with* the body. Even if the body was viewed as an instrumental good, it was favorably implicated in both systems as being worthy of specific attention and care. Maximizing longevity also required a degree of virtue, whether temperance (e.g., Cornaro's regime), or the cultivation of practical knowledge (e.g., Paracelsus's exhortation to discern the remedies given by God that were once perfectly perceived in the garden of Eden). These two schools of longevity were also working with theories of aging that respected boundaries in nature. Bacon, Paracelsus, and Cornaro routinely referenced the humoral aging theories of Aristotle (384–322 BCE), Galen (129–200 CE), and Avicenna (980–1037), which assumed that aging was a natural process (unlike disease, which was against nature) by which the body gradually loses heat.[54] Instead of adopting an Aristotelian cosmology that clearly distinguished heavenly, immortal

---

53. Gruman, "History of Ideas," 65.

54. Aristotle's theory is in line with the older Hippocratic understanding of aging as related to the four humors making up the human body. Hippocrates identified each humor with a stage of life, where old age was considered cold and moist and childhood hot and moist. Hippocrates, *Nature of Man*, 4:3–13, 279–81. Though Aristotle believed that old age was cold and *dry*, both held that aging occurs due to a loss of heat. Galen's theory of aging, which was also influential, could be read as a subtle modification of Aristotle's aging-as-drying thesis.

bodies from earthly, temporal human bodies, many Latin alchemists and hygienists adopted a cosmology based on the book of Genesis, expressing optimism concerning the prospect of retarding aging. Though Roger Bacon, for instance, agreed with the basic physiology of aging as understood by Aristotle and Galen, he criticized Galen's hygienic program for too readily accepting the maladies of old age instead of aggressively attempting to reverse the aging process.[55] Yet even here, Bacon's more radical suggestion that aging might be reversed required unlocking the quintessence of natural elements that might restore the body's ability to retain heat. Bacon hoped to extract the vital essence from nature in order to apply it to the body as a kind of medicine without violating the limit of life set by God after the fall.

Despite the recognized failure of alchemy and hygienic methods for securing a longer life, the idea of that life might be radically extended continued unabated into the eighteenth and nineteenth centuries, spurred on by key figures like Benjamin Franklin (1706–1790), whose own discoveries and inventions fueled belief in human progress. Franklin lamented the fact that he would miss the many discoveries that would eventually lengthen life as long as one wishes. In 1773 he suggested a method of embalming drowned persons so that they might be recalled back to life at some future time, anticipating current methods of suspended animation such as cryonic preservation.[56] The self-professed atheists William Godwin (1756–1836) and Marie Jean Antoine Nicolas Caritat, Marquis de Condorcet (1743–1794) expressed a similar faith in progress and human power over nature, believing that it was possible to achieve earthly immortality. Godwin's hope for immortality is a variant of the hygienic theme freed from the strictures of Christian dogma connecting human mortality with sin or the fall. Influenced by recent developments in psychology and with Franklin's suggestion that the mind might one day exercise omnipotence over matter, Godwin adopted a voluntarist perspective on aging. Physiological aging ultimately depended on one's mental state. If, as Luigi Cornaro taught, melancholy thoughts could shorten one's life, then preserving one's youth and vitality was merely a matter of cultivating positive mental habits.[57] The

55. Bacon, *Cure of Old Age*, 136. "But the things which are laid down by us in this Epistle, differ very much from the things laid down by the Ancients. First, because the *Ancients* Regiment of living, defends Men's Bodies from hastening to their End besides the Course of Nature: but *our* Regiment lays open by what Way Old Men and the well stricken in Years may easily be freed and defended from the Accidents of Old Age . . ." Bacon was also influenced by fanciful stories recounting the discovery of medicines and ointments that extended life by hundreds of years. See Gruman, "History of Ideas," 63.

56. Pepper, *Medical Side of Benjamin Franklin*, 61–62. See also Arrison, *100 Plus*, 17–18.

57. Haycock, *Mortal Coil*, 112–14.

first step towards immortality however involved overcoming the need to sleep. If, according to the Christian tradition, sleep afforded one daily the opportunity to both meditate on and prepare for one's own death, Godwin believed sleep was to be avoided as a means of overcoming death altogether. If the need for sleep were conquered *en masse*, Godwin believed that it would lead to a race of enlightened men and women, with no crime, war, disease, anxiety, melancholy, or submission to sexual urges, a description that mirrors the biblical description of heaven.[58] Though Godwin's thesis represents another form of hygienic longevity, his appeal to the sheer power of one's will in exercising control over the body marks a move toward a dualistic anthropology, for the mind is not only working with the body, but ever and always *against* it. Certainly much more will need to be said on this point, for while a theological anthropology confesses the goodness of embodiment, the Apostle Paul could speak of "buffeting" his body in order to make it his slave in the battle between the flesh and the spirit (1 Cor 9:27). We will take up this discussion in the context of Christian asceticism later on.

Like his English counterpart, the French philosopher and mathematician de Condorcet envisioned salvation though the mind, not as an expression of the naked will over one's body, but through the cultivation of practical knowledge. Condorcet emphasized the role of the human mind in exerting control over the natural order through the development of natural science, leading to the eventual perfection of man. Dividing the world history into ten epochs, Condorcet located himself and his fellow Jacobins in the penultimate ninth given humanity's nearly unlimited progress over nature, situated on the precipice of the apocalyptic tenth and final epoch described as heaven on earth. Medicine and hygiene would facilitate the radical prolongation of life, which would be passed on biologically to subsequent generations, a process that would later come to be known as Lamarckism, predecessor to Darwinism.[59] He echoed Francis Bacon in promulgating an organized, systematic investigation of all kinds of natural phenomena with a view of understanding the laws by which things operate, including the human body. Building too on René Descartes's (1596–1650) metaphor of the body as machine, Condorcet envisioned the discovery of laws that would enable physicians to keep the body in a state of permanent health, "as a watchmaker by his skill can keep a timepiece in perfect running order."[60] Advances in preventative medicine and hygiene would most surely put an

58. Godwin, *Enquiry Concerning Political Justice*, 2:398–402.
59. Gruman, "History of Ideas," 88.
60. Gruman, "History of Ideas," 88.

end to disease, promoting a longevity where "the average span between birth and decay will have no assignable value."[61] Indeed, he was reluctant to suggest limits to these developments, since it was generally unclear whether nature's laws themselves have dictated any as such.[62] Thus, where it was once possible to appeal both to limits set by God and nature (e.g., Roger Bacon), with God removed from the equation, nature by itself was largely mute on such matters. There was no primeval paradise, no garden of Eden to which humanity might return. Rather, the world was but a vacant lot ripe for development, ready to accommodate ever higher towers of Babel in the name of human progress.

The audacious claims put forward by Godwin and Condorcet were not readily received by all. The English theologian Thomas Malthus (1766–1834), whose own population theory provided the framework for Darwin's understanding of evolution, mockingly derided Godwin's and Condorcet's work as hopelessly utopian, pointing out the negative implications of their theses. According to Malthus, one might as well "suppose that the attraction of the earth will gradually be changed into repulsion, and that stones will ultimately rise instead of fall . . ."[63] Malthus criticized Condorcet's claims on theological grounds as well, pointing out that his program of indefinite earthly longevity was not only a rejection of a natural religion that "has indicated the future existence of the soul," but also a repudiation of biblical revelation which "absolutely promises eternal life in another state."[64] Such utopian claims invited criticism, though it hardly impeded the search for other more circumspect, empirically based quests for extending life by attenuating the aging process. Indeed, the late nineteenth and early twentieth centuries witnessed new and strange attempts to recapture youthfulness through techniques that would later be identified as the "great gland madness," described as the "first full-fledged world craze to spring from the application of modern science to the anti-aging quest."[65]

Though the findings of French neurologist Charles-Édouard Brown-Séquard (1817–1894) would eventually give birth to the field of endocrinology, they were initially employed for some rather unorthodox longevity treatments, instigated in part by Brown-Séquard's own reported rejuvenation after injecting himself with minced dog and guinea pig testicles. The Viennese endocrinologist Eugen Steinach (1861–1944) would

---

61. de Condorcet, *Sketch*, 200.
62. de Condorcet, *Sketch*, 200-1.
63. Malthus, *Essay on the Principle of Population*, 240.
64. Malthus, *Essay on the Principle of Population*, 241, 242.
65. Stipp, *Youth Pill*, 9.

later perform a vasectomy-like surgery in hopes of reactivating puberty. Steinach's clientele included the poet William Butler Yeats (1865–1939) and Sigmund Freud (1856–1939). Yeats claimed he felt reborn after being "Steinached," launching himself into several affairs with younger women and penning some fifty poems the last three years of his life. Freud too swore he felt years younger. Some hailed Steinach as one of the greatest biologists of his time. The American author Gertrude Atherton (1857–1948) claimed she felt thirty years younger after Steinach irradiated her ovaries with X-rays; her best-selling novel *Black Oxen* followed shortly thereafter. These success stories garnered considerable attention, inviting comparisons to prelapsarian Eden while reinvigorating notions of banishing death altogether. The writer George Sylvester Viereck (1884–1962) wondered whether Steinach's techniques for rejuvenation might not be the very knowledge the serpent promised Eve that would make her god, asking, "if we halt the insidious advance of Age, may we not, in time, challenge Death?"[66] Though Steinach himself dismissed such suggestions, he did hope to "stretch the span of man's usefulness" and eventually prolong life.[67]

More radical solutions came in the form of transplanting monkey gonads. The French-Russian surgeon Serge Voronoff (1866–1951) implanted testicular grafts from apes and other animals into thousands of old men. His work became so popular that he eventually established a monkey farm in Italy to accommodate the surging demand for gonads.[68] Though some would continue to promote expensive cellular rejuvenation therapies beyond the 1950s, the rejuvenation revolution was pronounced dead by the early twentieth century. Steinach's surgeries were yet another example of the "dangers of putting new wine into old bottles," for many of these "re-erotized old men" died shortly thereafter.[69] Not long afterwards physiologist and Nobel Prize laureate Alexis Carrel (1873–1944) lambasted the procedures of Steinach and Voronoff in the *New York Times*, concluding that the process of aging was irreversible. Steinach's work has since been described as "one of history's most sensational placebo effects."[70]

Indeed, though hormonal surgeries may have temporarily contributed to an increased energy, they did nothing to slow down aging. Despite the failure of these rejuvenation theories however, a subtle conceptual shift over the interpretation of human aging would appear. One of Steinach's

66. Viereck, *Glimpses of the Great*, 249; Viereck [Corners], *Rejuvenation*, vii, 1, 95.
67. Viereck, *Glimpses of the Great*, 250, quoting Steinach.
68. Stipp, *Youth Pill*, 8–9.
69. Warthin, *Old Age*, 173–74.
70. Stipp, *Youth Pill*, 7.

ardent supporters, surgeon Peter Schmidt (1892–1930), wrote a work entitled *The Conquest of Old Age*, in which he proclaimed that these limited breakthroughs had revealed aging itself as a disease. "We are now able to regard old age as an illness," mused Schmidt. Though he was not the first to assert as much—François Ranchin's 1627 *Opuscula medica* drew a distinction between "normal" and "accidental" senescence and the eighteenth-century German pharmacist Jakob Hutter wrote a book in 1732 entitled *Senectus ipsa morbus est, That Senescence Itself is an Illness*—Schmidt also declared "no longer shall we look upon senility as an unavoidable evil."[71] Moreover, he believed (correctly, to some degree) that diseases are caused by aging. Once science realizes that diseases "are themselves merely symptoms of a single more general disease, the disease of growing old, what can seem more obvious than that we have to treat old age itself as a disease . . . ?"[72] Hence, scientific efforts ought to be ultimately focused on the disease of aging itself; treating only the symptoms of old age is like trying to restore a dried-out leaf by simply painting it green. It is hardly surprising that this shift in the interpretation of aging was accompanied by a shift in attitudes towards the human body: with every scientific advance, the body was increasingly described as yielding to man's "indomitable will." At the height of Steinach's success, the biologist Paul Kammerer (1880–1926) famously declared that man "will at last become master of his own house." Just as the ability to rule others requires that one has first mastered one's own will, "so man, after he has acquired sovereignty over his own body, will achieve a heretofore unimagined new freedom to shape the future of mankind and attain true civilization."[73]

Continued developments of endocrinology and immunology, coupled with the birth of evolutionary biology and genetics, have contributed to a proliferation of theories on human aging. New discoveries would challenge the biblical account of human origins as recorded in the book of Genesis, exposing its mythological character. The biblical story of human origins was eventually displaced by Darwin's theory of evolution involving natural selection, armed with more explanatory power and backed by empirical evidence, fueling the growth of science itself and establishing the framework within which all subsequent theories of aging were to find a home.

---

71. Schäfer, "'That Senescence Itself is an Illness,'" 525. See Schmidt, *Conquest of Old Age*, 32. See also Sengoopta, "Dr. Steinach Coming to Make Old Young!," 126. Though Schmidt held out hope for a nearly indefinite extension of life, he shot himself while sitting at his desk at the age of thirty-eight, leaving a note declaring that he no longer found life worth living.

72. Schmidt, *Conquest of Old Age*, 64.

73. Kammerer, *Rejuvenation*, 226.

Nevertheless, the residue of hyperborean tales would occasionally influence newer theories of human aging.

The Russian biologist Élie Metchnikoff (1845–1916), the father of gerontology, speaks of the enduring presence of hyperborean thought in the modern era. Metchnikoff believed he had discovered a link between bodily bacteria and longevity. He thought that aging was caused by the secretion of toxins caused by bacteria in the gut, which also accounted for the large discrepancy between the maximum life-span (which he estimated at 150 years) and the much lower average life-span.[74] Convinced by reports of Bulgarian peasants whose diet of soured milk apparently enabled them to live well beyond a century, Metchnikoff experimented with his own soured milk. He credited it with destroying harmful intestinal microbes that wreaked havoc on the body by weakening the immune system and shortening life.[75] Metchnikoff actually experimented on himself, supplementing a regimen of sour milk with an austere diet in order to avoid introducing foreign bacteria into his body. Though he acknowledged that his regimen was basically hygienic, this new form of hygiene was no longer afflicted by legendary stories but rather firmly established by empirical science. Metchnikoff insisted that his study of "bacteriology has placed hygiene on a scientific foundation, so that the latter is now one of the exact sciences."[76] Later research would challenge the link between gut bacteria and aging; not only was some bacteria necessary for digesting food, but subsequent experiments showed that a deficiency of bacteria actually shortened life.

Though Metchnikoff's regimen for longevity represented another failure of the hygienic approach to aging, his construal of the human body signaled a departure from the basic humoral understanding of bodily health operative at the time, consistent with the *Corpus Hippocratum*, which interpreted health as a natural balance of the four humors united in the human body. Before Metchnikoff, one of the fundamental questions of medicine was, "How can disease be possible?"[77] But in the wake of Darwin's theory of evolution, health as a harmony of humors could no longer be accepted. "The conception which has come down from antiquity to modern times," claimed Metchnikoff, "of a harmonious activity of all the organs, is no

---

74. Metchnikoff unfortunately failed to check the facts behind some inflated estimations of longevity and other hearsay accounts while collecting data in France, leading to the conclusion that the maximum age for humans is 150 years. See Haycock, *Mortal Coil*, 162.

75. Kirkwood, *Time of Our Lives*, 76.

76. Metchnikoff, *Prolongation of Life*, 331.

77. Chernyak and Tauber, "Idea of Immunity," 190.

longer appropriate to mankind."[78] Indeed, Darwin's unique contribution to evolutionary theory was the concept of natural selection, where only the "fittest"—organisms best suited for reproductive efficacy—survived in a predatory and hostile environment that Darwin himself called "the war of nature."[79] According to Metchnikoff, the slow, painful development of man's higher intellectual facilities was accompanied by a lower, animal portion, "which happened to be not just needless, but directly harmful." In particular, "his animal nature has shortened life because of the chronic poisoning by toxins elaborated by bacteria of the intestinal flora."[80] Older theories of health and illness spoke in terms of bodily balance and imbalance; for Metchnikoff, man was little more than "ape's monster," an abnormal and sick creature in need of the powers of medicine.[81] For "human nature, as it is revealed to us by science," noted Metchnikoff, "does *not* demonstrate the presence of a special law of harmonious development of different parts."[82] Given this sick state of man, Metchnikoff believed that human nature itself must be modified by some ideal that could not be derived from nature itself.[83] He referred to this ideal as "orthobiosis," where the body "passes through a long period of old age in active and vigorous health, leading to the final period in which there shall be present a sense of satiety of life, and a wish for death."[84] Despite his insistence that orthobiosis could not be derived from nature, he nevertheless believed that the body had its own death program that gradually curtailed one's aspirations and ambitions when one reached a certain age.

Metchnikoff's hygienic program for greater longevity was no longer about living in accordance with the natural laws of humoral balance within the human body, but about killing the bacteria within the body thought to shorten human life.[85] With this move the body was conceptually redefined as more of an *adversary* than an ally, a largely passive, damaged object that must succumb to the human will and the ideal of orthobiosis. Once the

78. Metchnikoff, *Prolongation of Life*, 325.

79. Darwin, *Origin of the Species*, 408-9. The term "survival of the fittest" was first coined by one of Darwin's most vociferous supporters, Herbert Spencer (1820-1903).

80. Chernyak and Tauber, "Idea of Immunity," 196.

81. Chernyak and Tauber, "Idea of Immunity," 196-97.

82. Chernyak and Tauber, "Idea of Immunity," 196, emphasis mine.

83. Metchnikoff, *Prolongation of Life*, 325.

84. Metchnikoff, *Prolongation of Life*, 327.

85. Metchnikoff continued however to use the harmony-disharmony terminology; he only insisted that these terms be described strictly in accord with the human *ideal* of the bodily constitution. He vigorously rejected the charge that his claims were metaphysically based, claiming complete ignorance of the designs or motives of nature.

humoral theory of bodily harmony was replaced by a Darwinian conception of the human body as the product of undirected, wasteful processes, the body increasingly became a target for human technological intervention according to some ideal which, as Metchnikoff insisted, could not be derived from nature. Metchnikoff himself tended to speak of the body as an enemy, rife with disease. When the body is construed as such, the conceptual distance between aging and disease begins to narrow. Indeed, Metchnikoff went so far as to declare that "disease is in our essence."[86] Nevertheless, one would be wrong to conclude that he despised the body. On the contrary, Metchnikoff criticized Christianity for excluding hygiene from its religious code. He took particular aim at Jesus' apparent disregard for the welfare of the body as exemplified in his command to take no thought of one's life, food, or drink (Matt 6:25). This facile judgment rests on a rather thin reading of the New Testament, though to be sure the Christian tradition has a long and complicated relationship with the human body and the practices thought to benefit it, topics that will be addressed later on.

Metchnikoff's attempt to resituate the aging body within a Darwinian framework represented a fundamental shift in approaches to slowing down the aging body in part because the Darwinian framework did indeed possess an explanatory power that readily accommodated continuing advances in various scientific disciplines. With increasing knowledge of cellular biology and the advent of genetic technology, the human cell would become the new locus of research on aging. The German biologist August Weismann (1834–1914) suggested that death eventually occurs because the cells that make up the body (i.e., somatic cells) can only renew themselves through division a finite number of times, after which such cells die. Weismann's "wear and tear" theory of human aging represented the first developed explicitly from within a Darwinian framework. As such, he posited that aging and death are nature's way of keeping the old from competing with the young over scarce resources. Though the logic of his explanation would soon be challenged (e.g., how are the decrepit old a threat to the young?), Weismann's observations concerning the finite nature of somatic cell replication and his linkage of longevity with reproduction have proven enormously influential.[87] Eventually, aging would be described as a problem for cellular biology.

This turn toward the cellular economy of the body in combatting aging was evident in the work of author and physician Charles Asbury Stephens

---

86. Haycock, *Mortal Coil*, 165.

87. See Weismann, *Essays upon Heredity*. See also Olshansky and Carnes, *Quest*, 58; Stipp, *Youth Pill*, 16–18; Medvedev, "Rational Classification," 377.

(1844–1931). Echoing Weismann's theory of cellular replication, Stephens believed that the causes of old age "are to be sought within the cells rather than in the organism of the whole."[88] Stephens established one of the first laboratories in the United States to study the aging process in animals in hopes of expanding his laboratory into an institute of gerontology.[89] Unlike Metchnikoff, Stephens believed that science could significantly extend the human life-span, perhaps indefinitely. Influenced by the vitalist materialism of prominent German Darwinist Ernst Haeckel (1834–1919), Stephens believed that "enlightened man ... may possibly escape death by setting his wits to work to this end."[90] Stephens hoped to redirect the vast amounts of unused energy toward cell rejuvenation.[91] In 1896 he drew up a research proposal that included a comparison of both young and old capillaries, cerebral cells, blood, and organ tissues as well as psychical studies of the mental states of the young and old, plans, however, that were never carried out after the chief benefactor died unexpectedly.[92] It may not have mattered, for the preliminary results were generally unimpressive.[93]

Despite Stephens's interest on aging at the cellular level, his theories for slowing aging were largely hygienic in nature. He believed that aging stemmed from molecular imperfections in individual cells that could be corrected by ingesting specially engineered food. According to Stephens, the body was under constant attack by "microscopic life of a hostile and noxious character" both externally—through food, water, and air—and internally, penetrating to individual tissues and organs.[94] Life extension was a matter of increasing the rate of cellular repair to outpace the cell's mitochondrial waste production and eliminating deadly bacteria.[95] This

88. Stephens, *Immortal Life*, 68. Stephens was nevertheless critical of the view that nature is essentially locked in as the fate of inheritance, a view he attributed to Weismann and several other "histologists." See Stephens, *Natural Salvation*, 81.

89. Gruman, "C. A. Stephens," 660.

90. Stephens, *Natural Salvation*, 82. Gruman, "C. A. Stephens," 334. Stephen's medical school thesis entitled "Living matter" was an exposition of Haeckel's philosophy of biology.

91. Stephens, *Immortal Life*, 235. "Given vital energy at command, to use as needed, it is not believed here that the involution, or devolution, of the cell, known as 'old age,' will go on, or be initiated. A full head of vital energy in the organism, maintaining a strong aura of life, is the natural antidote to old-aging."

92. Stephens, *Long Life*, 13.

93. Gruman, "C. A. Stephens," 334.

94. Stephens, *Natural Salvation*, 84.

95. Stephens, *Natural Salvation*, 70: "Avoiding death is less a question of ultimate, incorruptible atoms than of making scientific repair expel natural waste." See also *Natural Salvation*, 65, 80.

improved cellular economy could be achieved by consuming biochemically engineered food, paving the way for eventual immortality.[96] Though Stephens believed that perfectly optimized nutrition would replace "vague religious aspirations for a spiritual body," he nevertheless described the body's gradual transformation as a "progressive spiritualization" where the body gradually became "less 'carnal,' less gross."[97]

Thus, there was a certain ascetic component to this transformation. Moreover, Stephens's description of proper digestion is suffused with biblical language. Consuming food for optimal cellular functioning would require a degree of discipline to curtail the animal impulses that serve the gratification of the mouth and stomach: "he who would pass from death to life *must eat with his brain* rather than his belly-greed."[98] Perfected digestion will be "sweet and clean to taste and smell." Even the internal cavity of the human body "may yet be made, a very penetralia of life, the sanctuary of a holy purity."[99] Where Metchnikoff posited a "death program," Stephens saw a growing sense of deathlessness which would quench the desire for both food and sex.[100] Though he rejected any possibility of life after death, Stephens freely appropriated the Apostle Paul's description of the resurrection body as a metaphor for natural salvation:

> . . . the eye of faith may even now reasonably foresee the day when these animal organisms of our inheritance shall be progressively transformed and transfigured to the more "spiritual" bodies of the apostle's vision, when, in very truth, "this corruptible shall put on incorruption" [1 Cor. 15:53].[101]

This was no transcendent window to immortality opened from above. Rather, "Man can reach this diviner life by his own exertions."[102]

In spite of Stephens's insistence on bodily immortality, his doctrine of natural salvation fostered a certain ambivalence with regard to one's body. Oddly enough, he defended the necessity of the body against his understanding of the Christian doctrine of the immortality of the soul. As he saw it, belief in some ethereal afterlife like heaven wrongly encouraged

---

96. Stephens, *Immortal Life*, 210.
97. Stephens, *Immortal Life*, 236.
98. Stephens, *Immortal Life*, 210.
99. Stephens, *Immortal Life*, 205.
100. Stephens, *Immortal Life*, 210.
101. Stephens, *Immortal Life*, 221–22.
102. Stephens, *Immortal Life*, 222.

Christians to "despise corporeal life and disdain the earth as an abiding place."[103] Yet Stephens's vision of bodily immorality exhibited threads of Gnostic thought.[104] The bodily spiritualization process of which he spoke was motivated in part by his disdain for material aspects of the aging body. "At present our bodies are a sad, strange mixture of foulness and putrefaction in which the sweeter, purer, etheric flame of life struggles and smoulders . . ."[105] To slow aging by consuming specially engineered food meant that one could gradually eliminate "the grossness, coarseness and ugliness of the human organism, often so repulsively exhibited as that organism ages."[106] Stephens's life-long revulsion over the aging body was also fueled by his profound fear of death that had afflicted him from childhood.[107] Hence, his evocative description of the body running on optimized nutrition hinted at the possibility of its transformation into something more spiritual than material, even though Stephens did not despise embodiment as such, it being the only possible mode of human existence. Either way, however, he was however far less sanguine about the aging body. Additional disparaging accounts of the aging body would come from others who saw aging primarily as a problem for biology. As will be clear shortly, by some accounts the body becomes disposable.

In 1951 Peter Medawar's (1915-1987) inaugural lecture as the chair of zoology at the University of London dealt with the subject of human aging. The lecture, entitled "An Unsolved Problem of Biology," implied that a solution was well within reach.[108] Medawar argued that from an evolutionary perspective, natural selection was primarily concerned with ensuring species' survivability until the age of reproduction, after which the deleterious effects of aging become increasingly pronounced. In short, Medawar believed that natural selection effectively delays the genetic expression of

103. Stephens, *Salvation by Science*, 4.

104. Stephens's interpretation of August Weismann's theory of cellular replication likely contributed to his disdain for the human body: "It is an error to regard the animal or human organism (soma) as the essential or important part. The reproductive tissue (germ-plasm) alone is of importance. The *soma* is subordinate and exists for the purpose of carrying forward the germ-plasm. It is its vehicle of life, exists for no other object, and has no other *raison d'être*." *Natural Salvation*, 68.

105. Stephens, *Immortal Life*, 236.

106. Stephens, *Immortal Life*, 235.

107. As Stephens reflected later on this experience, "I should have to die and look as that man looked and be buried in the ground. The thought of it caused me to gasp suddenly, and filled me with a sense of terror and despair so awful that I could scarcely restrain myself from crying out." See Stephens, *When Life Was Young*, 205.

108. Stipp, *Youth Pill*, 11.

harmful diseases into the post-reproductive period of life.[109] His work is largely credited with lending "unprecedented respectability to gerontology," deepening our understanding of the mechanisms involved in human aging.[110] Several years later, the evolutionary biologist George C. Williams (1926–2010) would develop and modify Medawar's idea of harmful genes with his own theory known as "antagonistic pleiotropy," where genes beneficial to an organism early in life mutate and harm the organism in later life.[111]

One of the most widely accepted contemporary theories explaining *why* we age is Tom Kirkwood's "disposable soma theory," employing the Greek word *sōma*, meaning "body."[112] We grow old and die, says Kirkwood, because our bodies, which are composed mostly of finite somatic cells, eventually become superfluous once our genes can be passed on through germ cells—such as egg and sperm cells—that are capable of replicating indefinitely.[113] The body, or *sōma*, is simply the egg's way of making another egg, and so on, indefinitely.[114] Once our bodies, composed primarily of somatic cells, reach sexual reproductive maturity, they are no longer required by our germ cells and hence, become "disposable." In other words, germ-line cells, which are replicatively immortal, no longer require the bodies into which they develop once the age of reproductive maturity occurs. Building on the work of Medawar and Williams, Kirkwood maintains that somatic maintenance is very costly. Therefore, once the germ line has had an opportunity to propagate through sexual reproduction, the resources required for continued maintenance of the body gradually fall off. Human life is a balance between the maintenance of our bodies and germ-line reproduction. Death, it seems, is the price humans pay for sex. According to Kirkwood then, we grow old and die because we are disposable; our genes don't need us.[115] In terms of aging, claims Kirkwood, "we are all, metaphorically speaking, in sinking ships."[116] In the wake of Kirkwood's hypothesis, others have described the human bodies that develop from the immortal germ cells as

---

109. Olshansky and Carnes, *Quest*, 59–61; Kirkwood, *Time of Our Lives*, 78–79.

110. Stipp, *Youth Pill*, 12.

111. Williams, "Pleiotropy, Natural Selection."

112. Kirkwood, *Time of Our Lives*, 65.

113. Incidentally, geneticist Ian Chambers named the gene associated with immortality "NanOg" after the mythological Celtic islands known as The Land of Youth (*Tír na nÓg*).

114. West, *Immortal Cell*, 228.

115. Kirkwood, *Time of Our Lives*, 63. "And the saddest thing is that this assessment of our disposability is made by none other than our very own genes."

116. Kirkwood, *Time of Our Lives*, 21.

"genetic transport vehicles" or "no more than disposable gene packages."[117] Michael West, founder of the Geron Corporation (originally established to slow the rate of cellular aging by exploiting research on telomeres) grasped the broader implications of Kirkwood's theory: "Not only does the theory of evolution deflate our view of the individual's significance in the biosphere, it adds insult to injury by implying that we are not even important enough to keep around after we have reproduced ourselves and brought up our children to do the same."[118]

Despite these pessimistic assessments, the disposable soma theory has proven to be quite powerful in describing more than simply why humans age. Indeed, one of the most effective predictors of longevity in women is the age at the onset of menopause, after which the very factors that enhance survival begin to gradually fall off.[119] However, evolutionary biologist Michael Rose has put Kirkwood's theory of aging to use, developing a line of fruit flies that live up to five times longer through a form of selective breeding based on Kirkwood's hypothesis. Rose boasts of his ability to "make tiny flying Methuselahs at will."[120] Not to be outdone by Kirkwood's evocative metaphors, Rose describes the natural selection process by which aging might be slowed as "a nursing home orderly waiting indifferently for his elderly charges to die."[121] His comments reveal much of the fear—not altogether unfounded—that animates the search for longer, healthier life. More importantly however, these construals of aging illustrate the reductionism such perspectives on aging are, as if *human* aging is largely identical to *biological* aging.

This is no less true of Kirkwood's disposable soma theory. Putting aside the obvious fact that genes, strictly speaking, are not individuals and therefore not capable of having any perspective, the metaphor of disposability is significant. Kirkwood claims that the body's disposability is a judgment rendered by our own germ cells. There may be nothing particularly objectionable to Kirkwood's depiction so long as it is restricted to that evolutionary framework. However, when he also states that *we* are disposable, he appears to be making a larger claim. While we are our bodies, we are also *more* than our biology; the human body is the site of human presence. It is reasonable to suspect that Kirkwood intended to restrict the metaphor

---

117. Olshansky and Carnes, *Quest*, 51; Stipp, *Youth Pill*, 24.
118. West, *Immortal Cell*, 228.
119. Ossewaarde et al., "Age at Menopause."
120. Rose, *Long Tomorrow*, 45. See also Rose, "Laboratory Evolution of Postponed Senescence"; Luckinbill et al., "Selection for Delayed Senescence."
121. Rose, *Long Tomorrow*, 35.

of disposability to this evolutionary perspective, given that his explanation of aging was intended for a wide audience. Nevertheless, it is possible that the metaphor of the disposable body—even when restricted to the realm of evolutionary biology—may foster the concept that science can manipulate and reshape the human body in any way thought to be desirable or useful.

Kirkwood's disposable soma theory has proven a powerful paradigm in helping understand the dynamics of human aging, most especially *why* humans age. The *how* of aging however remains a mystery. Since the work of Weismann and Medawar, the fields of evolutionary biology and gerontology have witnessed a proliferation of the number and range of aging theories that, according to one scientist, "rather stupefies the imagination."[122] Currently there are over 300 such theories that have been categorized along genetic, evolutionary, and cellular damage lines, though the ways these theories have been grouped nearly approaches the number of aging theories themselves.[123] This is particularly vexing to many scientists, for while aging is arguably the most common phenomenon in nature, it remains resistant to precise definition. Some have noted that "it is ironic that such a ubiquitous phenomenon as aging is so controversial regarding its definition and measurement."[124] There are other complex questions as well. For the human aging process is more than decline and decay; it also includes growth and development. Gerontologists are often anxious to point out that aging is not always an undesirable process—wine being a prime example. Though many believe that aging begins when one reaches reproductive maturity, others are not so sure. Even the most facile, straightforward, and seemingly innocuous descriptors of aging—e.g., that aging is a chronological phenomenon—are disputed.[125]

In spite of these issues, it is generally recognized that human aging is significantly influenced by cellular aging.[126] Commonly called "senescence," cellular aging occurs when the body's cells—somatic cells—gradually lose the ability to replicate. Eventually (in most cases) these senescent cells enter

122. Austad, *Why We Age*, 53.

123. Medvedev, "Rational Classification," 378. Some have divided aging theories into damage and programmed theories. See Banks and Fossel, "Telomeres, Cancer, and Aging," 1345. Others have divided evolutionary theories of aging into two classes: optimality and deleterious mutation. See Partridge and Barton, "Optimality, Mutation and the Evolution of Aging." Robert Arking classifies fourteen basic theories on aging in *Biology of Aging*. Other breakdowns include Esposito, *Obsolete Self*; Hart and Turturro, "Theories of Aging"; and Hayflick, "Theories of Biological Aging."

124. Ingram, "Is Aging Measurable?," 18.

125. See for instance Arking, *Biology of Aging*.

126. This includes even highly reductionistic definitions of aging that reduce the former to the latter.

a phase known as apoptosis, or cellular death, which over time negatively impacts the tissue or organ of which they consist. But even senescent cells can negatively impact the body's function as such cells cause inflammation, which is also related to the aging of an organism. In general, the relationship between cellular senescence, apoptosis, and human aging is far from clear.[127] Most gerontologists contend that cellular aging is not identical with an organism's aging, even though they are clearly related.[128] It is also widely accepted that aging has a genetic component. Progerias that lead to premature and accelerated aging like Werner's Syndrome and Hutchinson-Gilford Progeria Syndrome have been linked to specific genes, leading some to conclude that aging might be modulated by a manageable number of genes.[129] Nevertheless, most gerontologists are reticent to describe aging as a genetic program, much less identify particular genes that might influence aging. Many gerontologists acknowledge that since the aging process is stochastic, influenced by genetic, epigenetic, and environmental factors, any progress in extending the human life-span—if indeed any significant progress is possible—will be achieved through interdisciplinary effort.[130] However, despite the seemingly innumerable complexities involved in aging, scientists have demonstrated that the aging process in mammals and humans is amenable to technological intervention.

SLOWING AGING: FROM LEGEND TO LABORATORY

This brief survey of the history of attempts at human longevity bears witness to a still widely held view that considers attempts to attenuate or slow human aging as little more than ill-fated admixtures of pseudoscience, spirituality, and half-baked theories, or, as one author put it, an "endless parade of deluded dreamers and quacks."[131] Though some gerontologists

127. Kirkwood, *Time of Our Lives*, 97. "There is no evidence that ageing is driven by apoptosis, even though apoptosis does occur more readily with age in some tissues, probably because damage accumulates."

128. Austad, *Why We Age*, 225n37. See also Clark, *Means to an End*, 113, who observes, "understanding just how replicative senescence relates to aging in the entire organism will likely engage researchers for many years to come."

129. Clark, *Means to an End*, 93, has asserted that "the incredible spectrum of aging-like phenotypic changes wrought in the single-gene progerias suggests that the actual number of genes [associated with aging] may not have to be terribly large." Austad however contends that progeria is not the same as aging, but merely caricatures it. Moreover, geneticist George M. Martin has estimated that several thousand genes may influence aging. See Austad, *Why We Age*, 46–47.

130. Jazwinski, "Longevity, Genes, and Aging."

131. Stipp, *Youth Pill*, 26.

liken contemporary anti-aging science to "scientific porn," this perception has slowly changed as respected authorities within the field have produced empirical evidence of aging attenuation in the laboratory.[132] Nearly two decades ago, S. Jay Olshansky and Bruce Carnes—both well-respected researchers at the University of Chicago—refuted many of the myths surrounding aging attenuation in their book *The Quest for Immortality* (2001). At the same time however they readily acknowledged the "frenetic scientific search for biochemical keys that will unlock the secrets of aging," expressing optimism that there might be a few chemical compounds available for the youngest of the current generation.[133] Indeed, more recently scientists have announced "the unquestioned conviction that we cannot alter aging and the cellular underpinnings of the diseases that accompany the aging process is no longer strictly tenable."[134] Life extension has gone from legend to the laboratory, leading many in the fields of gerontology and molecular biology to acknowledge that, while the prospects of attenuating aging are difficult, the idea is much more than a hyped-up, vacuous notion. The mapping of the world as a result of exploratory efforts that would eventually expose hyperborean stories as mere legend have given way to the mapping of the human genome, opening up promising new vistas of greater longevity within the body. Gilgamesh has given way to the genome and molecular biology.

Within the last several years, for instance, scientists have been able to significantly extend the life-spans of mice, fruit flies, and other multicellular organisms such as the *Caenorhabditis elegans* (*C. elegans*), or nematode worm.[135] It is significant that these longer life spans have also extended the period of an organism's *health*. Though such organisms are considerably less complex than the human body, these experiments are considered the first step towards an eventual application to human beings. Among the most promising methods of aging attenuation are genetic manipulation, telomerase therapy, and caloric restriction.

132. Gavrilov, "Pieces of the Puzzle."

133. Olshansky and Carnes, *Quest for Immortality*, 148. Not all scientists are convinced. Leonard Hayflick, co-founder and name bearer of one of the most significant scientific discoveries in molecular biology this century—the Hayflick Limit—remains incredulous about the prospects of retarding the aging process, and whether this is even desirable. *How and Why*, 6.

134. Banks and Fossel, "Telomeres, Cancer, and Aging," 1348.

135. Two of the earlier studies of multicellular species, the *Drosophila melanogaster* and *Caenorhabditis elegans* are cited in Banks and Fossel, "Telomeres, Cancer, and Aging." Others include Ewbank et al., "Structural and Functional Conservation"; Lakowski and Hekimi, "Determination of Lifespan"; and Larsen et al., "Genes That Regulate Development." Since then, the number of studies confirming these findings has steadily grown.

At just 959 cells with an average life-span of thirteen days, the nematode worm *C. elegans* has proven an ideal candidate for slowing aging through genetic manipulation. Scientists are routinely uncovering the different genetic pathways and mechanisms that influence aging in the *C. elegans*, with the discovery of a gene implicated in slowing aging ("age-1") in 1988.[136] Other genes have been subsequently identified, adding to an ever-expanding class of "gerontogenes." Geneticist Cynthia Kenyon discovered a mutated gene, daf-2, that doubled the life-span of the *C. elegans*.[137] Daf-2 had been known to induce dormancy in larval worms, but when mutated, in produced famine-like responses from the worm as a survival mechanism. Subsequent research identified this gene as a component of a hormone system that transmits signals from a similarly structured growth hormone IGF-1. When the daf-2 is mutated, the worms produce less growth hormone and live longer. By altering two genes the effects have been even more pronounced; the *C. elegans* lived nearly *six* times longer than their unmodified counterparts.[138] While nematode worms are far less complex than the human body, these studies demonstrate that asging in multicellular organisms can be modified by relatively straightforward gene interventions.

An intriguing factor with these nematode worms is that their IGF-1 signaling pathway functions similarly in human beings. A human analogue occurs among sufferers of a rare genetic disorder known as Laron syndrome or Laron-type dwarfism, which produces significantly less IGF-1. In what might be considered a modern hyperborean tale with a genetic twist, the *New York Times* published a story of ninety-nine Ecuadorean villagers suffering from Laron syndrome who are remarkably youthful in appearance, and nearly immune to age-related diseases like cancer and diabetes in spite of their higher rate of obesity.[139] Though the death rate for these villagers is adversely affected by alcoholism and accidents, Dr. Jamie Guevara-Aguirre's decades-long endocrinological study has captured the attention of gerontologists in North America, who acknowledge that reducing the production of IGF-1 in adulthood has potential to lengthen the span of life. Andrzej Bartke, a well-respected gerontologist at Southern Illinois University, has already engineered mice that live twice as long as untreated mice by

---

136. See for instance Murphy et al., "Genes That Act Downstream." It is believed that there are at least five genomic regions with several genetic pathways that influence longevity. See Jazwinski, "Longevity, Genes, and Aging" and Friedman and Johnson, "Mutation in the Age-1 Gene."

137. See Kenyon et al., "*C. elegans* Mutant." See also Guarente and Kenyon, "Genetic Pathways"; Johnson, "Increased Life-Span of *age-1* Mutant," 908–12.

138. Banks and Fossel, "Telomeres," 1345.

139. Wade, "Ecuadorean Villagers."

manufacturing a defect in its growth hormone receptor gene. As we will see shortly, this "longevity pathway" of IGF-1 modulation can be activated by adopting a "fast mimicking diet," building on knowledge gained from the Ecuadorian studies.

Other potential genetic interventions into the aging process derive from the discovery of four genes known as Yamanaka factors (named after their discoverer, Shinya Yamanaka), that are capable of inducing adult cells to behave like embryonic pluripotent stem cells, or iPSCs. Stem cells can be coaxed to develop into any other human cell type. Yamanaka factors allow for partial reprogramming of cells to a pluripotent, embryo-like state, which actually reverses cellular aging by resetting the aging clock. A 2016 study tested the efficacy of Yamanaka factors on laboratory mice that were specially designed to age prematurely. By triggering their Yamanaka factors two days per week throughout their life-span, these mice lived 40 percent longer than their untreated counterparts.[140] More recently, scientists have regenerated optic nerves in mice by activating three Yamanaka factors (Oct4, Klf4, Sox2), leading to the possibility of arresting glaucoma and actually restoring vision.[141] Though questions remain over whether such results are translatable to humans, the once unquestioned assumption that cells undergo a unidirectional differentiation process from pluripotency to eventual apoptosis (cellular death) is no longer gospel. Researchers at the Salk Institute have noted that such findings demonstrate that "aging is a very dynamic and plastic process, and therefore will be more amenable to therapeutic interventions than what we previously thought."[142]

Still other promising genetic interventions are on the horizon. In 2000 Dr. Leonard Guarente and his colleagues at Massachusetts Institute of Technology discovered the genetic pathway that effectively mimics the longevity effects produced by caloric restriction (to be discussed shortly) in yeast.[143] Yeast given an extra copy of the gene SIR2—silent information regulator No. 2—lived longer. Gene silencing protects cell integrity and prevents the activation of other genes which have the potential to produce deleterious effects in organisms. Sirtuins, which derive their name from SIR2, are enzymes which serve epigenetic regulators, controlling reproduction and DNA repair and overseeing cellular reproduction. Sirtuins trade cellular reproduction for DNA repair, effectively ordering our bodies to "hunker

140. Ocampo et al., "In Vivo Amelioration." It was also observed however that increasing the dose even slightly proved toxic to the mice.

141. Sinclair and LaPlante, *Lifespan*, 167–72.

142. Salk Institute, "Turning Back Time."

143. Wade, "A Pill to Extend Life?," 2A, commenting on Lin et al., "Requirement of NAD and SIR2 for Life-Span Extension." See also Kaeberlein et al., "*SIR2/3/4* Complex."

down" in times of stress, affording added protection against the major diseases of aging such as diabetes, heart disease, Alzheimer's, osteoporosis, and cancer.[144] Mammals have seven sirtuin genes (SIRT1 to SIRT7) which are made by nearly every cell in the body. The decline in sirtuin activity as we grow older is thought to be a primary reason our bodies develop diseases as we age. Adding extra copies of the SIR2 gene to fruit flies and mice has extended their life-spans as these organisms are better equipped to deal with the epigenetic noise that brings on aging. Similar results have been attained by adding copies of SIRT6 from mice and beavers to human cells, showing that SIRT6 promotes double-strand DNA repair in breaks that inevitably increase with age.[145] Moreover, researchers discovered that SIRT6 is more efficient and stronger in longer-lived species—SIRT6 in beavers is more effective than the same gene in mice. There are now plans to examine the SIRT6 gene of bowhead whales—given their capability of living more than 200 years—to test its potency. Researchers hope to target interventions that delay the onset of cancer and other age-related degenerative diseases.

Significantly, more recent studies at the Max Plank Institute for Heart and Lung Research and Stanford University used sirtuins to prevent cellular senescence in humans.[146] Scientists have discovered several sirtuin activating compounds—STACs. One particularly promising STAC, known as NAD (nicotinamide adenine dinucleotide), boosts the activity of all seven mammalian sirtuin enzymes. In 2018 researchers treated elderly mice with a NAD-boosting molecule that activated the SIRT1 enzyme in the endothelial cells lining blood vessels, effectively reversing the effects of aging.[147] After receiving NAD, these elderly mice were running the equivalent of ultramarathons on the treadmill. This development has been characterized as one of the first exercise mimetics, and demonstrates that some aspects of aging reversal are indeed possible.[148] The linkage between sirtuins and cellular aging is a promising avenue of research for slowing aging at the cellular level.[149]

---

144. Sinclair and LaPlante, *Lifespan*, 24. Sinclair likens sirtuins to "directors of a multifaceted disaster response corps, sending out a variety of specialized emergency teams to address DNA stability, DNA repair, cell survivability, metabolism, and cell-to-cell communication." *Lifespan*, 45.

145. Tian et al., "SIRT6 Responsible for More Efficient DNA."

146. Ianni et al., "Sirt7 Stabilizes rDNA Heterochromatin"; Paredes et al., "Epigenetic Regulator SIRT7."

147. Das et al., "Impairment of an Endothelial NAD+-H2S Signaling."

148. Sinclair and LaPlante, *Lifespan*, 63.

149. See for instance Lee et al., "Sirtuin Signaling in Cellular Senescence."

Another prospect for longevity comes from the discovery of an enzyme called telomerase, named after telomeres, which are the unencoded tips of chromosomes making up somatic cells. Telomeres gradually shorten over time with repeated cell divisions until DNA duplication is no longer possible. This telomere shortening can lead to "chromosomal clumping," triggering the cell's damage control system to halt the replication process, leaving the cell in a state of senescence, before (eventually) entering apoptosis, or cellular death.[150] Thus, this process, known as "replicative senescence" or the "Hayflick Limit," which speaks to the finite number of divisions a somatic cell can perform, is largely the result of telomere shortening, and closely associated with aging, cellularly and phenotypically.[151] Though telomeres of somatic cells shorten over time through successive replications, germ cells exhibit no evidence of telomere shortening, enabling them to replicate indefinitely. In the 1980s Elizabeth Blackburn and Carol Greider, who would later receive the Nobel Prize for their work, discovered an enzyme which they originally called "terminal transferase," which preserves telomere length with repeated cell division.[152] In 1998 researchers transfected normal somatic cells with a gene that activates terminal transferase—now called "telomerase"—enabling the cells to continue dividing beyond the Hayflick Limit.[153] These transfected cells had elongated telomeres and exceeded their normal life-span by doubling at least twenty times beyond untreated cells.[154] Some have made rather startling claims concerning the promise of telomerase therapy. In the late 1990s Michael Fossel claimed that telomerase therapy would be widely available by 2015.[155] Blackburn herself claimed that the discovery of this enzyme "sort of translates into a fountain of youth," noting that "the number of years of living is related to telomere length."[156] Her co-authored book entitled *The Telomere Effect: A Revolutionary Approach to Living Younger, Healthier, Longer* (2017), joins a rapidly expanding list of recent offerings with titles such as *The Telomerase Revolution*, *The Telomere Miracle*, and *The Telomerase Diet*, all showing how to exploit our scientific

---

150. See Austad, *Why We Age*, 67–68; Clark, *Means*, 109–13; Hayflick, *How and Why*, 135–36; Kirkwood, *Time of Our Lives*, 156–58.

151. Hayflick and Moorhead, "Serial Cultivation of Human Diploid Strains."

152. Greider and Blackburn, "Identification of a Specific Telomere." See also Brady, *Elizabeth Blackburn and the Story of Telomeres*. Telomerase is also present in hair follicle cells, certain gut cells, and white blood cells.

153. Bodnar et al., "Extension of Life-Span." See also Hahn et al., "Inhibition of Telomerase"; Yang et al., "Human Endothelial Cell Life Extension."

154. Bodnar et al., "Extension of Life-Span," 349.

155. Fossel, *Reversing Human Aging*, 222.

156. Blackburn, "New Health Program."

knowledge of telomerase to "slow your genetic aging" or "turn back the clock on aging."[157] Other studies have explored psychological avenues to maintain telomere length, given that length is related to chronic stress and exposure to depression, while others have uncovered a link between telomere length and exercise.[158]

Not everyone is as optimistic, as it is still unclear if human aging itself has actually been attenuated. In addition, telomerase is known to inhibit a protein known as p53, which is responsible for detecting damaged DNA and initiating cellular apoptosis—the cell's death sequence. When cellular apoptosis functions poorly, the chances of developing cancer increase.[159] Indeed, telomerase is present in over 90 percent of all cancers.[160] It has also been discovered that mice with an overly active p53 protein age prematurely, even though they developed far fewer tumors than normal mice, raising the possibility that the same p53 mechanism that guards against cancer early in life may *accelerate* aging later on.[161] Finally, others point out that telomerase is not the answer to aging because most cells in the body do not divide a great majority of the time, and often reach the Hayflick Limit long before they eventually initiate apoptosis and die.[162] Other prominent researchers have also expressed doubt that this finding is of any real significance to forestalling the aging process.[163]

Despite these concerns, continued research has yielded promising results in understanding telomeres and telomerase as mediators of aging and disease. Harvard University scientists have actually reversed aging-related

---

157. Blackburn and Epel, *Telomere Effect*; Fossel, *Telomerase Revolution*; Park, *Telomere Miracle*; Moon, *Telomere Diet and Cookbook*.

158. Jacobs et al., "Intensive Meditation Training"; Epel et al., "Can Meditation Slow Rate of Cellular Aging?"; Tucker, "Physical Activity and Telomere Length." According to Tucker, "Adults with High activity were estimated to have a biologic aging advantage of 9 years (140 base pairs ÷ 15.6) over Sedentary adults. The difference in cell aging between those with High and Low activity was also significant, 8.8 years, as was the difference between those with High and Moderate PA [Physical Activity] (7.1 years)."

159. Ferbeyre and Lowe, "Price of Tumor Suppression?"

160. Clark, *Means*, 128–29.

161. Tyner et al., "p53 Mutant Mice"; Ferbeyre and Lowe, "Price of Tumor Suppression?," 27.

162. Clark, *Means*, 112.

163. Olshansky and Carnes, "No Truth to the Fountain of Youth," 80. "A single genetic intervention in an organism as complex as a human being would have little chance of combating the probably vast array of genes and biological activities that play subtle, unpredictable parts in the timing of our ultimate demise." See also Hayflick, *How and Why*, 6.

damage in mice through telomerase therapy.[164] After breeding mice to age prematurely (without the enzyme telomerase), they showed substantial improvement when they received telomerase—damaged tissues were repaired, and new brain neurons grew, indicators of reversing the signs of aging. Moreover, none of the mice developed cancer after treatment. The scientists conclude that this "unprecedented reversal of age-related decline in the central nervous system and other organs . . . justify exploration of telomere rejuvenation strategies for age-associated diseases."[165] Ronald DePinho, who led the Harvard Study, speculated that such treatment might be safe for humans if administered periodically to younger, cancer-free individuals.[166] Several years ago Geron Corporation, a biopharmaceutical firm in California, patented a human gene for telomerase in hopes of manufacturing a drug to slow aging, though they are now focused on developing telomerase-based cancer drugs. They have however licensed a supplement known as TA-65 through a company called T.A. Sciences, backed by clinical studies showing it activates telomerase enzymes in humans, lengthening telomeres.[167] Though such supplements—which start at $100 for thirty capsules—are not subject to the demanding constraints of the pharmaceutical industry, it remains to be seen whether longer telomeres will translate into longer, healthier life. Nevertheless, the advent of CRISPR/Cas-9 technology will enable scientists to quickly and efficiently track telomeres in ways at the systems level that were not possible just few years ago, affording researchers the ability to conduct *in vivo* studies of telomere damage in real time.[168]

Another major strand of aging exploration flowing out of the long history of hygienic practices falls under the more precise moniker of "caloric restriction," or CR, emphasizing the positive effects of *under*nutrition cellularly and phenotypically. Though hygiene has nearly always been associated with increased longevity, the link between longevity and dietary restriction was first confirmed in the modern era (1930) by Cornell University nutrition researcher Clive McCay (1898–1967). He demonstrated that rats lived much longer when placed on near-starvation diets.[169] Since then,

164. Jaskelioff et al., "Telomerase Reactivation."
165. Jaskelioff et al., "Telomerase Reactivation," 106.
166. Sample, "Harvard Scientists Reverse the Ageing Process in Mice—Now for Humans."
167. Harley et al., "Natural Product Telomerase." The researchers note however that there was no control group in this particular study.
168. Brane and Tollefsbol, "Targeting Telomeres."
169. McCay and Crowell, "Prolonging the Life Span." For a brief history of the discovery linking caloric restriction and longevity, see Cesario and Hollander, "Life Span Extension."

numerous studies have been conducted with promising results.[170] Generally speaking, animals fed 30 to 50 percent less than a normal caloric intake experienced an average life-span increase of approximately 33 percent, with small variations between different species.[171] Calorically restricted rats and mice are also more tumor resistant and maintain energy, immune system function, and memory for a longer period of time.[172] Limiting caloric intake reduces oxidative stress, allowing DNA to repair damage suffered by cells.[173] Others suggest that caloric restriction may reduce a process called "browning" (also known as the Maillard reaction)—where glucose attaches to proteins in unwanted places resulting in undesired and unalterable chemical structures.[174] CR activates a host of benefits for the body, including increased efficiency in DNA repair, more efficient protein synthesis, more effective cell replacement and regeneration, and fortification of the immune system.[175] In 2017, a long-term study at the University of Wisconsin has demonstrated that CR extends the median and maximum life-span of rhesus monkeys, who are genetically similar to humans.[176] Though their median life-span (in captivity) is twenty-six years with a 10 percent survival rate at thirty-five years, a 30 percent reduction in calories enabled six of the original twenty monkeys to live beyond *forty* years, including one forty-three-year-old monkey—a longevity record for this species, and the equivalent of a one-hundred-and-thirty-year-old human. The study also showed an overall reduction in aging-related pathologies and a twofold reduction in the risk for age-related morbidity. The researchers conclude that "it seems highly

170. See for instance de Cabo and Mattson, "Effects of Intermittent." See also Cheng et al., "Fasting-Mimicking Diet"; Cheng et al., "Prolonged Fasting Reduces IGF-1/PKA"; Mattison et al., "Caloric Restriction Improves Health,"; Nashiro et al., "Brain Structure,"; Park and Prolla, "Lessons Learned"; Cohen et al., "Calorie Restriction Promotes Mammalian Cell Survival."

171. Kirkwood, *Time of Our Lives*, 176.

172. Austad, *Why We Age*, 184; Clark, *Means*, 137–38.

173. Clark, *Means*, 139, 161. Clark however concedes that excess caloric intake may shorten life-span more than caloric restriction extends it. Leonard Hayflick has also argued that feeding animals *ad libitum* does not realistically mimic nature, and therefore actually *shortens* the life-span more than lengthening the life-span of the calorically restricted mice. See *How and Why*, 284. Kirkwood however cites studies that show gains in longevity even when calorically restricted animals' life-spans are compared to those on a controlled diet. See *Time of Our Lives*, 177; Austad, *Why We Age*, 189.

174. Austad, *Why We Age*, 137.

175. Rattan, "Gene Therapy for Ageing," 28; Rattan and Singh, "Progress and Prospects."

176. Mattison et al., "Caloric Restriction Improves Health." It should be noted that a similar study conducted at the National Institute on Aging did not produce the same results, though Mattison et al. offer several possible explanations for the discrepancy.

likely that the beneficial effects of CR would also be observed in humans. . . . and that aging itself presents a reasonable target for intervention."[177] This echoes the claims of gerontologists made a decade earlier, who estimated that a mere 30 percent reduction in caloric intake from age thirty would increase life expectancy by approximately seven years.[178] This is significant given that eliminating all forms of cancer and heart disease would increase life expectancy by only three years.

Walter Longo, a gerontologist at the University of Southern California who studied under one of the world's leading experts on nutrition, Dr. Roy Walford (1924–2004), has been actively exploring the science behind caloric restriction in hopes of developing a nutritional regimen to realize longer, healthier life-spans. He believes that our increasing understanding of maintaining the human body through the right combination of nutrition, fasting, and exercise will allow us to "stay fully functional into our nineties, hundreds, and beyond," primarily through "exploiting" the body's innate ability of cellular regeneration.[179] Having spent years studying the link between nutrition and the genes regulating cellular protection and regeneration, Longo promotes a "programmed longevity" approach combining specific nutrition with an occasional "fast-mimicking diet" (FMD) that will activate these rejuvenating cellular mechanisms necessary for longer, healthier life.[180] Longo is active in the nascent field of "nutritechnology" that treats ingredients found in normal food as a complex set of molecules, which, under the right conditions, can exhibit "drug-like beneficial properties" that can be harnessed to delay aging.[181] In short, an FMD is able to spur cell regeneration naturally by taking advantage of billions of years of evolution to activate the body's own self-healing program that resembles embryogenesis.[182] Longo believes that we can delay the onset of significant physiological decline one or two decades, from about forty or fifty to about sixty or seventy years. In 2018 he published a recommended diet in

177. Wei et al., "Fast-Mimicking Diet."

178. Speakman and Hambly, "Starving for Life." The promise of extending the healthspan through a reduced diet has led to the birth of the CR Society International (CRSI), and continues to produce steady stream of literature promoting proper consumption to live to 120 years, if not longer.

179. Longo, *Longevity Diet*, xii.

180. Longo's diet is situated within the disciplines he calls the Five Pillars of Longevity: (1) juventology—the study of youth, (2) epidemiology, (3) clinical studies, (4) studies of centenarians, and (5) the understanding of complex systems. See *Longevity Diet*, xv, 42, 47, 66–84.

181. Longo, *Longevity Diet*, 8. See Longo and Cortellino, "Enhancing Stem Cell Transplantation."

182. Longo, *Longevity Diet*, 109.

conjunction with his clinically-tested product ProLon, developed by his company L-Nutra.[183]

Longo's longevity diet is backed by the aforementioned data on the efficacy of caloric restriction. He worked with the endocrinologist Jaime Guevara-Aguirre, who spent decades studying a long-lived people in Ecuador suffering from Laron syndrome. These villagers lack the receptor for growth hormone, IGF-1, which while stunting their overall growth and stature, also dramatically reduces the incidences of cancer, diabetes, and Alzheimer's—despite heavy consumption of fried foods and unhealthy lifestyle choices.[184] The reduction in insulin-like growth factor 1 (IGF-1) has long been associated with tumor suppression and heightened longevity.[185] Longo notes that the mutation in the growth hormone receptor gene forces the body to remain in an "alternative longevity program," enhancing both cellular regeneration and resistance to disease; he duplicated the Laron syndrome in laboratory mice, observing a 50 percent increase in healthy life-span. While his lab is currently testing drugs to block IGF-1 in humans, Longo asserts that gene expressions driving cellular rejuvenation and disease resistance—"longevity genes"—can be effectively modulated by adopting his fast mimicking diet.[186] In particular, FMD switches all cells into a "protected anti-aging mode," which promotes autophagy—the self-consuming parts of a cell—as well as the replacement of damaged cell components with newly generated cells. The regimen, which mirrors a pescatarian diet, prescribes eating two meals a day, and a snack, coupled with a five-day FMD (at least) twice a year.[187]

A randomized study of 100 patients conducted at the Keck Medical Center at the University of Southern California yielded encouraging results. The participants followed Longo's five-day fast-mimicking cycle once per

---

183. Longo recommends the diet and ProLon product be used in conjunction with medical supervision. He also notes that he does not benefit financially from the sale of ProLon.

184. Nashiro et al., "Brain Structure and Function." Only one of Guevara-Aguirre's research subjects has died of cancer in his thirty years of observation. Moreover, their cognitive function mirrored that of younger individuals.

185. Tazearslan et al., "Impaired IGF1R Signaling." See also Sinclair and LaPlante, *Lifespan*, 96–98.

186. Cheng et al., "Prolonged Fasting." See also Cheng et al., "Fasting-Mimicking Diet."

187. Longo's diet actually involves eight guidelines: (1) adopting a pescatarian diet, (2) consuming low amounts of protein, (3) minimizing bad fats and sugars while maximizing good fats and complex carbohydrates, (4) being nourished, (5) eating a variety of food associated with one's ancestry, (6) eating twice a day plus a snack, (7) observing time-restrictive eating, and (8) practicing periodic prolonged fasting with FMD.

month, for three months, eating whatever they wanted the rest of the time. Though one quarter of the participants dropped out of the study for various reasons, the health benefits in the form of decreased body mass, better levels of glucose, triglycerides, and cholesterol, along with other factors, were observed, persisting to the third month *after* participants had returned full-time to a regular diet.[188] Longo concludes that this small study "may be responsible for the generation and rejuvenation occurring in multiple systems."[189] That is, he believes that a FMD can spur cell regeneration by taking advantage of billions of years of evolution to activate the body's own self-healing program, which, when operating well, resembles core features of embryogenesis, the generation of new cells.[190]

In his apologetic for pursuing nutritional changes coupled with FMD (utilizing ProLon), Longo seeks to situate his regimen between the extremes of fad dieting on the one hand and snake-oil remedies on the other. He points out the significance of religious fasting in human history to counter the notion that FMD is yet another fad in the weight loss battle. In addition, Longo asserts that FMD is preferable to drugs and stem-cell based therapies because is a "natural intervention," insofar as it operates in harmony with the evolutionary development of human metabolism.

> The major advantage of the FMD approach—compared with drug interventions and stem cell-based therapies—is that it awakens a highly coordinated response that is already built into the body but that has fallen dormant because of our steady and constant consumption of food.[191]

Longo also notes how the longevity diet in conjunction with an FMD can prevent, delay, treat, and even reverse the effects of specific diseases, including cancer treatment and prevention, diabetes prevention and treatment, cardiovascular disease, Alzheimer's, and other neurodegenerative diseases. While no studies conducted thus far—whether in rhesus monkeys or humans—would lead one to conclude that CR actually attenuates the aging process, they do show that the human *health* span can be modulated by behavioral changes.[192] Insofar as Longo remains firmly committed to a vision of longer, healthier life through better, scientifically informed

188. Wei et al., "Fast-Mimicking Diet."
189. Longo, *Longevity Diet*, 105.
190. Longo, *Longevity Diet*, 109.
191. Longo, *Longevity Diet*, 108.
192. There is also evidence that healthspan through CR mimetics may compress the period of morbidity before death. See Finch, *Biology of Human Longevity*, 185–86; Stipp, "Researchers Seek Key," A1.

nutrition, his work could be categorized as hygienic with respect to longevity. His views however, represent a minority position among scientists who are eager to understand the aging process in order to extend healthy life, who lean toward the development of drugs known as caloric restriction mimetics or other pharmacological interventions in order to produce more consistent, reliable results.

Indeed, many question whether long term CR or intermittent fasting is practical, much less possible. Rozalyn Anderson, lead researcher in the rhesus monkey study at the University of Wisconsin, stressed that neither she nor her colleagues are recommending humans adopt similar caloric restriction practices. She candidly admitted that a 30 percent reduction in calories on a long-term basis would be nothing short of a "bonkers diet."[193] Science writer Adam Piore, who tried the ProLon FMD for five days, quipped that even though caloric restriction might not make you live longer, "It'll certainly feel like longer," though he lost several pounds and felt much better.[194] A 2019 review of intermittent fasting in *The New England Journal of Medicine* put it rather bluntly: "Most people consume three meals a day plus snacks, so intermittent fasting does not occur."[195] Moreover, chronic caloric restriction has shown adverse effects for several mouse strains, and there is the potential to induce some humans into what some might consider a near anorexic state. Others in the field of eating disorders have noted negative outcomes as well.[196] Leslie Robert, biochemist and physician at the University of Paris, echoes these concerns over long-term health; she asserts that pharmaceutical approaches have greater anti-aging potential.[197] Robert's views reflect a growing consensus among researchers. In fact, developments in pharmacology over the last decade fuel hopes that scientists will indeed manufacture a pill capable of mimicking the beneficial effects of CR and FMD. "Until about the early 1990s, it was kind of laughable that you could develop a pill that would slow aging," noted Richard Miller, biogerontologist at the University of Michigan. "It was sort of a science fiction trope." However, he notes, "Recent research has shown that pessimism is wrong."[198] The same review in the *New England Journal of Medicine* that noted the unlikelihood of adhering to long-term caloric restriction drew a similar conclusion:

193. Conniff, "Hunger Gains."
194. See Piore, "Starvation Diet," 65.
195. de Cabo and Mattson, "Effects of Intermittent Fasting," 2541.
196. Di Francesco et al., "Time to Fast," 770. See also Liao et al., "Genetic Variation"; Walford et al., "Caloric Restriction in Biosphere 2"; Vitousek, "Case for Semi-Starvation."
197. Conniff, "Hunger Gains."
198. Taylor, "A 'Fountain of Youth' Pill?"

"By further understanding the processes that link intermittent fasting with the broad health benefits, we may be able to develop target pharmacologic therapies that mimic the effects of intermittent fasting without the need to substantially alter feeding habits."[199] Though some scientists' projections of the first anti-aging pill have yet to be realized, the consensus is, it seems, that a pill for slowing aging is on the horizon within the next decade if not sooner.[200]

Perhaps the most significant results in the field of CR mimetics occurred in 2009. In an Interventions Testing Program (ITP) sponsored by the National Institute on Aging, three laboratories reported that a drug known as rapamycin extended the life-span of mice in ways that closely mirrored the effects of caloric restriction.[201] First derived from an antifungal compound found in the actinobacterium *Streptomyces hygroscopicus* on a remote volcanic island, Rapa Nui (of the Easter Islands), rapamycin has been used as an immunosuppressant and is also known to have antitumor effects.[202] In the early 1990s scientists identified rapamycin's molecular targets as protein producing enzymes made by two related genes TOR1 and TOR2 ("target of rapamycin"). It was also known that nematode worms, flies, and mammals have genes that are very similar to TOR. Suppressing TOR in nematodes doubled their life-span, with similar effects on fruit flies.[203] Similarly, inhibiting the mammalian target of rapamycin (mTOR) pathway extends life-span in mice. mTOR is a set of genes that play a fundamental role in cellular function, regulating cellular growth and metabolism by sensing the local environment and either signaling cells to grow when conditions are good or shutting down reproduction in times of stress.[204] When inhibited, protein production in cells slowly significantly, reducing cells' energy requirements and the production of defective protein in cells that, over time, can contribute to cancer and other maladies associated with aging. In short, rapamycin seemed to mimic the effects of CR. What most surprised scientist however was the effectiveness of rapamycin on mice that were *already* very old (twenty months).[205] All three labs saw similar results: the

---

199. de Cabo and Mattson, "Effects of Intermittent Fasting," 2549.

200. For instance, S. Jay Olshansky et al. have asserted that scientists had garnered enough knowledge to produce a pill capable of delaying the onset of age-related diseases by seven years. See "Longevity Dividend." See also Taylor, "A 'Fountain of Youth' Pill?"

201. Harrison et al., "Rapamycin Fed Late in Life."

202. Stipp, *Youth Pill*, 207.

203. Vellai et al., "Influence of TOR Kinase"; Kapahi et al., "Regulation of Lifespan in *Drosophila*."

204. See Laplante and Sabatini, "mTOR Signaling."

205. Harrison et al., "Rapamycin Fed Late in Life."

maximum life-span was increased by 12 and 9 percent in females and males respectively. There is even stronger evidence that rapamycin can be effective later in life as well.[206] Moreover, these mice did not show the weight loss that CR mice normally experience. Still more recent studies have increased the life expectancy of middle-aged mice by 60 percent after three months of rapamycin, extending their healthy life-spans.[207] Rapamycin likely slows aging by rendering cellular senescence more efficient by stimulating autophagy, the process by which stubborn senescent cells, which cause inflammation and other problems, are effectively destroyed (called apoptosis). As we age, the mechanisms that clear away senescent cells gradually lose their effectiveness, allowing them to accumulate and produce inflammation in various tissues that, in the long term, become risk factors in conditions like heart disease and other age-related maladies. Hence, rapamycin could prove useful in diseases like Alzheimer's and Parkinson's where plaques accumulate in the brain.[208] Though there are concerns about potential side-effects—chiefly concerning rapamycin's immunosuppressive characteristics—it is reasonable to conclude that the drug can act as a CR mimetic in human beings.

As mentioned above, the push is on for developing a pill capable of slowing aging—whether it could be described as a caloric restriction mimetic or not. Human trails of rapamycin are already underway. Studies using derivatives of rapamycin called rapalogs have shown promise in ameliorating immunosenescence—detrimental changes in the immune system such as greater susceptibility to infection and reduced responses to vaccination—in older adults. In 2014 researchers led by Joan Mannick at Novartis Pharmaceuticals demonstrated the effectiveness of the mTOR inhibitor RAD001 (called everolimus). When administered to elderly patients over a six-week period, RAD001 enhanced the body's response to a seasonal influenza vaccine (by approximately 20 percent) and reduced the percentage of PD-1 positive T cells that accumulate with age and have a diminished antigen response.[209] In other words, patients' immune systems responded with a vigor found in much younger people. Though everolimus and its derivatives are not likely a panacea as high doses over extended periods of time has shown to be toxic to kidneys, the Mannick et al. study has been described as groundbreaking as it "sets the stage for testing drugs

---

206. Life expectancy at 600 days was increased by 38 percent and 28 percent in females and males respectively.
207. Bitto et al., "Transient Rapamycin Treatment."
208. Savage, "Growing Up."
209. Mannick et al., "mTOR Inhibition Improves Immune Function."

associated with delayed aging in older human populations."[210] Mannick currently serves as chief medical officer at resTORbio in Boston, a spin-off of Novartis, and is testing whether the same drug will help older adults ward off lung infections. Mannick believes that drugs are just a few years away, as she awaits the results of two phase three trials currently targeting the biology of aging.[211] Novartis has since shifted their research in another direction, selling the program to PureTech in exchange for an ownership stake in the new company. PureTech has committed millions to resTORbio in continuing efforts to reverse immunosenescence. Joseph Bolen, chief scientific officer of PureTech, has pointed out that such developments show that aging modulation "is actionable with a drug and not, say, calorie restriction."[212]

Trials are being conducted on drugs already on the market to test the efficacy of their abilities to modulate aging in humans. Metformin, currently used to manage diabetes, mimics the effects of caloric restriction by limiting metabolic reactions in mitochondria that are responsible for converting macronutrients into energy. In addition to inhibiting cancer cell formation, metformin also increases mitochondrial activity and removes misfolded proteins.[213] Indeed, there is ample evidence that metformin reduces the likelihood of a host of age-related maladies. A study of more than 41,000 metformin users between the ages of sixty-eight and eighty-one showed a reduced likelihood of dementia, cardiovascular disease, cancer, frailty, and depression.[214] A group study of frail subjects who took metformin over the course of nine years showed a reduction in dementia (4 percent), depression (16 percent), cardiovascular disease (19 percent), and frailty (24 percent). However, a recent study of healthy volunteers showed that the age of blood cells as measured by DNA methylation was actually *reversed* within one week after a single dose (850 mg) of metformin.[215] In late 2019 Nir Barzilai, geneticist at Albert Einstein College of Medicine in New York City conducted a study called TAME—Targeting Aging with Metformin—to administer metformin to patients already suffering from one age-related disease like cancer, heart disease, and Alzheimer's.[216] It appears that modulating aging on the cellular level leads to phenotypical benefits. As Barzilai says, "When

210. Kennedy and Pennypacker, "Aging Interventions Get Human," 591. More recently, similar results have been achieved by giving older dogs limited dosage of rapamycin. See Urfer et al., "Randomized Controlled Trial."
211. Hall, "Anti-Aging Drug around the Corner?"
212. Regalado, "Anti-Aging Pill We've All Been Waiting For?"
213. Sinclair and LaPlante, *Lifespan*, 125.
214. Wang et al., "Differential Effects of Metformin."
215. Elbere et al., "Significantly Altered Peripheral Blood."
216. Barzilai et al., "Metformin as a Tool."

you fix ageing on the cellular level, you fix a lot of other things."[217] Many hope that success here opens the door for the United States Food and Drug Administration to consider aging as a treatable condition.

Another promising pharmacological avenue in slowing human aging has been discovered in resveratrol, a natural molecule found in red wine. After it was shown to extend the healthy life-spans of fruit flies and laboratory mice by 20 percent, there was widespread speculation that drinking red wine may increase human longevity.[218] However, it was discovered that resveratrol does not have the same effect on humans, in part because it is not very soluble in the human gut. Nevertheless, there are other beneficial effects of resveratrol in terms of offsetting the negative effects of high caloric intake.[219] Moreover, the research did show that a molecule is capable of providing the benefits of caloric restriction, setting off a race to discover other molecules that produce similar effects. It also made the idea of manufacturing an anti-aging pill sound more credible, at least in some scientific circles.

Still more promising offerings are on the horizon with the development of senolytic drugs. The nascent field of senolytics focuses on cell-based strategies for greater longevity by clearing senescent cells with certain aging associated markers. Having earned the moniker "zombie cells" for their disruptive features and resistance to death, senescent cells are organisms' somatic cells that have reached the limit of their ability to divide (i.e. replicative arrest, or the Hayflick Limit) but do not enter the self-destructive phase known apoptosis. Senescent cells send out panic signals by secreting several pro-inflammatory and tissue remodeling molecules; they often accumulate in many aging tissues and at sites of pathology in chronic diseases. For instance, when scientists inject small numbers of senescent cells around the knee joints of mice, they induce an osteoarthritis-like condition resembling the non-injury osteoarthritis common in elderly humans.[220] Senolytic agents are designed to consume senescent cells, thereby counteracting the deleterious cellular and phenotypical effects of aging.[221] The first senolytic agents were discovered in 2015, and have since been used to ameliorate several chronic conditions in laboratory mice associated with aging such as frailty,

---

217. Savage, "Growing Up," S58.
218. Howitz et al., "Small Molecule Activators."
219. Mattison et al., "Resveratrol Prevents High Fat/Sucrose."
220. Xu et al., "Transplanted Senescent Cells," 780–85.
221. Justice et al., "Senolytics in Idiopathic Pulmonary Fibrosis." "Senolytic agents are drugs developed using a hypothesis-driven approach that selectively induce senescent cell apoptosis by transiently disabling the senescent cell anti-apoptotic pathways (SCAPs) that defend senescent cells against their own pro-apoptotic environment" (555).

cardiac dysfunction, vascular calcification, diabetes, liver steatosis, osteoporosis, vertebral disk degeneration, and pulmonary fibrosis.[222] Researchers however are also aware of the potential to fundamentally modulate aging at a cellular level will have an impact on numerous phenotypical aspects of human aging. Indeed, James L. Kirkland and his fellow researchers at the Mayo Clinic note the potential of senolytics to "transform geriatric medicine by enabling prevention or treatment of multiple diseases and functional deficits in parallel, instead of one at a time."[223]

The life-spans of laboratory mice have been extended with a combination of senolytic agents consisting of dastinib, a common chemotherapy drug, and the molecule quercetin, found in capers, kale, and red onions (D+Q).[224] When young mice (four months) were injected with senescent cells, they displayed impaired walking speed, muscle strength, physical endurance, and general daily activity within two weeks.[225] However, D+Q was effective in selectively consuming the senescent cells, and was shown to have attenuated the deterioration in walking speed, endurance, and grip strength. Older mice treated with D+Q intermittently alleviated normal age-related physical dysfunction, as indicated by higher walking speeds, treadmill endurance, grip strength, and daily activity. Remarkably, even very old mice (twenty-four to twenty-seven months) treated bi-weekly with D+Q experienced a 36 percent higher average post-treatment life-span than control mice, indicating that senolytics can reduce the risk of death in old mice. By clearing senescent cells with D+Q, physical dysfunction was alleviated and late-life survival increased in aged mice *without* extending morbidity.

More recently, promising results have been observed in humans. In 2018 researchers at the Mayo Clinic, in collaboration with Wake Forest School of Medicine and the University of Texas, conducted a safety and feasibility trial on fourteen patients with mild to severe idiopathic pulmonary fibrosis (IPF), a chronic, irreversible, progressive, and fatal senescence-associated disease resulting in the scarring of lung tissue.[226] The participants,

---

222. Zhu et al., "Achilles' Heel of Senescent Cells"; Kirkland et al., "Clinical Potential of Senolytic Drugs."

223. Kirkland et al., "Clinical Potential of Senolytic Drugs," 2297. This is also known as the "geroscience hypothesis."

224. Xu et al., "Senolytics Improve Physical Function"; National Institutes of Health, "Senolytic Drugs Reverse Damage Caused by Senescent Cells in Mice."

225. The study also indicated that the senescent cells spread rapidly and that this spread was exacerbated by a high-fat diet.

226. Justice et al., "Senolytics in Idiopathic Pulmonary Fibrosis." The median survival time for newly diagnosed individuals over sixty years of age is less than four years.

who received D+Q orally three days each week for three weeks, showed "a statistically significant and clinically meaningful" improvement in mobility as measured by a six-minute walk test, timed sitting to standing repetitions, and other benchmarks.[227] The authors conclude that these results "constitute preliminary proof-of-concept evidence that interventions designed to target senescent cells may alleviate functional consequences of aging-related diseases in humans, as is the case in mice."[228] Moreover, co-author Nicolas Musi, professor of medicine at University of Texas Health San Antonio and director of the university's Sam and Ann Barshop Institute for Longevity and Aging Studies noted that "cellular senescence is clearly emerging as a main player in aging."[229] Other researchers in the field of aging agree. Though it will likely be a few more years before enough is known about the effects and safety of these drugs to provide them for everyone, if they prove efficacious, their potential is vast.[230] These small but encouraging studies only fuel the push for more human trials to explore the anti-aging effects of drugs already on the market, with hopes of manufacturing more specific, efficacious anti-aging drugs in the future.

In 2019 researchers were surprised to discover that human aging had actually been *reversed* in patients who received a combination of drugs aimed at regenerating thymus tissue in adults.[231] For one year, a group of nine men took two growth hormone medications in conjunction with metformin, a powerful caloric restriction mimetic in mice. Geneticist Steve Horvath, one of several designers of the study at the University of California Los Angeles, expressed his surprise: "I'd expected to see slowing down of the clock, but not a reversal."[232] The aging reversal was indicated by four different epigenetic "clocks" measuring DNA methylation at specific sites on the genome (providing greater accuracy than chronological age).[233] On average,

---

See Raghu et al., "Idiopathic Pulmonary Fibrosis."

227. Justice et al., "Senolytics in Idiopathic Pulmonary Fibrosis," 561.

228. Justice et al., "Senolytics in Idiopathic Pulmonary Fibrosis," 562. There were some mild reactions to the drugs consistent with IPF symptoms; the retention rate was 100 percent.

229. University of Texas Health Science Center at San Antonio, "First-in-Human Trial of Senolytic Drugs Encouraging."

230. Sinclair and LaPlante, *Lifespan*, 154.

231. Fahy et al., "Reversal of Epigenetic Aging," e13028.

232. Abbott, "Trial Hints at Age-Clock Reversal."

233. The specific epigenetic clocks for the study were designed by Steve Horvath (DNAm age), G. Hannum et al. (DNAm age H), M. E. Levine et al. (DNAm PhenoAge), and A. T. Lu et al. (DNAm age G or "GrimAge"). The relationship between epigenetic clock indicators and chronological age remains a current topic of exploration. See Fransquet et al., "Epigenetic Clock as a Predictor."

the participants shed 2.5 years off their biological ages. Moreover, one of the epigenetic clocks known as the "GrimAge" predictor showed that the effects persisted six months after treatment was discontinued. "This is to our knowledge the first reported of an increase, based on an epigenetic age estimator, in predicted human lifespan by means of a currently accessible aging intervention."[234] Though these scientists acknowledge that this study reflects a small sample size, they too conclude that "the general prospects for meaningful amelioration of human aging appear to be remarkably promising."[235] This sentiment however has not gone uncontested. John Greally, professor of Genetics, Pediatrics, and Medicine at the Albert Einstein College of Medicine in New York City, points out that there is still no evidence showing that DNA methylation influences how cells age. That idea, says Greally, "has red flags all over it."[236]

Such skepticism however seems to have done little to dampen the hopes of slowing aging pharmacologically. Those who have the knowledge and the means are already experimenting on themselves. David Sinclair, professor of genetics at Harvard Medical School and one of the foremost figures in the field of slowing aging, admits to following his own anti-aging regimen consisting of one gram each of NMN (nicotinamide mononucleotide)[237]—a chemical found in avocado, broccoli, and cabbage shown to boost sirtuin activity in mammals—along with resveratrol, and metformin, and daily doses of vitamins D, K, and 83 mg of aspirin. In addition to regular exercise, he also tries to regularly skip a meal each day. Every few months his blood is analyzed for several biomarkers. Though Sinclair halfheartedly dampens the evangelistic tone in disclosing the effects of his regimen by warning that no program should be undertaken apart from proper medical supervision, he writes glowingly of his father's transformation, who, in his mid-seventies had just passed the type 2 diabetes threshold, was constantly tired and grumpy, and was slowly losing his hearing, eyesight, physical stamina, memory, and lust for life. But after six months of metformin for his borderline diabetes and daily dosage of NMN in small amounts, his father noticed a marked increase in energy and mental awareness; the normal aches and pains common to one's eighth decade diminished. His doctor was surprised to find that his liver enzymes had normalized after two decades of abnormality.[238] In reflecting

234. Fahy et al., "Reversal of Epigenetic Aging," e13028.
235. Fahy et al., "Reversal of Epigenetic Aging," e13028.
236. Hayasaki, "Mouse That Died," 28.
237. In his own lab, seven out of a group of forty mice put on NMN late in life were still alive, all of them having outlived the mice who did not receive it. See Sinclair and LaPlante, *Lifespan*, 136.
238. Sinclair and LaPlante, *Lifespan*, 142.

on his father's improvement, Sinclair employs the metaphor of war, deriving comfort from the "armies of chemists" at work against our adversary, aging:

> Maybe the research under way on any one of these molecular approaches [NMN, NAD] to battling aging will provide half a decade of additional health. Maybe a combination of these compounds and an optimal lifestyle will be the elixir that gets us a couple of extra decades. . . . [Nevertheless] Armies of chemists are now working to create and analyze natural and synthetic molecules that have the potential to be even better at suppressing epigenomic noise and resetting our epigenetic landscape.[239]

Sinclair understands critics who ask whether such a regimen is worth the potentially negative side effects, but replies, "I know exactly what is going to happen to me if I don't do anything at all—and it's not pretty."[240] Sinclair is hardly a lone ranger, however; he estimates that roughly one third of his colleagues working on solving aging are already taking metformin or an NAD (sirtuin-activating compound) booster.[241] Elizabeth Parrish, CEO of BioViva, reported that her telomeres had "grown younger" after three years of telomere therapy. A year earlier, Mikhail Blagosklonny, professor of oncology at the Roswell Park Cancer Institute published an article outlining an anti-aging formula consisting of rapalogs—such as rapamycin or everolimus—in conjunction with other clinically approved drugs like metformin, angiotensin II receptor blockers, statins, propranolol, aspirin, and a PDE5 inhibitor (commonly used to treat erectile dysfunction). Other reputable institutions like the Mayo Clinic have stoked the phenomenon with glowing press releases on the potentially "transformative" anti-aging effects coming from the Kirkland et al. study of dastinib and quercetin (D+Q) and a follow-up study on the effects of another promising drug called fisetin which has extended the life-span of mice by roughly 20 percent.[242] In a 2018 opinion piece in the *Journal of the American Medical Association*, Kirkland himself cautioned that "patients should be advised not to self-medicate with senolytic agents or other drugs that target fundamental aging processes in the expectation that conditions alleviated in mice will be alleviated in people."[243] There is little evidence to suggest Kirkland's warning is being heeded by anti-aging enthusiasts. James Clement, leader of the organization

---

239. Sinclair and LaPlante, *Lifespan*, 145.

240. Sinclair and LaPlante, *Lifespan*, 304.

241. Blagosklonny, "From Rapalogs to Anti-Aging Formula"; Blagosklonny, "Koschei the Immortal and Anti-Aging Drugs," e1552.

242. Yousefzadeh et al., "Fisetin is a Senotherapeutic."

243. Kirkland and Tchkonia, "Aging, Cell Senescence, and Chronic Disease," 1320.

BetterHumans, is financing four small human trials of a combination of rapamycin, NAD boosters, various senolytic compounds, and injections of plasma concentrated from umbilical cords.[244] Clement himself has taken the combination six times, and wears a steel wristband instructing anyone who comes across his dead body to notify the brain-freezing company Alcor. Others are unfazed by Kirkland's warning. One experimenter reported a doubling of the dosage of fisetin in Kirkland's study: "The Mayo clinic protocol called for 180mg, but I decided to [hit] those zombie cells harder."[245] Still others with means have gone to greater extremes to slow down the human aging clock.

Self-appointed lifestyle guru and biohacker Dave Asprey, inventor of "Bulletproof Coffee," runs a gym-like facility in Santa Monica, California filled with biohacking tools that include a cryogenic freezer, a float tank for meditation, and a Pulsed Electromagnetic Field machine (PEMF) that supposedly activates cell generation and circulation.[246] He has stem cells injected into his brain periodically. However, not all of his hacks have proven beneficial; Asprey suffered first-degree burns after an experiment with cold exposure went awry (he fell asleep), and he temporarily suffered from garbled speech after zapping himself with infrared light (in an attempt to learn faster).[247] Despite these setbacks, Asprey continues to promote his longevity regimen, releasing a book entitled *Superhuman: The Bulletproof Plan to Age Backward and Maybe Even Live Forever* (2019), which trades on the growing popularity of the transhumanist movement.[248]

These admittedly outlandish examples of prolongevity notwithstanding, the prospect of manufacturing a pill to increase one's healthy life-span by even a few years has captured the imagination of several well-known figures in the technology industry with deep pockets to fund their ambitions. Peter Thiel, co-founder of PayPal, plans on living to 120 years, a modest aim when compared to other tech billionaires like Dmitry Itskov, the "godfather" of the Russian Internet, who is aiming for 10,000. Google's founders Sergey Brin and Larry Page have pumped millions of dollars into Calico, a secretive health venture that aims to "solve death."[249] Other wealthy elites like Larry Ellison, co-founder of Oracle, finds human death deeply offensive, and has

---

244. Regalado, "Immortality Faith."

245. Regalado, "Immortality Faith," 73. The user reported a dosage of 300 mg.

246. Monroe, "Guru's Dilemma," 111.

247. Monroe, "Guru's Dilemma," 110.

248. Asprey, *Superhuman*.

249. Gabbatt, "Silicon Valley's Quest?" See Isaacson, "Silicon Valley Is Trying to Make Humans Immortal."

spent hundreds of millions to fund anti-aging research.[250] Life extension has moved to the laboratories of numerous well-respected universities, hospitals, and other centers of scientific inquiry. Academic institutions are increasingly partnering with start-up biotech companies—Juvenescence, Calico, Rejuvenate Bio, Sierra Sciences, Elysium, resTorbio, PureTech, AgeX, Turn Biotechnologies, GenuCure, and Life Biosciences—in order to slow human aging. Juvenescence is developing a range of therapies and technologies to increase human longevity, and has invested in several different companies such as AgeX Therapeutics, a California-based company working on developing stem cells to regenerate tissues that deteriorate with old age. Life Biosciences was founded in 2016 by scientists David Sinclair, professor in the Department of Genetics and co-director of the Paul F. Glenn Center for the Biology of Aging at Harvard Medical School, and global investor Tristan Edwards. The Boston-based company is investing in eight pathways of age-related decline.[251] In January of 2019 Life Biosciences raised fifty million dollars—double their initial target—to expand its portfolio of daughter companies dedicated to research and development. Rejuvenate Bio is another start-up, founded by George Church and Noah Davidsohn of Harvard Medical School. Church is currently testing some sixty different age-reversing gene therapies. The company claims it can reverse aging in animals by adding new DNA, and has carried out research on beagles. It has also planned a trial to combat mitral valve disease in Cavalier King Charles Spaniel dogs, a common malady caused by aging.[252] In November of 2019 they also reported that a single gene combination was capable of ameliorating several different age-related conditions in laboratory mice.[253]

Elysium, co-founded by Massachusetts Institute of Technology professor Leonard Guarente, is currently promoting NAD boosters as part of a growing "aging supplement" industry. Developed by the Harvard geneticist David Sinclair, a supplement known as "Basis" claims to slow aging as well as age-related diseases.[254] Supplements that have the backing of promising, peer-reviewed empirical studies carry a greater legitimacy in what has historically been a rather loosely regulated field. Indeed, Elysium boasts of an exclusive licensing agreement with Harvard University and the Mayo Clinic, while advertising their partnerships with Harvard, Cambridge, and Oxford Universities. While debates concerning the benefits, risks, and efficacy of

250. Bercovici, "How Peter Thiel Is Trying to Save the World."
251. See https://lifebiosciences.com/focus-areas/.
252. Saigol, "Companies Race to Find the Key to Eternal Life."
253. Davidson et al., "Single Combination Gene Therapy."
254. Taylor, "A 'Fountain of Youth' Pill?"

such substances will undoubtedly continue, these recent partnerships have raised questions about whether research institutions are sufficiently scrutinizing the financial interests and involvement of their faculty, and indeed their own institutions.[255] David Sinclair epitomizes such concerns; as of late 2019 he serves as either a founder, investor, equity holder, or consultant for more than twenty-five companies, eighteen of which are involved in slowing human aging.

The growing body of anti-aging research continues to fuel the hopes for longer, healthier lives. Even the moderate prospect of seven to ten years of healthy life and the possibility of avoiding a lengthy decline is enormously attractive. Certainly, if life is good and death the greatest threat to that good, it is difficult to criticize the desire to add a few years of health by attenuating aging and possibly reducing the period of morbidity before death, given especially the enormous financial, physical, and emotional strain of providing care in later life. But it is worth considering some of the subtle costs of slowing aging through technology, namely, how our attempts to modulate aging blur the distinction between aging and disease, and the impact this may have on our understanding of what it means to be embodied creatures. For it appears that with each discovery of a new pathway to longevity the distinction between aging and disease becomes more difficult to make. Researchers Leonard Guarente and Cynthia Kenyon are keenly aware of the power at their disposal, noting that "animals that should be old stay young" when even a single gene is altered. When confronted with such findings, they concede that "we begin to think of ageing as a disease that can be cured, or at least postponed."[256] There is enough evidence to suggest that the more aging is likened to a disease, the more we are inclined to view the body as an adversary, as something in our possession that must be brought into submission of the naked will through the growing arsenal of technologies currently at our disposal. Before bringing this chapter to a close, it is worth considering whether aging should be considered a disease, and how it may shape our understanding of embodiment.

IS AGING A DISEASE?

The Harvard researcher David Sinclair is unequivocal in his assertion. "Aging is a disease." For Sinclair this fact is so clear that "it seems almost insane that those four words need to be repeated again and again . . . aging is a disease. And not only is it a disease, but it is the mother of all diseases, and

---

255. Taylor, "A 'Fountain of Youth' Pill?"
256. Guarente and Kenyon, "Genetic Pathways," 261.

the one we all suffer from."²⁵⁷ According to Sinclair, we should be able to die whenever we want to. Hence, reframing aging as a disease is critical to his melioristic framework; for once aging is classified as a disease, vast sources of funding will become available for tackling particular diseases can be redirected to the one disease underlying them all.²⁵⁸ Sinclair is as much evangelist as he is scientist; he preaches good news to those fearful of decline, for we are on the precipice of solving the aging, deteriorating body, which he finds deeply offensive:

> Spend a day in a nursing home like my wife does every few days. Go feed people who can't chew. Wipe their bottoms. Bathe them with a sponge. Watch as they struggle to remember where they are and who they are. When you are done, I think you will agree that it would be negligent and cruel for you *not* to do what you can to combat your own age-related deterioration.²⁵⁹

When Sinclair reflects on the decline of his own grandmother, he is scarcely able to conceal his disdain for her stoic resignation to human finitude and death. After watching her gradually succumb to frailty, sedentariness, and sickness, he offers a chilling assessment: "the person she *truly* was had been dead many years."²⁶⁰ If, as Henri Nouwen and Walter Gaffney once noted, care for the elderly is predicated upon making ourselves available to the experience of becoming old, then Sinclair's abrasive rhetoric is understandable.²⁶¹ It is but a tiny leap from "anti-aging" to being against aging and aged people.²⁶² Sinclair has no patience for any other interpretation of human existence, especially those interpretations questioning the wisdom of living as long as one desires or those who argue that treating aging as a disease goes against the grain of nature. On the contrary, accepting our

---

257. Sinclair and LaPlante, *Lifespan*, 268.

258. Adam, "What If Aging Were A Disease?," 18. Adam observes, "Because aging isn't officially a disease, most research on these drugs exist in a gray area: they don't—or can't—officially tackle aging." The Healthy Life Extension Society is part of a group that petitioned the World Health Organization (WHO) to add aging to their latest revision of its official International Classification of Diseases, ICD-11. The WHO declined, but did list "aging-related" as an extension code that can be applied to a disease.

259. Sinclair and LaPlante, *Lifespan*, 302.

260. Sinclair and LaPlante, *Lifespan*, xiv.

261. Nouwen and Gaffney, *Aging*, 102. "Thus care for the elderly means, first of all, to make ourselves available to the experience of becoming old. Only he who has recognized the relativity of his own life can bring a smile to the face of a man who feels the closeness of death.... No guest will ever feel welcome when his host is not at home in his own house."

262. Aronson, *Elderhood*, 92.

biological limitations is *unnatural*, says Sinclair, for as a species we have always pushed against perceived boundaries. In fact, "our biology compels us to."[263] While he acknowledges that ending aging will upend nearly every idea of what it means to be human, history and biology push us forward. The future does not belong to the young, but to those who, with the help of technology, refuse to grow old.

In her work entitled *The Mansion of Happiness: A History of Life and Death*, Jill Lepore has observed that "the transformation of old age from a stage of life into a disease was a long time coming."[264] Aristotle ventured that disease might be described as "adventitious old age" and old age as "natural disease" before rejecting the notion.[265] Galen followed suit, arguing that aging was not a disease as it was not contrary to nature.[266] As our knowledge of nature increased however, it became more common to speak of aging as a disease. Those guided by Christian convictions were hardly immune to the sentiment. Roger Bacon's *The Cure of Old Age, and Preservation of Youth* suggests as much. In the forward to Bacon's work the Reverend Richard Browne anticipated a potential Christian objection to life extension in Jesus' words to the Pharisees, "The whole have no need of a Physician, but they that are sick" (Matt 9:12, Mark 2:17, Luke 5:21). Undaunted, Browne considered bodily *health* a "Pharisaical condition," given that body's inclines toward one disease or another from the moment of birth. "You make every day a considerable step toward Old Age, which is itself a Disease."[267] One of the more prescient and haunting statements on aging was made by Ralph Waldo Emerson (1803–1882): "Nature abhors the old, and old age seems the only disease; all others run into this one."[268] Emerson's quip captures the complex relationship between health and sickness, between aging and disease, while maintaining a distinction that inevitably seems to vanish as we age.

263. Sinclair and LaPlante, *Lifespan*, 243.
264. Lepore, *Mansion of Happiness*, 148.
265. Aristotle, *Generation of Animals* V.49 784b 33–34. Aristotle's statement is commonly interpreted as saying that old age, with all of its infirmities, is the natural outcome of healthy adulthood. See for instance Carrick, *Medical Ethics in Antiquity*, 29–30. Aristotle in *De caelo* did liken phthisis and old age as "beyond nature" (*para physin*), but only in comparison with the nature of the unchanging, eternal celestial element, later called quintessence (*quinta essentia*). Though Aristotle recognized that some diseases seem to mimic the effects of old age, he ultimately rejected the idea that aging itself was a disease. See Terence, *Phormio* IV.575, where Chremes declares "*Senectus ipsa morbus*"—"Old age is an illness in itself."
266. Green, *Translation of Galen's Hygiene*, 15–17.
267. Browne, "To the Reader," A3.
268. Emerson, "Circles," 11:319.

From the mid-seventeenth century onward it was not unusual to find the occasional scientist classifying aging as a disease, though contemporary medicine attributes the changes that accompany old age to individual illnesses and various pathological processes.[269] While it is generally accepted that aging is not a disease, it is nevertheless becoming increasingly difficult to distinguish one from the other as knowledge of pathologies and disease etiologies continues to grow.[270] Though the occasional scientist like Sinclair have argued that aging should be considered a disease,[271] two characteristics—its intrinsic nature and universality—would seem to carry enough weight to maintain the distinction.[272] Aging is intrinsic to our very biology, a condition universal to humanity itself. From this vantage point a distinction between aging and disease seems reasonable in its appeal to indisputable "facts" rooted in empirical observation. It seems too that the quest to attenuate aging can be described as treating aging *as if* it were a disease, which effectively sidesteps the question altogether. Hence, there may be little to gain in placing too much emphasis on this distinction.

There are however implications for this narrowing of the conceptual distance between aging and disease, namely, attempts to slow aging may very well lend a pathological dimension to *embodiment itself* as something to be remedied by our growing arsenal of technological abilities. Moreover, our understanding of the human body and its moral significance in the Christian life may be adversely affected by the narrowing of this conceptual distance. As more particular genes and genetic pathways are implicated in aging and thus treated as malfunctions in need of correction, the more likely the body will be seen as a problem. We have seen this in the steady progression of aging attenuation research, as hygienic practices that minimally recognized the body as an ally, though perhaps in an instrumental sense, gave way to increasingly invasive acts against the body when hygiene at best yielded only marginal gains in longevity. It is evident when Walter Longo speaks of the human body "as an army of cells at war," where "the enemy includes oxygen and other molecules that damage DNA and cells," and where the thick(er) practice of eating is reduced to an exercise in rearmament, ingesting the right nutrients to help the body remain vigilant in the interminable battle of homeostasis. "Like an army in need of rations,

---

269. Schäfer, "'That Senescence Itself is an Illness,'" 536, 545.

270. Blumenthal, "Aging/Disease Dichotomy."

271. See Blumenthal, "Aging/Disease Dichotomy," 144–45; Boorse, "On the Distinction between Illness and Disease"; Caplan, "The 'Unnaturalness' of Aging"; Hayflick, *How and Why*, 45, notes that some studies have found that more than 75 percent of those over the age of eighty-five have between three and nine pathological conditions.

272. Blumenthal, "Aging/Disease Dichotomy," 141.

ammunition, and equipment, the body needs proteins, essential fatty acids
... minerals, vitamins, and, yes, sufficient levels of sugar to fight the many
battles raging inside and outside cells."[273] In this expansion of knowledge,
the body has come to be seen as increasingly passive, with a greatly reduced
role as a constitutive part of the self. Indeed, as Brian Brock has noted, "the
techniques of modern technology are so internalized that individuals come
to conceive of themselves as managers of their own biology."[274] But there is
also a larger backstory that lends credibility to this shift regarding the body,
namely, the advent of neo-Darwinian thought and development of evolutionary biology. While evolutionary biology offers a powerful explanation
concerning why we age, it has also engendered darker descriptions of the
body as diseased (Metchnikoff) or disposable (Kirkwood), though equally
pessimistic statements have come from a Christian framework as well (e.g.,
Reverend Browne).

At this juncture it is crucial to grasp one very important point made by
Metchnikoff himself, for he readily grasped the significance of Darwinian
evolution for understanding the goals of humanity. Metchnikoff recognized
that if one accepts Darwin's explanation of how the human species has come
into existence as a metaphysical theory, then nature itself can offer no guidance on what specific goals should be pursued, much less how the human
body itself should be reshaped. Thus, Metchnikoff could insist on developing
some *ideal* like orthobiosis which, while supposedly not derived *from* nature,
could nevertheless be applied *to* it. The perceived purposelessness of Darwinian evolution enabled him to plead ignorance in regards to nature's plan.
Metchnikoff claimed, "I have not the remotest idea if nature has any ideal
and if the appearance of man on the earth were a part of such an ideal," insisting instead that his own concept of a normal life-span was derived solely
from some ideal of human aging. "When I have spoken of the normal cycle
of life or of physiological old age, I have used the words normal and physiological only in relation to *our ideal* of the human constitution."[275] According
to Metchnikoff, nature itself is mute. It cannot tell us anything about an appropriate span of life; that notion must come from somewhere else.

If nature is thought to be generally devoid of purpose, then there would
seem to be little objection to imposing our own ideals of a long life on to nature to the degree that our scientific abilities allow (save the consequentialist and utilitarian concerns endemic to an immanent ethic and the liberal
values of fairness and equal access that often underwrite such concerns).

---

273. Longo, *Longevity Diet*, 61.
274. Brock, *Christian Ethics*, 334.
275. Metchnikoff, *Prolongation of Life*, 333–34, emphasis mine.

But *some* view of embodiment is implicit in such ideals, and we may wonder whether the body vis-à-vis anti-aging technology could be viewed at best as morally neutral or at worst as despicable. The Scottish explorer and philosopher Winwood Reade (1838–1875), who took Darwin's claims to heart, serves as an early example of the latter. In his *The Martyrdom of Man*, Reade asserted that the human mind has outgrown our bodies, "which belong to the lower animals." Hence, "already we look upon them with contempt."[276] Reade's interpretation of the body was hardly a cultural indictment alone; contempt for the body was an inevitable by-product of the expansive power of the human mind by which the forces of nature could be mastered, where humans "become themselves architects of systems, manufacturers of worlds." Having thrown off death and decay, boasts Reade, "Man then will be perfect."[277] This perfection of man however entailed "the martyrdom of man," a title he also ascribed to universal history.[278] Reade's philosophy shares much in common with recent transhumanist thought, which, in its extreme iterations, privileges indefinite life extension by rejecting the body altogether as an unreliable substrate for consciousness, opting for uploading the digitized contents of the brain to a more reliable medium.[279]

But if Metchnikoff was correct in his assertion that no purpose could be discerned in nature, it seems he failed to recognize that Darwin's perspective represented one particular *interpretation* of the evolutionary process—albeit a very influential and useful one for contemporary science. For any interpretation regarding the significance of nature—including embodiment, aging, and appropriate life-span—must come from somewhere. Any kind of substantive or normative claims concerning aging, disease, how long life should be, or what the human body is for, are inevitably situated in some interpretation of reality that renders such claims intelligible. Though it can be claimed that aging is not a disease because it is a universal human phenomenon intrinsic to human existence, this fact alone is unable to answer the deeper questions concerning life, death, and aging, questions like what the body is *for*, and whether slowing down aging, while desirable, is actually something worth pursuing, and how we might proceed. Such questions require a metanarrative or myth, a story that "sees the empirical world and its happenings, and above all man and his action, in the light of a

---

276. Reade, *Martyrdom of Man*, 514.
277. Reade, *Martyrdom of Man*, 515.
278. Reade, *Martyrdom of Man*, 543.
279. See Young, *Designer Evolution*. The field of literature is rapidly expanding. See for instance Lee, ed., *Transhumanism Handbook*; More and More, eds., *Transhumanist Reader*.

reality which constitutes them . . . and at the same time transcends them."[280] Indeed, myths give "meaning and purpose to all actual being and happenings," and are crucial to understanding reality.[281] A Darwinian interpretation of evolution then is one myth among several—including the Christian faith—in which aging and human responses to it can be understood.

This should not be construed as an attack on science or a challenge of evolution as a scientific theory.[282] The principles of evolutionary biology have proven very effective in uncovering the processes of human aging and how it might be slowed. But when science itself considers aging as an enemy, it must appeal to myth. It is perfectly legitimate to uncover the operations of nature; Christians have long endorsed this practice as a way of learning more about creation and God. But determining what should be manipulated or repaired requires something more than sound scientific methodology can rightfully supply. When scientists for example justify slowing human aging by appealing to Darwinian evolution or some notion of progress or the good life, they invariably import metaphysical assumptions in supplying the necessary myth—though often unarticulated—without realizing it. That we require some metanarrative or myth to make sense of reality is not the problem. The problem, as Allen Verhey once observed, is that bad myths exist.[283] This does not necessarily mean that the conclusion reached by aging researchers is wrong, nor should it be too readily concluded that the Christian myth—the metanarrative of reality as disclosed in the revelation of Jesus Christ as attested in Scripture—precludes any interventions aimed at slowing aging. As this brief survey has shown, and the next two chapters will make clear, the quest for longer life by slowing aging has indeed been promoted along theological lines, often in reference to the creation narratives in Genesis.

In determining whether aging is a disease, it may not be altogether necessary to appeal to transcendent categories; as suggested earlier, empirical observation that confirms aging as a universal and intrinsic phenomenon seems adequate to the task. Considering however whether aging should be treated *as* a disease in order to fulfill our desire for longer life—a desire that appears perfectly justifiable—requires a story that speaks to the nature

280. Fries, "Myth," 1011–12.

281. Fries, "Myth," 1012, 1014.

282. See Plantinga, *Where the Conflict Really Lies*, xii. Plantinga notes that there is no real conflict between theism and the *scientific* theory of evolution. There is however conflict between theistic religion and a "philosophical gloss or add-on" to the scientific doctrine of evolution insofar as evolution is claimed to be *"undirected,* unguided, unorchestrated by God (or anyone else)."

283. Verhey, *Nature and Altering It*, 15.

of things and the purposes of humanity. A thicker account of aging and attempts to slow it requires some understanding of how aging fits in with the larger interpretation of reality—a metanarrative or myth—that, while offering some account of nature and biology, also transcends it, which includes normative claims concerning aging and the human body, claims that may help determine what interventions may or may not be wise, and why. In other words, appeals to intervene in nature requires some larger interpretive framework that can account for why such intervention is desirable, whether or not it should be pursued, and the potential effects following.

CONCLUSION

The quest for longer life is as old as humanity itself. Though the history of life extension reads as a catalogue of spectacular failures, recent discoveries of the mechanisms and processes associated with aging, backed by laboratory results, have engendered new hope that human aging might be brought under human control. As the search for the means to retain a youthful body has moved from alchemy to hygiene to modern science, it becomes increasingly difficult to draw a conceptual distinction between aging and disease. The story of aging attenuation as narrated by evolutionary biology and genetics suggests that the human body is nearly infinitely malleable or even disposable. With the development of modern medicine and science, the body has tended to be viewed as morally neutral at best, and at worst as a biological adversary that threatens not only to cut existence short, but to inflict increasing levels of suffering and limitation along the way. While this dominant myth rightly encourages research and interventions in the body to relieve suffering and improve the quality of life, such amorphous concepts are easily incorporated into a voluntarist calculus, where the concepts of suffering and quality of life are understood primarily in reference to the individual will. Each new breakthrough in aging attenuation encourages an increasingly expansive notion of what constitutes suffering, tempting us to treat our bodies as more of an adversary than ally. Indeed, even this way of putting it might suggest that the human body is little more than something we possess rather than constituting who we are. The story of aging and the human body as narrated by modern science encourages us to think about embodiment in ways that must be examined from a Christian perspective. These concerns will be given considerable attention in chapters 4 and 5.

The quest for longevity has moved from legend to laboratory. Gilgamesh has given way to the genome, yet myths have persisted, and are necessary in order to make sense of aging and disease.[284] Though the current myth that treats aging as a problem for technology is a dominant one, it also underwrites the notion that our bodies are primarily aging, passive recipients at best—and adversaries at worst—of the human will, and hence in need of some form of technological intervention. While the Darwinian perspective of embodiment, aging, and death may very well have displaced earlier religious understandings, it would be presumptive to interpret the development of aging-attenuation research as a secular movement arising primarily from this displacement. Though this chapter has narrated one part of the story, perhaps even a significant one, there are other strands in this narrative that implicate Christian doctrine in the development of the modern quest to slow human aging. Before offering a theological response to the modern life extension project in chapters 4 and 5, we will first attend to this theological strand of the story of subduing human aging in order to gain a better understanding of the interpretive and critically important ethical question, "What is going on?" This will be the subject of the next two chapters.

284. See Midgley, *Science as Salvation*.

Chapter 2

Theology and the Development of Aging as a Medical Problem

> There is something of the Image of God in age.... In respect of their Age there is a stamp of God among Old Men, more than upon others. He is called *the Ancient of Days*...And Christ in respect of His Eternity is represented as having *His head and his hair white like wooll, as white as snow*... Old Age bears the fairest Image of Eternity.
>
> —Increase Mather

> When thinking about life and death moved from the library to the laboratory, the light of history dimmed. The future trumped the past. Youth vanquished old age, and death grew unthinkable. The more secular ideas about immortality have become, the less well anyone, including and maybe especially doctors and scientists, has accepted dying, or even growing old.
>
> —Jill Lepore

Aging has not always been the enemy. Though the quest for longer life may be as old as humanity itself, aging has not always engendered a battle against it, whether through hyperborean quests, hygiene, alchemy, or genetic intervention. There was a time in the early modern era when aging was considered a reality of human existence that lay utterly beyond human control, an inevitability whose reality gradually, but persistently, stole upon human powers, inscribing the circle of one's activities, interests, and relationships ever inward, closing one off from the world. Though old age often meant being wracked with illness and physical misery, those fortunate enough to reach it were afforded an opportunity to prepare for death and the life to come. Aging was not a phenomenon to be avoided, but a by-product of fallen existence. Similarly, old age demanded an attitude of patient acceptance; as something to be endured it demanded the diligent exercise of one's moral and rational faculties, an exercise made all the more difficult when confronted with a failing body and mind. Though aging was once regarded as inevitable, the reasons for this stance toward aging and old age were probably more theological than technological. Certainly, the story of how the quest for longer life has moved from legend to the laboratory can be narrated as the progressive march of science, but there are other threads to this story. The next two chapters consider the theological shifts that informed and contributed to changing perspectives on aging, namely from one of acceptance to the prevailing view that aging is primarily a problem for contemporary science and medicine.

By drawing on insights from Thomas R. Cole's cultural-historical investigation of aging in America, it will possible to outline discernible shifts in attitudes toward aging—attitudes, it should be noted, that were no less influenced by theology. Cole chronicles the changing attitudes toward old age and aging itself over the last two centuries as these phenomena have gradually come under the domain of medicine. In particular, he traces the shift away from a Calvinist view that was capable of sustaining the tension of old age as both a gift from God and a time of suffering, toward an increasingly negative perspective of old age and aging as an undesirable phenomenon that might be forestalled by new advances in science and medicine. Though this analysis follows the major cultural shifts of aging as identified by Cole, it focuses more narrowly on the theology behind these cultural shifts, particularly as aging came to be increasingly understood as a problem for medicine. Nevertheless, Cole's cultural historical account will help illustrate a complex relationship between the scientific quest to conquer aging and the theology that informed these quests, challenging the notion that our increasingly medical perspective on aging has filled the void left by the gradual demise of religious perspectives.

AGING AND OLD AGE IN EARLY AMERICA

One of the least controversial statements on aging has been made by historian David Hackett Fischer, who noted that as "old age came to be more common, it also came to be regarded with increasing contempt."[1] This generalization, as Fischer himself is well aware, conceals the cultural, religious, medical, technological, environmental, and social factors that contributed to the development of a decidedly more pessimistic view of old age. Nevertheless, Fischer detected an attitudinal shift in the late eighteenth century away from the veneration of old age toward a cult of youth. Thomas R. Cole's exploration of the meaning and significance of human aging in the modern era can be seen as a further development of Fischer's thesis. Cole has shown that the story of how aging became to be a problem for medicine is in large part a story of how Christian theology was shaped and eventually overwhelmed by powerful cultural forces. In *The Journey of Life*, he traces the theological, cultural, and scientific shifts that have impacted the interpretation of human aging, from the Puritans in early America to the advent of the aging industry in the late twentieth century. Cole believes that the fear, evasion, and hostility surrounding aging can be traced back to a collapse of the "late Calvinist" understanding of aging and death that maintained a degree of "existential integrity" in facing the tension between the inevitable and inexorable decline of the aging body and the hope of heaven.[2] This tension would evaporate with the rise of Romantic evangelicals and various health reformers who emphasized the role of individual behavior in influencing—for better or worse—the way one aged, resulting in a dualistic vision of aging and death. On the positive side, long life followed by a brief dying was seen as God's reward for proper behavior. On the other hand, the disobedient could expect an early, disease-ridden, and drawn-out death for having ignored God's commands. It would soon become clear however that the link between behavior and length of life was not so straightforward; godly behavior did not always lead to a longer life, nor did immoral behavior necessarily shorten it. The eventual disintegration of the relationship between behavior and longevity, coupled with continuing scientific advances and a declining belief in the afterlife, led to an emphasis on what Cole calls the "negative pole" of aging, which stressed the suffering that accompanies physiological and mental decline—whether natural or pathological—leaving aging as a problem for scientists and medical researchers. Thus, the dominant view of aging as primarily a scientific problem has supplanted

---

1. Fischer, *Growing Old*, 114.
2. Cole, *Journey*, xxv.

earlier interpretations that recognized both the inevitability of aging and its intractable nature. Moreover, the older belief that aging was intractable was not so much a reflection of humanity's limited power, but rather a confession of God's absolute, yet mysterious, sovereignty over life and death. As we will see, the strongest objections to life extension were rooted in theological principles of Puritan thought.

THE LATE CALVINIST IDEAL OF AGING: "DEATH WITHOUT ORDER"

For the Puritans in early America, aging and death were inevitable components of fallen existence. Many Puritans, notes Cole, embraced aging as part of a sacred pilgrimage to God and the final judgment, a belief partly informed by the conviction that the establishment of new colonies was an "errand in the wilderness." This sentiment however, should not be overstated. Increase Mather (1639–1723), for instance, was acutely aware of the desire for more life, even amongst those who were in misery. "So lothe are most Men to leave the Earth," observed Mather, "that it would be very superfluous to perswade them to be willing to stay here." Indeed, were God to entrust us with the ability to determine the time of our passing, heaven would be largely vacant with "more Men here below than the Earth could contain."[3] Mather preached in an era when the challenging conditions of life made death very unpredictable, where growing old was by no means a guarantee. Those who did survive into old age were often wracked with pain and illness as constant companions. Nearly a century later, the elderly clergyman Eliab Stone (1737–1822) wondered whether the protracted life "is not so properly called living, as dying a lingering death."[4] Calvinist thought however was well-equipped for the harsh living conditions of early America, where the uncertainties of life dovetailed nicely with a God whose decrees concerning the length of one's life and eternal destiny were as inscrutable as they were irrevocable. Death was an absolute certainty; the timing and manner however by which it would arrive were more difficult to discern. Cole identifies the last vestiges of an existential integrity regarding aging and death among the "late Calvinists" in New England who managed to navigate the tension between utilizing every day as an opportunity to demonstrate one's election and the recognition that every new day might be their last. These Calvinists retained the *Ars moriendi* of the Middle Ages, where the deathbed practices of penance, prayer, and renouncing vices—especially the desire to remain

3. Mather, *Dignity and Duty*, 136–37.
4. Stone, *Discourse*, 8.

on earth—were crucial given the imminence of God's impending judgment where one would be required to give an account for how one spent their time on earth.[5] According to Cole, God's absolute and inscrutable sovereignty over all things—a hallmark of Calvinist theology—provided the rich theological soil in which a new perspective to life and death could take root, cultivating an existential integrity concerning life and death that recognized both life's giftedness and the frailty that accompanied old age.

The last remnants of a Calvinist view of death and aging are on full display in the preaching of Puritan divine Nathanael Emmons (1745–1840), where, says Cole, "death remained the last bastion of Calvinism's absolute, incomprehensible, and sovereign God."[6] Cole describes Emmons's understanding of death as being utterly "without order," which demanded a daily preparation for death. Just as God has inscrutably elected and damned all individuals before the foundations of the earth were laid, so too has he determined the number of our days. In a funeral sermon entitled "Death Without Order," Emmons warns young and old alike against placing hope for long life in earthly circumstances. "God discovers no order in calling men out of the world. As he gave them life, so he takes it away at his pleasure."[7] He has determined the day of our death so as to "baffle all human hopes, desires, and expectations."[8] The young are especially vulnerable to thinking themselves far from the grave, notes Emmons, while in reality they "may be the next to be covered with the clods of the valley."[9]

Though the timing and circumstances of one's death were beyond knowing, Emmons asserted that God's sovereignty over life and death was ultimately a reflection of God's mercy.

> The oldest person on earth cannot give a reason why he did not die in infancy, or in childhood, or in any period or circumstance of life in which others have died. The living are a wonder to

---

5. Jacques Choron observes that in the Middle Ages "the moment of death became of the utmost importance, since the deathbed came to be seen as the battleground of the last and desperate fight which the Devil and his cohorts waged for the soul of man. Because of this contest between the forces of Good and Evil in the last hour it was indispensable to avail oneself of the help the Church was ready to extend . . ." See Choron, *Death and Western Thought*, 92. While it is generally affirmed that the Puritans faced death with an unmatched intensity, they also shared a sentiment expressed by the English divine John Donne, namely, that the most critical day is not the day we die, but the entire course of our life. See Donne, "Death's Duel," 58. See also Stannard, *Puritan Way of Death*, ix.

6. Cole, *Journey*, 61.

7. Cole, *Journey*, 61, quoting Emmons, "Death Without Order," in *WNE*, 5:428.

8. Emmons, "Divine Sovereignty," in *WNE*, 5:720–21.

9. Emmons, "Death Without Order," in *WNE*, 5:435.

themselves. They can assign no reason why they have not, before now, been numbered with the dead. They are the monuments of God's sparing, distinguishing and sovereign mercy.[10]

If there is no order to be discerned in death, neither can any order be discerned by considering one's bodily constitution, upright character, education, circumstances, or religion.

> God is continually calling the human race out of time into eternity, without any apparent regard to their age, their character, or their condition in life. . . . He promiscuously takes away the useless and the useful, the learned and the unlearned, the rich and the poor, the religious and the irreligious. He apparently disregards the desires, the hopes, the expectations, and even the prayers of the dying, and those of their nearest and dearest friends. As God gives and preserves, so he takes away life, by his particular providence.[11]

Perhaps the most difficult deaths to reconcile with God's goodness and mercy are those of infants. But even here Emmons proclaims God's sovereignty in not preventing the deaths of millions of infants and young children.[12] In funerals he often reminded parents that Martha's complaint that Jesus could have prevented her brother's death was unwarranted (John 11:21). On the contrary, "God was present, and has done his pleasure; which is a solid ground, not only of submission, but of consolation."[13] It is better to be still and silent, "for God has done it, and done it in perfect wisdom and goodness."[14] Though seemingly harsh, Emmons's dictums were hardly those of a detached spectator. He was intimately acquainted with grief, for his wife died one year after the birth of their second child. Shortly both of their children succumbed to dysentery within hours of one another. Though bereaved of his entire family over the span of a few months, Emmons found consolation in submitting to God's will. Under God's "correcting hand of Providence," he realized his love for his children had been idolatrous. "I

---

10. Cole, *Journey*, 61–62, quoting Emmons, "Death Without Order," 434.

11. See also Emmons, "Sermon LIV," in *WNE*, 5:813.

12. Emmons, "Power of God to Prevent Death," in *WNE*, 5:689. Though God is able to prevent anyone from dying at a particular age, "he does not see fit to prevent millions of infants from dying in infancy, nor millions of children from dying in childhood, nor millions of youth from dying before they arrive at manhood or old age."

13. Emmons, "Power of God to Prevent Death," in *WNE*, 5:700.

14. Emmons, "Power of God to Prevent Death," in *WNE*, 5:699.

loved them to excess; and God saw it was not safe for them, nor for me, that they should long continue in my hands."[15]

In the face of a sovereign God who sweeps away infants and children for his own glory and our own good, Emmons had special advice for the old, who ought to be acutely aware of God's sustaining mercy in their lives. According to Emmons, piety was the only proper response for those fortunate enough to have reached old age, and the only compensation to the physical and mental losses that accompany aging.[16] Piety was inextricably tied to a righteousness grounded in the gospel.[17] Aged piety is a purified, refined piety, says Emmons, which spreads a "peculiar glory" over those who have survived the storms of life in service to God, and "are waiting for their appointed change."[18] While Emmons candidly admits that the very old are a spectacle from which we often turn away in pain or disgust, piety goes a long way in covering over the maladies afflicting mind and body.

> You can hardly bear to see a man, with whom you have been acquainted in his better days, after he has lost his bodily activity, his hearing, his seeing, his memory, and all his sociability. . . . in a greater or lesser degree; and there are certainly great corporeal and mental imperfections, which need something to cover them. But there is nothing that can cover these imperfections, but vital piety . . .[19]

Any attempt to cover the imperfections of age with cosmetics or clothing, rather than sound character, would certainly have earned Emmons's scorn. The aged Apostle John, feeble in mind and body, who reminds us to "love one another," served as an example for the elderly. According to Emmons, John's piety shone through his decrepit body, eliciting an amiable response from his listeners who might otherwise have turned away in horror. Fitting words, it seems, somehow cloaked the deformities of age. "Who could see, or despise his decays of nature," asks Emmons, "which

---

15. Park, "Memoir of Nathanael Emmons," in *WNE*, 1:87. Emmons would employ these arresting pastoral reflections when preaching to bereaved parents. See for instance, Emmons, "Death in Early Life," in *WNE*, 5:777–92, where Emmons speculates that God sometimes takes children to spare them from a greater evil, or for the spiritual edification of the parents.

16. Emmons, "Piety an Ornament," in *WNE*, 6:676–78. Even those who did not demonstrate piety deserved to be treated with "respect and tenderness."

17. Emmons, "Piety an Ornament," in *WNE*, 6:674. The doctrines of the gospel included everything Scripture teaches about God, salvation, future rewards and punishments, and the two natures of Christ in one person.

18. Emmons, "Piety an Ornament," in *WNE*, 6:676.

19. Emmons, "Piety an Ornament," in *WNE*, 6:676–77.

were adorned with the beauties of holiness?"[20] He thus recognized a tension between the body and the soul. Though the body slowly breaks down and succumbs to the afflictions of age, the spirit aided by piety enabled one to gracefully bear up under these failings. A refined piety also had the power to cure the psychological ills that attend old age, such as melancholy, disappointment, disgust, and a querulous spirit.[21] Such piety makes the aged "happy in themselves and pleasant to others," and renders them useful to the world.[22] They serve as "visible monuments of sovereign grace" when the things of the world no longer satisfy desires or alleviate burdens.[23]

If an "aged piety" was based on the gospel and the promise of the resurrection, it was no less informed by God's sovereign mercy that allows anyone to reach old age. Though God occasionally allowed this, the hope for a long life was nevertheless "the strongest and most fatal practical error," and a common cause of neglecting spiritual concerns.[24] This is especially true because God often *shortens* life, depriving many of "the residue of their years."[25] Indeed, Emmons was convinced that God would "continue to sweep off myriads and myriads of mankind, before they have filled their days, and reached the natural bounds of life."[26] Vain or hopeful calculations that place one's death in the distant future may give God a reason "for shortening their days, and blasting their hopes and purposes."[27] Apart from these speculations, Emmons generally believed that God had been gradually curtailing the human life-span since the time of the biblical patriarchs. Though the early chapters of Genesis recorded lives that spanned several centuries, by the time Moses penned Psalm 90, God had shortened the life span to a mere seventy years or so.[28] Though such beliefs were common, it does expose a curious feature of Emmons's theology, for he firmly believed that the human body was still capable of sustaining life for several centuries were it not for God's active intervention in frustrating the laws of nature. The occasional eighty- and ninety-year-old served as evidence that the laws of nature themselves do not limit life to three score and ten. In fact,

---

20. Emmons, "Piety an Ornament," in *WNE*, 6:677.
21. Emmons, "Piety an Ornament," in *WNE*, 6:679.
22. Emmons, "Piety an Ornament," in *WNE*, 6:679.
23. Emmons, "Piety an Ornament," in *WNE*, 6:678.
24. Emmons, "Shortening of Human Life," in *WNE*, 5:490. Emmons however also acknowledges that one's choices in life can greatly extend one's life.
25. Emmons, "Shortening of Human Life," *WNE*, 5:481.
26. Emmons, "Shortening of Human Life," in *WNE*, 5:484.
27. Emmons, "Death in the Midst of Life," in *WNE*, 5:650.
28. Emmons, "Expectation of Long Life Unwise," in *WNE*, 5:812–13.

Emmons could still say that these octo- and nonagenarians were deprived of their remaining days for failing to reach "the bounds of life which are imposed by the laws of nature."[29] Indeed, Emmons asserted that God has a thousand ways to obstruct nature and shorten human life without recourse to any miraculous intervention.[30]

When Emmons speculated that God shortened life, then, the number of forfeited additional years was hardly negligible. Though he thought the natural limit to life ranged from 120 to 150 years, he also surmised that nature might "*always* extend the bounds of life, if it were not obstructed by either sickness, violence, or casualty."[31] Later in life Emmons reiterated his claim that there was nothing in the general laws of nature preventing human life-spans from approaching lengths of the antediluvian patriarchs, which spanned several centuries, including Methuselah's.[32] This gave the length of life a deeply voluntarist cast.

> Though Methuselah lived nine hundred and sixty-nine years, yet he [God] could have prevented his dying so soon, and caused him to live to this time, if he had pleased. . . . And it is equally true that he can preserve any man's life, and prevent any man's death, as long as he pleases, without any miraculous interposition in the case.[33]

Emmons also acknowledged however that the laws of nature place an absolute limit on humanity. Because the "seeds of mortality" have been implanted in our constitution, our "bodies must, according to a fixed law, return to the dust from which they were taken."[34] A self-described "thor-

---

29. Emmons, "Shortening of Human Life," *WNE*, 5:483. Emmons also conceded that the laws of nature were not fully understood.

30. Emmons, "Shortening of Human Life," *WNE*, 5:489. In another sermon Emmons asserts that God uses "innumerable causes to counteract the general laws of nature, which once amazingly prolonged the lives of men." See Emmons, "Expectation of Long Life Unwise," *WNE*, 5:814.

31. Emmons, "Shortening of Human Life," *WNE*, 5:483, emphasis mine. Emmons's biographer has observed, "His own favorite theory was, that 'not one in a thousand or a million of the human race reaches the bounds of life which nature has set;' that 'the course of nature may extend these bounds an hundred and twenty, or thirty, or forty, or fifty years; and perhaps would always do so, if it were not obstructed by some incident interfering with the laws of our physical constitution." See Park, "Memoir," *WNE*, 1:112. God can frustrate nature by causing one natural law to oppose another.

32. Emmons, "Expectation of Long Life Unwise," *WNE*, 5:813. "The general laws by which God governs the natural world allow men to live much longer in the world than they commonly do."

33. Emmons, "Power of God to Prevent Death," *WNE*, 5:687-88.

34. Emmons, "Shortening of Human Life," *WNE*, 5:483.

ough Calvinist," Emmons could not speak of human finitude without also acknowledging a moral dimension to human death.[35] Humanity stood under a sentence of mortality on account of Adam's sin (Gen 3, Rom 5:12–21). "God passed a sentence of mortality upon Adam, and in consequence of it, death has reigned over mankind, in every age and part of the world."[36] Indeed, "Adam undoubtedly conveyed to his posterity a corrupt body, or a body subject to wounds, bruises and putrefying sores."[37] Apart from this sentence of death however, God "might have carried them all to old age, and brought them to the grave as a shock of corn fully ripe in its season."[38]

In terms of human longevity then, what was possible by nature was often forbidden by God's sovereignty. Yet, within the tension between the laws of nature on the one hand and the will of God on the other, Emmons acknowledged a degree of human agency in influencing the length of life that mirrored the limited agency he affirmed in effecting one's salvation.[39] First, he encouraged Christians to pray that one's life might be extended in accordance with God's will. "We ought always to pray that God would lengthen out our own lives, and the lives of others, as long as they can fulfil the designs of providence," even when the last spark of life remains, including those who through sickness or disease are breathing their last.[40] Prayer is encouraged in all such cases, since we are unable to know when any person has reached nature's boundary.[41] Though it is only proper that the dying should long for their departure, Emmons condemns the idea that anyone—especially the aged—should pray that God shorten life. On the contrary, prayers for longevity are the natural outflow of a righteous life.[42] At the same time however, Emmons recognized the tension between the prayer of middle-aged King David—"take me not away in the midst of my days" (Ps 102:24 KJV)—and that of the aged Simeon—"Lord, now lettest thou thy

35. Emmons, "Reasons for Being a Thorough Calvinist," *WNE*, 6:731–35.

36. Emmons, "Adam the Public Head," *WNE*, 2:607. By declaring Adam head of humankind, Emmons explicitly rejected the idea that Adam conveyed *only* a morally corrupt nature to his posterity; we are also *guilty* on account of our relationship with Adam.

37. Emmons, "Original Sin," *WNE*, 2:592.

38. Emmons, "Shortening of Human Life," *WNE*, 5:484. See also Emmons, "Good Men Wait for the Day of Their Death," *WNE*, 5:601.

39. See Park, "Memoir," *WNE*, 1:428. Towards the end of his life Emmons affirmed that humans have freedom under divine agency, and that "men are active and not passive in regeneration."

40. Emmons, "Shortening of Human Life," *WNE*, 5:489; "Power of God to Prevent Death," *WNE*, 5:694.

41. Emmons, "Shortening of Human Life," *WNE*, 5:488.

42. Emmons, "Piety," *WNE*, 6:680.

servant depart in peace, according to thy word" (Luke 2:29 KJV). All except the very aged ought to pray as David did, while the very old should cultivate the desire to die. "But in his old age, when his exertions and usefulness are failing, he ought to have a prevailing, though submissive desire to die."[43] To think otherwise betrays too great an attachment to the world and too little preparation for death. Questions remain however concerning how one discerns old age from very old age.

In addition to prayer, Emmons also acknowledged some ability to modulate aging through hygienic practices as evidenced in his criticism of those who neglected proper care of their bodies. If the masses were denied a "natural death" by God's inscrutable will, which easily overrides the laws of nature, others aged prematurely through "improvidence, intemperance, and excessive labors and fatigues."[44] These "bring upon themselves a premature and painful old age, which they might retard and render vastly more easy, pleasant, and useful."[45] Emmons attempted to practice what he preached. When, at the age of ninety, he became convinced that his lifelong tobacco habit was immoral, he committed to abstinence, even though his physician warned that abandoning a "habit so long indulged" at his age might cause more harm than good. It was likely too late; Emmons succumbed to cancer five years later. Emmons's biographer appears to have accepted his views on aging, insisting that he did not die of old age, even at ninety-five.[46] Like myriads of others, God in his sovereignty had seen fit to deprive Emmons the residue of his years.

While Emmons conceded that we have some measure of control over our aging bodies, his interests were squarely focused on being spiritually prepared for a death that might come at any moment according to God's providential and inscrutable determination of the timing, circumstances, and means of death. He thus construes God's sovereignty in relation to the length of life along voluntarist lines. Like divine election and reprobation, there was no going beyond the hidden will of God when it came to the length of one's life, whether it spans a few minutes or a few centuries. Even the moral component to longevity was under God's control as Adam's sin, which brought the curse of death (Gen 3), was willed by God and carried out through God's agency.[47] Though some found his teachings difficult, Emmons

---

43. Emmons, "Piety," *WNE*, 6:686.

44. Emmons, "Expectation of Long Life Unwise," *WNE*, 5:813.

45. Emmons, "Expectation of Long Life Unwise," *WNE*, 5:813.

46. Park, "Memoir," *WNE*, 1:111.

47. Emmons, "Primitive Rectitude of Adam," *WNE*, 2:553. See Calvin, *Institutes* 3.23.4, 951. "Adam fell by predestination of God, . . . I admit that in this miserable condition wherein men are now bound, all of Adam's children have fallen by God's will."

disdained all sophisticated "ambages and circumgyrations" that avoided the fact that God makes peace and creates evil. God not only stood by the criminal, but moved him to the crime.[48] Such theological voluntarism left little room for the working of nature itself. In the face of God's will, it did not matter much whether nature's laws allowed human life to span one century or ten. Moreover, when God shortens life by bringing the laws of nature into conflict with one another, it becomes increasingly difficult to distinguish between God and nature. Emmons's thought approaches the stoic *Deus, sive natura*—God, or nature—which even Calvin defended in a limited sense.[49] Indeed, so sparse were Emmons's reflections on nature that several charged him with denying that it existed separately from God. "On principle," says Emmons's biographer Park, "he said less of the powers with which the Creator has enriched the earth, than of the riches of power remaining in the Creator himself."[50] Emmons was more content to look *through* nature than *at* it.

Emmons's perspective on aging is greatly admired by Cole, who discerns an existential integrity that acknowledges the tension between the limitedness of bodily life and our unlimited desires, between one's self and one's fragile, decaying body.[51] But Cole also recognizes that such tensions are ultimately rooted in Emmons's Calvinism.[52] Indeed, because God is sovereign over the length of life, one should live each day as if it were the last, ever mindful of the judgment to come. Even though for Emmons the human body possessed the natural resources to flourish for several centuries, God has inscrutably determined that most will never reach Methuselah's span for God's own glory and our own good. Though it was prudent to care for one's body, it was foolish to trust in hygienic practices to ensure a longer life, for one could never assume that God had granted it. Better to be ready for death than to try to extend life, for the length of one's life was as certain and fixed as one's eternal destiny; what God had decreed would irrevocably come to pass.

48. Park, "Memoir," *WNE*, 1:301–302.

49. The phrase was coined by Baruch Spinoza (1632–1677) long after the birth of Stoicism, though the concept is quite ancient. Calvin acknowledged that there is a sense in which *Deus sive natura* holds true, though not strictly so. See *Institutes* 1.5.5, 58. "I confess, of course, that it can be said reverently, provided that it proceeds from a reverent mind, that nature is God; but because it is a harsh and improper saying, since nature is rather the order prescribed by God, it is harmful in such weighty matters, in which special devotion is due, to involve God confusedly in the inferior course of his works."

50. Park, "Memoir," *WNE*, 1:386. Emmons was "wonderful for his habit of looking through nature up to nature's God."

51. Cole, *Journey*, 63.

52. Cole however holds out hope for a return to this kind of existential integrity without the theological baggage.

REVIVALISM AND HEALTH REFORM, AND THE DUALISTIC VISION OF AGING

This late-Calvinist view of aging as exemplified by Emmons would eventually split into a more dualistic understanding that was unable to sustain the aforementioned tension between the limited body and one's limited desires, giving way to a Victorian ideal of aging that separated strength from frailty, and growth from degeneration.[53] The length of life was no longer solely determined by God's sovereignty, but increasingly became a matter of human responsibility. During the Great Awakenings, Calvin's doctrine of sovereignty would be challenged by the revivalist preaching of George Whitefield (1714–1770) and Jonathan Edwards (1703–1758), who stressed that assurance of one's election could be attained through active piety.[54] This new emphasis on personal behavior and responsibility in determining one's salvation fit nicely with the advances of several health reformers of the time who drew freely upon the theological language of sin and salvation in arguing that aging could be forestalled through the virtues of self-reliance and proper living. As Cole observes, however, these developments led to a dualistic vision of aging. The righteous could look forward to a long, healthy life and easy death, while the lazy and indulgent could expect a short(er) life marked by disease, sickness, decline, and general decrepitude.[55]

Cole observes a notable shift away from the Calvinist understanding of divine election during the Second Great Awakening in the revivalist preaching of Charles Grandison Finney (1792–1875), who not only rejected Calvin's doctrine of predestination, but was equally dismissive of the doctrine of original sin.[56] In his *Lectures on Revival of Religion* (1835), Finney applied the commonsense rationality employed in discerning the laws of nature to the concept of revival.[57] If God has established nature's laws that operate through cause and effect, it followed that God did the same for the spiritual world. Because Finney believed that men were free to obey God and the call of the gospel, he emphasized the importance of the human will

---

53. Cole, *Journey*, xxvi.

54. Cole, *Journey*, 60–61; Stannard, *Puritan Way of Death*, 154n55.

55. Cole, *Journey*, 91, 106. Cole summarizes the history of aging from this point forward as oscillating between these two poles.

56. See Hewitt, *Regeneration and Morality*, ch. 2; Weddle, *Law as Gospel*. David Stannard also located a similar shift, citing the Congregational clergyman Charles Chauncy (1705–1787), who, in opposing the Puritan construct of salvation through stages, asserted that salvation "might well be with the individual from birth." See Stannard, *Puritan Way of Death*, 153.

57. Noll, *America's God*, 235–36.

in exercising personal faith.[58] By stressing the need to accept the gospel, he effectively compressed the Puritan morphology of conversion to Christ, adding a strong voluntarist element. While the Puritans considered conversion as something one gradually discerns over time through daily activities whereby one demonstrates one's election (e.g., John Bunyan's *Pilgrim's Progress*), Finney stressed personal conversion as necessary to *begin* one's spiritual journey. Though Finney employed the language of eternal election and reprobation, he understood them as conditional upon human response.

If one's eternal destiny depended in part on human decision, so too did the length of one's life. Cole observes that "just as salvation had become a matter of personal volition, length of life and quality of old age came to hinge on self-discipline."[59] In the matters of salvation and lengthening life, Finney would stress both God's sovereignty and human volition. Reprobates, for instance, are not considered as such on account of God's eternal will, as if God had irrevocably decreed them as such before the earth's foundations were laid, but rather "*become* reprobates when they pertinaciously, and finally refuse to accept eternal life on the terms of the Gospel."[60] Finney applied the same logic to the length of life. Even though God determines the limits of a person's life, he nevertheless asserted that the length of one's span was under human control.

> [M]an's life and death are all fixed, and his days are numbered. God has set the bounds of his habitation that he cannot pass, and all the circumstances of his life and death are settled; yet, who does not know that the time of man's death ... is a matter of entire contingency; that his days may be lengthened or shortened by his own conduct; that years, or scores of years, may be added to or subtracted from, his life, through the instrumentality of his own agency.[61]

This shift towards the human instrumentality in controlling one's aging also paved the way for the concept of a "natural death," a dying of old age that "complemented the evangelical certainty of supernatural salvation."[62] At the same time however, the revival emphasis on personal conversion and proper hygiene had other implications for both the young and old alike.

Though Finney emphasized the power of the human will, he also believed that this power waned with old age. He warned the old sinner how

58. Finney, *Lectures on Systematic Theology*, 2:14–19.
59. Cole, *Journey*, 83.
60. Finney, "Reprobation," in *Sermons on Important Subjects*, 242, emphasis mine.
61. Finney, "Reprobation," in *Sermons on Important Subjects*, 242.
62. Cole, *Journey*, 106.

difficult it was to be converted, given especially that the vast majority of converts were under the age of twenty-five.

> Sinner, are you forty years old? Now look over the list of conversions in the last revival; how few among them are of your age? Perhaps some of you are fifty or sixty! How seldom can you find one of your age converted. There is only here and there one; they are few and far between, like beacons on distant mountain tops, scattered sparsely along, just to keep old sinners from absolute despair. Aged sinner, there are more than fifty chances to one that you are a reprobate.[63]

The energetic Presbyterian minister Albert Barnes (1798–1870), renowned for successfully closing down the taverns in Morristown, New Jersey, echoed Finney's sentiments. "The chills and frosts of age are about as unfavorable to conversion to God as the frosts and snows of December are to the cultivation of the earth."[64] This revivalist theology implicitly favored youth in adopting an increasingly instrumental stance toward aging, which clearly carried unfavorable implications for the aged. Moreover, while the opponents of Finney's reforms continued to stress the Augustinian linkage of aging and death with sin, Finney emphasized human instrumentality with regards to both sin and aging.

Cole asserts that later Romantic evangelicals unwittingly embraced a "civilized" or Victorian morality inherent in Finney's theology, which stressed personal responsibility and self-restraint. This morality dovetailed nicely with the image of healthy old age portrayed by several health reformers of this time, who, as Cole describes, adopted "a hygienic utilitarianism that had little room for either the vicissitudes of old age or the glory of God."[65] Christianity and medicine found a natural alliance in the health reformers William P. Alcott (1798–1859) and Sylvester Graham (1794–1851), who, along with Harvey Kellogg (1814–1872), developer of the corn flake, would later be heralded as "crusaders of fitness."[66] Alcott, a physician, and Graham, a Presbyterian minister, joined forces to create a Christian hygienic program that promoted vegetarianism to extend the human life-span. It is hardly surprising that longevity became a central focus for the health reformers, given that the life expectancy for women and men hovered in the low forties. Both Alcott and Graham saw a moral equivalency between morality and long life, between virtue and health. Alcott identified a causal

---

63. Finney, *Lectures on Systematic Theology*, 2:456.
64. Cole, *Journey*, 81, citing Barnes, "The Harvest Past," 349–50.
65. Cole, *Journey*, 78.
66. Jonsen, *Short History of Medical Ethics*, 76.

connection between longevity and righteousness in the very heart of the moral code established by God, for the Decalogue spoke of long life as one's rightful reward for honoring one's parents (Exod 20:12). Conversely, since God actually cuts short the days of the wicked, the righteous could expect to have their time extended.[67]

Graham, a convert to Christianity during the Second Great Awakening, also considered the Holy Scriptures the absolute authority on longevity. He asserted that good dietary habits would not only prolong life to several hundred years, but would also ensure "a much greater degree of youthfulness" throughout one's life.[68] Since Adam and Eve were created with a constitution perfectly adapted for their environment, where "food from the bosom of nature" was abundant, their bodies required "very little or no artificial preparation."[69] A natural diet with moderate exercise would not only promote longevity, but also reduce the body's impulses that wage war on the soul, especially sexual impulses. Graham disdained nutrient-deprived white bread and developed his high-fiber cracker with the belief that it would promote health and its dry consistency would help curb sexual urges.[70] Since intemperance regarding food and sex was the primary cause of life-shortening diseases, a righteous life and a proper diet ensured a long life and easy passage to the next world.

> If mankind always lived precisely as they ought to live, they would—as a general rule—most certainly pass through several stages of life, from infancy to extreme old age, without sickness and distress, enjoying, through their long protracted years, health, and serenity, and peace, and individual and social happiness, and gradually wear out their vital energies, and finally lie down and fall asleep in death, without an agony—without pain.[71]

A generation earlier Eliab Stone begrudgingly spoke of the protracted life as little more than "lingering death," unpalatable yet unavoidable because the Ancient of Days had irrevocably determined the length of life if not the physiological conditions of old age. By Graham's estimation of things, such sentiments would likely be interpreted as defeatist, if not immoral. Those who found themselves suffering in old age had only themselves to blame.

---

67. Alcott, *Laws of Health*, 9.

68. Cole, *Journey*, 97, 101–2, in reference to Graham, *Lectures on Science*, 264, 266–67. See also Graham, *Lecture to Young Men on Chastity*.

69. Graham, *Lectures on Science*, 71.

70. Grumett and Muers, *Theology on the Menu*, 67.

71. Graham, *Lecture to Young Men*, 34–35.

Graham's rhetoric resonated with many, and even garnered support from the medical community. The physician William Alcott was equally convinced that a greatly extended life was largely under one's control: "If five years are desirable, why not fifty? And if fifty, why not a hundred, or even five hundred?"[72] For Alcott the medical and moral were inseparable. Drawing on the prophet Isaiah (65:20)—"one who dies at a hundred years will be considered a youth"—Alcott believed that life could be significantly extended by simply obeying the laws of the human body and the laws of God:

> Isaiah has indicated a period in human history when the child shall die a hundred years old. I see no reason at all why we should be required to wait many centuries for the realization of this blessed promise, would but men follow out the path of pure and perfect obedience, physically and morally.[73]

He dismissed concerns that any additional years would accrue only at the end of one's life, resulting in a miserable and protracted decline. Alcott thought it perfectly possible to extend the peak of one's powers, denying any necessary connection between suffering and old age.

Nathanael Emmons, the great Calvinist preacher who lived nearly a century, was a case in point, noted Alcott. For Emmons did not die of old age, but from stomach cancer, an ailment that could strike at any moment in one's life.[74] One is left with the sense that Emmons's cancer cut his life far too short. Indeed, Methuselah himself need not have suffered from any physiological decline.

> If Methuselah suffered from what we call the infirmities of age, it was his own fault. God, his Creator, never intended it. The very common belief, that old age necessarily brings with it bodily infirmities, besides being a great mistake, reflects dishonor on God.[75]

Though we were made to wear out eventually, says Alcott, we can engage in practices that prevent us from aging prematurely. The key to longevity and avoiding the infirmities of age lay in recognizing the body's own system of renewal and the practices that influence it. In his *Laws of Health* (1859), Alcott assembled an exhaustive catalogue of practices for promoting longevity, including regulating one's diet, exercise techniques, skin care, and the type

---

72. Alcott, *Laws of Health*, 9.
73. Alcott, *Laws of Health*, 18.
74. Alcott, *Laws of Health*, 18.
75. Alcott, *Laws of Health*, 10.

of clothing one should wear. He even set down particular laws of bathing. However, Alcott's first directive for securing long life came from the "Divine laws" of Holy Scripture, the first of which called for abandoning wickedness. "It is one of the plainest inferences which can possibly be made, that if the wicked shorten their days by their wickedness, they must, in order to secure long life, leave off their wickedness."[76] This entailed more than avoiding evil, but required that one actively serve Christ. The sinner who ceases from evil and does good should expect "his prospect of long life . . . therefore greatly increased."[77]

This increasingly tight linkage between moral practices and longevity led to a bifurcated image of aging, which earned either praise or scorn. If righteous living and proper hygiene promised a long life and peaceful passing, wickedness, sloth, and indulgence were nearly synonymous with premature aging and a disease-ridden death. As Cole observes, a sinful life could easily lead to a "bad" old age, including the physical suffering of disease and general infirmity.[78] Alcott's own theory of bodily rejuvenation was intimately tied to particular practices. The healthy, active, and morally upright adult benefitted from a more rapid renewal than "the lazy, stupid, corpulent man, who seldom stirs from his chair . . . having little more true activity of body or mind than a statue."[79] Alcott reminded physicians that they must "impress upon the public the realization that illness is sin; it comes only from the transgression of divine laws."[80] Graham was haunted by a recurring apocalyptic vision of myriads of children being raised without proper moral instruction. He took particular aim at the practice of masturbation, which was an indication of profound moral failure, inviting punishment, numerous ailments, and even death. The consequences of this "self-pollution" included the loss of eyesight; heart, lung, and kidney disease; memory loss; and brain damage—traits that mimicked old age.[81] For these thinkers sin was not so much a condition, but rather a set of discrete actions or at worst a concatenation of actions in opposition to God's law. Thus, while Alcott thought it appropriate to speak of illness as sin, he did not seem to consider sin as an illness, as the chronic condition of a disordered will. Hence, there is a discernible humanist element in theological

76. Alcott, *Laws of Health*, 10.
77. Alcott, *Laws of Health*, 8. "As he has ceased to do evil, it is to be presumed he will now do good."
78. Cole, *Journey*, 94.
79. Alcott, *Laws of Health*, 7.
80. Whorton, *Crusaders for Fitness*, 111.
81. Lepore, *Mansion of Happiness*, 71–72, in reference to Graham, *Lecture to Young Men*, 102–26.

anthropology underwriting this new moral hygiene. True, some connection between sin and death was still maintained by these health reformers. But by subtly shifting sin from the metaphysical to the moral plane, slowing aging was no more difficult than breaking a bad habit, which, though doubtless inconvenient, was merely a matter of exercising one's will. More generally, "Grahamism" has been described as marking a turning point away from the religious understanding of the good life toward a medical one, where "the wages of sin became the stages of life."[82] As Jill Lepore has aptly noted, "though Graham believed in Christ, death, and eternal life; he just didn't believe in sex, sickness, or aging."[83]

Later on Romantic evangelicals, notes Cole, would reinforce this bifurcated image of later life by stressing the love of God over against the electing and damning God of Calvinism. Such teachings were exemplified in the Congregationalist clergyman Henry Ward Beecher (1813–1887). Haunted by a fear of damnation and his inability to satisfy his father's demands for conversion, Beecher would reject Calvin's understanding of divine election and even milder forms of the doctrine of original sin. Beecher referred to Christianity as "the science of right living," the "*new manship* of the world ... whose end is perfect manhood in Christ Jesus."[84] Not only did man possess the ability to repent and turn to Christ, he is also "made to ... go on, and on, and up, and onward, steadily emerging from the controlling power of the physical and animal conditions in which he was born ... and ending in the glorious liberty of the sons of God."[85] He considered it "a beautiful thing" when man arrives at old age with "no more preparation to make."[86] Older spiritual practices such as imagining one's death were not only unhelpful, but a "supreme folly."[87] Beecher did promote a kind of spiritual preparation for old age, yet he showed little interest in reflection, self-examination, or meditation on the challenges that accompany it.[88] Better to remember God in one's youth by obeying his commandments so that "the misery of old age shall be escaped, and a brighter day be awarded you."[89]

---

82. Lepore, *Mansion of Happiness*, 72.
83. Lepore, *Mansion of Happiness*, 73.
84. Beecher, "Science of Right Living," in *Sermons in Plymouth Church*, 330.
85. Beecher, *Beecher*, 190.
86. Beecher, "Treasures in Heaven," in *Forty-Eight Sermons*, 2:8.
87. Beecher, "Strength According to Days," in *Forty-Eight Sermons*, 1:15–16.
88. Cole, *Journey*, 135.
89. Beecher, "Old Age," in *Sermons by Henry Ward Beecher*, 2:323.

For Beecher, long life was a natural right that belonged to everyone. Thus, "men are defrauded if they do not possess it."[90] Lifelong temperance was a core feature of Beecher's teaching on longevity, by which he meant submission to the laws of nature. These were "nourishing laws," for "nature is congenial . . . nature is the universal nurse, the universal physician of our race."[91] Unlike as with Alcott and Graham, however, nature was no less generous than God. The man who led a temperate life in accordance with nature's economy could rightfully expect to reach the biblical three score and ten or perhaps three score and twenty years.[92] Although one could expect some diminishment in old age, Beecher romanticized it. Old age was not designed to be mournful, but beautiful. As a part of the scheme of life, Beecher likened old age to the closing movement of a symphony, "beautiful in its inception, rolling on grandly and terminating in a climax of sublimity."[93] But if temperance enabled one to reach three score and ten or perhaps twenty years, intemperance—especially in youth—would eventually mitigate against a long life. Echoing earlier health reformers, Beecher asserted that the wicked would not live out half their days (Ps 55:23). Wasting one's youth was particularly scandalous. "Perhaps there is nothing more disreputable than for a young man to present himself a miserable wreck of what he might have been, and a burden to the state and to the age in which he lives . . ."[94] While life might be occasionally shortened through the sin of one's parents or through accidents, "the greatest number . . . are deprived of a good old age by their own ignorance or by their own misconduct." Those who do manage to live intemperately into old age find it "a land of sorrow."[95] Beecher warned against drawing excessively upon the treasure of youth and exhausting its supply through riotous living, for this robs from the finite capital necessary for a healthy old age: "Every man that transcends nature's laws in youth is taking beforehand those treasures that are stored up for his old age."[96] Far better to cut the staff in one's youth so that it can be leaned upon in old age.[97]

In the hands of the health reformers and some Romantic evangelicals, long life was not so much a gift from God as it was a right to be exercised.

90. Beecher, "Old Age," 2:324.
91. Beecher, *Beecher*, 148–49.
92. Beecher, *Beecher*, 148.
93. Beecher, "Old Age," 2:325.
94. Beecher, *Beecher*, 147.
95. Beecher, "Old Age," 2:324.
96. Beecher, *Beecher*, 148.
97. Beecher, "Old Age," 2:243.

Once under the domain of God's sovereignty, aging had entered the domain of personal responsibility. In contrast to the late Calvinists, who were more inclined to accept disease and suffering as inevitable by-products of a fallen world, Romantic evangelicals resurrected a Pelagian perspective in asserting that the infirm elderly *were responsible for their own sicknesses and maladies in old age*. Whereas earlier the doctrine of original sin indiscriminately ensured that aging, decline, and death were the lot of all Adam's children, the Victorian vision of "civilized morality" judged the elderly for failing to age well. Aging was no longer linked (however construed) to Adam's transgression, but was increasingly interpreted as a sign of immanent personal moral failure. Cole concludes, "Piety was transformed into the sum of civilized behavior; longevity into the dividend of properly invested physical capital; and death into a natural and peaceful transition from old age to eternal youth."[98]

In spite of the growing sense that life could be extended through proper spiritual discipline and care of the body, such optimism was nevertheless tempered by the life to come, which far outweighed any suffering one might endure in this life.[99] Even amidst these shifts, notes Cole, the tensions necessary to discern the proper meaning of aging—tensions between this life and the next, between human instrumentality and God's sovereignty which brings "death without order"—were still present. The rapid progress of science however would gradually collapse this tension altogether.

THE RISE OF SCIENCE AND THE SHIFT TOWARDS THE NEGATIVE POLE OF AGING

The Romantic notion that one could grow old in a state of relative health and self-reliance through virtue and temperance would persist late into the nineteenth century. Improvements in public sanitation and a reduction in infant mortality would significantly impact life expectancy. But several cultural trends and developments, observes Cole, would contribute to a shift toward the negative pole of aging by the end of the century: rapid demographic and sociogenic aging of urban immigrants, perceptions of an accumulation of older industrial workers, the recognition of old age as a distinct period of life, and the beginnings of an epidemiologic transition from infectious to degenerative diseases—all helped ensure this transition.[100] Though decline, dependency, and physiological decay were likely no more abhorrent to a civilized Victorian morality than those who were not under such influences, the

---

98. Cole, *Journey*, 139.
99. Cole, *Journey*, 155.
100. Cole, *Journey*, 163.

stark realities of aging and old age would gradually dispel romantic notions that aging could be modulated to one's liking. Aging would reassert itself as an inevitable component of earthly, embodied life.

The beginnings of this shift can be detected in the work of George Miller Beard (1839–1883), a New York physician who published a series of articles on the harsh realities of old age. Cole accords him the dubious distinction as the first to "scientifically legitimate the reduction of human beings to their productive capacities."[101] After conducting a massive biographical study of the greatest names in history, Beard determined that the median age for most discoveries and great work was approximately forty, after which one could expect a gradual and irretrievable diminishment of mental abilities that came with the breakdown of the body's nervous, muscular, and osseous systems. For Beard, old age was not "a gentle cessation of unimpaired function, but a ten- to fifteen-year period of decline beginning with cerebral disease."[102] The grim prospects of aging however did not engender compassion, but scorn. Beard was sharply critical of "undue reverence" based on one's age; it was a "barbarian folly" to believe that the aged were capable of governing others when "their own brains have begun to degenerate and the fires of youth have spent half their force."[103] Therefore, it might be "a blessed thing to die young, or at least before extreme old age."[104]

Under Beard's influence, aging would come to be viewed as an inevitable period of reduced productivity, accelerating decline, and increased dependency. Cole notes that the older imagery of animals, seasons, salvation, damnation, and eternity that formerly described the stages of life would be replaced by "the rise and fall of productive capacities as the sole criterion of meaning and value."[105] Though Beard's methods were methodologically sloppy by contemporary standards and generally lacking in clinical evidence, American physicians would soon accept and elaborate on his position.[106] William Osler (1849–1919), for instance, one of the most well-known physicians of the early twentieth century, echoed Beard's assessment. If men over forty were comparatively useless, men over sixty were absolutely

101. Cole, *Journey*, 168. See also Ballenger, *Self, Senility, and Alzheimer's*, 20–35.
102. Cole, *Journey*, 166.
103. Cole, *Journey*, 165–166, quoting Beard, *Legal Responsibility in Old Age*, 22.
104. Cole, *Journey*, 168, quoting Beard, "On the Decline of the Moral Faculties," 4.
105. Cole, *Journey*, 165.
106. Cole, *Journey*, 167. Cole notes that this move was facilitated by Jean M. Charcot's landmark study *Clinical Lectures on the Diseases of Old Age*. While respecting the limits of science, Charcot asserted that physiology "absolutely refuses to look upon life as a mysterious and supernatural influence which acts as its caprice dictates, freeing itself from all law." See Charcot, *Clinical Lectures*, 13.

so. "Nearly all the great mistakes," claimed Osler, "may be traced back to the sexagenarians."[107] He practiced what he preached, retiring from the Medical School at Johns Hopkins at the age of fifty-six. In his final speech Osler lamented the aging university faculty and urged them to set an age limit of sixty years or so in order to exploit the collective wealth of younger, more creative faculty. He ruefully entertained the "admirable scheme" of chloroforming those over sixty as depicted in Anthony Trollop's futuristic, necrophilous novel *The Fixed Period*, in order to spare them the "calamities which may befall men during the seventh and eighth decades."[108] Osler himself was spared this fate, dying at the biblical age of three score and ten.

Though the negative pole of aging had largely taken hold by the early twentieth century, it did not go entirely unopposed. The defenders of a civilized morality considered Osler's stance toward old age a direct assault on the moral teachings of earlier health reformers who encouraged the young to conserve one's limited supply of energy through temperate living in order to be well stocked later in life. From this perspective Osler's advice was considered foolishly burning the candle at both ends. The physician James Crichton-Browne (1840-1938) took exception to Osler's views on aging, asserting that reasonable people could live to one hundred if they managed their powers wisely, echoing the advice of Alcott, Graham, and Beecher.[109] Yet, Crichton-Browne made his claims without any appealing to God's sovereignty, or general theological truths, or any necessary linkage between moral behavior and longevity. Indeed, he insisted that any appeal to God as determining the number of man's days "is no explanation."[110] Valid explanations of aging must appeal to truths identifiable in the laboratory. Thus, hygiene and vital chemistry would help conserve the "vital impulse," preventing it from being exhausted prematurely.[111] If the ages of the biblical patriarchs were too fantastic for modern sensibilities, exemplars of healthy old age were readily available in contemporary literature. According to Crichton-Browne, the epitome of bodily conservation was found in the servant Adam of Shakespeare's *As You Like It*, who, at eighty could still boast of his "strong and lusty" old age and the means by which he attained it: "For in my youth I never did apply Hot and rebellious liquids to my blood; Nor did

107. Osler, "Fixed Period," 382-83.
108. Cole, *Journey*, 171, citing Osler, "Fixed Period," 381-83.
109. Crichton-Browne, "Prevention of Senility," 39, 59.
110. Crichton-Browne, "Prevention of Senility," 43.

111. Crichton-Browne, "Prevention of Senility," 61. He was also intrigued by Metchnikoff's theory of aging that linked longevity to intestinal bacteria, though he was skeptical that "sour milk" would so easily combat the aging process.

not with unbashful forehead woo the means of wickedness and debility."[112] Crichton-Browne effectively displaced prelapsarian Adam as the archetypal man for modern science and preventative medicine:

> It is the business of preventative medicine, applying these principles in the light of modern science, to give us hosts of old Adams, not of the Biblical, but the Shakespearian stamp, up to a hundred years, leading a serene, an useful, and honoured old age . . ."[113]

Though Crichton-Browne recognized that there was some reward for proper bodily behavior, the linkage between longevity and morality was slowly becoming untethered as the virtues of hygiene were less efficacious than the practices of "preventative medicine."

Advances in science in the late nineteenth and early twentieth centuries facilitated a shift toward the negative pole of aging. As Cole observes, "scientific investigation now revealed old age as an inevitable casualty in the great 'race of life,'" ensuring that appropriate standards of care would be increasingly provided by medical expertise.[114] The early twentieth century would witness a renewed interest in prolongevity, spurred on in part by the damning indictments of old age proffered by Beard and Osler. Though there was a continued emphasis on hygiene, other methods based on professional knowledge—such as the glandular surgeries discussed in the last chapter—were promoted along with a host of fringe rejuvenation techniques perpetrated by quacks and medical hustlers.[115] Nevertheless, prolongevity advocates in the ensuing decades adopted an increasingly hostile stance toward old age. As Cole observes, prolongevitists of the late nineteenth and early twentieth century levied "unambivalent hostility toward weakness and illness in old age," declaring "infirm old age . . . an unacceptable condition."[116] The coupling of such hostility with a diminishing expectation of an afterlife only underscored the urgency to find a scientific solution for the problem of old age and death. Charles Asbury Stephens (1844–1931) and Élie Metchnikoff (1845–1916) worked under such assumptions, though, as we will see, unencumbered by Christian convictions.

As we saw in the last chapter, one of the influential figures of prolongevity in this era was Charles Asbury Stephens. He saw himself as inhabiting an era situated between the death of religious hope and the realization of a

112. Crichton-Browne, "Prevention of Senility," 68, quoting Shakespeare, *As You Like It*, Act 2, Scene 3, lines 49–52.
113. Crichton-Browne, "Prevention of Senility," 68.
114. Cole, *Journey*, 164.
115. Cole, *Journey*, 169.
116. Cole, *Journey*, 175.

scientifically based salvation: "We live too late to be buoyed and comforted by the illusions of religion, too soon to reach the goal and snatch our lives from the grasp of death."[117] Though he shared the same disdain with Beard and Osler over romantic notions of a "healthy old age," Stephens's study of aging and death took on an added urgency with rejection of the Christian doctrine of eternal life. Death was no longer the ladder to heaven, but brings one to a state of permanent unconsciousness.[118] Science had undoubtedly "added a pang to death for all her children."[119] As Stephens saw things, any former refuge in the pleasant illusions of such creeds had been ruthlessly swept away by science and evolution: "If the doctrine of evolution and all that we know of life and living matter teach anything whatever, it is that the dissolution of the brain and spinal cord is the end of the conscious and subconscious life that subsisted there."[120]

Not only was the Christian faith poisoned with the "false eschatology" of a heavenly afterlife, it offered absolutely no initiative for achieving natural salvation through science.[121] Stephens however did believe that science need not be opposed to religion as such, but believed that traditional faith must be replaced with a natural religion or "Promethean Faith."[122] This Promethean faith had little patience for the existential or spiritual aspects of aging that viewed it as a potential source of spiritual reflection or preparation for the life to come. Rather, aging was a problem that could one day be solved by placing faith and trust in our own scientific capabilities, which will enable us to shape nature according to our natural desire for indefinite life.

> It is to our sciences—the superior intelligence of brain—that we look for aid in prolonging our lives. Man has already passed the point where he relies for his progress on the tedious course of terrestrial nature unassisted. He reaches forth a Promethean arm and . . . bends lower nature to his wishes.[123]

With the loss of heaven, the metaphysical aspects of aging evaporated, leaving it as a physical problem. As such, its proper domain was science, not

---

117. Stephens, *Natural Salvation*, 127.
118. Stephens, *Natural Salvation*, 113; Stephens, *Salvation by Science*, 4–5.
119. Stephens, *Natural Salvation*, 122.
120. Stephens, *Natural Salvation*, 113; also 112, 126; Stephens, *Salvation by Science*, 12.
121. Stephens, *Natural Salvation*, 53, 61. "The belief that this earth is merely a place of probation for heaven after the death of the body is the worst possible initiative for the achievement of that natural salvation which is, and has ever been, the real goal of life."
122. Stephens, *Salvation by Science*, 16.
123. Stephens, *Natural Salvation*, 80.

religion. The issues surrounding aging are "purely physical problems and properly the subjects of scientific research," problems that could be resolved by turning our collective scientific gaze toward the processes of cellular aging.[124] By utilizing "the superior intelligence of the brain," we will be able to greatly extend life by working at the cellular level and assisting the cell's regenerating powers.[125]

Nevertheless, Stephens was quite comfortable in drawing upon religious imagery, particularly the metaphor of salvation. Indeed, his message of "salvation by science"—the title of his 1913 work on immortality—was "good news" for those who believed that aging and death were inevitable. Stephens considered his scientific program a "greater, grander gospel of manly endeavor and achievement," which would eventually lead to eternal life on earth.[126] This new gospel effectively pitted evolution and nature against "Heaven" and "God" by reinterpreting and immanentizing the latter into new doctrines.[127] Heaven and immortality were no longer to be sought as a source of comfort in the face of finitude and death, but rather "ideals to be realized by human effort."[128] Earthly immortality was now within human grasp.

> Immortal life will be won by applied knowledge. Man will save his own soul. Earth is to be made "heaven." "Salvation" is to come from knowledge and the apotheosis of the race. This is what evolution means. This is what life on earth is struggling upward to win ...[129]

No longer in the hands of a transcendent God, eternal life was in the capable hands of scientists.

This earthly salvation would require a sustained assault on nature, rendering it subservient to human desire. In *Natural Salvation*, Stephens draws on the biblical imagery of Eden in articulating his desire to see earth made heaven, transforming it into one of "the garden spots" of the universe by controlling the environment to facilitate longer life. Subduing

---

124. Stephens, *Natural Salvation*, 65, 82, 84.

125. Stephens, *Natural Salvation*, 80.

126. Stephens, *Natural Salvation*, 123.

127. Stephens, *Long Life*, 95. "But that is our present difficulty with 'Heaven' and 'God,' as contrasted with evolution and nature; the one scheme is hind side before to the other and becomes more so every day. 'God' and evolution are like two inverse ratios, side by side, which diverge faster and farther on either hand, as the fog of our ignorance lifts."

128. Stephens, *Long Life*, 91.

129. Stephens, *Long Life*, 91; *Natural Salvation*, 127. "Immortal life will be achieved by the aid of applied science; it is what the whole scheme of evolution moves forward to."

wind currents and rainfall would "bring about that physical paradisation of the earth, needful to redeem it from the imputation ... of being 'a dreary bourne' and a place of exile to homesick souls who long to flee away to some better land."[130] For Stephens however, there was no lost paradise. Though nature was in need of redemption, it was hardly due to God's curse. The only imputation leveled against nature comes from the judgment of humanity itself. Continuing to exploit the imagery of Eden, the tree of knowledge did not reveal our sin and nakedness, claimed Stephens, but rather opened our eyes to the bankruptcy of any theological doctrine of immortality and hence a much harsher reality.

> It is, therefore, a sterner gospel into which we of this generation have to be baptized. We have partaken of the tree of knowledge.... We face Nature's hard law with no fairy tale to disguise its inclemency.[131]

Now that our eyes have been opened to the truth of things, a new, "sterner gospel" of human achievement would be required. The good news is no longer a gift, but a task—or, more accurately, a project.[132] In order to prolong life, humanity must enlist all of its technological resources to bring nature under control.

Despite Stephens's rejection of the resurrection, he denied that salvation through science was meant to replace the Christian faith: "No such purpose to supplant Christianity exists."[133] To the contrary, Stephens considered the project of immortality through science "a scientific *renaissance of Christianity*."[134] But this renaissance took a highly rationalistic cast. He repeatedly attacked the supernatural elements of "church Christianity" as the most significant obstacles to human progress; they must therefore be obliterated.[135] These included the misguided beliefs that God has woven human finitude into the very order of the universe by his will, and that God has predestined humans to disembodied life after death in either heaven or hell.[136] Similarly, Stephens believed that Jesus' actual teachings had

---

130. Stephens, *Natural Salvation*, 82; Stephens, *Salvation by Science*, 93, 258–259.

131. Stephens, *Natural Salvation*, 126.

132. Brague, *Curing Mad Truths*, 4, 9–16. Brague understands a "project" as a *human* undertaking, while a "task" is entrusted to us by some higher power, whether nature (paganly) or God (biblically).

133. Stephens, *Immortal Life*, 12.

134. Stephens, *Immortal Life*, iii.

135. Stephens, *Salvation by Science*, 13, 14, 87, 89, especially 91. "Supernaturalism and everything connected with it must go, *in toto*."

136. Stephens, *Immortal Life*, 12–13, 222.

been distorted and idealized over the centuries through accretions of supernaturalism, especially through church synods and conferences, polluting the real message of Jesus with elements of "blood-guiltiness, ordeal, revenge, and merciless retribution."[137] The remedy for sin is not Christ's sacrifice, but a "deathless life," for sin simply *is* death, that which is "hopeless and brutal."[138] The greatest error of all however was ascribing divinity to the man from Nazareth. In the vein of the nineteenth-century liberal theological tradition, Stephens contended the church had essentially idealized and deified Jesus, recasting him as the Son of God incarnate who as intercessor bore the sins of the world on the cross, assuaging Jehovah's wrath.[139] But in doing so the church failed to grasp the true significance of Jesus' personage. "How sadly do those belittle him who teach that he was a God," asserted Stephens, for as one who truly embodied the ideals for humanity, Jesus "is infinitely greater and grander as a man."[140]

What was this ideal, and what did it have to do with earthly immortality? According to Stephens, the doctrines Jesus *really* held and taught concerned the coming kingdom of God as a fulfillment of Old Testament prophecy, but a thoroughly earthly kingdom stripped of its apocalyptic elements, one that would be realized through the communal practices of brotherly love, mercy, and cooperation.[141] Jesus taught that "immortal life for the sons of men, would come through moral purity, . . . living for our fellow-men, merging our lives, without reserve, in the larger life of our race."[142] This moral purity entailed meekness, mercy, unselfishness, and right living. Stephens asked, yet left unanswered the question concerning whether Jesus could have intuitively perceived the biological knowledge that has taken science such a long time to learn.[143] Nevertheless, these "great humane doctrines of Jesus" will enable us to "realize the Messianic ideal of a 'kingdom of God on earth.'"[144] This divine ideal espoused by Jesus awaits

137. Stephens, *Salvation by Science*, 89, 91.

138. Stephens, *Immortal Life*, 223.

139. Stephens, *Salvation by Science*, 90. Stephens alluded to Joseph Ernest Renan's *Life of Jesus* (1863), which portrayed Jesus as a human being with lofty religious ideals. However, even Renan occasionally confused the "real" human Jesus with the divinized Jesus created by the church, claimed Stephens.

140. Stephens, *Salvation by Science*, 88.

141. Particularly, Isaiah, Daniel, and Jeremiah, though he gives no specific references.

142. Stephens, *Salvation by Science*, 88.

143. Stephens, *Salvation by Science*, 89.

144. Stephens, *Salvation by Science*, 5. Elsewhere Stephens spoke of the Messianic Ideal as "a loving brotherhood of pan-humanity on earth." *Salvation by Science*, 91.

fulfillment in our era, for "the full grandeur of the Idea has as yet scarcely dawned in the minds of men."[145] The prerequisite for realizing the immortal life of which Jesus spoke requires a united humanity, a pooling of resources in defeating the unmitigated enemy of death. Only by fully embracing Jesus' divine ideal will heaven be brought to earth:

> For there will never be any real peace on earth and good-will among men till we all accept this ideal, till every man of us merges his selfishness and accepts pot luck with his fellow. Then—when we all stand together, shoulder to shoulder, heart to heart—then will begin that commune life of great works which will transform earth to Heaven, transfigure and spiritualize the human organism and win immortal life.... By perfecting this communal life of pan-humanity... the life of the individual man may be prolonged a thousand times.[146]

Cooperation is the only way to gain control over nature and achieve a natural salvation from disease, "sin," and death.[147] In this spirit the modern biologist must "revert with renewed respect to the real ideas of the Youth of Nazareth."[148]

By embracing elements of the liberal theological tradition, Stephens's functional, largely Ebionite Christology could be readily accommodated to his utopian project for biological immortality, for his affirmation of Christ's divinity was not so much a metaphysical claim as a value judgment. Jesus was God because he held to divine ideals, and thus "lives on still in the communal life of Man."[149] Stephens's message of natural salvation echoed an earlier interpretation of the kingdom as the "Fatherhood of God and the brotherhood of man," put forward by Albrecht Ritschl (1822–1889) and Adolf von Harnack (1851–1930).[150] Indeed, Ritschl's articulation of the kingdom of God as the "uninterrupted reciprocation of action springing from the motive of love" might describe Stephens's new community of scientists whose brotherly collaboration would lead the way to natural salvation.[151] Unsurprisingly then, Stephens had little use for the bodily resurrection of Jesus. Rather, Jesus is divine "only because he is first human,

---

145. Stephens, *Salvation by Science*, 89.
146. Stephens, *Salvation by Science*, 91, 93.
147. Stephens, *Salvation by Science*, 93.
148. Stephens, *Immortal Life*, 223.
149. Stephens, *Salvation by Science*, 88.
150. Ritschl, *Christian Doctrine of Justification*, 49; von Harnack, *History of Dogma*, 1:70.
151. Ritschl, *Christian Doctrine of Justification*, 334.

and what we may all become, the evolution of Godhood within us."[152] By doing so, Stephens transmuted the doctrine of salvation as God's activity in and through Christ into a collective scientific activity, where sin is no longer the "sting of death," but is recast as disease, hopelessness, and ultimately death itself. Sin does not give death its power; rather, death empowers sin. Only when immortal life is achieved will sin, animated by finitude and the shortness of life, cease altogether. Moreover, Stephens's Christology fostered an anthropology that affirmed the divine within humanity; that which was stripped from the incarnation resurfaced as an intrinsic feature of human existence itself. Jesus' power did not stem from his being, but his message. Here Stephens found the moral currency for his program of natural salvation through science. Whether or not his own Christology was clear, his core message was simple, rational, and attractive. "Shall we demonstrate the spirit, intent and real meaning of the doctrines of Jesus Christ, or see these grand doctrines lapse into a vacuous ritual?"[153] Stephens was more prophet than scientist, but his melioristic attitude toward the aging body lives on among many transhumanist thinkers whose scientific abilities far surpass those of Stephens. If, however, Stephens thought he distilled the essence of the Christian faith to fit his vision of hyperlongevity, others believed it was altogether unnecessary.

The Nobel Prize (1908) recipient immunologist Élie Metchnikoff, professor at the Pasteur Institute in Paris, shared Stephens's horror at the specter of old age. "Old age, death, toxins and the prolongation of life," notes Ann Dally, "Metchnikoff is deeply involved in them all."[154] Unlike Stephens however, Metchnikoff had no interest in rescuing Christian doctrine from the church, much less defending a religion that demanded "an uncritical faith as the means of curing the ills which afflict humanity" while ultimately failing to deliver on such promises.[155] He was convinced that early Christianity had fostered a toxic dualism as evidenced in its uncritical embrace of asceticism, a dualism that ultimately "led to the depreciation of the body as compared with the soul."[156] Metchnikoff also shared Stephen's belief that science was the only means to extend the human life-span—though not indefinitely—in the face of the widely discredited religious doctrines of immortality, including the Christian doctrine of bodily resurrection. Though Metchnikoff's research contributed much to science in the fields of

152. Stephens, *Salvation by Science*, 91.
153. Stephens, *Salvation by Science*, 15.
154. Dally, *Fantasy Surgery*, 133.
155. Metchnikoff, *Prolongation of Life*, 332.
156. Metchnikoff, *Nature of Man*, 10.

bacteriology and immunology, he was obsessed with the underlying agenda that has been described as restoring "the old man to his rightful position in the world."[157] It is well known that Metchnikoff was a neurotic adult, plagued with depression and other psychosomatic symptoms.[158] Following two suicide attempts in his youth, he was obsessed with the idea of death and profoundly fearful of aging, two factors that would animate his promotion of science as the only legitimate means to extend the human life-span.

Like Stephens, Metchnikoff had little good to say about the aging body. "We are greatly disturbed by the appearances of wrinkles and grey hair." In general, old age is "marked by ugly features, and often by repugnant or even horrible characters."[159] Though old age was "horrible and useless, and at best no more than to be tolerated," he embraced the instinctive drive for life to continue.[160] Metchnikoff believed that evolution had left man a "disharmonious organism," and therefore ill-equipped for long-term survival.[161] The large intestine, for instance, which harbors harmful bacteria, was hardly necessary. The development of his theory of phagocytosis—the ingestion of bacteria and foreign matter by phagocytes—played a helpful role in the body's functioning. In general, he believed that restoring the body to a relative state of harmony, which involved mitigating the effects of macrophages—which he defined as a type of phagocyte—that promoted "senile decay," was the way forward.[162] In fact, "so universal a symptom of old age is the invasion of the tissues by macrophags, that it must be regarded as immense importance."[163] The language of "invasion" implies something stronger than mere "disharmony," and suggests that the body is at war with itself, and the product of a larger, violent, evolutionary epic of survival.

But the disharmonious constitution of humanity was as much psychological as it was physical. According to Metchnikoff's assessment of the human condition, we are all "tormented by the contradiction between the desire of life and the inevitability of death." It is therefore perfectly reasonable to "demand some solution to the problem" beyond merely learning to be content with our lot.[164] For Metchnikoff, the solution must come from

157. Cole, *Journey*, 190, quoting McFarlane, "Prolonging the Prime of Life," 551.

158. Dally, *Fantasy Surgery*, 123.

159. Metchnikoff, *Nature of Man*, 129.

160. Metchnikoff, *Nature of Man*, 130. The desire for long life was rooted in the twin instincts of the love of life and the fear of death. According to Metchnikoff, all religious doctrines of immortality were the product of these instincts.

161. Metchnikoff, *Nature of Man*, 63.

162. Metchnikoff, *Nature of Man*, 240.

163. Metchnikoff, *Nature of Man*, 242.

164. Metchnikoff, *Nature of Man*, 228.

a more expansive science. Indeed, treating death itself is no less warranted than treating diabetes:

> If a man complains to his physician of uncontrollable hunger and thirst, he is not told that it is wrong to be so greedy, and that that fault could be mastered by strength of mind. The doctor carefully examines the patient and does what he can for the distressing symptoms, which, indeed, in this case are generally due to diabetes. Those who hunger and thirst after eternal life, ought to be similarly treated by men of science whose duty it is to ameliorate their sufferings as much as possible.[165]

However, though science had proven able to successfully treat disease through prevention and cure, Metchnikoff lamented that science was still powerless before old age and death: "Not only is no remedy for old age known to science, but little or nothing is known with regard to that period in the lives of men and animals."[166] Nevertheless, he was confident that science would open up the doors to longer, healthier life, making decrepit old age a thing of the past. Metchnikoff's ideas would be widely circulated in America, serving as to counter more pessimistic stances on aging, such as that of Osler.

Metchnikoff considered himself a man of faith, and insisted that humankind could not live without it. Once again, however, the only valid object of one's faith was science, a science that would more adequately occupy the role(s) that traditional religions were unable to fill. For, like Stephens, Metchnikoff believed that the age of faith in religious doctrines of immortality had been put to rest. In *The Nature of Man*, Metchnikoff boasted of a new faith in science: "If it be true that man cannot live without faith, this volume, when the age of faith seemed gone by, has provided a new faith, that in the all-powerfulness of science."[167] Metchnikoff's supreme confidence in the expanding power of scientific knowledge precluded any suggestion that this science would lead to a loss of hope over the ability to push back aging and death. If this were the case, it would be better to abandon this science altogether: "If science do no more than to destroy faith and to teach us that the whole living world is moving towards a knowledge of inevitable old age and death, it becomes necessary to ask if the perilous march of science should not be stayed."[168] Any scientific creed proclaiming the inevitability of aging and death was no less outmoded than religious beliefs that arrived

165. Metchnikoff, *Nature of Man*, 228–29.
166. Metchnikoff, *Nature of Man*, 229.
167. Cole, *Journey*, 187, quoting Metchnikoff, *Nature of Man*, vii.
168. Metchnikoff, *Nature of Man*, 227.

at the same conclusion, like the myth of Prometheus. Metchnikoff also traced this dogma to the threat of death attached to the forbidden tree of knowledge in the garden of Eden (Gen 2:17), which, in his view, was little more than "the invention of the words of Jahveh."[169] If Stephens comfortably employed the language of Genesis, Metchnikoff rejected it altogether. Even though Metchnikoff rejected traditional consolations offered by religion in the face of old age and decrepitude, the hope offered by science was no less religious. Under Metchnikoff's care, the Pasteur Institute was likened to a mediaeval religious community, where "the new Order of priests of science . . . forsook things of the world . . . under the compulsion of a great idea . . . sharing their goods and their work" while conducting ceaseless "vigils of the laboratory" for the future of humanity.[170] Though Metchnikoff's claims for longer life were modest by Stephens's standards, his program was no less religious, even as it was shorn of anything that might be mistaken for theology. Little wonder then that his second wife, Olga, could say "his worship of Science and of Reason made of him an inspired apostle."[171]

By the early twentieth century, observes Cole, aging had been largely freed from its religious and cosmological moorings, allowing scientists to focus nearly exclusively on the biological causes of aging, whether cellular or genetic.[172] This shift toward the negative pole of aging was also facilitated by the failure of hygienic programs for longevity, which fostered the belief that aging could only be slowed by more invasive, technologically sophisticated measures that transcended behavior-related technique.[173] Cole laments the loss of any larger narrative in which aging might be situated, one capable of accommodating aging's physical and spiritual elements, one that might also account for decline and growth. He also detects the remnants of the Victorian, dualistic vision of aging in the fields of geriatrics and gerontology, which examine the pathological and normal causes of aging respectively. Cole concludes that the development of these disciplines has "helped complete the long-term cultural shift from conceiving aging primarily as a mystery or an existential problem to viewing it primarily as a scientific and technical problem."[174] Concerns about *why* humans age have

---

169. Metchnikoff, *Nature of Man*, 226.

170. P. Chalmers Mitchell, "Editor's Introduction," in Metchnikoff, *Nature of Man*, iii, vii. The idea of Adam as the priest of creation can be traced back to Maximus the Confessor (580-662). See chapter 1 of Torrance, *Ground and Grammar of Theology*, entitled "Man, the Priest of Creation," 1-14.

171. Metchnikoff, *Life of Elie Metchnikoff*, 96.

172. Cole, *Journey*, 193-94.

173. Cole, *Journey*, 174-75.

174. Cole, *Journey*, 195. While Cole admires the existential integrity in Calvinist

been supplanted by questions concerning *how* we age. Troubling existential and ideological questions concerning aging have seemingly been resolved in the more familiar terms of "bodily economy," under the assumption that biology—and bodies in particular—are value-free.[175] As Gerald McKenny has observed, nature is no longer viewed as the source for reflection or soul searching, much less a source that might tell us something about God and his providence, but has instead been reduced to an object of responsibility.

> While the loss of ideas of providence or a meaningful cosmic order removes the incentive to find any religious or cosmic meaning for suffering, the mechanization of nature means that suffering from natural causes is no longer an inevitable feature of the world but is, to the extent that human beings are capable of controlling nature, an object of human responsibility.[176]

Under such conditions the universal process of aging is increasingly perceived as something we should be able to learn to control, a project whose failure represents an affront to our scientific sensibilities.[177] We expect solutions to the limitations that come with being human creatures as such. Indeed, our wider therapeutic culture frequently operates under the self-deception "that death can be avoided if we work hard enough and sufficiently trust our rational scientific abilities."[178] The longing for transcendence—including the desire to grow older without aging—has become a problem for technology.

CONCLUSION

In light of this survey, one might conclude that the pervasive influence of the current biotechnological metanarrative with its myopic, reductionist vision of aging as a "problem" requiring a technical solution is the inevitable result of the demise of religious beliefs, particularly the doctrines of original sin, the sovereignty of God, and eternal life. Certainly this explanation accounts for a significant portion of how aging has come to be seen as a problem for science and a medical profession dedicated to the proposition

---

theology of Emmons, he hopes for the development of postmodern narratives of meaning capable of sustaining the tension between one's limited body and one's limitless desires.

175. Cole, *Journey*, 179, 194.
176. McKenny, *Relieve the Human Condition*, 19.
177. Shuster, *Fall and Sin*, 236–37. Aging becomes "something we *should* surely be able to learn to control: the very idea that we could not is a kind of affront."
178. Meador and Henson, "Growing Old in a Therapeutic Culture," 90.

that prolonging life is unequivocally good.[179] At the same time, however, this survey has also shown how Christian doctrine could be reinterpreted in ways that were easily amenable to radical life extension, though one might argue that the resultant doctrines were little more than—to borrow Feuerbach's critique—humanity's most exalted thoughts about humanity projected and ascribed to revered figures in Scripture.[180] In light of these events, one might alternatively conclude that the modern project of aging attenuation can only be theologically justified by so rationalizing the content of Christian doctrine, that in the end it proves unnecessary, as it merely affirms conclusions that could be justified on (supposedly) non-religious grounds. This conclusion may not be entirely unwarranted either, though perhaps it too readily assumes the older, traditional Calvinist perspective of aging and death unequivocally foreclosed all attempts to secure a longer life by slowing aging is all that might be said on the matter.

In fact, this last conclusion may be more questionable after considering the work of another Puritan thinker. Indeed, the modern quest to slow aging has theological origins. At the risk of further complicating the story of how aging has become primarily a problem for medicine, it will be useful to examine the work of Francis Bacon (1561–1626), who called for a new scientific methodology bent on rendering practical knowledge to alleviate human suffering by conquering disease, primarily, by slowing the aging process. Though Bacon is often credited with the birth of the modern biomedical project that seeks to eliminate all forms of human suffering—including the condition of aging itself—his claims that aging might be overcome were rooted in the Christian narrative bounded by creation, the fall, and redemption of humanity. Bacon found the moral justification necessary for his program by casting a vision of redemption from the fall as a return to prelapsarian Eden, a theme that can be traced back to the Church Fathers, and will warrant more attention later on in this work. The next chapter considers Bacon's program for longevity and the theology that informed it.

---

179. Fukuyama, *Posthuman Future*, 67.
180. See Feuerbach, *Essence of Christianity*.

Chapter 3

Relief of Man's Estate

Francis Bacon and the Theological Origins of the Modern Quest to Slow Aging

> And therefore it is not the pleasure of curiosity, . . . but it is a restitution and reinvesting, in great part, of man to the sovereignty and power . . . which he had in his first state of creation. And to speak plainly and clearly, it is a discovery of all operations and all possibility of operations from immortality, if it were possible, to the meanest mechanical practice.
>
> —Francis Bacon

> These Western dreams of embodied near-immortality could only emerge against a theological background that more or less endorsed them. . . . [T]he initial conceptual context for a scientific assault on aging itself is a religious one.
>
> —Stephen G. Post

In the last chapter we considered the story of how aging came to be a problem for medicine by examining cultural and theological shifts from a late-Calvinist perspective, which recognized the polarities of aging and old age, toward an increasingly negative view of aging by the nineteenth century. Though this particular narration may have appeared to support the widely accepted secularization thesis, which views scientific attempts to defeat aging and death as an inevitable response to the loss or demythologization of the Christian doctrines of sin and eternal life, there are other theological strands to this story. One would in fact be left with a distorted account of theology's role in this narrative were not Francis Bacon's contribution taken into consideration. This chapter considers the theological roots of the modern quest to slow the aging process by examining Bacon's program to extend life, a goal which was inseparable from his call for a new scientific methodology aimed at cultivating useful knowledge. Indeed, Bacon's work can be considered the fountainhead of contemporary attempts to forestall aging, if not the larger biomedical project of improving the human condition. That contemporary medicine is often described as "Baconian," insofar as it aims to eliminate suffering and expand choice, suggests that his project has influenced contemporary medicine to a considerable degree.[1] Though Bacon might be considered the originator of the modern scientific approach to aging attenuation, it should also be noted that both Bacon's understanding of God's relation to the world and his approach to Scripture were products of prior theological shifts, shifts that enabled his particular approach to life extension. Where appropriate, these will be mentioned in order to place Bacon in proper context.

Bacon sought to reorient medicine toward the goal of conquering aging itself through a new kind of science founded on the development and cultivation of practical rationality in order to "relieve man's estate." However, Bacon's justification for slowing aging through science was inextricably tied to his understanding of God's sovereignty and the divine mandate given to humanity to fill and subdue the earth (Gen 1:28–30).[2] By focusing his atten-

---

1. McKenny, *Relieve the Human Condition*, 2; Verhey, *Christian Art of Dying*, 31; Verhey, *Nature and Altering It*, 22–26.

2. A related question beyond the scope of this chapter concerns assessing the sincerity of Bacon's theological convictions, though a few brief comments are warranted. Responses to this modern question have ranged from portraying Bacon as an atheist who twisted Christianity for secular ends on one hand, to claims that he was a "sincere Christian" on the other. See Matthews, *Theology and Science in the Thought of Francis Bacon*, vii. Skeptical readings of Bacon's religious motivation include Faulkner, *Francis Bacon and the Project of Progress*; Paterson, "On the Role of Christianity in the Political Philosophy of Francis Bacon"; Weinberger, *Science, Faith, and Politics*; and White, *Peace among the Willows*. It has been noted that these conflicting images of Bacon were nonexistent before the Enlightenment, reflecting the concerns of later generations that may have been tempted to recast Bacon in a different light. See Henry, *Knowledge is Power*, 83. Recent studies of Bacon as a creature of his religious context have bolstered the notion that Bacon's theological claims were indeed genuine. See Gaukroger, *Francis Bacon and the Transformation of Early-Modern Philosophy*; Harrison, *Bible, Protestantism, and*

tion on the early chapters of Genesis, he was able to formulate an aggressive stance on aging that the late Calvinist perspective in America—even two centuries later—was unwilling to consider. This difference can be explained in part by noting that Bacon's interpretation of Calvin's theology at particular points was less enthusiastic than the Puritan preachers in antebellum America. Moreover, by emphasizing the role of humanity in overcoming the effects of the fall, Bacon could interpret aging as both a punishment from God and a phenomenon amenable to manipulation as part of a larger moral project construed as return to prelapsarian Eden. With these theological moves, Bacon was able to take aging out of the hands of God without challenging God's authority as the final arbiter of life and death. While theological differences between Bacon and the late Calvinism of Emmons will be noted at points, this chapter will focus on Bacon's critical reception of Calvin's theology, which provided him enough space for a scientific assault on aging within the Christian narrative. But if Bacon's reception of Calvin could be described as cool, he was openly hostile to Aristotle insofar as the Aristotelian perspective of science represented an outmoded approach to understanding how the world works.

INSTRUMENTAL KNOWLEDGE AND A RETURN TO EDEN

Modern thought, it has been said, began with the sharp criticism and repudiation of the Aristotelian perspective on the natural world and our understanding of it.[3] Building upon the Socratic tradition, Aristotle (384–322 BCE) understood the world primarily by deduction, examining the various causes in order to give a complete explanation of phenomena in nature with a view toward cultivating contemplative knowledge, *theoria*. Aristotle considered what are now commonly referred to as "Aristotelian" causes—the material, efficient, formal, and final causes—as necessary for a full explanation of any observable phenomenon in nature or the cosmos.[4] This Aristote-

---

the *Rise of Modern Science*; Matthews, *Theology and the Science in the Thought of Francis Bacon*; McKnight, *The Religious Foundations of Francis Bacon's Thought*; and Zagorin, *Francis Bacon*. Apart from the claims of these more recent studies, it is reasonable to conclude that Bacon spoke to a culture where religious arguments were required and indeed inseparable from natural philosophy or science. Though some continue to question the *sincerity* of Bacon's religious convictions—despite mounting evidence to the contrary—there is little doubt *that* Bacon relied on theological arguments for his program.

3. Baillie, *Natural Science and the Spiritual Life*, 18.
4. Aristotle, *Physics* 2.3.194b15–195a3. "Aristotelian" is placed in scare quotes as

lian perspective had largely dominated science up through the early Middle Ages.[5] In Greek thought the study of nature that led to contemplation was intimately connected with and directed toward God's very being. Because nature itself was "a perceptible God made in the image of the Intelligible," Plato, for instance, believed that men could discern the divine, eternal principle or Idea in nature through the exercise of reason, being an activity of the soul which also had some share in the divine.[6] Though Aristotle would reject Plato's concept of eternal Forms in favor of an Unmoved Mover and an eternal cosmos, he too considered the contemplation of nature as a divine activity patterned after the contemplation of the distinct Intelligence or gods that eternally move the heavenly spheres.[7] The man who cultivates the intellect through contemplation is the happiest of all creatures, and "dearest to the gods."[8] Thus, Aristotle's theological interpretation of the world was essentially at one with his philosophical and scientific explanation.[9] Though Aristotle did not consider the divine Intelligence as the efficient cause of the cosmos, God and nature were nevertheless so closely aligned that it

---

Aristotle himself did not employ this terminology, even though "final," "formal," "efficient," and "material" causes have been widely used by others. Aristotle's "material cause" is simply "that out of which a thing comes to be and which persists," while the term "formal cause" is a statement of a thing's essence, or "what it is to be something." What is commonly known as "efficient cause" concerns "the primary source of the change or rest," and the contemporary term "final cause" speaks of "that for the sake of which a thing is done," as, for example, "health is the cause of walking about."

5. Aristotle's sense of the "end," or, "that for the sake of which a thing is"—first dubbed "teleology" by the German philosopher Christian von Wolff (1679-1754)—was not greatly concerned with any overarching pattern in the universe or necessarily seeks after the purpose of objects outside themselves. A thing's "end" was often internal to the object and intimately connected with a thing's form—the essential nature of a thing—and which determines matter.

6. Plato, *Timaeus* 92c, in *Plato* 9:253. See Plato, *Phaedrus* 247; Plato, *Phaedo* 80. See also Foster, *Mystery and Philosophy*, 33. Étienne Gilson has remarked that according to Plato, "a philosopher is a human soul which remembers its own divinity and behaves as becomes a god." See Gilson, *God and Philosophy*, 29.

7. Aristotle, *Metaphysics* 12.7.1072a23-26, in *Complete Works of Aristotle*. According to R. J. Hankinson, "Aristotle is no atheist . . . his God does play a role in the continuing unfolding of the world-order. But God is neither the creator of that order, nor its continued efficient cause." See Hankinson, "Philosophy of Science," 127.

8. Aristotle, *Nicomachean Ethics* 10.8.1179a. See also *Nicomachean Ethics* 10.7.1177b-1178a, 195-96. "If the intellect, then, is something divine compared with the human being, the life in accordance with it will also be divine compared with human life. . . . We ought rather to take on immortality as much as possible, and do all that we can to live in accordance with the highest element within us; for even if its bulk is small, in its power and value it far exceeds everything."

9. Gilson, *God and Philosophy*, 33.

approached a kind of pantheism or a *deus sive natura*, where "God, or nature" were nearly interchangeable.

The early Christian doctrinal development of creation *ex nihilo* sought to guard against any identification of God with the cosmos, rejecting both the eternality of the universe and its divinity. Nevertheless, under the lingering influence of Neoplatonic and Aristotelian thought, the created order was largely construed as the material counterpart of the universe as patterned in the mind of an impassible, unmoving, and changeless God, and thus had significance only insofar as it reflected or illustrated these eternal patterns.[10] Those working in natural philosophy followed suit. Galileo (1564–1642), for instance, considered the laws of nature and nature's God as one and the same thing.[11] Whatever knowledge might be gained about nature was ultimately considered significant, not because it could tell us something about the world, but because it was capable of revealing something about *God*.[12] As a result, many believe that science in the Middle Ages suffered. As T. F. Torrance observed, "so long as this view of the natural world and its changeless and timeless bond to the divine mind prevailed, the rise of empirical science was severely handicapped."[13]

Early in his education at Trinity College, Cambridge, Bacon's suspicion of Aristotle's view of nature would later develop into a full-blown criticism.[14] According to Bacon, Aristotle's statement "Nature does nothing in vain" had made nature so pregnant with final causes that he "had no further need of a God."[15] But Bacon also found fault with Aristotle's emphasis on final causes that were aimed at understanding, which Bacon saw as unfruitful knowledge. Far better to focus on putting knowledge of the natural world *to good use*—specifically, to restore humankind to its original state of power and sovereignty over nature before the fall (Gen 3), which included lifespans that were routinely measured in centuries (Gen 5—11). Whence this criticism of Aristotle? The sources of Bacon's critique of Aristotelian science and his call for a new methodology were distinctly theological in nature, informed by the Reformation with its different perspectives on the interpretation of Scripture, the nature of salvation, and the relationship between God and creation. It will be worth pausing briefly to see how Bacon's new

10. Torrance, *Theology in Reconstruction*, 65; Torrance, *Theological Science*, 66–67.

11. Becker, *Heavenly City*, 21.

12. See Foster, "Christian Doctrine of Creation," 453. "The medieval philosopher had of course believed the Christian doctrine that nature is created. But the belief had been efficacious only in his theology."

13. Torrance, *Theological Science*, 60.

14. Peltonen, "Introduction," in *Cambridge Companion to Bacon*, 3.

15. Bacon, *De Augmentis Scientiarum* 3.4, WFB, 4:365.

program of science aimed at the restoration of human power over nature was a product of Reformation thought.

While there were numerous areas of doctrinal, political, and social conflict that gave birth to the Reformation, it marked, among other things, a return to the Scriptures as the source of God's revelation to humankind. In this return to Scripture a new emphasis on God's covenant with creation and God's creatures would draw attention to the *contingency* in nature itself, a contingency that would eventually enable science to flourish. Before the Reformation, the relationship between God and nature was so tightly knotted that nothing less than a new conception God and God's relation to the world could loosen this bond.[16] The Reformation provided this by emphasizing God's grace in freely creating the world that, while dependent on God's upholding power, was nevertheless distinct from God in a way that recognized the freedom to explore nature for itself. This theological shift effectively decoupled earlier theological understandings that unintentionally construed God's sovereignty over the world in *deus sive natura* fashion.[17] Moreover, this new emphasis on the contingency of creation opened up space for humanity to serve as God's vice regents, as God's image bearers charged to exercise dominion over the earth as the recipients of his grace, having been created in God's image (Gen 1:26–28). Hence, Bacon was able to break away from Aristotelian, deductive science for reasons that were no less theological than scientific; science would never be the same.[18]

If then Francis Bacon's criticisms of Aristotelian science were religious in nature, so too was the goal toward which science should be directed—the relief of man's estate. Utility was to replace contemplation as the new end of knowledge. Such knowledge must be "subject to that use for which God hath granted it; which is the benefit and relief of the state and society of man," by which he meant "an improvement in man's estate, and an enlargement of his power over nature."[19] Bacon believed this amplification of power over the

---

16. Torrance, *Theology in Reconstruction*, 64; see Baillie, *Natural Science and the Spiritual Life*, 25. "The reason why ancient science was so little observational, and hardly at all experimental, was that in holding so fast to the intelligibility of the world it failed to do justice to its contingency."

17. Torrance, *Theological Science*, 68. In other words, the relational structure between God and the world was no longer seen as organic, as in much medieval theology, but as covenantal, reflecting the biblical language. Other medieval thinkers would challenge this view, most notably William of Ockham (1287–1347).

18. Baillie, *Natural Science and the Spiritual Life*, 18; Foster, "The Christian Doctrine of Creation," 448. It should however be noted that Bacon's influence on science remains a point of dispute.

19. Bacon, *Valerius Terminus* 1, *WFB*, 3:221–22; Bacon, *Novum Organum* 2.52, *WFB*, 4:247. Elsewhere Bacon asserts that "human life be endowed with new discoveries

world had been assigned to man by God himself.[20] If properly and humbly pursued, such knowledge would also lead to a greater exaltation of God's glory.[21] Without this specific goal, asserted Bacon, it would be impossible to properly advance scientific knowledge.[22] This was the problem with the current scientific methodology; it produced little *useful* knowledge, being too focused on cultivating a contemplative *understanding* of nature. Those men of experiment or dogmas only sought knowledge for itself, thought Bacon, rather than "for the benefit or ostentation or any practical enablement in the course of their life."[23] If the experimenters are like ants that heap up their store in piles, the men of dogma are like spiders spinning out their own webs. Far better is the bee that not only gathers material from the field, but transforms and digests it by exercising its own power. Hence, a proper philosophy ought to form "a closer and purer league between these two faculties, the experimental and the rational."[24]

Rather than follow the "Aristotelian," deductive path burdened by final and formal causes, Bacon asserted that science must begin inductively with renewed attention to observation and the particular.[25] The former path was like looking at nature from a high tower, which created too much distance between the natural philosopher and the natural world. The latter, by way of contrast, entailed "a closer and more accurate view of things themselves," rendering profitable knowledge.[26] The former, easier path has led only to a trackless wasteland, while the latter path, though more difficult and yet untried, would lead into the open country.[27] Bacon criticized the ancient Greeks like Plato, Aristotle, and Epicurus, who, in pursuing contemplative understanding through the consideration of final causes, have "sought in knowledge a couch" rather than using knowledge to build "a

---

and powers" through science, though such discoveries are aimed at the relief of suffering. *Novum Organum* 1.81, WFB, 4:79.

20. Bacon, *Valerius Terminus* 1, WFB, 3:223; Bacon, *Novum Organum* 1.129, WFB, 4:114.

21. Bacon, *Valerius Terminus* 1, WFB, 3:221. Elsewhere Bacon declared "*scientia inflat,*" that "knowledge puffs up." Bacon, *Proficience and Advancement of Learning* 1, WFB, 3:264.

22. Bacon, *Novum Organum* 1.81, WFB, 4:79.

23. Bacon, *Valerius Terminus* 9, WFB, 3:232.

24. Bacon, *Novum Organum* 1.95, WFB, 4:93.

25. Aristotle, *Physics* 2.3.194b15–195a3. See footnote 4 above for an explanation of the use of scare quotes for "Aristotelian."

26. Bacon, *De Argumentis Scientiarum* 4.2, WFB, 4:382.

27. Bacon, *Proemium*, WFB, 4:8; Bacon, *Aphorisms* 1:19, WFB, 4:50.

rich storehouse, for the glory of the Creator, and the relief of man's estate."[28] Indeed, there was scarcely a single experiment in the Aristotelian way of science that might yield knowledge to elevate or assist humankind.[29] According to Bacon, the pursuit of final and formal causes, with their focus on purpose and essence respectively, hindered diligent inquiry of physical causes—material and efficient causes—"to the great arrest and prejudice of further discovery."[30] To conclude, for instance, that eyelids serve as a fence for one's eyes, or that the purpose of skin is to defend internal organs against the extremities of heat and cold, or that the bones serve as the structure upon which living bodies are built, is to engage in questions of metaphysics, asserted Bacon, which are impertinent to physics.[31] Indeed, "the inquisition of Final Causes is barren, and like a virgin consecrated to God produces nothing."[32] Equally intrusive is the inclusion of formal causes in the realm of physics. Moreover, the study of forms was so perplexed and complicated that it was hardly worth the trouble. If, for example, one investigates the cause of the whiteness of snow, a perfectly suitable explanation is given that its whiteness comes from the intermixture of air and water (e.g., the efficient and material causes). But considering the *form* of whiteness is another question altogether, since the mixing of two very different substances may result in whiteness.[33] Abstract questions such as these had no place in the realm of physics, for the question of forms was a question of the general nature or essence of things, which again offered no help in putting specific knowledge *to use*.

For reasons of utility then, Bacon assigned the study of formal and final causes to the discipline of metaphysics, reserving the study of efficient and material causes to the branch of physics.[34] The former dealt with "that which is abstracted and fixed ... which supposeth further in nature a reason, understanding, and platform," while the latter was concerned with what was

---

28. Bacon, *Advancement of Learning* 1, WFB, 3:294. Bacon preferred the more ancient Greeks like Empedocles, Democritus, and Heraclitus, for they "more silently and simply and severely,—that is, with less affection and parade,—betook themselves to inquisition of truth." Bacon, *Novum Organum* 1.71, WFB, 4:72.

29. Bacon, *Novum Organum* 1.73.

30. Bacon, *Advancement of Learning* 2, WFB, 3:357-58.

31. Bacon, *Advancement in Learning* 2, WFB, 3:358.

32. Bacon, *Augmentis Scientiarum* 3.5, WFB, 4:365.

33. Bacon, *Augmentis Scientiarum* 3.4, WFB, 4:361.

34. "The second part of Metaphysic is the inquiry of final causes, which I am moved to report not as omitted, but as misplaced." Bacon, *Augmentis Scientiarum* 3.4, WFB, 4:363.

"inherent in matter and therefore transitory."[35] Bacon of course recognized that the study of final causes was not entirely useless, or necessarily opposed to other causes. That eyelids and eyelashes were for the protection of the eye, and skin for protecting internal organs from the extremities was beneficial in a certain sense, and did not contradict material and efficient causes, such as how eyelids provide lubricant to the eye, or how the pores of animal skin function.[36] Formal causes could also be useful in the realm of metaphysics, so long as forms were constructed from the ground up and rooted in material reality, rather than empty apprehension abstracted from matter, which was Plato's fundamental error.[37] Nevertheless, as long as the study of final causes was allowed a place in the study of natural phenomena, they would continue to muddy the waters and hinder the development of useful knowledge that could be garnered through the study of only material and efficient causes.[38] Far better to throw off any preconceived notions of the form and function of things that have taken experience hostage so that we might humbly meditate on nature and perceive it as it *actually* is, with "minds washed clean from opinions to study it in purity and integrity."[39] Proper observation "depends on keeping the eye steadily fixed upon the facts of nature and so receiving their images simply as they are."[40] Bacon frequently likens his new method to Jesus' command to "become as little children" (Matt 19:14, Mark 10:14, Luke 18:16–17; see also 1 John 5:21), which meant casting away the "idols of the mind" that inevitably cloud our interpretation of nature by imposing some pattern of thought upon it.[41] Indeed, the only way to uncover nature's secrets is through "a childlike inquiry and a readiness to learn from what is actually given to us in the world of nature."[42]

This separation of metaphysics and physics effectively separated the study of the natural world from the study of God, benefitting both fields of inquiry. It has been noted that Bacon's separation of material and efficient causes from formal and final causes was not so much a methodological dispute, but a *theological* one. In short, Bacon (and others like Descartes) were working with a doctrine of God and God's relationship to the created

---

35. Bacon, *Advancement of Learning* 2, WFB, 3:353–54. In the later edition of this work, Bacon asserted that metaphysics "supposes also a mind and idea." Bacon, *Augmentis Scientiarum* 3.4, 346.

36. Bacon, *Augmentis Scientiarum* 3.4, WFB, 4:364.

37. Bacon, *Augmentis Scientiarum* 3.4, WFB, 4:360.

38. Bacon, *Augmentis Scientiarum* 3.4, WFB, 4:364.

39. Bacon, *Natural and Experimental History*, WFB, 5:132.

40. Bacon, "Plan of the Work," WFB, 4:32.

41. Bacon, *Novum Organum* 1.39, 68.

42. Torrance, *Theology in Reconstruction*, 67. See Torrance, *Theological Science*.

order inherited from the Reformation, one which was at odds with Aristotle.[43] God's free decision to create and preserve a world entirely dependent on God's will and wisdom, while nevertheless being utterly distinct from himself, allowed the world to be rightly interpreted in its distinctness and in its natural processes without direct reference to God.[44] As T. F. Torrance has noted, "God has kept the Godward side of nature hidden, that is, He has kept final causes or the ultimate law of nature 'within His own curtain,' but whatever is not-God is laid open by God for man's investigation and comprehension."[45] Once again, this separation of causes "directed Bacon to the pursuit of natural science as a religious duty."[46] Moreover, it allowed Bacon to acknowledge God as the fountain of final causes, while also insisting that the study of final causes in nature posed no threat to divine providence but only confirmed it.[47] As Bacon himself observed, just as a skilled politician is able to make his constituents instruments of his will without fully acquainting them with his purposes, "so does the wisdom of God shine forth more admirably when Nature intends one thing and Providence draws forth another."[48] Bacon could argue that the investigation of material and efficient causes was to be free from the constraints of final causes on account of the distinction between God and the world, for God's hidden will could never be fully read off the book of nature, but was rather disclosed in God's holy book. The heavens, noted Bacon, do not reveal God's *will*, but God's *glory* (Ps 19:1).[49] Comingling causes was to confuse divine and human knowledge, impairing both. "For if any man shall think by view and inquiry into these sensible and material things, to attain to any light

43. Baillie, *Natural Science and the Spiritual Life*, 18. "The real reason why both Bacon and Descartes broke with the authority of Aristotle was a reason of faith rather than a reason of science.... [T]hey found themselves working with a different conception of God and of His relation to the world."

44. Torrance, *Theological Science*, 67.

45. Torrance, *Theological Science*, 69, quoting Bacon, *Valerius Terminus* 1, *WFB*, 3:220. "And although the highest generality of motion or summary law of nature God should still reserve within his own curtain, yet many and noble are the inferior and secondary operations which are within man's sounding."

46. Torrance, *Theology in Reconstruction*, 66.

47. Bacon, *Augmentis Scientiarum* 3.4, *WFB*, 4:364.

48. Bacon, *Augmentis Scientiarum* 3.4, *WFB*, 4:364. Elsewhere Bacon noted that God conceals certain matters for his own glory (Prov 25:2). See Bacon, *Valerius Terminus* 1 and *Novum Organum* 1.29.

49. Bacon, *Advancement of Learning* 2, *WFB*, 3:478. "Wherefore we conclude that sacred Theology (which in our idiom we call Divinity) is grounded only upon the word and oracle of God, and not upon the light of nature: for it is written, 'Coeli enarrant gloriam Dei [the heavens declare the glory of God]' but it is not written, 'Coeli enarrant voluntatem Dei [the heavens declare the will of God].'"

for the revealing of the nature or will of God, he shall dangerously abuse himself."[50] In spite of this distinction in knowledge however, Bacon readily affirmed that "*all knowledge is to be limited by religion, and to be referred to use and action*," meaning Christian charity.[51] Though each sphere had its own kind of knowledge and study—whether the book of God or the book of nature—Bacon's valuation of knowledge for its usefulness in relieving human suffering was doubtless theologically rooted.[52] His arguments for the cultivation of useful knowledge were hardly "casual exploitations of the familiar religious vernacular," but were informed by theological convictions in an attempt to flesh out Christian hope.[53]

THE FALL, LONGEVITY, AND THE RETURN TO EDEN

Bacon's argument for the cultivation of useful knowledge was situated within the Christian drama of the fall, redemption, and restoration. Though significant strides were made in improving humanity's lot, disease and death were still dominant powers that marred human existence and cut life short. According to Bacon, the memory of Eden cast a shadow on human existence, giving it a tragic dimension. Every death, every admission of the limited power of medicine, was a forfeiture of potential, a failure made more tragic because things need not be this way. For Bacon, the opening chapter of Genesis did not attest so much to what had been *lost*, but what might be *restored*, namely, power over creation and longer life. Bacon believed that man's manifold ignorance of things could be readily remedied through the judicious use of practical knowledge, so that the earth "might be restored to its perfect and original condition," or at least brought to "a better condition than that in which it now is."[54] Bacon's great instauration spoke of the manifold ways in which humanity might once again enjoy the fruits of Eden.

Bacon's program depended on a particular reading of Genesis, namely, an assumption that the events recorded there actually took place as described. In this regard Bacon largely follows in the footsteps of Luther and

50. Bacon, *Valerius Terminius* 1, *WFB*, 3:218.

51. Bacon, *Valerius Terminius* 1, *WFB*, 3:218; Bacon, *Advancement of Learning* 2, *WFB*, 3:442, 472. According to the Apostle Paul, if knowledge is not guided by charity, it will only puff up (1 Cor 8:1). The same goes for faith: even if we have faith enough to move mountains, but have not love, we are nothing (Matt 17:20). Bacon, *Valerius Terminius* 1, *WFB*, 3:222.

52. For Bacon's description of these two books, see *Valerius Terminius* 1, *WFB*, 3:218–24.

53. Briggs, "Bacon's Science and Religion," 176.

54. Bacon, *Proemium*, *WFB*, 4:7.

Calvin.[55] Thus, the garden of Eden was in the vicinity of Mesopotamia and the fall was an event in history that occurred in or around 4004 BC.[56] The Reformation focus on the literal interpretation to the exclusion of allegorical readings represented a new approach to Scripture that was more circumscribed than the patristic and medieval eras. Origen (185–253/4), for instance, derided those who were "so silly as to believe that God, after the manner of a farmer, 'planted a paradise eastward in Eden,'" noting instead that Genesis contained figurative expressions describing certain mysteries through "a semblance of history and not through actual events."[57] In the patristic and scholastic eras the creation accounts were read as a kind of moral fable, or tropologically. Genesis 1:26-28, for instance, was often interpreted psychologically—one must learn to exercise dominion over the "beasts within," over one's body and passions—and only secondarily in a physical sense.[58] Peter Harrison has provocatively argued that this shift in scriptural interpretation helped usher in modern scientific inquiry. By effectively "flattening out" the world to which Scripture referred, the referential character of creation was considerably limited; elements of the text that were once pregnant with rich sources of *meaning* were reduced to mere objects of *manipulation*. Harrison thus links the dominance of literal exegesis to the development of modern scientific spirit. In the hands of the Protestant Reformers, "the biblical narratives of creation and Fall . . . cannot be read other than enjoining upon the human race the necessity of re-establishing its dominion over nature."[59]

In this regard Bacon was no exception. Nevertheless, his interpretation of the events in early Genesis enabled him to adopt a melioristic program in regard to nature and the pursuit of immortality that stood in contrast to both Calvinist interpretations of his day, and earlier scholastic interpretations. For instance, Calvin identified that before the fall there was a threefold purpose for Adam and Eve: to behold the wonderful works of creation as the theatre of God's glory; to use the earth in developing obedience toward

---

55. Martin Luther famously derided allegorical interpretation as tending to "make a mockery of the scriptures," favoring rather "the simplest meaning as far as possible." See Luther, *Babylonian Captivity*, 146, 241. Luther did allow allegorical readings, but only if "the context manifestly compels it." Many Reformers shared Luther's judgment, including Philip Melanchthon, John Calvin, and Martin Brucer. Huldrych Zwingli was a notable exception.

56. See Harrison, *Bible, Protestantism*, 226. This was in large part due to the work of Bishop James Ussher (1581–1656).

57. Harrison, *Bible, Protestantism*, 207n3, quoting Origen, *On First Principles* 4.3.1.

58. Harrison, *Bible, Protestantism*, 209. Origen, Chrysostom, Jerome, Gregory of Nyssa, Ambrose, and Augustine offered similar interpretations.

59. Harrison, *Bible, Protestantism*, 208.

God; and to employ their rationality in meditating on a better life "that they might tend directly towards God."[60] Within this context Adam's work consisted of cultivating the garden which was so pleasant and sweet that Calvin was able to say that in a sense Adam "might be said to play."[61] Calvin thus adhered closely to the agrarian language in Genesis in describing Adam as a farmer cultivating the earth, being content to use the land with moderation and frugality. While the tree of the knowledge of good and evil afforded the opportunity for obedience, it also served as a restraint for licentiousness, given that man had been "adorned and enriched with so many excellent gifts."[62] But this tree also served as a check on the thirst for knowledge, "lest Adam should desire to be wise above measure."[63] Calvin was not opposed to the idea that Adam might increase in knowledge, only that it come at expense of dependence on God. For earlier in Genesis Calvin had noted that in abstaining from the tree of knowledge, Adam "might become wise only by his own obedience."[64] Nevertheless, Adam and Eve ate the forbidden fruit by which they forfeited God's supernatural gift of righteousness and faith, bringing the promised threat of death (Gen 2:17), and with it a disorder of heart, mind, and soul, leaving the rest of creation in a state of frustration and disorder (Gen 3).

It is worth noting that Calvin's discussion of Adam's knowledge in the creation accounts occurs primarily in the context of the fall. Though Calvin and other Protestant interpreters hardly disparaged the attainment of natural knowledge as good, they nevertheless considered such a task fraught with danger. Calvin had great respect for science and medicine and praised the remarkable and penetrating insights of "natural men" (1 Cor 2:14), though he harbored suspicions concerning the powers of the human mind to grasp even the earthly, lower realities.[65] This hesitancy can be traced to his description of the fall as being caused by an inordinate desire for knowledge.[66] Calvin and other Reformers believed that Eve relied too heavily on her senses when beholding this tree, fostering a hunger for more knowledge than God permitted.[67] Adam too, was not content with his lot, and

60. Calvin, *Commentaries on the First Book of Moses*, 1:64–65.

61. Calvin, *Commentaries on the First Book of Moses*, 3:17, 1:174; also Gen 2:15, 1:125.

62. Calvin, *Commentaries on the First Book of Moses* 2:17, 1:126.

63. Calvin, *Commentaries on the First Book of Moses* 2:17, 1:126.

64. Calvin, *Commentaries on the First Book of Moses* 2:9, 1:118.

65. Calvin, *Institutes* 2.2.13–16, 1:271–75.

66. Calvin recognizes that the root of the fall was unfaithfulness, which gave birth to pride wherein Adam sought more than was granted to him. *Institutes* 2.1.4, 1:245.

67. Calvin, *Commentarie of John Calvine*, 91; Calvin, *Institutes* 2.1.4, 1:245.

"had tried to ascend higher than was lawful; as if it had been said, 'See now whither thy ambition and thy perverse appetite for illicit knowledge have precipitated thee.'"[68] If Adam's inordinate desire for knowledge precipitated the fall, a postlapsarian desire for knowledge could hardly be less culpable. Moreover, the very capacity to cultivate knowledge could only suffer as the result of it, for after the fall man's reason has been significantly impaired. Though a glimmer of understanding and judgment remain to distinguish man from the beasts, our minds are now "plunged into deep darkness" and "choked with dense ignorance, so that it cannot come forth effectively."[69] Moreover, creation itself suffered on account of Adam's sin. Almost immediately "degenerate and noxious fruits" appeared in the land which would suffer still further damage in the deluge.[70]

For Calvin and many Reformers then, the inordinate desire for knowledge rooted in human pride precipitated the fall of Adam, which in turn brought death to humankind and disorder to creation itself. In short, all forms of death were the result of original sin.[71] As such, death was an intrusion into God's good creation. Indeed, Calvin seemed to reject the notion of a "natural" death before the fall through gradual bodily corruption, or aging.[72] According to Calvin, it was hardly possible to understand death—even at the physiological level—without delineating its relationship to sin at the same time. Though medicine might help cure disease, Christ was the only medicine for the soul, the only hope for both restoring God's image in humanity and creation itself. In this respect Calvin's interpretation of the tree of life is noteworthy. Though he criticized Origen's allegorical

---

68. Calvin, *Commentaries on the First Book of Moses* 3:22, 1:183.

69. Calvin, *Institutes*, 2.12.12, 1:270. As Torrance has noted, "the words that Calvin constantly uses to describe this state in fallen man are *perversity, depravity,* and *corruption.*" Torrance, *Calvin's Doctrine of Man*, 92.

70. Calvin, *Commentaries on the First Book of Moses* 1:30, 1:100.

71. Calvin, *Institutes* 2.1.8, 1:251. "Original sin, therefore, seems to be a hereditary depravity and corruption of our nature, diffused into all parts of the soul, which first makes us liable to God's wrath, then also brings forth in us those works which Scripture calls 'works of the flesh' [Gal 5:19]." Moreover, Calvin observed that those who defined original sin as "the lack of the original righteousness, which ought to reside in us" did not go far enough in describing its power and energy. "For our nature is not only destitute and empty of good, but so fertile and fruitful of every evil that it cannot be idle." *Institutes* 2.1.8, 1:252.

72. Calvin, *Commentaries on the First Book of Moses* 2:17, 1:127. "He [Adam] was in every respect, happy; his life, therefore, had alike respect to his body and his soul, since in his soul a right judgment and a proper government of the affections prevailed, there also life reigned; in his body there was no defect, wherefore he was wholly free from death. His earthly life truly would have been temporal; yet he would have passed into heaven without death, and without injury."

reading of the creation accounts and generally had little patience for reading the Scriptures in such a fanciful manner, Calvin nevertheless followed Augustine's interpretation of the tree of life as a figure of Christ.[73] He had no quarrel with interpretations that ascribed a "quickening power" to this tree as a means to forestall aging—a view that Augustine himself endorsed—but preferred the deeper spiritual meaning of the tree in the narrative, namely, that without Christ, "nothing remains for us but death."[74] Whatever might be said regarding bodily corruption, for Calvin and the Reformers in general, knowledge of theological truths was far more interesting than knowledge of nature.[75] Though, as noted earlier, he could indeed marvel at the findings of learned scientists, given the crippling noetic limitations of the fall, Calvin showed little interest in the restoration of the human mind—much less things in nature—apart from the spiritual renewal of the soul mediated in and through Christ. Finally, it should be briefly noted that Calvin's description of fallen humanity was a deliberate rejection of the scholastic and Tridentine position that viewed the fall as a loss of the supernatural gift of grace, rendering Adam subject to death while leaving the powers of his soul neither destroyed nor diminished, and therefore more capable to scientific inquiry.[76] He resolutely rejected any interpretation of the fall as a *defectio boni*, speaking instead of a corruption or perversion in man's nature. If Aquinas could speak of the fall in terms of human *deprivation*, Calvin and the Reformers spoke much more darkly of *depravation*.

Bacon's interpretation of the creation narratives in many respects represents a middle path between earlier scholastic understandings on the one hand and Reformation readings on the other, for he allowed for the recovery of natural knowledge and the possibility of indefinitely extended life. If, for instance, earlier interpretations viewed Adam's immortality as a supernatural gift (*donum superadditum*) forfeited at the fall, there might be little reason to hope for even a partial recovery of this gift, even if human rationality was left unscathed and fully capable of uncovering the secrets of nature. Yet, according to medieval Catholicism, there was a spiritual route toward immortality that culminated in the beatific vision, a pathway alighted by wisdom and the sacraments that mediated a measure of divine grace and a partial realization of this future reality. Hence, Ignatius of Antioch could describe the bread as the "medicine of immortality, and

---

73. Calvin, *Commentaries on the First Book of Moses* 2:9, 1:117. Calvin also credits Eucherius of Lyon (380–449) with this interpretation.

74. Calvin, *Commentaries on the First Book of Moses* 2:9, 1:117.

75. Harrison, *Fall of Man and the Foundations of Science*, 64.

76. See for instance Aquinas, *Summa Theologica* IaIIae, q. 85, art. 1–3.

the antidote which prevents us from dying."[77] For Calvin on the other hand, Adam's initial immortality was *not* considered a supernatural gift but part of Adam's original constitution as created by God, yet something considerably—indeed irrevocably—damaged after Adam's sin. After the fall there was little point in pursuing the mysteries of nature or longer life, given the resultant depravity of the human mind and the distortion of nature itself.[78] Human rationality was subsequently so perverted that there was little hope that man could gain an intellectual grasp of the things of nature, much less things spiritual. Bacon's approach rejected both options. Against Rome he observed that the patriarchs lived several hundred years before the flood, rejecting the idea that such longevity was "imputed to grace or to the holy line."[79] But Bacon also rejected Calvin's pessimism concerning the attainment and use of natural knowledge to restore human capacities, including significantly longer life-spans. Indeed, the protocols that Bacon sought to initiate in science parallel the sacramental system that aimed at restoring corrupted Adamic abilities.[80] Indeed, as we will see, Bacon construed the scientist's role in sacerdotal terms.

Historically the church interpreted prelapsarian Adam as a farmer, whose primary work involved tilling and cultivating. Bacon portrayed Adam as a proto-scientist of sorts, whose appointed purpose in the garden was nothing but "exercise and experiment." If Calvin felt comfortable in describing Adam's prelapsarian labor as "play," Bacon's Adam was busying himself with active experimentation from the start.[81] Before the fall, however, Adam's experimentation would have been aimed only at contemplation; there would have been no need to put such knowledge to use, for nature had not yet been made the object of God's curse. Bacon thus interpreted "tending the garden" as cultivating *contemplative* knowledge in the Aristotelian sense, where naming creatures was akin to identifying formal causes.[82] In this original state of innocence knowledge was cultivated for its own sake; it was a "matter of delight in the experiment, and not [a] matter of labour

---

77. Ignatius of Antioch, *Epistle of Ignatius to the Ephesians* 20, in *ANF*, 1:57, longer version. See also Aquinas, *Summa Theologica* IIIa, q. 61, art. 2. On wisdom and immortality, see Aquinas, *Summa Contra Gentiles*, 1.2. Aquinas relied on the Wisdom of Solomon: "Therefore if you delight in thrones and scepters, O monarchs over the peoples, honor wisdom, that you may reign forever" (Wis 6:21 RSV).

78. As will become clear, Calvin had other reasons for eschewing any desire to extend human life, namely, God's sovereignty.

79. Bacon, *History of Life and Death*, *WFB*, 5:243.

80. Harrison, *Fall of Man*, 170.

81. Calvin, *Commentaries on the First Book of Moses* 3:17, 1:174.

82. Matthews, *Theology and Science*, 62.

for the use."[83] As Bacon saw things, prelapsarian Adam knew more than the average seventeenth-century scientist.

Bacon's interpretation of prelapsarian life and the fall is markedly different from Calvin's, and harkens back to Irenaeus's (130–202) description of the garden as a place where Adam and Eve could grow from a kind of infantile and innocent naiveté to maturity, developing in both grace and knowledge.[84] In this respect Bacon's position would also differ from later interpretations that commonly ascribed near omniscience to Adam. A generation later the English Restorationist Robert South (1634–1716), for instance, asserted that Adam could view the essences of things and even discern effects yet unborn by causes; in short, Adam "was ignorant of nothing but sin."[85] Though Bacon was more circumspect in his assessment of Adam's knowledge before the fall, he was also far less suspicious of natural knowledge, and fully aware that his own stance on Adam's knowledge—both before the fall and after—was at odds with his Puritan contemporaries. Bacon defended his own account of Adam's rationality by drawing a distinction between moral and natural knowledge, arguing that the fall came through Adam's inordinate desire for *moral* knowledge, not through an overly inquisitive pursuit of natural knowledge.[86] After all, the forbidden tree offered knowledge of *good* and *evil*. There was no doubt that Adam and Eve forfeited their dominion by disobeying God, distorting human nature and ushering in disease, decay, and death; Bacon simply refused to blame the fall on Adam's overly ambitious pursuit of natural knowledge.[87] More importantly however, God did not leave Adam and Eve without hope in this fallen condition. It was possible to at least partially regain and repair what was lost at the fall.

Bacon's Protestant sensibilities concerning the effects of the fall remained largely intact, with the exception of Adam's rationality. When it

---

83. Bacon, *Advancement of Learning* 1, WFB, 3:296.

84. Irenaeus, *Against Heresies* 4.38–39.

85. Harrison, *Fall of Man*, 155, quoting South, "Man Was Made in God's Image," 127–28. Harrison observes that the origins of this particular interpretation of Adam's prelapsarian abilities can be identified as early as Luther.

86. Bacon, *Novum Organum* 2.52, WFB, 4:247–48. "For behold it was not that pure light of natural knowledge, whereby man in paradise was able to give unto every living creature a name according to his propriety, which gave occasion to the fall; but it was an aspiring desire to attain to that part of moral knowledge which defineth of good and evil, whereby to dispute God's commandments and not to depend upon the revelation of his will." See also *Valerius Terminus* 1, WFB, 3:219.

87. Bacon, *Novum Organum* 2.52, WFB, 4:247–48. While the fall resulted in a disruption in numerous relationships—the relationship between humanity and God, Adam and Eve, and humanity and nature, Bacon is primarily interested in the relationship between humanity and nature.

came to the noetic effects of sin, Bacon was less pessimistic than his Puritan forebears. Here once again he forged his own path between the extremes of scholasticism and Calvinism. Bacon spurned the Tridentine position that Adam's rational capacities were left unscathed on the one hand, yet denied that the human mind was utterly depraved apart from divine assistance on the other. Though the fall did indeed occasion a twofold loss—the love of God and dominion over nature—Bacon believed that *both* could be partially recovered in this life by religion and science respectively. Bacon's estimation of human potentiality was thus more sanguine than Calvin and the Puritan tradition in which Bacon was raised. Where Calvin preached a renewal of the mind by the power of the Holy Spirit, Bacon believed that man "is the most susceptible of help, improvement, and alteration . . . not only in his body, but in his mind and spirit."[88] Creation could still be subdued, for God's curse of creation had not rendered it entirely rebellious or intransigent.[89] However, this subjugation must now be accomplished through labor, toil, and sweat. Bacon read God's denouncement in Genesis 3:19—"In the sweat of thy face shalt thou eat bread"—as a *command* and not a curse, reasoning that sweat would not have been required before the fall.[90] But the work of restoring man's dominion over creation was more a sweat of brow than body, of the brain, rather than the exercise of brute force. Mere strength, while useful, must also be directed by the power of the mind—through invention and execution—in order to recapture man's original state of perfection.[91] Putting the knowledge of nature to good use in overcoming the effects of the fall would surely lead to the kind of increase of knowledge (*scientia*) as foretold by the prophet Daniel: "Many shall pass to and fro, and science shall be increased."[92]

Bacon's frequent references to Daniel's prophecy reveal a strand of millennialism in his theology, the beginning of a special dispensation of God's power and influence over the world which would improve man's condition. The true ancients were not the Greeks and Romans, but the scientists of his

---

88. Bacon, "A Letter to Sir Henry Savill," *WFB*, 7:99. Bacon goes on to describe victories over the body through the sheer exercise of the will, whether long periods of fasting, enduring extreme cold, holding one's breath under water, or maintaining breath in extreme heat without suffocation.

89. Bacon, *Novum Organum* 2.52, *WFB*, 4:248. "Both of these losses however can even in this life be in some part repaired; the former by religion and faith, the latter by arts and sciences."

90. Bacon, *Novum Organum* 2.52, *WFB*, 4:248.

91. Bacon, *Valerius Terminus* 1, *WFB*, 3:223.

92. Bacon, *Valerius Terminus* 1, *WFB*, 3:221, quoting Daniel 12:4.

own era.⁹³ Bacon saw his generation as the time of fulfillment; the promise of long life as recorded in the Old Testament was now being realized "after our Saviour's days," with the beloved disciple John and the long-lived holy monks and hermits among the first fruits of the promise.⁹⁴ God had providentially appointed Bacon's era, this particular "autumn of the world," for the flourishing of science.⁹⁵ Thus, the call for the cultivation of practical, useful knowledge was indeed limited by religion, as Bacon had claimed was necessary, for his theological vision was deeply rooted in the book of Genesis.

This practical science was not to serve the will of man for any vision of perfection, but was only aimed at restoring what had been *lost*. At the same time however, Bacon's religious vision for the renewal of all things as set forth in *The Great Instauration*—a term in the Vulgate used to speak of the rebuilding of the temple—was breathtakingly expansive.⁹⁶ For the Bible contained not only the teachings that could help man regain some measure of innocence lost at the fall, but it also supplied the ground and vision to go beyond *reading* the book of nature by *interrogating* it.⁹⁷ By "putting the question to nature" through a new science focused on material and efficient causes, useful knowledge could be developed to help humanity forge a path back to Eden, storming its gates and regaining a degree of dominion over creation that man had enjoyed before the fall.⁹⁸

Of the various aspects of this prelapsarian existence, no feature warranted more attention or proved more alluring than potential immortality.

---

93. Bacon, *Novum Organum* 1.84, *WFB*, 4:81–82. See also Rossi, *Francis Bacon*, 128. "Bacon's theory of present-day man's superiority to past generations was related to his refutation of traditional philosophy in which he saw a form of pride akin to the original sin of the old Adam." See also Becker, *Heavenly City*, 132.

94. Bacon, *History of Life and Death*, *WFB*, 5:217. Even the prophetess Anna provided Bacon with a New Testament exemplar in this regard (Luke 2:36–37), who, on Bacon's reading, was widowed for eighty-four years, and therefore must have lived to at least a century. See Bacon, *History of Life and Death*, *WFB*, 5:245.

95. Webster, *Great Instauration*, provides an exhaustive account of how the Puritan mission to restore Paradise was predicated upon a literal millennium, which in turn reflects a literal interpretation of Scripture, particularly, the book of Revelation.

96. Whitney, "Francis Bacon's Instauratio." See Matthews, *Theology and Science*, 51. This term was also used to speak of the establishment of God's covenant, and of recapitulation in Ephesians, from which Irenaeus derived his doctrine.

97. George Tovey notes that for Bacon "the Bible . . . appears no less explicit in its description of the method to be followed for combating the loss of Paradise than it is in its description of this loss itself." See Tovey, "Toward a New Understanding," 573.

98. Foster describes Bacon's new proposed methodology as "putting the question to nature" for new ends—the restoration of man's dominion over nature. See Foster, *Mystery and Philosophy*, 56, 58.

Just as the tree of life was at the center of the garden, so the radical prolongation of life was at the center of Bacon's program. Bacon believed that cultivating natural knowledge would enable humanity to make significant inroads against the conditions of fallen, embodied existence marked by diseases, maladies, and shortness of life. Though the cultivation of such knowledge could be used in ways counter to God's will, the true purpose of such cultivation entailed "a restitution and reinvesting (in great part) of man to the sovereignty and power . . . which he had in his first state of creation."[99] The pathway to paradise would be paved with the limitless growth of natural knowledge whose breadth was as far as the East is from the West, ranging from "a discovery of all operations and possibilities of operations from immortality (if it were possible) to the meanest mechanical practice."[100] Hence, medicine was foremost in Bacon's mind as the most important of several fields of inquiry that desperately required an infusion of useful knowledge, for it was a science "more professed than laboured, and yet more laboured than advanced."[101] Indeed, medicine often did more harm than good, asserted Bacon, and was very far from exercising any kind of sovereignty over the body.[102] He particularly loathed pronouncing any disease "incurable," for it "gives a legal sanction as it were to neglect and inattention, and exempts ignorance from discredit."[103] Bacon hoped that calling no disease incurable might draw attention to this need, that "some physicians of eminence and magnanimity may be stirred up to take this work."[104] In time, he hoped that knowledge of the human body would lead to cures for diseases once considered incurable, and eventually banish the term from the lexicon of medicine altogether.

But Bacon was not content with merely curing the incurable; he also called for an expansion of medicine to include inquiry into the human aging process itself in order to slow its progress. By doing so he sharpened the distinction between death that comes by disease and death by aging, which he understood as the decay of the whole body. If physicians were at fault for presuming that some diseases were incurable, they were equally culpable for failing to uncover the various mechanisms of aging, the processes which could be modulated to extend the human life-span. "But the lengthening of the thread of life itself, and the postponement for a time of that death which

---

99. Bacon, *Valerius Terminus* 1, *WFB*, 3:222.
100. Bacon, *Valerius Terminus* 1, *WFB*, 3:222.
101. Bacon, *Augmentis Scientiarum* 4.2, *WFB*, 4:383.
102. Bacon, *Advancement of Learning* 2, *WFB*, 3:377.
103. Bacon, *Augmentis Scientiarum* 4.2, *WFB*, 4:387.
104. Bacon, *Augmentis Scientiarum* 4.2, *WFB*, 4:387.

gradually steals on by natural dissolution and the decay of age," asserted Bacon, "is a subject which no physician has handled in proportion to its dignity."[105] On the contrary, if physicians would devote themselves to this task they would more properly learn to consider themselves as "instruments and dispensers of God's power and mercy in prolonging and renewing the life of man."[106]

At the same time however, Bacon was unflinching in his belief that Divine Providence determines not only *when* men die, but *how* they die, reflecting the Puritan emphasis on God's sovereignty. On this particular point both Bacon and Calvin recognized that God is active in all of creation, and that nothing occurs that has not been foreordained by God. Yet, Bacon differed with Calvin over the particular way in which God's sovereignty was exercised. Calvin allowed no room for any distinction between "general providence," understood as the natural order or activity of the cosmos, and "special providence," by which God was free to circumvent normal chains of causality to accomplish God's own purposes.[107] That is, for Calvin God was *immediately* involved in all events that take place, including the first occurrence of sin. God did not merely permit sin, but indeed brought about all the conditions to make human avoidance of sin impossible.[108] Bacon rejected Calvin at this point, believing that his construal of God's sovereignty was not only too deterministic, but implicated God in evil.[109] Unlike Calvin, he attributed sin and the fall to human freedom while affirming that this event was "eternally known" according to God's own prescience.[110] Bacon saw no necessary identity between God's decree and God's foreordaining activity, allowing that God authored events "by links and subordinate degrees."[111] By construing God's sovereignty as operating through a chain of causes, he proffered a more Augustinian understanding that prevented God from

105. Bacon, *Augmentis Scientiarum* 4.2, WFB, 4:383.

106. Bacon, *History of Life and Death*, WFB, 5:215.

107. Matthews, *Theology and Science*, 34–35; Calvin, *Institutes* 1.16.2–4.

108. Calvin, *Institutes* 1.18.1–3.

109. Bacon, *Meditationes Sacrae* 11, WFB, 7:253–54. "But the fact is that whatever does not depend upon God as author and principle, by links and subordinate degrees, the same will be instead of God, and a new principle and kind of usurping God. And therefore that opinion is rightly rejected as treason against the majesty and power of God. And yet for all that it is very truly said that God is not the author of evil; not because he is not author,—but because not of evil." According to Calvin, God did not merely *permit* sin, but arranged matters in such a way to make sin unavoidable. After all, God hardened Pharaoh's heart. See Calvin, *Institutes* 1.16.2.

110. Bacon, *Confession of Faith*, WFB, 7:220. God "removed from himself the beginning of all evil and vanity into the liberty of the creature."

111. Bacon, *Meditationes Sacrae* 11, WFB, 7:253.

being the author of evil, a theological move which also left enough room for the cultivation of practical knowledge in order to relieve man's estate. Bacon could thus affirm that God's providence "no doubt directs all kinds of death alike, whether from violence or disease or the decay of age"; however, he also acknowledged that God's providence "does not on that account exclude the use of preventions and remedies."[112] By this same logic Bacon extolled God's sovereignty in commencing the great instauration during his era (in fulfillment of Daniel 12:4) while also urging humankind to forge a new scientific path in order to make the great instauration a reality.[113] Indeed, it was imperative that humanity *choose* the advancement of science to make this a reality.[114] Bacon could confess God's sovereignty and control on the one hand, while underwriting a search into the mechanisms of aging on the other, all without the fear that humans were running the risk of trespassing on sacred ground in their attempted return to Eden.

To understand the novelty of Bacon's thought, it is helpful to recall that nearly two centuries later, the Puritan preacher Nathanael Emmons (1745–1840) was still following Calvin's doctrine of God's sovereignty closely. Though Emmons also believed that a return to Methuselah-like life-spans was possible, it would only come if God willed it, apart from human effort, save perhaps the effort to live a moral life. Emmons preferred to leave human longevity to God's sovereignty; Bacon saw extending life as a divinely ordained activity that also required significant human effort. Where Emmons would stress God's ability to bring death without order, Bacon sought a new kind of science in order to avoid death as long as possible. While Emmons seemed to embrace a radical theological voluntarism, Bacon emphasized the *human* will, whose distinctive feature was the power of choice.[115] As we saw in the last chapter, Bacon's melioristic stance towards aging would be echoed in the teachings of subsequent health reformers who were equally convinced that aging could be modulated by exercising the human will—not through a new kind of science—but through better living.

If, as Bacon saw things, humanity's attempt to regain Methuselah-like life-spans through the cultivation of natural knowledge did not run afoul of God's sovereignty, neither was there any perceived conflict between

---

112. Bacon, *Augmentis Scientiarum* 4.2, *WFB*, 4:383–84.

113. Bacon, *Novum Organum*, Aphorisms 93, 94, *WFB*, 4:91–92. Matthews has also noted that if "the event of the Instauration was decreed by God, it was also the result of human will and effort, for it is the humans themselves who go 'to and fro' for the increase of knowledge." Matthews, *Theology and Science*, 52.

114. Matthews, *Theology and Science*, 39.

115. See Wallace, *Francis Bacon on the Nature of Man*, 140; Bacon, *Letter and Discourse to Sir Henry Savill*, *WFB*, 7:101.

the temporal and the eternal, between a longer life here on earth and the promise of eternal life. Indeed, Bacon warned Christians against gazing too intently into the mysterious glories of heaven, lest long life be too lightly esteemed. Even though life is marred by sin, a longer life would provide more opportunity to pursue charity. "For though the life of man is only a mass and accumulation of sins and sorrows, and they who aspire to eternity set little value on life; yet even we Christians should not despise the continuance of works and charity."[116] Though Christians do indeed look forward to the promise of heaven, Bacon also recognized that it is only natural for us to esteem long life as the "greatest blessing."[117] By acknowledging human instrumentality within the bounds of God's sovereignty, Bacon believed that any success in slowing aging could never come solely from the cultivation of natural knowledge apart from God's gracious provision. Once again Bacon was able to navigate the tension between this life and the next in a way that his Puritan contemporaries seemed incapable:

> For although we Christians ever aspire and pant after that land of promise, yet meanwhile it will be a mark of God's favour if in our pilgrimage through the wilderness of this world, these our shoes and garments (I mean our frail bodies) are as little worn out as possible.[118]

For Bacon the difficulties of this life and the promise of a better life to come presented no real theological impediment to the development of an inductive science that would gradually replace useless opinions and reports with useful knowledge concerning the mysteries of aging and its attenuation. On the contrary, long life was inextricably related to our calling as Christians to bring an end to sickness and suffering through the cultivation of instrumental knowledge, regaining a degree of prelapsarian paradise even as we move inexorably toward our heavenly home.

The culmination of Bacon's vision for new knowledge is found in his unfinished *The New Atlantis* (1627), a religious allegory brimming with Old Testament symbolism and eschatological imagery.[119] Despite its utopian

116. Bacon, *History of Life and Death*, WFB, 5:217.

117. Bacon, *History of Life and Death*, WFB, 5:217. Bacon was certainly aware of human propensity to make an idol of long life, yet it appears that he was more concerned with being led astray by incorrect theories of aging that have been corrupted with false opinions and vain reports.

118. Bacon, *History of Life and Death*, WFB, 5:215.

119. See McKnight, *Religious Foundations of Francis Bacon's Thought*, 10–44. There are competing interpretations of this particular work that argue that Bacon here is developing a secular, materialistic view of progress. However, as McKnight shows, such interpretations rest upon highly selective readings.

flavor, *New Atlantis* is "not of an ideal world released from the natural conditions to which ours is subject, but of our own world as it might be made if we did our duty by it."[120] With expansive language Bacon described an academy called Solomon's House—or the College of the Six Days' Works—on the island of Bensalem, the epicenter of scientific inquiry devoted to uncovering "the knowledge of Causes and the secret motions of things; and the enlarging of the bounds of Human Empire, to the effecting of all things possible."[121] Here there was no distinction between the sacred and the scientific, between prayer and parsing nature. Bacon construed the role of the scientist in sacerdotal terms. By conducting experiments on nature, Bacon believed he himself was "perform[ing] the office of a true priest of the sense . . . and a not unskillful interpreter of its oracles."[122] Indeed, if inquiry into the causes of nature was an act of worship, the laboratory was a cathedral. The brethren of Solomon's House sung hymns and offered daily prayers of thanksgiving to God for his marvelous works along with petitions for the blessing of their labors, which in turn might be fashioned "into good and holy uses."[123]

Moreover, Bacon noted that research into the production of new metals and research into curing diseases was carried out in deep caves under the tutelage of hermits, who served as sources of scientific learning and spiritual encouragement.[124] Bacon's allusion to hermits, who in the Christian tradition were known for exceptional longevity, points to extending life as the primary goal of Solomon's House.[125] Bacon was well aware of St. Antony, Paul the Hermit, and Simeon Stylites, who, through the spiritual disciplines of continual self-examination, penance, and fasting were able to extend their lives to an extraordinary degree.[126] Just as the anchorites

---

120. Spedding, "Preface," *WFB*, 3:122.
121. Bacon, *New Atlantis*, *WFB*, 3:156.
122. Bacon, "Plan of the Work," *WFB*, 4:27.
123. Bacon, *New Atlantis*, *WFB*, 3:166.
124. Bacon, *New Atlantis*, *WFB*, 3:157. Bacon generally believed that the monks lived a life conducive to longevity. See Bacon, *Sylva Sylvarum* Century 3, *WFB*, 2:437.
125. McKnight, *Religious Foundations of Francis Bacon's Thought*, 165–66 n. 20.
126. Bacon, *History of Life and Death*, *WFB*, 5:261, 262. "A life spent in religious and holy offices seems to contribute to longevity. . . . [C]ontinued renewals, by observances, penances and atonements, which have all a strong tendency to prolong life. And if besides these there is a strict diet to harden the substance of the body, and lower the spirits, no wonder if remarkable longevity ensue; like that of Paul the Hermit, Simeon Stylites the columnar anchorite, and many other hermits and anchorites." See also Bacon, *History of Life and Death*, 277, 283–84, 291. Bacon generally acknowledged that a well-regulated diet contributed to longevity, whereby a sharper appetite is maintained in favor of leaving the stomach "absolutely empty." See Bacon, *History of Life and Death*, *WFB*, 5:294.

served as beacons of hope for the church, the hermits of Solomon's House helped illuminate the book of nature, assisting with scientific inquiry; piety and practical knowledge went hand in hand.[127] In a new hyperborean twist, Bacon envisioned the development of a drink that harkened back to Eden called the "Water of Paradise," with properties to promote health and prolong life.[128] Little wonder then that some have described Bacon's program as "the new asceticism," where the spiritual monks in the desert have been replaced by scientists.[129] Whether or not Bacon would have recognized such a distinction, it is interesting to recall from the last chapter that the Pasteur Institute under Metchnikoff's guidance was similarly likened to a religious community of sorts, where the priests of science conducted ceaseless vigils of the laboratory for the future of humankind.

Bacon's depiction of scientific inquiry in *New Atlantis* appears fantastic, yet he was under no illusions concerning the difficulties of this noble venture; he readily conceded that slowing aging would be far from easy. His fundamental apologetic for including aging attenuation as the primary goal of medicine is contained in *The History of Life and Death* (1622–23), where, with the assistance of "the Author of Life and Truth," he might inquire "about the means of prolonging the life of man."[130] Though he originally intended this to be the last of six total installments in his *Natural and Experimental History*, Bacon made this the second offering, believing it would have more immediate impact by directing those in medicine to aim at something higher than merely "curing a few diseases, and pronouncing the rest incurable."[131] Bacon had little positive to say about medicine as traditionally practiced, and was equally critical of the various theories of aging at the time. If humoral theories of aging based on radical moisture and innate heat were nothing but "mere fictions," the "extravagant praises of chemical medicines only raise men's hopes to disappoint them."[132] Alchemy also earned particular scorn. Those attempting to create potable solutions of metal and stone, asserted Bacon, were foolish to imagine that "delaying and turning back the course of nature can be effected by a morning draught

127. Matthews, *Theology and Science*, 105. "Just as Bacon saw it necessary within the Church to have some, like monastics, who were dedicated to a life of prayer, the Order of Salomon's House is dedicated to a life of hermits in order to read the book of nature."
128. Bacon, *New Atlantis*, WFB, 3:158.
129. Tovey, "Toward a New Understanding," 574.
130. Bacon, *History of Life and Death*, WFB, 5:217.
131. Spedding, WFB, 14:398.
132. Bacon, *History of Life and Death*, WFB, 5:217; Bacon, *Augmentis Scientiarum* 4.2, WFB, 4:379–80.

or by the use of some precious drug; by potable gold, or essence of pearls, or suchlike toys."[133] Bacon's own theory of aging however differed little from the traditional humoral theory, which attributed aging to a loss of heat and moisture, though, unlike others, he expressed optimism that our finite quantity of moisture could eventually be repaired and even increased.[134]

The problem, as Bacon saw it, was that some bodily organs were more amenable to repair than others. Blood, flesh and fat were still easily repaired, while the drier parts of the body like nerves, arteries, bones, and bowels were repaired with more difficulty.[135] As the body aged, this disparity of rates of repair became more pronounced, eventually reaching a point where even the organs more amenable to repair begin to fail by their connection with other bodily parts that were "hardly repairable," leaving the whole body in a state of dissolution and irrevocable disrepair.[136] Bacon likened this state of uneven repair to the "torture of Mezentius" in Virgil's *Aeneid*, where living captives were bound face to face with rotting corpses until "the oozy foulness and corruption of the dreadful embrace so slay them by a lingering death."[137] For Bacon, the aging body was at war with itself, its various members and organs locked in a gruesome, tortuous embrace. He speculated that aging might be treated by addressing the body's repair functions, easing this disequilibrium. If this could be accomplished, the whole body might endure much longer, if not indefinitely: "whatever can be repaired gradually without destroying the original whole is, like the vestal

---

133. Bacon, *Augmentis Scientiarum* 4.2, WFB, 4:391. Though Bacon remained critical of the alchemist's designs on potable gold, he did acknowledge that some had achieved limited success, but probably on account of the salt by which the gold is dissolved. He did exhort the use of cordials containing the powder of fine pearls, precious stones and various spices, but only in moderation, "not heap[ing] them promiscuously together, as is usually done." See Bacon, *History of Life and Death*, WFB, 5:264.

134. Bacon, *History of Dense and Rare*, WFB, 5:399. "Age brings bodies either to putrefaction or dryness."

135. Bacon's belief that the material or animal soul resided mainly in the head, which ran along the nerves and was refreshed by arterial blood owes much to Bernardino Telesio (1509-1588). See also Bacon, *History of Life and Death*, WFB, 5:321-23. Bacon's theory of aging has been aptly described as an eclectic mix of Aristotle, Avicenna, Paracelsus, Telesio, and Neoplatonic philosophy. See Rees, "Introduction," in *Oxford Francis Bacon*, 6:lxix.

136. Bacon, *History of Life and Death*, WFB, 5:218. "The cause of the termination is this; the spirit which like a gentle flame is ever preying on the body, and the external air which likewise sucks and dries bodies, conspiring with the spirit, do in the end destroy the workshop of the body with its machines and organs, and make them incapable of performing the work of repair. Such then are the true ways of natural death."

137. Bacon, *History of Life and Death*, WFB, 5:218; Virgil, *Aeneid* 8.485, 162.

fire, potentially eternal."¹³⁸ Just as a youthful body not only repairs itself entirely but actually increases in both quantity and quality, asserted Bacon, "the matter whereby they [parts of the body] are repaired would be eternal, if the manner of repairing them did not fail."¹³⁹ With Bacon's speculation concerning earthly immortality, the tension between this life and the next all but evaporates. Though elsewhere Bacon acknowledges that human life is finite, he was curiously silent on the curse of death (Gen 2:17; 3:19) in his many references to the fall. Little wonder that some see Bacon arguing for an earthly immortality of sorts.

If Bacon genuinely believed that the human life-span might be extended indefinitely, his optimism was certainly also informed by his reading of Scripture. Following the lead of Church Fathers Augustine and Jerome, Bacon interpreted the genealogical accounts of Genesis literally.¹⁴⁰ He was perfectly content with a naturalistic explanation for the steady decrease in life-spans from several centuries in the early chapters of Genesis to a mere threescore and ten by the time of Moses (Ps 90:10), attributing this phenomenon to the flood, without much further speculation.¹⁴¹ He saw no reason to take Moses's allusion of life's brevity in Psalm 90 as an irrevocable by-product of God's wrath, nor was he willing to attribute the patriarchs' longevity to a special dispensation of God's grace. There were more than enough examples in the history of the church—including the centenarians Paul the Hermit and Antony—to conclude that regaining longer life was a matter of re-establishing dominion over nature. He also drew on contemporary examples, recalling a recent Morris dance performed by eight men in Herefordshire whose collective age totaled 800 years.¹⁴² In spite of his protestations against the fables and fallacious calculations of the heathen however, Bacon proved no less susceptible to the hyperborean tales than

---

138. Bacon, *History of Life and Death*, WFB, 5:218.

139. Bacon, *History of Life and Death*, WFB, 5:218.

140. Bacon, *History of Life and Death*, WFB, 5:245. Both Jerome and Augustine took pains to account for the apparent fact that Methuselah would have died fourteen years *after* the flood in for him to reach 969 years. See also Augustine, *City of God* 15.11. Earlier on in his career, Bacon made this same point by appealing to early Greek tales like the story of Prometheus. According to Bacon, we learn from the forfeited gift of youth bestowed by Jupiter that the "methods and medicines for the retardation of age and the prolongation of life were by the ancients not despaired of, but reckoned rather among those things which men once had and by sloth and negligence let slip, than among those which were wholly denied or never offered." Bacon, *Wisdom of the Ancients* 26, WFB, 6:749.

141. Bacon, *History of Life and Death*, WFB, 5:256. He did however reject the idea that this curtailment in longevity was simply due to the passing of generations.

142. Bacon, *History of Life and Death*, WFB, 5:255–56.

his predecessors, happily accepting reports of 150-year-old dwellers in the mountains of Ethiopia as no less reliable than the ages of the patriarchs recorded in the book of Genesis.[143]

Such anecdotal accounts in *The History of Life and Death* are commonplace, reflecting an expansive, gregarious inquisitiveness into the factors influencing longevity, whether for good or ill. Bacon left no stone unturned in his attempt to identify contributing factors to human aging. He examined longevity in plants, animals, and reports of long-lived men and women throughout history, giving thoughtful consideration to potential contributing factors, including physiology, birthplace, the length and time of nativity (whether in the morning, afternoon, or evening, in January, June, or July), family history, psychological constitution, affections of the mind, habit, diet, particular mannerisms, and even climate.[144] For instance, he attributed the exceptional longevity of the Ethiopian and Abyssinian mountain-dwellers to the air quality and soil composition. Bacon's reflection on the particular means by which aging might be slowed was equally expansive, which he divided into three basic categories of the prevention of consumption, perfecting repair, and the renovation of decay.[145] These included the use of potable precious metals and stones (in spite of his criticism of alchemy), a moderately spare diet, and the right cultivation of the "affections and passions of the mind." The latter entailed cultivating love, hope, and admiration while avoiding envy, strife, and anger. Though his many suggestions for longevity strike modern ears as odd—the use of opiates in the month of May, or the application of warm kitten blood to help rejuvenate the skin—Bacon's *History of Life and Death* has been rightly described as a "prodigious texture of medical, pharmaceutical, botanical, historical and antiquarian erudition."[146] Nevertheless, while Bacon railed sharply against the methods of traditional medicine and alchemy, his own suggested solutions did not depart significantly from the medicine and methods he so sharply criticized, and represent "a kind of practical, bet-hedging eclecticism coupled with a measure of intellectual 'slippage' forgivable in one struggling to escape from received ideas."[147]

---

143. Bacon, *History of Life and Death*, WFB, 5:257.

144. Bacon, *History of Life and Death*, WFB, 5:220-21.

145. Bacon, *History of Life and Death*, WFB, 5:268.

146. Gemelli, "History of Life and Death," 155; Bacon, *History of Life and Death*, WFB, 5:271, 277, 279, 307.

147. Rees, "Introduction," 6:lxviii. Georges Minois described Bacon's work as oscillating "between alchemy and popular potions in his search for remedies prolonging life." Minois, *History of Old Age*, 274.

While Bacon's *History of Life and Death* contributed little by way of knowledge into human aging, his urgent call for the inquiry into its causes with the view of bringing it under discrete human control as man's God-given vocation lent considerable prestige to the idea of prolonging life through the inductive study of God's book of nature. Bacon's call to emphasize material and efficient causes over formal and final causes was inseparable from his goal of prolonging human life. From the earliest published essays such as "Of Regiment of Health" (1597) to *The History of Life and Death* (1623) and *New Atlantis* (1627), Bacon placed considerable emphasis on the role of medicine in alleviating suffering and finding new cures not only for disease, but for radically prolonging life by attenuating the aging process.[148] Unlike previous searches for longevity, however, which consisted largely of primitive fountain legends, alchemy, and hygienic methods, Bacon called for relentless inductive research into the mechanisms of the human aging process, aware of its highly complex, intransigent nature. His call for the pursuit of practical knowledge that required relocating formal and final causes to another sphere of inquiry would profoundly reshape science and medicine. Insofar as modern medicine rejects the notion that any disease is fundamentally incurable, and remains dedicated the prolongation of life—whether through treating diseases or treating aging as a disease—it reflects the expansive powers of diligent human inquiry envisioned by Bacon. Indeed, Bacon's influence has also shaped the nature of contemporary gerontology.[149] Certainly, recent advances in both science and medicine give much cause for celebration and optimism, and bear witness to the tremendous fruit cultivated by the empirical, inductive investigation of nature on its own terms, unencumbered by the metaphysical baggage of formal and final causes. The eradication of many diseases along with the general improvement in both the quality and length of life attest to the power of Bacon's approach. However, concerns have been raised about the fruit borne out by the Baconian approach to science and medicine, and how the quest to reshape nature—including our very selves—in order to secure radically longer life, shapes us morally.

---

148. Gemelli, "History of Life and Death," 134–57, shows how the theme of longevity is constant throughout the entire Baconian corpus. For "Of Regiment of Health," see Bacon, *Essays*, *WFB*, 6:530–31. In addition, the first few lines of Bacon's *Magnalia Naturae* (1627) read as follows: "The prolongation of life. The restitution of youth in some degree. The retardation of age. The curing of diseases incurable. The mitigation of pain." Bacon, *Magnalia Naturae*, *WFB*, 3:167. This work was later added as an appendix to *The New Atlantis*.

149. Gruman, "History of Ideas," 82. See also Achenbaum, *Crossing Frontiers*, 7.

BACON'S QUEST AND THE BACONIAN PROJECT

It is no accident that contemporary quests to extend life by slowing aging itself have been described as "Baconian." According to Gerald McKenny, the "Baconian Project" is nothing less than the attempt "to relieve the human condition of subjection to the whims of fortune or the bonds of natural necessity," evidenced especially in attempts to manipulate the aging process.[150] It often serves as a shorthand notation for the Promethean effort to eliminate nearly all forms of suffering—including human mortality—through the use of technology.[151] As McKenny observes, when Bacon removed final causes from the investigation of the physical world, nature itself would come to be construed in a new way. Specifically, the concepts of nature as being ordered by a final cause (*telos*), or governed by providence, gave way to constructs of nature as "a neutral instrument that is brought into the realm of human ends by technology."[152] This represents a departure from the attitude of Greek scientists, whose "intellectualized from of nature worship" rendered the idea that nature might be subjected to human will, much less human mastery, unthinkable.[153] In addition, McKenny sees modern discourse on medicine as the natural outflow of Bacon's program where "moral convictions about the place of illness and health in a morally worthy life are replaced by moral convictions about the relief of suffering and the expansion of choice."[154] But understanding or describing "a morally worthy life" requires some metanarrative in which medicine and its roles can be situated. Such a narrative ought to allow ample space for working out the degree to which some suffering might be endured for higher purposes (i.e., in alignment with a morally worthy life) while acknowledging other kinds of suffering against which our medical resources ought to be enlisted. McKenny's point speaks to the dominance of Bacon's perspective, which tends to view all suffering as inimical to human flourishing, including the suffering of old age.

---

150. McKenny, *To Relieve the Human Condition*, 2.

151. McKenny, *To Relieve the Human Condition*, 2.

152. McKenny, *To Relieve the Human Condition*, 21.

153. Foster, "Some Remarks," 6. "The idea that it [nature] might be subjected to mastery by the human will could hardly have been entertained by a Greek thinker." See also Baillie, *Natural Science and the Spiritual Life*, 29.

154. McKenny, *To Relieve the Human Condition*, 21. Several years earlier Leon Kass made a similar observation, describing the modern project as the "conquest of nature for the relief of man's estate," with the implicit goal of reversing the curses of Adam and Eve or restoring access to the tree of life through the tree of knowledge. See Kass, *Toward a More Natural Science*, 34n31; 69.

Two hallmarks encapsulate the basic thrust of the Baconian Project: the relief of suffering and the expansion of choice. While neither are necessarily problematic in and of themselves, they nevertheless invite questions regarding the nature of human limits and the place of suffering in living a morally worthy life. As McKenny observes, when these two aims are pursued in an attempt to escape "our subjection to fortune and finitude," the project takes on a utopian flavor.[155] Since the Baconian Project tends to interpret the human body as neutral, then one must supposedly look elsewhere for a framework or metanarrative that might provide guidance in discerning between the *kinds* of suffering we should attempt to alleviate and the kinds of suffering that might serve higher ends—precisely the type of discernment that is generally foreign to utopian narratives. Does the aging process itself qualify as a form of suffering that demands relief at the hands of our instrumental, technological control? Technology itself cannot of course provide the answer, nor is it necessarily the problem. On the contrary, technology has helped us overcome disease, hunger, and toil. But if medicine and technology are unable to answer this question, it seems that nature cannot either since, in the Baconian scheme, it has been reinterpreted as something to be controlled rather than contemplated.[156]

We are left with the remnants of a threadbare framework of eliminating suffering and expanding choice, without reference to the teleological question that asks what nature and our bodies are for, and without Bacon's theological vision that provided some guidance on questions of ultimate purpose. The contemporary Baconian framework leaves questions concerning what particular kinds of suffering should be eliminated unanswered (indeed, unasked). Nature has also been rendered neutral, reduced to a mere given, and therefore silent on such matters. Though nature may be construed as neutral with regards to particular *ends*, it is difficult to see how nature can remain neutral with regards to our *desires* that are often cultivated and shaped by new technologies. That is, when nature is made subject to our ideals of perfection that often entail increasingly expansive understanding of what constitutes suffering, it will tend to be treated as the enemy. Indeed, the Baconian Project encourages us to view nature itself—including the body—as the enemy, with human finitude itself as our fundamental flaw.[157] In this Baconian framework, what counts as suffering is often left to an individual's subjective needs, while the choices over how to address such suffering will likely continue to expand. Of course, careful

---

155. McKenny, *To Relieve the Human Condition*, 5.
156. McKenny, *To Relieve the Human Condition*, 18.
157. Verhey, *Nature and Altering It*, 72.

consideration of one's needs and properly exercising one's will in the pursuit of health and longevity is entirely appropriate to a degree. Yet, what constitutes "proper" or "appropriate" with respect to aging and its attenuation is far from clear without the teleological questions that arise naturally within a larger metanarrative that articulates the purposes for existence. As Oliver O'Donovan has noted, with a loss of teleology we are more likely to misjudge not only our place in this world, but also the means by which we extend our time in it.[158]

The Baconian Project and its clarion call to put knowledge to use in relieving humanity's estate by exercising and establishing power over nature remains the driving force underwriting the practice of scientific research and medicine long after the theological moorings that might have placed limits on this project have given way. However, the "Baconian Project" should not be confused with Bacon's own agenda, for there are at least two notable areas of divergence. First, Bacon at least recognized that there were appropriate and inappropriate reasons for pursuing longevity. He utterly rejected the notion that longevity could be pursued for longevity's sake. Indeed, he asserted instead that the duties of life were preferable to life itself.[159] Though Bacon himself never specified these duties, he was critical of those who aimed at long life itself as the ultimate goal, singling out the cave-dweller Epimenides, who supposedly slept many years in a hibernation-like state without the need for food.[160] He was equally critical of those who relied on "exact regulation of food and diet which makes the preservation of life its sole object, to the neglect of everything else."[161] Bacon also referenced the hypochondriac Herodicus in Plato's *Republic*, who earned scorn for strictly following a regimen in order maintain health for health's sake rather than putting the power of medicine at the disposal of fulfilling one's vocation as a citizen of the state.[162] He was only slightly less critical of his contemporary Luigi Cornaro, whose regimen was considered more modest. There is little reason to think that Bacon would have responded much differently to Roy Walford's *The 120 Year Diet* and his subsequent *Beyond the 120 Year Diet*,

---

158. O'Donovan, *Resurrection and Moral Order*, 52.
159. Bacon, *History of Life and Death*, WFB, 5:266.
160. Bacon, *History of Life and Death*, WFB, 5:277, 283.
161. Bacon, *History of Life and Death*, WFB, 5:266. Bacon was also likely aware of Taoist practices of the Chinese, whom he criticized for having "a mania for long life." See *History of Life and Death*, WFB, 5:257.
162. Plato, *Republic* 406a–d; Plato, *Phaedrus* 227d. Bacon also considered love and hope as key qualities in promoting longevity. Some goal is needed in life to prolong it, and it must be a good one, lest it is too easily achieved, after which the desire to live wanes. Bacon, *History of Life and Death*, WFB, 5:279–280.

even if his regimen proved fully efficacious, for it betrays the notion that longevity itself is the main goal under which all other potential activities must compete for time. Bacon, by contrast, sought to put forward remedies and principles that "will neither prevent the duties of life, nor hinder and embarrass them too much."[163] Though once again he was not concerned to delineate particular duties, so long as the goal of restoring man's estate was guided by charity, he recognized that there were duties in life worth pursuing, whether or not one lived long enough to fulfill them. Long life was indeed a worthy goal, but it was no absolute ethical lord demanding that all activities be directed towards its service.

The second notable difference between the "Baconian Project" and Bacon's own program concerns the way nature itself is construed. While the Baconian Project treats nature as neutral at best and sloppy or inefficient at worst, and therefore capable of being manipulated in nearly any way we see fit, Bacon's understanding was more complex. For Bacon, nature was neither neutral nor immutable, for his interpretation of nature was allied to a Christian faith, which was shaped by the relationship between God and the world.[164] Nature was simply that which operated according to God's law; nature is "nothing but the laws of the creation."[165] Though some laws had been partially revoked on account of the curse (Gen 3), they nevertheless remained in place, governing inviolably until the end of the world.[166] As such, nature itself had built-in limits ordered and established by God's wisdom which, despite the efforts of humankind, could not be violated. When for instance Bacon hoped to stir up physicians by publicly declaring no disease incurable, he parenthetically conceded that even the best physicians could only progress "as far as the nature of things permits."[167] Similarly, when it came to altering nature, Bacon believed man was incapable of doing anything beyond observation and interpretation, "for the chain of causes cannot by any force be loosed or broken."[168] This could hardly be construed as an excuse for inactivity, however. On the contrary, as we have seen, Bacon asserted that nature has been placed under human dominion by God. Yet, this rule could only be properly exercised after man had correctly

---

163. Bacon, *History of Life and Death*, WFB, 5:266.

164. Torrance, *Theological Science*, 73.

165. Bacon, *Confession of Faith*, WFB, 7:221.

166. Bacon, *Confession of Faith*, WFB, 7:221. According to Bacon, these laws have undergone three changes: (1) matter was created without form, (2) the imposition of form on matter, the "interim of perfection of every day's work," followed by (3) the curse, which has adversely affected nature. The final phase of nature has yet to be revealed.

167. Bacon, *Augmentis Scientiarum* 4.2, WFB, 4:387.

168. Bacon, "Plan of the Work," WFB, 4:32.

interpreted nature by *submitting* to it. Nature cannot be commanded, says Bacon, "except by being obeyed."[169] Here the twin forces of human knowledge and human power "do really meet in one."[170] Yet, our ignorance of causes significantly limited what humans might accomplish. "All that man can do is to put together or put asunder natural bodies. The rest is done by nature working within."[171] Hence, Bacon could liken nature to a lyre in need of careful tuning.[172] Therefore, we are not nature's shapers, but its servants. Though nature's laws were considered immutable, clearly Bacon believed that man could inductively uncover the laws of creation and attain *useful* knowledge that would allow for aging to be slowed down, all while (somehow) working within the bounds of nature, as established by God.

Closely related to this point is Bacon's rejection of imposing any template on nature derived from our own imagination, as if nature were a passive lump of clay ready to be shaped according to our grand ideals. While the Baconian Project sees nature as an object to be manipulated in ways that conform to human desires and ideals of perfection, Bacon recognized that nature was still under God's control through immutable laws that could not and must not be transgressed by vain human imagination. "God forbid," declared Bacon, "that we should give out a dream of our own imagination for a pattern of the world."[173] For in doing so "we create worlds, we direct and domineer over nature, we will have it that all things are as in our folly we think they should be, not as seems fittest to the Divine wisdom, or as they are found to be in fact."[174] Indeed, to see nature as capable of being reshaped to fit human desire was not only to repeat the sin of Adam and Eve, but to perpetuate and extend this initial transgression. Though our first parents sinned in their desire to be like God, claimed Bacon, "their posterity desire to be even greater."[175] But man actually forfeits his dominion by assert-

---

169. Bacon, "Plan of the Work," *WFB*, 4:32; Bacon, *True Directions Concerning the Interpretation of Nature* 1.1, *WFB*, 4:47.

170. Bacon, "Plan of the Work," *WFB*, 4:32. Though the mantra "Knowledge is power" appropriately describes Bacon's scientific program, the only time he is known to have used anything close to this phrase occurred in a parenthetical remark—"(for knowledge itself is power)"—in regard to the distinction between God's foreknowledge and foreordination. See Bacon, *Religious Meditations*, *WFB*, 7:253.

171. Bacon, *True Directions Concerning the Interpretation of Nature* 1.4, *WFB*, 4:47.

172. Bacon, *Wisdom of the Ancients* 11, *WFB*, 6:721. Similarly, Bacon describes the role of the physician as one of exercising the skill of stretching and tuning the harp of man's body in an attempt to keep it from "all harshness and discord." Bacon, *Augmentis Scientiarum* 4.2, *WFB*, 4:380.

173. Bacon, "The Plan of the Work," *WFB*, 4:32-33.

174. Bacon, *Natural and Experimental History*, *WFB*, 5:132.

175. Bacon, *Natural and Experimental History*, *WFB*, 5:132.

ing it in this fashion, for such vain imaginations inevitably *distort* man's interpretation of nature.[176] Truly useful knowledge could only be attained by fixing one's attention on the particulars of nature and seeing things as they really are (a quintessentially modern assertion), apart from any preconceived abstract notions of its operations, much less a pattern conceived in the mind of man.[177] This is why Bacon asserted that man has fallen doubly—first by desiring to be like God, and secondly by adhering to an Aristotelian philosophy that inevitably distorted one's apprehension of nature.

Bacon therefore would have strongly objected to the contemporary project that bears his name. Though he insisted that man must exert his power over nature, this dominion could hardly be described as remaking nature, much less the human body, according to our own desires. Whatever Bacon meant when he referred to reversing the effects of aging as "turning back the course of nature," he did not consider this a revolt against nature's laws or a fundamental alteration of nature itself.[178] That was no more possible than removing God from his throne.[179] Bacon's hope of reversing aging did however accord with his understanding of man's ability in this sphere as limited to the "rending asunder" and "putting together" of natural bodies, the remainder being accomplished by "nature working within."[180] Subsequent developments in science have shown the human body to be considerably more complex than Bacon could have possibly envisioned, leaving us to wonder what he might have said about current attempts to slow down human aging. Whether, for instance, Bacon would have considered genes or a chromosomal pair on a strand of DNA as natural bodies, and whether their manipulation would have been a violation of nature's workings "from within" is hard to say. For in one sense, "nature," understood in the modern sense as simply as "what is there," remains nature all the way down, regardless of the increasing complexity uncovered with each new discovery.[181] It seems plausible that Bacon could have interpreted genetic manipulation as simply another instance of putting natural bodies together in ways that allowed enough room for nature to "work from within." Indeed, it is hard to see how such manipulations could be interpreted as contrary to Bacon's theological commitments that supplied the warrant for slowing aging.

176. Bacon, *Natural and Experimental History*, WFB, 5:132.

177. Bacon, "The Plan of the Work," WFB, 4:32–33.

178. Bacon, *Augmentis Scientiarum* 4.2, WFB, 4:391; Bacon, *History of Life and Death*, WFB, 5:269, 330.

179. Bacon, *History of Life and Death*, WFB, 5:269; 330.

180. Bacon, *True Directions Concerning the Interpretation of Nature*, 1.4, WFB, 4:47.

181. Moreover, the very concepts "nature" and "natural" are very slippery and imprecise, amenable to multiple interpretations depending on the context.

It is significant however that the contemporary Baconian Project seems to leave little room for his concept of "nature working within," which, according Bacon, was a realm beyond human intervention. Late modern science, with its quest for mastery, recognizes no such inviolable boundary or category, but is intent on investigating the particulars of nature in its increasing complexity in hopes of bringing "nature working within" under discrete control. Indeed, the greatest potential of science, we are often told, hinges precisely on our ability to work "from within," where breathtaking, transformative power resides, whether through the creation of stem cells, genetic manipulation, synthetic biology, or nanotechnology. One should not belittle or minimize the tremendous good that has and may come as a result of medicine's ability to work "from within;" advances produced by the systematic, disciplined inquiry into the workings of nature along material and causal lines have produced significant victories over disease and suffering. However, as McKenny points out, contemporary medicine has difficulties recognizing any boundaries—beyond those imposed by the limits of our technology—because it has no controlling narrative that might qualify and limit the somewhat abstract and free-floating principles of eliminating suffering and expanding choice. Modern medicine lacks a framework to help determine what marks a worthy life, what kinds of suffering should be mitigated, and whether the effects of aging itself should be meliorated by slowing the process.

Bacon's program, by contrast, avoided earlier Greek understandings of nature as at least partly divine and therefore largely immutable on the one hand, and the contemporary view of nature as infinitely mutable on the other. His theological understanding of nature as fallen, yet created and ordered by God, was informed by the biblical mandate to fill and subdue the earth (Gen 1:28–30). Because nature was God's creation, it was thus limited by God's immutable laws of operation, even if many of these laws had yet to be discovered. Though Bacon insisted that the pursuit of natural knowledge should be free from interfering questions of essence and purpose (i.e., formal and final causes), the search into the workings of nature was guided by his theological conviction that all discoveries be ordered towards the goal of restoring what was lost at the fall.[182] In other words, Bacon asserted that the study of nature (known then as natural philosophy) should not be *invaded* by revealed theology in the Bible, but rather be *bounded* by it.[183] Bacon's suspicion of imposing our ideal on nature was not directed against the notion

---

182. Bacon, *Valerius Terminius* 1, WFB, 3:218; Bacon, *Advancement of Learning* 2, WFB, 3:442, 472.

183. Rees, "Introduction," 6:xlix; Bacon, *Valerius Terminus* 1, WFB, 3:218–19.

of having an ideal or template as such, but against the template's *source*. Any ideal of the world apart from God's revelation in Scripture could only come from man's "vain imagination." For Bacon, the template of humanity drawn from the first few chapters of Genesis supplied the particular ends to which useful knowledge could be put, namely, the restoration of man's power and sovereignty over nature which included extending life by slowing the aging process. Hence, Bacon's insistence that man exert his power over nature in exercising dominion could hardly be described as remaking nature, much less the human body, according to *man's* image or ideal, for the biblical Adam was God's archetypal image-bearer (Gen 1:26–27). This Adam served as the ideal of humanity as it was meant to be and could be again, by inductively uncovering God's laws in nature and putting them to use. A gradual return to Methuselah-like life-spans would serve as a primary indicator that men had regained a portion of Adam's prelapsarian existence.

BACON'S ADAM

There is little doubt that Bacon's program was informed by his understanding of the Christian faith, yet questions remain surrounding his theological justification for slowing the aging process, particularly his use of Adam as the ideal for man. Though Bacon viewed the fall as a crucial point in the history of humankind, his silence on the effects of sin, which include expulsion from the garden and access to the tree of life, is curious (Gen 3:22–24). After all, the fact that the Augustinian understanding of original sin, which held that Adam's potential immortality was forfeited on account of sin, was still largely accepted within the Puritan tradition, makes Bacon's omission all the more intriguing.[184] Moreover, by focusing primarily on the first Adam, one wonders whether Bacon's project of slowing aging is a sufficiently *Christian* account. It is hard to see whether Bacon's quest to relieve man's estate by attenuating aging was sufficiently informed by God's purposes for humanity as discerned in Christ. For in the Christian tradition Adam has been identified as the one who brought death into the world, consequences that the last Adam, Jesus Christ, came to remedy (Rom 5:12–21; 1 Cor 15:45–57). Though Scripture certainly bears witness to the *first* Adam of the garden,

---

184. Augustine, *City of God*, 13.20. Had Adam and Eve continued in their obedience, God would have eventually granted them immortality, living "eternally with their bodies," *City of God*, 13.19; 12.22; 22.30. Augustine also acknowledged however that before the fall the tree of life kept them from "declining into old age." *City of God*, 13.20. The way in which Augustine connected Adam's sin with the rest of humanity, particularly in reference to our corruption (*vitium*) and guilt (*reatus*), proved far more controversial.

Adam's story has been taken up and redeemed in light of the *last* Adam of Golgotha, Jesus Christ. Bacon's picture of the prelapsarian Adam as ideal human—including his longevity—is in need of incarnational qualification in light of the advent of Jesus Christ, the man from above, the God who took on human flesh. Reflecting on the morality of slowing aging with reference to Jesus Christ poses challenges to Bacon's use of the first Adam in justifying his program, especially the understanding of embodiment implicit in Bacon's account.

Though Bacon worked within a broad Christian framework that recognized both the limits of bodily existence and the resurrection to come, it is difficult to escape the conclusion that he tended to view the human body as an object of study and manipulation, even if these manipulations were to be guided by charity and ultimately serve the glory of God. At the same time, however, Bacon's desire to live longer by slowing the body down cannot be universally condemned. If extending life by battling disease is a morally worthy project, it is not immediately clear why extending life by slowing aging should be considered any more problematic. However, with his belief that inductive knowledge should be practically applied to slow the aging process in a return to Paradise, Bacon largely failed to consider *who* we might become through our efforts to restore human sovereignty and power; he offered no account of how our attempts to reform our bodies to the ideal of Eden might impact our spiritual development as creatures before God.[185] Bacon's understanding of postlapsarian humanity might account for this, for his interpretation of Adam's sin and its effects was not nearly as pessimistic as Calvin and his Puritan contemporaries. Though Bacon acknowledged that sin "defaced" the image of God in humankind and brought death into the world, he said little concerning its effects, situating sin in the context of Christ's work.[186] In his *Confession of Faith* Bacon focused more on the transforming effects that Christ's victory over sin had on and in humanity. As mediator, Christ "accomplished the whole work of the redemption and restitution of man to a state superior to the Angels, whereas the state of his creation was inferior . . ."[187] Bacon's description of the incarnation hints at *theōsis*—our participating the divine nature of Christ while remaining fully human ourselves (2 Pet 1:3-4)—when he refers to the Son's taking on flesh as a ladder "whereby God might descend to his creatures, and his creatures might ascend to God."[188] In this regard Ba-

---

185. Bacon, *Valerius Terminus* 1; Bacon, *Novum Organum* 2.52.
186. Bacon, *Confession of Faith*, WFB, 7:222.
187. Bacon, *Confession of Faith*, WFB, 7:223.
188. Bacon, *Confession of Faith*, WFB, 7:219. Both Luther and Calvin of course

con's theology was more aligned with the Christianity of late antiquity than the Reformation, though, as will become clear in the next chapter, Christ's incarnation informed bodily practices necessary for spiritual formation that also lead to longer life.

It is helpful to remember that before the advent of Baconian science nature was perceived largely as an unchangeable given that required humanity to learn to live within the dictates of this reality, conforming to the conditions it imposed.[189] With the advent of modern science, however, we are now confronted with the temptation of shaping reality in accordance with our most deeply held desires and wishes. If, as C. S. Lewis observed in *The Abolition of Man*, the old problem concerned conforming one's soul to reality through the pursuit of knowledge, self-discipline, and virtue, then any attempts to remake nature—including our bodies—in accordance with our desires will inevitably shape our character as well. But the growth in knowledge afforded by our technological projects has a way of displacing some of these older practices by which virtue might be cultivated. In a prescient remark, the English philosopher C. E. M. Joad (1891–1953) observed that our increased knowledge has engendered a new attitude toward human life where we have effectively substituted a problem of morals for one of technique: "For a problem of morals, a problem of discipline and control— how to govern the human soul—there has been substituted a problem of technique—how to alter reality in ways which are agreeable to man."[190] We must not however be deceived into thinking that we are left with a binary choice—either submit to the limits of nature for the benefit of the soul, or reshape nature according to our desires and thereby put the soul at risk. As Bacon recognized, God's command to fill and subdue creation (Gen 1:28–30) implies that some interventions in nature are appropriate. Herein lies the crux of the matter. The real challenge in formulating a Christian account of nature and human interaction with or even against nature (including ourselves) requires discerning precisely *what* kinds of interventions are warranted and the particular *means* by which such interventions are carried out. Guidance in these matters must rely on a faithful interpretation of Scripture, especially the creation accounts in Genesis and the life and work

---

occasionally employed *theōsis* or divinization as one metaphor for salvation where the believer participates in, or is made one with Christ. Recently, a new interpretation of Luther headed by Tuomo Mannermaa has attempted to move *theōsis* to the center of Luther's understanding of justification, but not without controversy. See Braaten and Jenson, eds., *Union with Christ*.

189. The survey in chapter 1 also showed that the desire to transcend human finitude is as old as humanity itself.

190. Joad, *Recovery of Belief*, 53–54.

of Jesus Christ as attested in the Gospels. The significance of Jesus Christ as it relates to aging attenuation will be developed later in this book.

Nevertheless, as has been suggested, Bacon overlooked the ways in which manipulating the human body to improve its functioning might impact one's spiritual formation. In particular, Bacon largely ignored the ways in which the body's limits might prove useful and even necessary in refining one's soul and shaping one's character. While Bacon helpfully asserted that all of our scientific endeavors should be guided by love or charity, he did not make it entirely clear how this love that marks and shapes the Christian life was to be developed, much less what role, if any, the body was to play in its cultivation. To be fair, such concerns were hardly central to his theological argument, which was aimed primarily at the development of practical knowledge for the relief of the human condition. This emphasis also seemed to fit his understanding of the efficacy of the incarnation, whereby humanity had already in a sense been remade in ways that surpassed prelapsarian existence. At the same time however Bacon implicitly assigned the human body an unacceptably narrow role in God's plan of redemption, reducing it to a passive recipient of human technical intervention. His call for the discovery and cultivation of practical knowledge would signal a shift in understanding concerning nature and the human body. The continued development of practical, natural knowledge initiated in part by Bacon's apologetic has fostered a conception of the human body primarily as problem for science to the degree that it remains resistant to certain forms of intervention or manipulation. This is in marked contrast to earlier conceptions of the body that recognized its inherent limitedness as an opportunity to cultivate discipline and spiritual development. In other words, the problems posed by the aging body that were once seen as conditions in and by which character might continue to be formed are now seen primarily as issues for science. If the body was once implicated in the formation of character by placing limits *on* human desire, the body now tends to be perceived as an object *of* desire—desires that range from lauding to loathing. It should not be surprising then to find that in the modern Baconian Project "the body as object of spiritual and moral practices is replaced by the body as object of practices of technological control."[191] Moreover, not only has the body become an object of technological control; it has also become the enemy.[192] As we have seen, laboratory success in slowing aging has tended to bolster enthusiasm for this project while simultaneously encouraging hostile stances toward the aging body. Once an ally for spiritual growth and a reminder to prepare

---

191. McKenny, *To Relieve the Human Condition*, 21.

192. Verhey, *Christian Art of Dying*, 37.

for the life to come, the aging body becomes an increasingly hostile and unforgiving reminder of what has been irretrievably lost, that our desires will always outpace the body's ability to instantiate them.

CONCLUSION

Though neither a mathematician nor a metaphysician, Francis Bacon has been described as a *buccinator novi temporis*—the herald of a new era—arguing for both a new method and purpose for science.[193] Earlier Greek methods of investigation that focused on contemplation of nature were inadequate to what Bacon saw as the true purpose of science—the relief of man's estate through the exercise of proper dominion over nature. In arguing for slowing human aging through a renewed and more circumscribed focus on material and efficient causality, Bacon drew upon the heritage of the Reformation that recognized nature's contingency vis-à-vis the God who made a covenant with humankind to rule and subdue the earth. This development allowed Bacon to criticize the older Greek concept of science as contemplation with its metaphysical abstractions in favor of practical activity aimed at restoring key features of human existence before the fall, significantly longer life being the most important. Bacon's literal reading of the biblical account of Adam in the garden that presented nature as both fallen yet subservient to God's will, coupled with God's command to fill and subdue the earth (Gen 1:28–30), enabled him to forge a path between earlier Greek conceptions of nature as largely immutable and the contemporary scientific view that sees nature as devoid of purpose and nearly infinitely mutable. Bacon carved out a space for the cultivation of useful knowledge through the disciplined inductive study of nature even while acknowledging man's limited ability to reshape it, for nature was still God's creation operating according to God's laws. Though this fallen nature threatened humanity with death and misery, nature could nevertheless be mastered through the wise application of knowledge and power, allowing humanity to once again taste the glory of Eden.

With its quest for mastery over the human body and the continual battle against disease and death, modern medicine owes its development in large part to the methodology so eloquently articulated by Bacon.[194] Nevertheless, contemporary medicine has considerable difficulty coming to grips with the limits of healing and the mortality of the body. As McKenny notes,

---

193. Willey, *Seventeenth Century Background*, 24.

194. See Taylor, *Sources of the Self*, 221–32; Weber, *Protestant Ethic and the Spirit of Capitalism*; Webster, *Great Instauration*.

modern medicine is Baconian to the degree that it has succumbed to Bacon's admonition "to call no disease incurable and, even more presciently, to orient medical knowledge to the prolongation of life."[195] If contemporary medicine seems bereft of resources to address human finitude and the role that the body with its inherent limitations might play in transforming the soul, Bacon's arguments offer little help. Though he put forward a theological justification for slowing aging, his construal of aging as primarily a problem for the new science left little room for other stances toward the aging body that might be formative in more positive ways. He failed to consider how attempts to secure longer life might impact one's character, and how the body's limitations and subjection to finitude might serve as a source of moral transformation. As will be seen in the next chapter, however, earlier, premodern interpretations of aging attenuation within the Christian tradition offered a more theologically robust account of the body and its role in moral formation. These will prove useful in building upon the redemptive elements of Bacon's account of slowing aging, recognizing that attempts to gain a longer life by attenuating the aging process cannot be dismissed so quickly.[196]

Despite Bacon's inattentiveness to the body and the role(s) its limitedness might play in shaping one's character, he was nevertheless appropriately suspicious of a Calvinist rendering of God's sovereignty that all but rejected human efforts to slow aging. Indeed, it is difficult to criticize Bacon for his desire to recapture extended longevity, for if the fall has altered nature in some way, there are ample theological warrants for overcoming such effects in the life and ministry of Jesus Christ as attested in Scripture. If Jesus healed disease and even brought the dead back to life, it is difficult to see why aging itself should not also be a candidate for technological manipulation, even if it remains conceptually distinct from disease. Bacon looked to prelapsarian Adam (and the longevity of the biblical patriarchs) in order to determine that aging had somehow been adversely affected by the fall. However, his is one of several such accounts in the Christian tradition. The next chapter will examine a much earlier account of a return to Eden put forward by Athanasius (296–373), who offered an alternative interpretation of aging retardation with a more theologically robust interpretation of the body and its role in the formation of virtue. Athanasius's rendering of a return to prelapsarian Adam will be the first of two chapters aimed at theologically repairing Bacon's account in acknowledgment that the desire to live longer by slowing aging is not necessarily a self-centered, narcissistic

195. McKenny, *To Relieve the Human Condition*, 19.
196. See Meilaender, *Should We Live Forever?*, 3–19, who deftly uncovers the many ambiguities of slowing aging from a Christian perspective.

enterprise. Athanasius's account of regaining the first Adam however will also require some modification by attending to the last Adam, Jesus Christ, the subject of chapter 5. Together, these chapters will address the role of the body in character formation as it relates to aging retardation, highlighting the potential dangers of Bacon's project.

Chapter 4

Adam Again

Theōsis and the Ascetically Ageless Body

> There is no hell but this—a body without a soul, or a soul without a body.
>
> —Oscar Wilde

> For not only are the souls of the saints different from those of sinners, but also their bodies.
>
> —John of Shmūn

As we have seen, the belief that life could be prolonged by slowing aging is not foreign to Christian thought and practice. Bacon's program of slowing aging is one of several accounts that construe the Christian life as a return to prelapsarian Eden, though his program was unique in calling for a new scientific methodology by which aging might be attenuated. Bacon's theories on aging and how it might be attenuated were hardly novel; however, recent laboratory breakthroughs that are largely the product of a Baconian methodology suffer from the same issues that afflicted Bacon's approach, namely, inattention to the body and its role in character formation. In other words, there are dangers inherent in the scientific approach to aging first proffered by Bacon and the technology required to make slowing aging possible. For the teleological questions—questions of purpose—that

Bacon stripped from the investigation of nature are still valid and necessary in considering life extension from a Christian perspective. Questions such as "What is a body for?" must be brought to bear on our technological attempts to forestall aging. In order to explore this question more fully, we will investigate a much earlier account of slowing aging put forward by Athanasius of Alexandria (296–373), who also situated aging within the narrative of a return to Eden. Athanasius's account however lends considerable attention to the role or purpose of the body from within the ascetic tradition.

In the third century in Alexandria, there were several key ascetic figures whose longevity surpassed the life expectancies of those around them. Perhaps no one was more well-known than Antony of Egypt (251–356), who, even in his eleventh decade, served as a pillar of Christian virtue, the very instantiation of Jesus' claim to surrender one's possessions and indeed whole self to Christ. Antony's fame can be credited to Athanasius's hagiographical *Life of Antony*, where the eremitic dweller is portrayed as the ideal Christian ascetic who attained victory over the impulses of his own body, withstanding disease, defeating demonic forces, and outwitting peripatetic purveyors of Greek philosophy.[1] Apart from the occasional polemical elements, Athanasius hoped his work would inspire Christians to imitate Antony's pattern of discipline. His aims were certainly fulfilled. Through Athanasius's artistry, Antony has been described as "the man on the boundary [who] appealed to many in the center," symbolizing 'the type of the Christian, the ideal portrait of the human being, as he should be.'"[2] The *Life of Antony* records the life of a man who at an early age renounced the pleasures of wealth and the world, who, through his gradual retreat into the desert, continually and successfully battled the temptations arising from his own bodily impulses through fasting and prayer, continually renewing his efforts until his body was explicitly under the control of his soul.[3] Of particular interest however is both Antony's longevity and manner

---

1. It is important to understand "biographical" in its ancient sense. *The Life of Antony* is similar in genre to the Greco-Roman *encomium*—a work relating the life and deeds of a celebrated person who has died. See Anatolios, *Athanasius*, 166–67; Harmless, *Desert Christians*, 68–69; Gregg, ed., "Introduction," in *Athanasius: The Life of Antony*, 5–6. See also Vivian, ed., "Introduction," in *Life of Antony*, xxv, who notes: "Recent studies have shown that the picture of Antony given to us in the *Life* cannot be written off as 'mere' hagiography or dismissed as an implausible glorification of an ideal: whether or not the details of Antony in the *Life* are 'biographically correct,' the Antony who lives and breathes in these pages is, on the whole, true to the way the early monks lived, thought, and believed."

2. Gregg, "Introduction," 6, quoting Dörries, *Die Vita Antonii*, 389.

3. For the historical setting surrounding St. Antony's life, see Kannengiesser, "Athanasius of Alexandria."

of death. Athanasius reports that Antony lived to the ripe age of 105, suggesting that Antony's ascetic regime substantially impeded the physiological deterioration of his own body.[4] Here we explore the theological commitments behind Antony's asceticism, commitments that encouraged bodily longevity. Indeed, as will be evident shortly, there was the belief that specific ascetic practices enabled the ascetic to remake his or her body.

ATHANASIUS'S THEOLOGICAL ANTHROPOLOGY

Athanasius's conception of remaking the body was firmly rooted in the biblical narrative of creation, redemption, and bodily resurrection. Through ascetic discipline, Athanasius believed the Christian might approach the original state of human existence before the fall. In order to understand what that means, we must look to Athanasius's understanding of prelapsarian existence. It is noteworthy that Athanasius's discussion of the first couple in Eden occurs in the context of the redemption wrought through the divine Word having taken on human flesh. In the opening chapters of *On the Incarnation*, Athanasius lays out God's original creation, how Adam and Eve went astray, and what God has done through Christ to restore what had been forfeited through sin.

Athanasius asserted that from the very beginning of creation, Adam and Eve were mortal creatures, subject to decay. There never was a time when they were *not* aging, even before sin entered the world. Athanasius reasoned that since Adam was created *ex nihilo*, he could only be mortal and subject to bodily decay, "inasmuch as he is made out of what is not."[5] Hence, the first couple was mortal by *nature*. Despite this tendency towards bodily decay, however, Adam and Eve had the means at their disposal by which to slow this natural corruption, namely, fellowship with God. "For because of the Word dwelling with them, even their natural corruption did not come near them."[6] Moreover, having created Adam and Eve in God's image (*imago Dei*), God gave them "a portion even of the power of His own Word; so that having as it were a kind of reflexion of the Word, and being made rational, they might be able to abide ever in blessedness . . ."[7] By this rationality Adam and Eve were able to contemplate the mysteries of God. Elsewhere Athanasius likened the contemplation of God's eternity as a means by which Adam could preserve his nature intact, thereby "living the

---

4. Athanasius, *Life of Antony* 89, 91, NPNF2, 4:219–21.
5. Athanasius, *On the Incarnation* 3.4; 4.6, NPNF2, 4:37, 38 respectively.
6. Athanasius, *On the Incarnation* 3.4, NPNF2, 4:38.
7. Athanasius, *On the Incarnation* 3.3, NPNF2, 4:37.

life of immortality unharmed and truly blessed."[8] It was only this constant attention to God that "prevented the body from decaying into non-being."[9] This rationality was not devoid of desire, however, for Athanasius spoke of the mind "taking pleasure in contemplating Him, and gaining renewal by its desire toward Him."[10]

While it is not difficult to detect the influence of Origen and certain elements of Neoplatonic philosophy in Athanasius's description, these efforts were nevertheless *embodied* activities. Unlike Origen's creation account where bodies were repositories of fallen contemplative minds that had "cooled" into souls, Athanasius asserts that man was created with a body and soul for contemplating God. This life-prolonging, corruption-staying activity, however, was interrupted when Adam turned away from the contemplation of God and spiritual things towards his body, breaking the law that God had established in the garden, eating from the fruit of the tree of knowledge. Athanasius employs the metaphor of mixing or entanglement of the body and soul in describing this shift in contemplation:

> But nearer to themselves were the body and its senses; so that while removing their mind from the things perceived by thought, they began to regard themselves; and so doing, and holding to the body and the other things of sense, and deceived as it were in their own surroundings, they fell into lust of themselves, . . . they entangled their soul with bodily pleasures, vexed and turbid with all kind of lusts, while they wholly forgot the power they originally had from God.[11]

Having been lured away from the contemplation of God toward bodily desires, "the soul became subject to cowardice and alarms, and pleasures and thoughts of mortality."[12] Hereafter the prospect of death became exceedingly dreadful. In echoes of Plato, Athanasius likened the soul to the charioteer that has turned away from God, thus "driving the members of the body beyond what is proper."[13] This first sin of Adam has been repeated by

---

8. Athanasius, *Against the Heathen* 2.2, NPNF2, 4:5.

9. Brakke, *Athanasius and the Politics of Asceticism*, 147. See Athanasius, *Against the Heathen* 33.1–4, NPNF2, 4:21–22.

10. Athanasius, *Against the Heathen* 2.3, NPNF2, 4:5

11. Athanasius, *Against the Heathen* 3.2, NPNF2, 4:5.

12. Athanasius, *Against the Heathen* 3.4, NPNF2, 4:5. It is important to observe that Athanasius uses the terms *mind* and *soul* to emphasize one's universal relationship to God and one's analytical relationship to the body, respectively. For a helpful description of Athanasius's use of the terms *nous*, *psychē*, and *sōma*, see Anatolios, *Athanasius*, 61–63.

13. Athanasius, *Against the Heathen* 5.2, NPNF2, 4:6.

humanity ever since. "But men, making light of better things, and holding back from apprehending them, began to seek in preference things nearer to themselves."[14] This contemplative turn toward the body not only ushered in a new fear over one's impending death, but also hastened the bodily decay, or aging, natural to man. Hence, "men began to die while corruption thenceforward prevailed against them, gaining even more than its natural power over the whole race."[15] While keeping the law in the garden meant life "without sorrow or pain or care," disobeying God meant that they would incur "that corruption in death which was theirs by nature."[16] Had Adam remained in a proper state of contemplation, appropriately unhindered by the desires of the body, his natural corruption would have been somehow reduced—"he would *stay* his natural corruption, and remain incorrupt."[17]

Moreover, the possibility of remaining with God in the garden and "staying" the corruption natural to man was closed down after Adam turned his attention from the incorruptible God to the corruptible body.

> But men, having rejected things eternal, and, by counsel of the devil, turned to the things of corruption, became the cause of their own corruption and death, being, as I said before, by nature corruptible, but destined, by the grace following from partaking of the Word, to have escaped their natural state, had they remained good.[18]

Though never free from the bodily decay of aging, humankind originally possessed the means by which this decay could be attenuated through the contemplation of God. After their sin however, Adam and Eve were "stripped of the protective clothing of divine contemplation"; they were now "exposed to the process of corruption and death natural to them."[19] What was once natural to humankind now had a legal hold over human existence after God's command (Gen 2:17) had been violated. It is precisely this condition, says Athanasius, that the incarnate Word, Jesus Christ, came to rectify.

---

14. Athanasius, *Against the Heathen* 3.1, NPNF2, 4:5.

15. Athanasius, *On the Incarnation* 5.2, NPNF2, 4:38.

16. Athanasius, *On the Incarnation* 3.4, NPNF2, 4:38. See Athanasius, *On the Incarnation* 6.2, NPNF2, 4:39.

17. Athanasius, *On the Incarnation* 4.6, NPNF2, 4:38, emphasis mine. See Athanasius, *On the Incarnation* 4.4, NPNF2, 4:38.

18. Athanasius, *On the Incarnation* 5.1, NPNF2, 4:38. See also Kelly, *Early Christian Doctrines*, 346–48.

19. Brakke, *Athanasius and the Politics of Asceticism*, 148.

Though Athanasius occasionally speaks of redemption with reference to Christ's death, his primary focus is on the redemptive force of the incarnation.[20] Drawing on 2 Peter 1:4, Athanasius says that Christ "was made man that we might be made God," a concept commonly understood as *theōsis*.[21] Significantly, Athanasius suggests that *theōsis* is also bodily in nature. "For therefore did He [Christ] assume the body originate and human, that having renewed it as its Framer, He might deify it in Himself, and thus might introduce us all into the kingdom of heaven after his likeness."[22] Athanasius asserts that Christ has taken on sin and corruption—things pertaining to the flesh—and destroyed them. Moreover, because Christ has appropriated what pertains to the flesh, "no longer do these things touch the body, because of the Word who has come in it, but they are destroyed by Him."[23]

In *theōsis* Christ is as much physician as savior. These roles however require the incarnation, by which the divine Word has become human. In arguing for the necessity of the incarnation, Athanasius asks why the divine Word could not have simply healed his own creation through speech. Indeed, if humanity has been created *ex nihilo* by a spoken word, could not healing just as easily come by another?[24] While he acknowledges the power of God "to save mankind ... by a mere fiat," the fact that humankind now has its own existence as something made requires also that the remedy also be made, and not simply spoken into existence. "For it was not things without being that needed salvation, so that a bare command should suffice, but man, already in existence, [who] was going to corruption and ruin."[25] Hence, the divine Word has become man. In the incarnation the Word uses his very body, says Athanasius, as an instrument of healing. Such a scandalous description of the Word understandably incited Arian objections. Nevertheless, the cure for human sin and death required nothing less:

---

20. See Athanasius, *On the Incarnation* 20, *NPNF2*, 4:38; Athanasius, *Four Discourses against the Arians* 1.4, 1.60, 2.69, and 3.3, *NPNF2*, 4:308, 341, 386, and 395 respectively; Athanasius, *Defence of the Nicene Definition* 3.14, *NPNF2*, 4:158–59.

21. Athanasius, *On the Incarnation* 54.3, *NPNF2*, 4:65. Elsewhere he says "for He has become Man, that He might deify us in Himself." Athanasius, *Ad Adelphium* 4, *NPNF2*, 4:576.

22. Athanasius, *Four Discourses* 2.70, *NPNF2*, 4:386.

23. Athanasius, *Four Discourses* 2.69, *NPNF2*, 4:386. See also Athanasius, *On the Incarnation* 44.6, *NPNF2*, 4:60.

24. Athanasius, *On the Incarnation* 44.1, *NPNF2*, 4:60. "As God made man by a word, why not restore him by a word?" This question was often posed by the Arians.

25. Athanasius, *On the Incarnation* 44.2, *NPNF2*, 4:60.

> But when man had once been made, and necessity demanded a cure, not for things that were not, but for things that had come to be, it was naturally consequent that the Physician and Saviour should appear in what had come to be, in order to cure the things that were. For this cause, then, He has become man, and used His body as a human instrument.[26]

Moreover, just as a heightened corruption and decay had been engendered in the human body through sin, so must life be engendered in the body through the incarnation. In the incarnation the divine Word mysteriously undoes the corruption internal to our bodies by taking on a corruptible body and the desires that come from it, thereby "winding life close to the body."[27]

A summary of Athanasius's understanding of the incarnation can be found in his arguments against the Arians, who held that the divine Word, or Logos (John 1:1), was *not* God, but God's first and greatest creation. Though Athanasius's description of the Word occasionally lent itself to such misunderstandings, his description of Mary as *theotokos*—"God-bearer"—was meant to head off any suggestion that the incarnation was somehow one step removed from the full divinity of God. Indeed, only God in the flesh can redeem us from within, the God who in Christ transfers our origin to himself in order that we may share in God's eternal, divine life:

> Whence also, whereas the flesh is born of Mary Bearer of God [*theotokos*], He Himself is said to have been born, who furnishes to others an origin of being; in order that He may transfer our origin into Himself, and we may no longer, as mere earth, return to earth, but as being knit into the Word from heaven, may be carried to heaven by Him. Therefore in like manner not without reason has He transferred to Himself the other affections of the body also; that we, no longer as being men, but as proper to the Word, may have a share in eternal life. For no longer according to our former origin in Adam do we die; but henceforward our origin and all infirmity of flesh being transferred to the Word, we rise from the earth, the curse from sin being removed, because of Him who is in us, and who has become a curse for us.[28]

Elsewhere Athanasius speaks of Christ as clothing us with immortality and incorruption.[29] The Word has taken on flesh, and by dwelling among

---

26. Athanasius, *On the Incarnation* 44.2, NPNF2, 4:60
27. Athanasius, *On the Incarnation* 44.2, NPNF2, 4:60.
28. Athanasius, *Four Discourses* 3.33, NPNF2, 4:411–12.
29. Athanasius, *On the Incarnation* 9, NPNF2, 4:40–41.

us the Word has opened up a pathway back to God, transforming the body in the process.

Often Athanasius speaks as if this incorruptibility has been transferred to all humankind, failing to distinguish between Christ's material body and the bodies of individuals. Under the influence of Platonic thought, at times Athanasius could speak as if Christ's taking on flesh has affected all humankind consubstantially, while at other times *theōsis* is described as a function of the Holy Spirit, baptism, or the Eucharist.[30] Elsewhere Athanasius draws upon adoption language in reference to the incorruptibility that has come through the incarnation.[31] While Athanasius does not seem terribly concerned in articulating the specifics by which we share in Christ's incorruption before the resurrection, he nevertheless continually asserts that Christ as God incarnate has taken on human flesh in order to undo the bodily corruption natural to humans, a corruption that has only increased due to Adam's sin. Yet, as several have noted, this deification, which in principle extends to all humanity, is not without human actions in appropriating what has been initiated by the divine Word through the incarnation.[32] If there is ambiguity surrounding how the incarnation has impacted human nature in the abstract, the bodily effects of *theōsis* are no less amenable to numerous interpretations.

In this regard, Norman Russell has drawn a helpful distinction between the *ontological* and *ethical* aspects of *theōsis*, the former invoking participatory language with the divine by which transformation occurs and

---

30. Kelly, *Early Christian Doctrines*, 379, referring to Athanasius, *Four Discourses* 2.61, and *Ad Serapionem* 2.6. But Alvyn Pettersen has aptly noted that though the Logos assumed a human body, "there is no sense in which Athanasius is so literal in his understanding of the Logos having assumed 'our body' that he believed that all who shared the assumed body were necessarily saved." See Pettersen, *Athanasius and the Human Body*, 93, also 35–39. Athanasius hints at baptism as one means of inheriting incorruption in *Four Discourses* 3.33, NPNF2, 4:412, where he says that "for as we are all from the earth and die in Adam, so being regenerated from above of water and Spirit, in the Christ we are all quickened; the flesh being no longer earthly, but being henceforth made Word, by reason of the God's Word who for our sake 'became flesh.'" See Brakke, *Athanasius and the Politics of Asceticism*, 150–51. See also Athanasius, *Ad Maximum Philosophum* 2, NPNF2, 4:578–79, where Athanasius expresses eucharistic overtones in relation to incorruptibility. "And we are deified not by partaking of the body of some man, but by receiving the Body of the Word Himself."

31. Athanasius, *Four Discourses* 1.38, 3.25, NPNF2, 4:329, 407 respectively. See Russell, *Doctrine of Deification*, 177, who observes that the terms "adoption, renewal, salvation, sanctification, grace, transcendence, illumination, and vivification are all presented as equivalents to deification."

32. See Russell, *Doctrine of Deification*, 1–15; 166–88; Anatolios, *Athanasius*, 135–63; Brakke, *Athanasius and the Politics of Asceticism*, 151–52; Pettersen, *Athanasius and the Human Body*, 106–7.

the latter involving becoming like God through *imitation*.³³ According to Russell, Athanasius develops both the ontological and the ethical aspects of deification in parallel. Athanasius speaks of ontological deification as the objective work of Word in divinizing human flesh by assuming a human body, likely appropriated through baptism though only fully realized eschatologically; he speaks of ethical deification when he speaks of the ascetic and contemplative life.³⁴ As we will see, the *Life of Antony* largely focuses on the ethical, imitative aspects of deification or *theōsis*.³⁵ Athanasius's Antony serves as a paragon of ethical deification, whose bodily incorruption is on display. Indeed, as Russell has rightly pointed out, "the eschatological nature of deification does not mean that its beginnings are not discernable in this life."³⁶ At the same time, however, Athanasius could describe this deification as becoming fully human again, as was prelapsarian Adam. Thus, in spite of the dangers and misunderstanding surrounding the word "*theōsis*" (much less the contemporary term "deification"), Athanasius consistently maintains the distinction between God and man, a point made especially evident in his anti-Arian writings. For Athanasius, "the grace of sonship and deification does not collapse the difference between God and creation into a strict equality."³⁷ Here it is important to emphasize that the remainder of this chapter will focus primarily on the ethical dimensions of *deification* as found in Athanasius's Antony, who sought to put on Christ through the spiritual disciplines of fasting and prayer, even as these disciplines afforded Antony a physiological transformation approaching that of prelapsarian Adam.

To briefly summarize, in Athanasius's theological anthropology humans are created by God, body and soul, *ex nihilo* for fellowship with the divine Word, a fellowship that enabled the naturally moral body a heightened degree of resistance to decay. While Adam and Eve were initially created as finite creatures, tending toward dissolution and nonbeing by their very nature, they were nevertheless capable of enjoying the contemplation of God, having been created in God's image, which afforded the body greater resistance to the decay natural to it. Over time, however, Adam and Eve were lured away from the contemplation of God toward the needs of the body,

---

33. Reed, *Genesis of Ethics*, xxix, serves as an example of the latter in likening the goal of Christian ethics to *theōsis*, understood as "achieving our potential in Christ" by primarily concerning oneself with "imitative incarnations in daily life of what we know in Jesus Christ of divine love."

34. Russell, *Doctrine of Deification*, 9, 184.

35. Russell, *Doctrine of Deification*, 184 n. 23.

36. Russell, *Doctrine of Deification*, 184.

37. Anatolios, *Athanasius*, 131.

engendering a fear of death. When Adam and Eve ate from the forbidden tree, they brought God's pronouncement of death, hastening bodily decay natural to embodied, created existence. Christ's incarnation has restored our bodies to incorruptibility by sharing in our humanity, and at the same time sanctifying or divinizing our bodies, enabling us to participate in the divine nature (2 Pet 1:4), a process that will reach its ontological fulfillment in the eschaton at the final resurrection.

Having established the general theological framework within which Athanasius situated his anthropology, it will be helpful to look more closely at Athanasius's treatment of asceticism in the *Life of Antony*, paying particular attention to its relationship to longevity and aging. Despite Athanasius's systematic inconsistency, the ascetic life remained the primary means by which it was possible to appropriate bodily incorruptibility. In particular, the discipline of fasting was thought to enhance the body's resistance to corruption and decay. Though generally speaking Athanasius focuses on the notion of contemplation, says David Brakke, the prelapsarian Adam of *On the Incarnation* was "not merely a contemplative; he was also an ascetic in full control of his body."[38] If Bacon interpreted Adam as a scientist, Athanasius portrayed him as an ascetic from the very beginning.

ATHANASIUS'S *LIFE OF ANTONY*

Athanasius records that Antony was born to wealthy parents in the middle of the third century near Heracleopolis Magna in Fayum (ancient Upper Egypt). Having lost his parents at the age of twenty, he found himself anxious to model his life after the apostles, after hearing Jesus' words to the rich young ruler one morning, "If you want to be perfect, go, sell your possessions, and give to the poor" (Matt 19:21 NIV). Antony felt as if God were speaking to him directly, so he sold all of his possessions to pursue a life of asceticism, seeking seclusion at a nearby tomb, where he would battle demons and wild beasts that would inflict heavy blows on his flesh. Several years later Antony retreated farther into the desert in pursuit of absolute solitude, crossing the Nile and residing on a mountain near the east bank now known as Der el Memum, spending the next twenty years in absolute solitude before surprising a colony of disciples in 305 when he decided to pay them a visit. Athanasius observes that Antony appeared surprisingly healthy and vigorous in both body and mind. Antony would go

---

38. Brakke, *Athanasius and the Politics of Asceticism*, 147; see Anatolios, *Athanasius*, 59–60. This stands in stark contrast to other more allegorical accounts where Adam was thought not to need food. See for instance Ambrose, *De Paradiso* 42, 42:320–21.

on to instruct these disciples for several years before retreating still deeper into the desert, spending his remaining years in seclusion before his death at the age of 105.

Athanasius goes to considerable lengths to show that fasting is a critical element in Antony's asceticism. Fasting was not an activity that weakened the body, but actually strengthened it. When tempted by the love of money or pleasures of the table, Antony continued to "fortify his body with faith, prayers, and fasting."[39] Yet, Athanasius eagerly notes that Antony was able to resist these temptations through divine enablement. "For the Lord was working with Antony—the Lord who for our sake took on flesh and gave the body victory over the devil, so that all who truly fight can say, 'not I but the grace of God which was with me.'"[40] Nevertheless, Athanasius observes that Antony's initial success over temptation led him to adopt a more severe mode of living. Antony allowed himself scant portions of salt or bread once each day, occasionally going two to four days with no food at all, remaining ever vigilant against allowing the desire for food to cloud one's mind and rule the passions, lest one be "deceived by the fulness of the belly."[41] He slept on a rush mat and avoided anointing his body with oil lest he somehow arouse bodily passions in the process. By this strict regimen, reasons Athanasius, "the fibre of the soul is then sound when the pleasures of the body are diminished."[42]

Antony's second milestone came at the age of thirty-five after he enclosed himself for many days in the tombs where he endured the bodily torment of several demons. But this success only precipitated another retreat to the desert, where he vanished out of sight for nearly twenty years. When his disciples were finally able to find him, they wrenched the door off his cell, where, says Athanasius, he emerged "as from a shrine."

> And they, when they saw him, wondered at the sight, for he had the same habit of body as before, and was neither fat, like a man without exercise, nor lean from fasting and striving with the demons, but he was just the same as they had known him before his retirement.... abiding in a natural [*physin*] state.[43]

Surprisingly, Antony's physical health had not deteriorated during this difficult training, but had actually improved. His rigorous asceticism had

---

39. Athanasius, *Life of Antony* 5, NPNF2, 4:197.
40. Athanasius, *Life of Antony* 5, NPNF2, 4:197.
41. Athanasius, *Life of Antony* 55, NPNF2, 4:210.
42. Athanasius, *Life of Antony* 7, NPNF2, 4:198.
43. Athanasius, *Life of Antony* 14, NPNF2, 4:200.

appeared to preserve his body in a healthy state. As the desert gradually became colonized by monks, Antony's subsequent exhortations portray the ascetic life as one requiring a discipline of both body and soul.

Antony encouraged the monks to daily increase in their earnestness and virtue by engaging in practices that allowed one's soul to return to its "natural state," by which he meant "as created."[44] In this natural state the soul fixed on God rightly regulated the body, thereby minimizing the effects of aging. Fasting enabled one to repair the soul; the soul that had been lured into vice by attending to the things of sense could also be drawn back towards its original virtuous state by contemplating God. Indeed, repairing one's soul required continual prayer, the singing of psalms, and careful attention to the works of the saints as recorded in Scripture so that "souls being put in remembrance of the commandments may be brought into harmony with the zeal of the saints."[45] Antony also suggested collecting an inventory of the thoughts, actions, and impulses of one's soul, imagining the resulting shame and embarrassment were such records displayed before fellow monks.[46] Better to continually seek pure thoughts in order to preserve one's soul for the Lord, "that He may recognize His work as being the same as He made it."[47] Cultivating pure thoughts was a thoroughly *embodied* exercise; it could only be accomplished by continual fasting, by sleeplessness, meekness, quietness, and piety towards Christ.[48]

Though Athanasius reports that Antony steadily increased in his discipline, one might be left with a sense that Athanasius harbored a hostile attitude towards the body and its materiality.[49] He reports that Antony "used to eat and sleep, and go about all other bodily necessities with shame when he thought of the spiritual faculties of the soul."[50] Antony was also "covered with shame" when eating in the presence of his brothers, preferring to partake by himself.[51] Athanasius unflinchingly records practices more commonly associated with bodily abuse or neglect. For instance, Antony donned a hair shirt throughout his entire life in the desert, and "neither bathed his body with water to free himself from filth," refusing even to

---

44. Athanasius, *Life of Antony* 20, *NPNF2*, 4:201.
45. Athanasius, *Life of Antony* 55, *NPNF2*, 4:211.
46. Athanasius, *Life of Antony* 55, *NPNF2*, 4:211.
47. Athanasius, *Life of Antony* 20, *NPNF2*, 4:201.
48. Athanasius, *Life of Antony* 30, *NPNF2*, 4:204.
49. Athanasius, *Life of Antony* 45, 47, *NPNF2*, 4:208, 209 respectively.
50. Athanasius, *Life of Antony* 45, *NPNF2*, 4:208.
51. Athanasius, *Life of Antony* 45, *NPNF2*, 4:208.

wash his feet "unless compelled by necessity."[52] Indeed, focusing only on Athanasius's account of Antony tends to underwrite unhelpful caricatures of asceticism and the body, inviting comparisons with Platonic and Gnostic thought that seemed to disparage the body insofar as it hindered the proper activities of the soul. We will address these concerns later on in this chapter.

If Antony's life served as an example for Christians to follow, so too was his death. Aware that his end was imminent, Antony continued to exhort his followers to "live as though dying daily" and to "zealously guard the soul from foul thoughts."[53] He gave instructions to have his body buried in secret, somewhere underground, consistent with the manner of Jesus' burial, knowing that he would receive it back "incorruptible from the Saviour" at the resurrection.[54] Athanasius hints that Antony had already received a portion of bodily incorruptibility on this earth, for he announces that Antony was nearly "a hundred and five years old."[55] But even at such an advanced age, Athanasius notes that his body

> remained entirely free from harm. His eyes were undimmed and quite sound and he saw clearly; of his teeth he had not lost one, but they had become worn to the gums through the great age of the old man. He remained strong both in hands and feet; and while all men were using various foods, and washings and divers garments, he appeared more cheerful and of greater strength.[56]

Even the manner of his death was exceedingly peaceful. Athanasius describes Antony's death in language befitting the biblical patriarchs, echoing the death of Moses, who died at a similar age, his teeth remaining unmoved (Deut 34:7 in the Vulgate; *nec dentes illius moti sunt*).[57] When making his final visit to the monks, Athanasius contrasts their intense sorrow with the joy of Antony, who spoke rapturously "as though sailing from a foreign city to his own," urging his disciples to continue in their labors.[58] When Antony died, his countenance appeared joyful as he was "gathered to the fathers."[59]

---

52. Athanasius, *Life of Antony* 47, NPNF2, 4:209.
53. Athanasius, *Life of Antony* 89, 91, NPNF2, 4:219, 220 respectively.
54. Athanasius, *Life of Antony* 91, NPNF2, 4:220.
55. Athanasius, *Life of Antony* 89, NPNF2, 4:219.
56. Athanasius, *Life of Antony* 93, NPNF2, 4:221. It should be noted however, that Antony also had two disciples attending him for the last fifteen years of his life, "on account of his age." Athanasius, *Life of Antony* 91, NPNF2, 4:220.
57. See Wilkinson, *Bible and Healing*, 35.
58. Athanasius, *Life of Antony* 89, NPNF2, 4:219.
59. Athanasius, *Life of Antony* 92, NPNF2, 4:220. There are parallels here between Athanasius's recording of Antony's death, and the idea of a "natural death" put forward

Athanasius thus presents Antony as one worthy of imitation, whose victory over the demons and his own body proved a model for all Christians. His flight into the desert and ascetic regime allowed him to slowly remake his body and refine his soul, restoring it to its rightful place as governor of this newly formed body. While it is tempting to demythologize Athanasius's account, which certainly reveals as much about his hagiographical interests as it does Antony's own understanding of asceticism, it will be helpful to balance this account with Antony's own letters addressed to unnamed monks and fellow ascetics. There is certainly continuity between Antony's letters and Athanasius's account, though Antony emphasized particular features of the ascetic life that were largely absent in Athanasius's account.

Antony's first letter has been described as "a carefully planned treatise on repentance and purification."[60] Unlike Athanasius's *Life of Antony*, Antony places considerable emphasis on the role of God's Spirit in formation, who instructs the ascetic in the course of repentance, working on the mind, soul, and body. This Spirit, says Antony, "sets for them a rule for how to repent in their bodies and souls," instructing those who wish to follow the way back to God, giving them "control over their souls and bodies in order that both may be sanctified and inherit together."[61] Echoing Athanasius, the *telos* of this repentance is described as a return to Adam's prelapsarian condition whereby his bodily movements were under the guidance of his soul, unencumbered by bodily desires. Certain practices were prescribed to free the soul from the various motions of the body—especially gluttony—which not only needlessly stirred up the body from within, but also invited demonic attacks from without.[62] When armed with the knowledge of these bodily movements, the Spirit teaches man to perform the sweet work of repentance, enabling the ascetic to return to one's "natural" state, where bodily movement occurs only with the soul's consent.[63]

Antony understands repentance primarily as an exercise of discernment and disentanglement, where the cloudy becomes clear, a process where the mind (which may be understood as the higher functions of the soul) under the Spirit's control, learns to discriminate between body and soul. Under the Spirit's influence, says Antony, the mind

---

by the health reformer Nicholas de Condorcet.

60. Rubenson, *Letters of St. Antony*, 52.

61. Antony, Letter 1:20, 22, in Rubenson, *Letters*, 198.

62. Antony, Letter 1:41, in Rubenson, *Letters*, 199. See Ward, ed., *Apophthegmata Patrum*, Antony 22, 6. For an introduction to the *Apophthegmata Patrum*, see Harmless, *Desert Christians*, chs. 6–8. See also Rubenson, *Letters*, 144–52.

63. Antony, Letter 1:19, in Rubenson, *Letters*, 198–99.

guides us in the actions of the body and soul, purifying both of them, separating the fruits of the flesh from what is natural to the body, in which they were mingled, and through which the transgression came to be, and leads each member of the body back to its original condition.[64]

Though Antony credits the Spirit with helping the ascetic discriminate between the body and soul, he claims that this involves a purification of *both*. In fact, attention is first focused on purifying the body by fasting, vigils, prayer, and the study of Scripture.[65] Citing the Apostle Paul's declaration "but I pommel my body and subdue it" (1 Cor 9:27a RSV), Antony observes that in so doing "the body is thus brought under the authority of the mind and is taught by the Spirit."[66] Fasting and prayer enable the ascetic to purify the members of one's body, bringing them under the authority of one's Spirit-led mind. For when the mind accepts this struggle between body and soul, keeping the "commands which the Spirit has delivered," the Spirit develops "a loving partnership" with the mind.[67] According to Antony, the Spirit sets rules of purification for the members of the body, including the eyes, ears, tongue, hands, belly, genitals, and even feet. Though he does not elaborate on these rules, the goal is that "the *whole body* may be changed and placed under the authority of the Spirit."[68] Instead of looking back to prelapsarian Adam, here Antony looks forward, noting that these exercises enable the body to take on the nature of our spiritual body at the resurrection.[69] Moreover, in addition to purifying the body, the Spirit is equally at work on the mind itself, teaching it how to "heal all wounds of the soul, and to rid itself of every one," purifying the soul from pride, hatred, and impatience. In the practice of all of these disciplines, notes Antony, God has mercy on the soul and the body, giving aid to both.

In their respective accounts of asceticism, Athanasius and Antony speak of the disorder in the relationship between one's body and soul, a condition which can however be rectified in part through fasting and bodily discipline. If Antony places a stronger emphasis on the Holy Spirit's guidance or the "Spirit of Repentance," Athanasius's treatment is more christological. Yet both believed that it was possible to return to one's "natural state,"

---

64. Antony, Letter 1:28-30, in Rubenson, *Letters*, 199.

65. Antony, Letter 1:28-30, 77, in Rubenson, *Letters*, 199, 202 respectively.

66. Antony, Letter 1:32, in Rubenson, *Letters*, 199. Antony cites this verse again in line 40.

67. Chitty, *Desert a City*, 3. See also Antony, Letter 1:44.

68. Antony, Letter 1:70, in Rubenson, *Letters*, 201. Emphasis mine.

69. Antony, Letter 1:71, in Rubenson, *Letters*, 201-2.

understood as a proper headship of the soul over the body. While Antony never explicitly describes one's "natural state" as involving a heightened resistance to bodily decay, Athanasius makes this an enduring theme, enlisting Antony as a contemporary realization of the archetypal prelapsarian Adam. Not only was Antony able to conquer demons and disease, he was able to conquer *himself*. Antony showed the Christian how to regain Eden.

As mentioned above, with their respective emphases on harsh treatment of the body as it relates to distinguishing it from the soul, it may be difficult to discern how their approach to moral formation is all that different from other systems of thought that harbor more pessimistic views of the body common to their social, philosophical, and cultural milieu, namely Gnosticism and Platonic thought. It may be useful here to take a brief detour to consider these other systems of thought on the issue of embodiment in order to appreciate how Athanasius's and Antony's program diverges from these systems in significant ways, even as the latter occasionally employ language used by the Gnostics, Plato, and Plotinus. Those who are not particularly interested in this detour may skip ahead to the section entitled "Early Christian Asceticism in Historical Context," where we return to Athanasius and Antony in light of these findings.

SOUL AND BODY IN THE PHILOSOPHICAL MILIEU

Gnostic and Manichaean Thought

Gnosticism, which has been a source of scorn and temptation to the Christian faith, represented an extremely dualistic, highly syncretistic religious movement espousing salvation through revelatory knowledge (*gnōsis*).[70] Asceticism is a common theme among the many strands of Gnostic thought, though, unlike the Genesis cosmogony, it is rooted in a radically dualistic cosmology marked by eternal conflict where the acosmic transcendent god Light (or Father, Life, or Spirit) opposed the tyrannical and ambitious Demiurge who created the earth as a prison for a portion of the divine substance, spirit (*pneuma*).[71] Gnostic soteriology was predicated upon the se-

---

70. For an English translation of the recently discovered Gnostic texts, see Robinson, ed., *Nag Hammadi Library in English*. See also Grant and Freedman, eds., *Secret Sayings of Jesus*; Grant, *Gnosticism: An Anthology*; Grant, *Gnosticism and Early Christianity*; Jonas, *Gnostic Religion*; King, *Gnostics and Their Remains*; Pagels, *Gnostic Gospels*; Wilson, *Gnostic Problem*.

71. This Demiurge is the result of a fall within the *pleroma*, or the graded hypostases of the Father. In some versions of Gnosticism the presence of this divine substance or spark is attributed to the Demiurge himself; in other versions, it is attributed to the

cret knowledge that the real, spiritual self, that divine spark, was imprisoned in an evil material body designed by the Demiurge. The pneumatics—those few who had attained this privileged knowledge—were required to cultivate contempt for the material world, including the body, which was likened to a "prison that will perish."[72] Gnostic anthropology is known for fostering two basic responses to the body: libertinism and asceticism. If the former indulged the body as a paradoxical form of salvation by affirming that true spirit is unaffected by the actions of the body, the latter sought to disengage the inner person from the body as much as possible by abstaining from those practices deeply rooted in one's material nature, namely, eating and sex. In *The Book of Thomas* for instance, the savior condemns those who are at the mercy of bodily powers, who "love intimacy with womankind and polluted intercourse with them."[73] Adherents were thus encouraged to watch and pray that they not "come to be in the flesh," but rather "come forth from the bondage of the bitterness of this life . . . from the suffering and passions of the body."[74] Treating the body harshly could only assist the soul's ascent to the Father. This should not be overstated however. Elsewhere adherents were encouraged to attend to any seeker's bodily needs, to "make firm the foot of those who have stumbled and stretch out your hands to those who are ill." Adherents were also instructed to feed the hungry, give rest to the weary, and "raise up those who wish to rise."[75] Nevertheless, salvation in either form—hedonism or asceticism—was a highly self-referential, inward journey that pitted the body against the soul, construing salvation as the latter's release from the former.

Manichaeism shared a similar dualistic cosmology where the human body is a product of light and darkness, with fragments of divine light trapped in and susceptible to the affections of the human body. In this condition the body serves as the battleground for good and evil. According to Mani, Jesus was sent to reveal the true nature of humanity and to promote the ascetic practices necessary to attain salvation from the flesh, which involved a strict diet of vegetables—food free from trapped particles of

---

higher powers in the *pleroma*, who secretly implant this seed in humankind as a means to secure salvation.

72. Turner, *Thomas the Contender* 143.11, 16, in Robinson, ed., *Nag Hammadi Library*, 205.

73. Turner, *Thomas the Contender* 144.10–15, in Robinson, ed., *Nag Hammadi Library*, 206.

74. Turner, *Thomas the Contender* 144.10–16, in Robinson, ed., *Nag Hammadi Library*, 207.

75. Attridge and MacRae, trans., *Gospel of Truth* 1.32.35–1.33.11, in Robinson, ed., *Nag Hammadi Library*, 47.

light—punctuated by set periods of fasting.[76] Marriage and procreation were also forbidden as the propagation of the species only protracted the drama of salvation by further dispersing particles of light. If Antony restricted the quantity of food, Manichaean thought was more concerned with the type of food consumed. Augustine would eventually criticize this approach to fasting, observing that one could engage in gluttonous behavior so long as the correct food was consumed (i.e., food not ensouled with particles of light).[77] The primary aim of such practices however was to separate the soul from the body—good from the evil—given that the body was a composite of both.[78] Indeed, Manichaean thought presents the body "at the intersection of good and evil, containing the richest concentrations of both substances, each attempting to gain ascendancy over the other."[79] Fasting both reduced the influence of dark powers in the body while simultaneously sustaining and nourishing it, enabling both the elect and the auditors to engage in meditation and prayer.[80] Ultimately however, it allowed only for a "reconstitution of the defective body by the separation of its antagonistic components."[81]

While the cosmologies and cosmogonies of Gnostic and Manichaean thought differed, both systems of thought encouraged ascetic practices based upon a largely negative construal of the material order. Abstinence from food and sex were thoroughly rooted in the metaphysical assumption that the body threatened the welfare of the soul. As such, it was thought impossible—indeed deeply abhorrent—to construe salvation as a redemption *of* the body. Rather, in these systems of thought, salvation could only come by escape *from* the body. Athanasius and Antony on the other hand understood salvation as a proper joining of body and soul, though they employ war-like imagery as freely as their Gnostic and Manichaean counterparts. If these systems are readily distinguishable from Christian thought, Platonic philosophy is more subtle. Indeed, Platonic thinking has long influenced Christian doctrine, for good or for ill.

---

76. According to Augustine, the Manichaeans allowed eating plants and vegetables, but prohibited eating any meat as it defiles the one eating it. See Augustine, *Morals of the Manichaeans* 15.36–37, NPNF1, 4:79. By eating vegetables, one was thought to avoid the ensouled food of meat and thereby avoiding injuring the particles of light trapped therein.
77. Augustine, *Morals of the Manichaeans* 14.35, NPNF1, 4:79.
78. Buckley, "Tools and Tasks."
79. BeDuhn, *Manichaean Body*, 88.
80. BeDuhn, *Manichaean Body*, 102.
81. BeDuhn, *Manichaean Body*, 99, 121.

Platonic and Neoplatonic Thought

Plato himself regarded the human body with a sense of ambivalence. Though the body at times appeared at odds with the soul—when Plato occasionally likened the body (*sōma*) as a tomb (*sēma*) for the soul—it is important to remember that these less than favorable descriptions occurred primarily in discussions surrounding the soul's ascent.[82] For Plato the soul as the seat of subjectivity is certainly of more value than the decaying body—though the soul too undergoes changes—for only the disembodied soul could fully apprehend the world of Forms.[83] "While we live, we shall be closest to knowledge if we refrain as much as possible from association with the body . . . escap[ing] the contamination of the body's folly."[84] Yet, none of these things could prevent Plato from acknowledging that the body is unmistakably beautiful and *good*.[85] Human beings were fashioned from preexistent matter, body and soul. The Demiurge sowed the seed of an immortal, incorporeal, rational soul to rule over the lower mortal portions of the soul that governed things like anger, courage, and sexual and nutritive desires (i.e., the irascible and concupiscible soul, respectively).[86] Plato described this rational soul as God's special guardian spirit (*daimonia*) that "raises us—seeing that we are not an earthly but a heavenly plant—up from earth toward our kindred in the heaven."[87] Given that creation, including the human body, is the product of a benevolent Demiurge, Plato's understanding of the relationship between the body and soul is more nuanced than Gnostic or Manichaean conceptions. Knowing for example that gluttony would both hinder the pursuit of philosophy and harm the body, the gods fashioned the lower abdomen to store excess food and drink, lest man hasten his demise.[88] Those posing the gravest danger to the soul are excessive pleasures and pains. For instance, Plato suggests that sexual overindulgence is caused by the "stuff" which flows in the body on account of the porousness of the

---

82. Plato, *Cratylus* 400c; Plato, *Gorgias* 493a; Plato, *Phaedrus* 250c. See also Plato, *Gorgias* 524b; Plato, *Phaedo* 64c, 67d; Plato, *Timaeus* 81d–82.

83. Plato, *Sophist* 249a; Plato, *Phaedo* 64c–67d, 72e–77d, 80a–84a, 102d–107b.

84. Plato, *Phaedo* 66e–67a, in Cooper and Hutchinson, eds., *Plato*, 58.

85. Plato, *Timaeus* 29a–30b, 34c–36e, 92c.

86. Plato, *Timaeus* 41c–d, 69b–72d, 89e; Plato, *Republic* 4.435–442; Plato, *Phaedrus* 253c–254e. For instance, in beholding a beautiful boy, the rational soul must pull back on the reins of both horses who desire to have sex with him—the irascible soul obeying while the concupiscible soul hurls insults at the rational soul—until the boy's beauty may be properly beheld with reverence and awe. See Plato, *Phaedrus* 254–256b; 249a

87. Plato, *Timaeus* 90a.

88. Plato, *Timaeus* 73a.

bones.[89] People should not be reproached for this, says Plato, for no one is willfully evil. On the contrary, "the wicked man becomes wicked by reason of some evil condition of body and unskilled nurture."[90]

When considering human creatures as "that compound of soul and body," Plato stresses a healthy proportionality between them.[91] Just as an overpowering soul can churn up or set fire to the body, tricking doctors into misdiagnoses, so too an overpowering body can render the higher functions of the soul dull, stupid, and forgetful, leading to perhaps the most serious malady of all, ignorance.[92] Thus, Plato counsels that salvation comes from avoiding both extremes, "neither to exercise the soul without the body nor the body without the soul, so that they may be evenly matched and in sound health."[93] Plato hardly sounds suspicious of the body. In fact, Plato's Socrates asserts that gymnastics and medicine are superior to other professions devoted to food production such as baking bread, or making wine, for the latter professions serve the appetite only while the former serve bodily excellence through discipline.[94] Moreover, medicine is good if it quickly cures the diseased body as it enabled *polis*-dwellers to fulfill their roles. At the same time however, it was a disgrace to require medical attention on account of inactivity.[95] Generally, Plato warned against an exaggerated concern for the body because it threatened the pursuit of daily activities, not to mention "the practice and study of virtue."[96] Thus, the wise person will engage in learning which benefits the *soul*, since its welfare was more important than that of the body, though the body too needed "tuning" for self-discipline which benefited one's soul.[97] One should neither leave the body behind in the pursuit of wisdom, nor direct inordinate attention to it by excessive asceticism or overindulgence, but rather consider the exercising of *both* in becoming the type of person worthy of citizenship in the *polis*.

---

89. Plato, *Timaeus* 86b–e; Plato, *Republic* 9.571d; Plato, *Sophist* 228a; Plato, *Laws* 3.689a–b.

90. Plato, *Timaeus* 86e.

91. Plato, *Timaeus* 88a–c, in Goold, ed., *Plato*, 239.

92. Plato, *Timaeus* 87c–88c. The wrong kind of food hinders the body, and the soul's capacity for thought and self-control. See Plato, *Republic* 8.559b–c.

93. Plato, *Timaeus* 88b, in Goold, ed., *Plato*, 241; Plato, *Republic* 4.442a. Better is the fortunate individual who has a beautiful soul and an equally beautiful body, *Republic* 3.402d.

94. Plato, *Gorgias* 517e–519b.

95. Plato, *Republic* 3.403c–407b; Plato, *Timaeus* 89b–c.

96. Plato, *Republic* 3.407c, in Ferrari, ed., *Plato*, 99. See Plato, *Republic* 3.406b; 4.425e–426b.

97. Plato, *Republic* 9.591d, in Ferrari, ed., *Plato*, 311.

Nevertheless, the rational soul had preeminence on account of its kinship with the divine; a good soul benefited the body more than a good body benefited the soul. While the excellence of a healthy body did not necessarily benefit the soul, a good soul could "make a body as good as it is capable of being."[98] Though ultimately salvation meant liberation from the body, Plato recognized a degree of excellence in the body that could be made still more excellent if properly guided and directed by one's soul. Plato's discussions of bodily discipline were not rooted in any supposed hatred of the body, but with the understanding that the desires stemming from it could wage war on one's soul, hindering one's pursuit of knowledge, which was the pathway to salvation.

Like Plato, for Plotinus (204/5–270) the soul was considered more significant than the body, though unlike Plato, he espoused a radically monistic cosmology. If Plato's soul carried the spark of the divine, for Plotinus the soul was a lower hypostasis or instantiation of the ineffable, unknowable, unchanging, and utterly transcendent One. All that exists emanated from this One in successively lower and increasingly diffuse gradations of being, the Intellect or Mind (*nous*) being the first emanation from which the Soul is derived. The Soul's hypostasis is comprised of the world soul, which in turn gave birth to the universe, including individual souls and their bodies.[99] Just as Intellect derives from the One, so too the Soul's individually divided hypostasis derives its being from the Intellect, gaining in multiplicity along the way. However, because Soul emanates from Intellect and ultimately the One, there is beauty, goodness, and order in the universe, which as an archetype of Intellect, is free of evil.[100] This is a core point, for even though the body is furthest removed from the One, it could hardly be considered evil.

Once again, for Plotinus, Soul is the lowest of the three divine hypostases comprising all that exists.[101] As the lowest gradation of being, the body is assigned the lowest status in Plotinus's thought. If for Plato the body was intentionally composed of eternal matter by the Demiurge, for Plotinus the body was not a product of creative activity at all, but rather the last remnants of what must inevitably overflow from the One. Thus, Plotinus can say that the soul "does not belong to the body, but the body belongs to it."[102] The

---

98. Plato, *Republic* 3.403d, in Ferrari ed., *Plato*, 94. Good physicians use the mind to treat the body. See Plato, *Republic* 3.408e.

99. Plotinus, *Ennead* 4.8.3.11, in Page, ed., *Plotinus*, 4:407. (All subsequent quotes from Plotinus are from the Page edition.) See also Plotinus, *Ennead* 5.1.6–7; 5.2.1.14–18.

100. Plotinus, *Ennead* 5.9.10.

101. Plotinus, *Ennead* 5.1.

102. Plotinus, *Ennead* 4.8.2.46–48.

body was utterly contingent. Since all material things share in Soul, notes Plotinus, for the individual this means that if the "body did not exist, it would make no difference to soul."[103] Like Plato, Plotinus could speak of the activities of the soul with respect to the body both positively and pejoratively. On the one hand, Plotinus speaks of the universe that emanated from Soul as a perfectly fitting occurrence, describing the individual soul's descent as a result of a "natural principle." When the Soul gives birth to the universe, each individual soul "comes down to a body made ready for it . . . one soul to a human being and others to different kind of animals." Hence, "There is no need of anyone to send it or bring it into body at a particular time, or into this or that particular body, but when its moment comes to it it descends and enters where it must as if of its own accord."[104] Once again, the human body is not the result of any divine will, but simply what happens by nature.

At other times however Plotinus describes the soul's descent (or emanation) into a body in decidedly negative terms, as a spontaneous jumping or a passionate desire for a sexual union or more generally as a falling away.[105] Soul gave rise to bodies in its desire to break away from Intellect and govern, thereby dispersing and immersing as souls in individual bodies.[106] As such, the human soul is torn between returning to Intellect and attending to the world.[107] Plotinus employs Plato's metaphor of the molting soul to describe the soul's descent, where such souls flee from the One and no longer look toward the intelligible. In this state the soul

> has become a part and is isolated and weak and fuses and looks towards a part and in its separation from the whole it embarks on one single thing and flies from everything else; . . . it has left the whole and directs the individual part with great difficulty; it is by now applying itself to and caring for things outside and is present and sinks deep into the individual part.[108]

Though this fallen soul is now "in the fetters of the body," it nevertheless remains transcendent, and to some degree invulnerable to change, since the soul always retains something of the Intellect.[109] Thus, in one sense then

---

103. Plotinus, *Ennead* 4.3.9.36–45.
104. Plotinus, *Ennead* 4.4.12.36–39; 4.4.13.1–10.
105. Plotinus, *Ennead* 4.3.13.20–24. Plotinus also speaks of the emanation of Intellect from the One in similarly disparaging terms. See *Ennead* 6.5.1.29.
106. Plotinus, *Ennead* 4.8.1.
107. Plotinus, *Ennead* 4.8.4.1–5.
108. Plotinus, *Ennead* 4.8.4.13–22. See also *Ennead* 5.1.1.
109. Plotinus, *Ennead* 4.8.8.3–6. See also *Ennead* 2.9.2.

there is no descent of the soul into bodies, for these three hypostases—Soul, Intellect, and the One—are in the human creature. "And just as in nature there are these three of which we have spoken," notes Plotinus, "so we ought to think that they are present also in ourselves."[110]

When these accounts of the soul and the bodies that Soul inevitably engenders are taken together, both Porphyry's observation that Plotinus seemed ashamed at being in the body and Julian's conclusion that the body was "more worthless than dirt" are somewhat curious.[111] For in order to speak of the body as *only* a fetter of the soul, one must ignore Plotinus's frequent mention of the universe—including human bodies—as a unitary living being reflecting Intellect in which there is no evil. Even as a fetter, the body *itself* is not evil. On the contrary, Plotinus equated unformed matter in the world of sense with primary evil, understood as the privation of the good, absolute negativity, or nonbeing, though not in an absolute sense.[112] Thus, the body (*sōma*) was not evil *per se*, but only to the extent that it participated in matter that proved resistant to form.[113] "Ugliness is matter not mastered by form."[114] Though human bodies were the result of matter that had accepted form, they were only considered "secondarily evil" insofar as they hindered the soul's activity. Indeed, "Bodies have a sort of form which is not true form, and they are deprived of life, and in their disorderly motion they destroy each other, and hinder the soul in its proper activity, ... being secondary evil."[115] At the same time, however, Plotinus urged his followers not to despise undefined, shapeless matter precisely because it was the very "stuff" with which Intellect worked, (via Soul), bringing form in its wake.[116] Simply put, matter was needed for beings that might come into existence. Indeed, in what appears as a humorous understatement, it "makes the greatest contribution to the formation of bodies."[117] It must be this way,

---

110. Plotinus, *Ennead* 5.1.10.5–7.

111. Porphyry, *Life of Plotinus* 1, in Page, ed., *Plotinus*, 1:3.

112. Plotinus, *Ennead* 4.8.1–8.3; Plotinus, *Ennead* 2.4.14; 4.16.

113. Plotinus, *Ennead* 1.8.4.1–2; 8.3.6–10. See Julian, *Orationes* 7.226c, in Wright, ed., *Julian*, 2:129.

114. Plotinus, *Ennead* 1.8.5.24–25. See *Ennead* 1.8.8.20–30; 2.4.16.16–25. See also O'Meara, *Plotinus: An Introduction*, 82.

115. Plotinus, *Ennead* 1.8.4.2–6. See also *Ennead* 2.4.2.11–12.

116. Plotinus, *Ennead* 2.4.3.1–4. "We must say that we should not in every case despise the undefined or anything of which the very idea implies shapelessness, if it is going to offer itself to the principles before it and to the best of beings." See Miles, *Plotinus on Body and Beauty*, 94.

117. Plotinus, *Ennead* 2.4.12.1–2.

for matter existed in the Intellect, which was utterly devoid of evil, though in Intellect matter was without dimension or size.[118]

In light of these tensions, Plotinus offered two reasons why the "soul's fellowship [*koinōnia*] with the body is displeasing."[119] First, following Plato, the body hindered thought or contemplation. The soul is damaged in its reasoning part since it is "fused with matter" and thus focused on *becoming* (i.e., focused on things of the visible world) rather than *being* (Intellect).

But if the part [of the soul] which is in the world of sense-perception gets control, and thrown into confusion [by the body], it prevents us from perceiving the things which the upper part of the soul contemplates.[120]

Second, the body's sense experience stimulated passions that filled the soul with "pleasures, desires, and grief."[121] The soul then becomes ugly, loving vice, filled with lust, and "living a life which consists of bodily sensations," hindering the soul from "seeing what a soul ought to see."[122] Plotinus spoke of the ugly soul as "getting muddy" by involving itself in "alien matter," when it ought to be directing itself toward Intellect.[123]

But Plotinus also insisted that the soul could perceive the affections of the body without being affected itself.[124] He rejected any Stoic striving for *apatheia*. "Why, then, ought we to seek to make the soul free from affections by means of philosophy when it is not affected to begin with?"[125] He defended this premise by positing a distinction between activity and affection; the soul was capable of conducting an activity and being affected without changing, while the body could not be affected without also changing. Though "sense perceptions" were activities (*energeia*) or judgments of the higher part of the soul while affections like grief, anger, pleasure, or desire were activities the lower part, the soul did not undergo change in carrying out these functions.[126] Thus, the soul caused the body to move and grow (and hence, change) while remaining free from change in its activity.[127] Only

---

118. Plotinus, *Ennead* 2.4.1, 4.2–4.4, 4.8, 4.12.
119. Plotinus, *Ennead* 4.8.2.42–45.
120. Plotinus, *Ennead* 4.8.8.2–6.
121. Plotinus, *Ennead* 4.8.2.44–45.
122. Plotinus, *Ennead* 1.6.5.26–36. Indeed, different souls look at different things, becoming what they look at, *Ennead* 4.9.3.
123. Plotinus, *Ennead* 1.6.5.45–50; *Ennead* 1.4.4.27–31.
124. Plotinus, *Ennead* 4.4.19.13.
125. Plotinus, *Ennead* 3.6.5.1–2.
126. Plotinus, *Ennead* 3.6.1, 3.6.3, 3.6.4.
127. Plotinus, *Ennead* 3.6.4.38–42. Similarly, while the lower part of the soul may

a soul present in every part of the body (like Stoicism) could be affected by the body. In Plotinus's cosmology, however, this could not be, since bodies derived from Soul; Soul transcended body, though every individual soul had "something of what is below, in the direction of the body, and of what is above, in the direction of the Intellect."[128] Given this distinction, Plotinus asserted that the individual soul could actually *benefit* by "plunging into" the body, for example, as a way of experiencing evil in order to give one clearer knowledge of the Good.[129] He also believed that the soul cared for the body, just as Soul cares for that which emanates from Soul. Plotinus likened the embodied soul to a gardener tending a plant, "concerned about the maggots in the plant and anxiously caring for it."[130] Once again however, this benefit—even if described as movement from vice to virtue—could not be properly described as change.[131] In contrast to a Gnostic mind-set where "men fly from the body since they hate it from a distance," Plotinus likened the body to a house "built for us by a good sister soul."[132] While the soul's role of caretaker was not considered a burdensome task, excessive concern about one's body—whether in treating illness, through ascetic regime, or concern over aging—was thought to pull the soul away from its most proper activity, the contemplation of Intellect.

In Plotinus's anthropology then there is a clear tension between competing duties of the soul: on the one hand the soul is the rightful caretaker of the body (and not necessarily its taskmaster), while on the other hand the soul strives toward Intellect, a striving that is hindered somewhat by the body's need for attention. When the soul "looks to what comes before [i.e., the Intellect] it exercises its intelligence, when it looks to itself it sets in order what comes after it [the body] and directs and rules it."[133] This tension is maintained, if not strengthened, by Plotinus's rejection of

---

form an "opinion" on an approaching evil giving rise to fear in the soul, the soul nevertheless forms this opinion without changing; the accompanying bodily response—"disturbance and shock"—is also strictly limited to the body.

128. Plotinus, *Ennead* 4.8.8.13–14; *Ennead* 2.9.2.5–10.

129. Plotinus, *Ennead* 4.8.7. The soul must seek the One through Intellect, lest it face a transmigratory existence. *Ennead* 3.2.13.11–15, 3.4.2.

130. Plotinus, *Ennead* 4.3.4.31–32.

131. Plotinus, *Ennead* 3.6.2. Nor does the soul does change in moving from virtue to vice.

132. Plotinus, *Ennead* 2.9.18.1–2; 15–16. Based on Porphyry's *Life of Plotinus*, Robinson asserts that Plotinus was likely familiar with the Gnostic works *Allogenes*, *The Three Tales of Seth*, *Trimorphic Protennoia*, and *Zostrianos*. See Robinson, ed., *Nag Hammadi Library*, 8.

133. Plotinus, *Ennead* 4.8.3.26–29.

the Platonic notion of man as a composite of body and soul.[134] Either way, Plotinus insisted that "we ourselves are not it [body], nor are we clear of it, but it depends upon and is attached to us."[135] Nevertheless, the good man will strive to pursue contemplation by first quieting bodily impulses so that body and soul can go their separate ways (a strikingly similar description to Antony's explanation of the mind's discrimination between body and soul). He must "gradually extinguish his bodily advantages by neglect" so as not to be altogether deprived of illness or pain.[136] Porphyry noted for instance that Plotinus refused to take an enema for his diseased bowels, feeling it improper for a man of his age.[137] As long as the body and soul are together however, there will be the tendency "to swing up and down" between excessive concern for the body on one hand and a longing for communion with Intellect on the other.[138] Thus, it not surprising that this ambiguous relationship between the soul and the body has been appropriately described as a "Platonic insouciance."[139]

It is not difficult to see that Athanasius's account of prelapsarian man in *Against the Heathen* draws on the language and imagery employed in Neoplatonic thought, particularly his description of man's fall from the contemplation of things divine, a fall precipitated by lending inordinate attention to the lure of the body.[140] Athanasius's descriptions of the fallen condition of humanity also echoes Socrates's admonitions in *Phaedo,* where the purification of the soul involves distancing it from the influences of the visible, corruptible body that constantly pull one away from the contemplation of the divine.[141] However, it is also clear that Athanasius believed the body itself could be refined, and marked the entry point for the refinement of the soul. Though the fall may have been occasioned by inordinate attention to the material, the way back to paradise begins by attending to the body. The ambivalence over the body inherent in Platonic and Neoplatonic thought is decidedly absent in Athanasius, though with Plato and Plotinus, he affirmed that a healthy body is not an end in itself.

---

134. Plotinus, *Ennead* 1.4.14.1–4.

135. Plotinus, *Ennead* 4.4.18.114–15.

136. Plotinus, *Ennead* 1.4.14.21–24.

137. Porphyry, *Life of Plotinus* 2, in Page, ed., *Plotinus*. Porphyry notes that Plotinus also refused certain medicines containing the flesh of wild animals.

138. Plotinus, *Ennead* IV.4.18.35–36.

139. Miles, *Plotinus on Body and Beauty*, 69.

140. Athanasius, *Against the Heathen* 2–8, NPNF2, 4:5–8. See Plato, *Phaedrus* 246c–247c; Louth, *The Origins of the Christian Mystical Tradition*, 77.

141. Plato, *Phaedo* 64c–67e; *Theatetus* 176a–b.

EARLY CHRISTIAN ASCETICISM
IN HISTORICAL CONTEXT

In spite of these similarities, however, Athanasius's affirmation that God created the soul *ex nihilo* established a clear ontological distinction between Creator and the created, a distinction considerably blurred in Plato and denied altogether by Plotinus. Though Athanasius speaks of humanity becoming divine, this assertion was certainly not rooted in a connaturality between God and humankind.[142] Athanasius had no trouble acknowledging God's intention that human creatures be composed of a body and soul, an assertion that Plotinus found untenable. Whenever Athanasius spoke of the soul as something other than the creaturely body, he was making a functional distinction, not a substantial one.[143] As Alvyn Pettersen observed,

> Pure human life for Athanasius lies not in the separation from sensible things, but in detachment from a *wrong relationship* of soul and body. The soul was created unadulterated by, but not separated from, its body. The one good God is the Creator and Sustainer of both, and the created body is then not to be fled. The human soul is not to be careless of its body: it is to recognize its God-given relationship to it.[144]

As we have seen, Antony too echoed the Platonic tripartite soul of which the mind (*nous*) is the highest part. His description of the mind's role in discriminating body from soul is similar to Plotinus's description of the soul's turning to Intellect and Plato's metaphor of the rational soul (*nous*) as a charioteer driving the lower parts of the soul.[145] Antony also saw passions originating in a "soul no longer guided by reason," which then "affect[s] man by being mingled with the members of the body, or the will."[146] Though both Athanasius and Antony made use of the imagery and expressions common to Platonic and Neoplatonic philosophy, which, should not be entirely unexpected, nevertheless affirmed the goodness of the body, fully recognizing the crucial role it plays in the refinement of one's soul. They both in fact

---

142. Pettersen, *Athanasius*, 42–44; Pettersen, *Athanasius and the Human Body*, 19.

143. Pettersen, *Athanasius*, 43.

144. Pettersen, *Athanasius*, 43, emphasis mine.

145. Plato, *Phaedrus* 245c–256b; Plato, *Timaeus* 69c–e. Rubenson also identifies the influence of Origen and Clement of Alexandria. See Clement of Alexandria, *On Spiritual Perfection* (*Stromateis* 3) 36–40, 115–18. See also Brown, *Body and Society*, 127–30.

146. Rubenson, *Letters*, 70. Athanasius too likens the soul that forgets God to a charioteer who pays no attention to the goal, driving the chariot at will. Athanasius, *Against the Heathen* 5.2, NPNF2, 4:6.

went beyond this by noting that a proper ascetic regime could *sanctify* the body and actually slow aging down.

Both Athanasius and Antony situated their ascetic regime in a Christian framework that affirmed the goodness of creation, thereby rejecting any construal of salvation as escape from the body. Nevertheless, Athanasius's unbridled exhortation of Antony's harsh and at times abusive ascetic regime appears to betray a Gnostic or Manichaean influence. Antony might be numbered with other Desert Fathers who called for harsh treatment of the body, for questionable examples abound. The oft-quoted Dorotheus of Gaza (505–565), who described bodily mortification as killing the body, would appear to confirm popular notions of asceticism as a repressive regime rooted in a hatred of the fallen body.[147] Others desecrated their food: Isaac of Cellia spread post eucharistic ashes over his food while Joseph of Panephō was known to have deliberately tainted his fresh water with sea water.[148] Contemporary Ethiopian ascetics whose lineage can be traced back to the Desert Fathers engaged in self-flagellation, stuck sharp objects into the body, and wore painful leather belts and chains.[149] It must be admitted that the Desert Fathers' withdrawal from society and the severe disciplining of their bodies suggests that "matter was a hindrance to those seeking to be true soldiers of Christ."[150]

Antony's ascetic regime cannot be so easily vindicated by simply condemning the more extreme measures occasionally undertaken by others. Antony himself urged Christians to "hate all peace that comes from the flesh . . . Suffer hunger, thirst, nakedness, be watchful and sorrowful . . . despise the flesh, so that you may preserve your souls."[151] Elsewhere he spoke of the body in Platonic terms as "heavy," and as something we may leave behind with God's assistance.[152] Both Antony and Athanasius alluded to mortification in their writings, following the Apostle Paul, who beat his body that he might keep it in order to make it his servant (1 Cor 9:27). Athanasius

---

147. Ware, "Way of the Ascetics," 9, quoting Palladius, *Lausiac History* 2.17. William Bushell has conducted a contemporary study of Ethiopian ascetics, and found similar statements. His spiritual father (*manafasawi abbat*) said of Jesus, "he was patient . . . like a lamb, he received all his torture to teach us that we have to receive all torture and to torture ourselves." See Bushell, "Psychophysiological and Comparative Analysis," 281.

148. Ware, "Way of the Ascetics,"10; Musurillo, "Problem of Ascetical Fasting," 25n7. However, the eucharistic ashes might also be seen as sanctifying one's food.

149. Bushell, "Psychophysiological and Comparative Analysis," 105.

150. Pettersen, *Athanasius and the Human Body*, 1.

151. Ward, ed., *Sayings of the Desert Fathers*, 8.

152. Antony, Letter 6:42, in Rubenson, *Letters*, 219. "And he [God] visits us by resolving us from the heaviness of this body, that we may leave it." See Antony, Letter 6:61, in Rubenson, *Letters*, 220.

noted that Antony "more and more . . . mortified the body and kept it under subjection, so that he would not, after conquering some challenges, trip up in others."[153] But Athanasius also likened prayer and fasting to bodily fortification grounded in the "Lord who for our sake took flesh and gave the body victory over the devil."[154] Antony's exhortation to subdue the body often occurred in the context of restricting particular movements of the body such as gluttony—and not the body itself. When he referred to Paul's admonition to "*Mortify your members*," he meant activities of the body, such as "*fornication, uncleanness, and evil desires*, and so forth."[155] Antony himself asserted that the purpose of these mortifications was "so that the whole body may be changed and placed under the authority of the Spirit."[156]

It should also be remembered that Antony chastised ascetics who treated the body too harshly. "Some have afflicted their bodies by asceticism," notes Antony, "but they lack discernment, and so they are far from God."[157] Indeed, the Spirit who guides one in sanctification assigns a rule of "moderation after the power of the body."[158] Though here undoubtedly influenced by Neoplatonic thought, he believed the materiality of the body simultaneously served as the source of temptation and as the precondition for spiritual progress and growth in virtue.[159] Antony carefully spelled out instructions for purifying the members of the body, enabling one to move towards the fully transformed body at the resurrection. That the body might be transformed presupposes, to some extent, its inherent goodness. Samuel Rubenson rightly recognizes that

> [Antony] did not share the contempt for the body manifest both in Plotinus and in Gnosticism. The body is to him not an irrelevant piece of matter, nor a prison of the soul, but a home to be cleansed, a sacrifice to be purified. . . . The body is to Antony not evil *per se*, nor is it responsible for its misuse; it is created for a good purpose, and only needs to be brought back to its

---

153. Pettersen, "Athanasius' Presentation," 441; Antony, Letter 1:40, in Rubenson, *Letters*, 199.

154. Athanasius, *Life of Antony* 5, 197.

155. Antony, Letter 1:68, in Rubenson, *Letters*, 201, in reference to Colossians 3:5, from the Greek *nekroō*.

156. Antony, Letter 1:70, in Rubenson, *Letters*, 201.

157. Ward, ed., *Sayings of the Desert Fathers*, 3. Rubenson notes the parallel with Letter 6:106. "Truly, my children, I also want you to know that there are many who have endured great struggle in this way of life, but have been killed by lack of discernment." Rubenson, *Letters*, 224.

158. Antony, Letter 1:63, in Rubenson, *Letters*, 201.

159. Rubenson, *Letters*, 67.

original nature. The body is not simply to be discarded; it can be transformed.[160]

Though Antony and Athanasius employed Platonic concepts in their respective anthropologies, they recognized the body's goodness, even in its fallen state.

If the goodness of human embodiment was preserved by the doctrine of creation *ex nihilo*, embodiment was most fully affirmed in the incarnation. Athanasius puts this eloquently in *Against the Heathen*: "But the reason why the Word, the Word of God, has united Himself with created things is truly wonderful, and teaches us that the present order of things is none otherwise than is fitting."[161] Moreover, the incarnation sets a limit to both the practice of and motivation for asceticism. Kallistos Ware has proven particularly helpful in discerning the motivations, and hence the moral standing of ascetic practices by making a distinction between natural and unnatural asceticism.[162] The former is creation-affirming, while the latter is creation-denying. According to Ware, unnatural asceticism "evinces either explicitly or implicitly a distinct hatred for God's creation, and particularly the body."[163] Unnatural asceticism seeks out special forms of mortification, inflicting gratuitous pain on the body. Those who wore spikes to pierce the flesh or chained themselves in iron fetters were likely guilty of this. Tolstoy's account of the hermit Sergius who impulsively lopped off his left index finger with an axe in a desperate attempt to calm his lust, serves as a contemporary example.[164] Natural asceticism on the other hand reduces physical needs to a minimum. If unnatural asceticism involves starving the body and weakening it to the point where one is no longer able serve others, or intentionally making food and drink repulsive, natural asceticism involves limiting one's diet to vegetables and water while avoiding such foods as wine or meat.[165]

Ware claims that this general stance toward asceticism has been adopted as the official attitude of the church from the fourth century onwards. He argues that the early church recognized the legitimacy of voluntary asceticism, not as a denial of one's body, but in affirmation of the body and of God's creation in general. Indeed, the *Apostolic Canons* (400) warned against

---

160. Rubenson, *Letters*, 71. Rubenson does concede that Antony believed that such a bodily transformation involves making the body less material and more spiritual, and is thus more closely aligned to Origen.

161. Athanasius, *Against the Heathen* 41.2, NPNF2, 4:26.

162. Ware, "Way of the Ascetics," 9.

163. Ware, "Way of the Ascetics," 10.

164. Tolstoy, *Father Sergius*, in *Tolstoy: Master and Man*, 33–42.

165. Ware, "Way of the Ascetics," 9.

forms of abstinence based on a suspicion of the body, drawing a fundamental distinction between proper asceticism and an abstinence stemming from hatred or dislike of material things, which was viewed as blasphemous.

> If any bishop, presbyter or deacon, or any other member of the clergy, abstains from marriage, or from meat and wine, not by way of asceticism (*askēsis*) but out of abhorrence for these things, forgetting that God made "all things altogether good and beautiful" (Gen 1:31), and that "he created humankind male and female" (Gen 1:27), and so blaspheming the work of creation, let him be corrected, or else be deposed and cast out of the Church. The same applies also to a lay person.[166]

Ware defends contemporary ascetic practices as a way to gain control over one's body while also highlighting the social dimensions of abstinence.

> We fast, not out of hatred for God's creation, but so as to control the body; also fasting enables us to help the poor, for the food that we ourselves refrain from eating can be given to others who are in need. Natural asceticism, it can be argued, is warfare not against the body but *for* the body.[167]

He traces the early church's stance on asceticism to Antony and specifically Athanasius's *Life of Antony*, which "adopts a markedly positive attitude towards the body."[168]

Though the body is good in itself as created by God, it is also a fallen body, and thus a source of passions that must be held in check.[169] As Athanasius stressed in the opening chapters of *Against the Heathen* and *On the Incarnation*, embodiment itself was not a lesser state of being, but simply represented the *possibility* of a fall that need not have taken place had Adam kept appropriate control of his bodily desires. If Platonic thought could in one sense regard materiality with a kind of semi-ambivalent suspicion, Athanasius saw embodiment only as granting that possibility.[170] As mentioned earlier, Athanasius presents Adam as an ascetic whose soul for a time

---

166. Ware, "Way of the Ascetics," 10, paraphrasing *Canons of the Holy and Altogether August Apostles* 51, NPNF2, 14:597.

167. Ware, "Way of the Ascetics," 10, italics mine.

168. Ware, "Way of the Ascetics," 11.

169. See Athanasius, *Against the Heathen* 2–3 and *On the Incarnation* 1–3. Both Pettersen and Brakke observe that this move was motivated in part by Athanasius's desire to safeguard Christ's divinity in his dispute with the Arians, who asserted that Christ was the first and greatest of God's creation. Thus, the passions stem from Jesus' body, and not his soul.

170. Pettersen, *Athanasius*, 86.

was in control of his body until his contemplation of God was interrupted by the passions of the body. That Adam abused his freedom by turning his attention toward his body in no way signals that the body is in some way inferior to the soul. As Pettersen has noted, the body may indeed be *associated* with sin, but is never equated with sin. "The body is the victim and not the origin of sin."[171] However, as stated at the beginning of this chapter, Christ's incarnation has opened a way to transform the body and regain a heightened resistance against the decay natural to it. This transformation required an ascetic regime by which the passions of the body might be brought under control of one's soul. The practice of fasting in particular was rooted in Scripture and the narrative of redemption that involved a foretaste of the final transformation to be received at the resurrection. As such, it was always enabled by and directed toward Christ.

Pettersen's rich discussion examines the theological roots of Athanasius's understanding of embodiment and the role fasting played in its formation. Echoing what has been said above, Pettersen notes that asceticism was much more than a simple denial of the body, but involved "relating it to the lordly and enlivening Logos, (therein finding its truly creaturely status and role)."[172] The body thus has both a *symbolic* function of expressing the divine mind and an *instrumental* function in effecting the purposes of God.[173] "A person, as it were, brings God to mankind by interpreting God 'incarnate' in his or her own body, and the same person directs and offers that body to God."[174] Indeed, on multiple occasions Antony exhorts his followers to offer their bodies as living sacrifices to the Lord.[175] Pettersen refers to the body in this sense as a "sacramental body," where the one's body is revered and recognized as the locus of God's activity in the world as "God's media of incarnate expression," even as such expressions are simultaneously directed toward God.[176] Thus, on the one hand, "a person is to play a priestly role towards himself or herself as a body," while on the other, "each [person] is to contemplate God's purposes and intentions, and, in the light of such

---

171. Pettersen, *Athanasius and the Human Body*, 101.

172. Pettersen, *Athanasius and the Human Body*, 3.

173. Pettersen, *Athanasius and the Human Body*, 3.

174. Pettersen, *Athanasius and the Human Body*, 84.

175. Antony, Letter 3:38, in Rubenson, *Letters*, 208; also from Rubenson, *Letters*, see Letter 5:7, in *Letters*, 212; Letter 6:83, in *Letters*, 222; Letter 6:93, *Letters*, 223; Letter 7:52, *Letters*, 228; Letter 7:58n, *Letters*, 230.

176. Pettersen, *Athanasius and the Human Body*, 99. "The body *is* rather than *has* a material means of expression. It is the vehicle or instrument through which the soul relates to the world and the world to the soul," 112.

reflection, to be active through his or her body towards the created world."[177] While the body certainly requires discipline, it is ultimately necessary to accomplish God's purposes in the world. This is most certainly incarnational thought. Pettersen's allusion to the body as a sacramental is apposite here, for the asceticism was also underwritten by the belief that the body could be transformed through various practices. Subduing the body's impulses was not simply for the benefit of one's soul, but transformed the body itself. Fasting in particular represented one possible means by which humans were able to regain a degree of bodily incorruptibility, interpreted as a return to prelapsarian Eden. For Athanasius and Antony, *theōsis* marked the way back to Eden.

ON FASTING AND REMAKING THE BODY

The belief that the body could be transformed by pursuing certain practices was common among Christians from at least the third century onwards. Peter Brown has observed that the notion of remaking the body was wholly consistent with theories of bodily functioning and operation at this time, which tended to view the body as a closed or autarkic system, capable of conserving its own energy indefinitely (from the Greek *autos*, meaning "self" and *arkein*, meaning "to be sufficient"). Adam and Eve were archetypes in this regard, especially before the fall. Thus, notes Brown,

> In ideal conditions it [the body] was thought capable of running on its own "heat"; it would need only enough nourishment to keep that heat alive. In its "natural" state—a state with which the ascetics tended to identify the bodies of Adam and Eve—the body had acted like a finely tuned engine, capable of "idling" indefinitely.[178]

Athanasius and Antony shared in the belief that asceticism allowed one to remake the body, thereby returning it to its natural (*physis*), prelapsarian state. Derwas J. Chitty has observed that the ascetic's aim "is the recovery of Adam's condition before the Fall . . . man's fallen condition being *para physin*—'*un*natural.'"[179] Thus, there is little doubt that there was a

---

177. Pettersen, *Athanasius and the Human Body*, 84, 99.

178. Brown, *Body and Society*, 223. Brown observes that this view of the body is espoused by Gregory of Nyssa, *On the Making of Man* 30, NPNF2 5:422–27. See also Brakke, *Athanasius and the Politics of Asceticism*, 241.

179. Chitty, *Desert a City*, 4. See Ware, "Way of the Ascetics," 3–15. Ware says, "asceticism has not subverted Antony's physicality but restored it to its 'natural state,' that is to say, to its true and proper condition as intended by God. This natural state

widespread belief that ascetic practices were instrumental in the recovery of Adam's original state. Brown notes that "the body-image which the ascetics brought with them into the desert gave considerable cognitive and emotional support to their hope for change through self-mortification."[180] But the discipline of fasting was thought to hold promise for not only shaping one's soul, but one's body, transforming it into a finely tuned engine.

Fasting as a Return to Eden

As we have seen, Athanasius and Antony both believed fasting enabled the disciple to return to a more natural, prelapsarian body Adam and Eve enjoyed before the fall. The importance of fasting for the Church Fathers can hardly be overstated, particularly for those who endured the challenging conditions of the nearly uninhabitable desert. As Brown observes,

> Once they had faced out the terrible risks involved in remaining human in a nonhuman environment, the men of the desert were thought capable of recovering, in the hushed silence of that dead landscape, a touch of the unimaginable glory of Adam's first state. Hence the importance of fasting in the world of the Desert Fathers.[181]

If, as, many believed, Adam's sin was related to his belly, denying the impulses of one's stomach marked the pathway back to Eden. To fast was to relive and conquer the first temptation to eat from the tree of knowledge.[182] All Christians were in fact encouraged to fast at various times throughout the year. Even a Lenten fast, for instance, "was to undo a little of the fateful sin of Adam."[183] Ascetics however were forced to endure what Brown calls the "Cold Turkey Treatment," by driving excessive dependence on food and sex far from the body.[184] Brown notes that fasting allowed the ascetic to

---

continues up to the end of Antony's long life." "Way of the Ascetics," 11.

180. Brown, *Body and Society*, 223.

181. Brown, *Body and Society*, 220.

182. Brown, *Body and Society*, 221. Indeed, Brown observes that it was widely believed in Egypt that the first sin of Adam and Eve was not sexual in nature, but was the sin of "ravenous greed." *Body and Society*, 220.

183. Brown, *Body and Society*, 220.

184. Brown observes that Clement of Alexandria approvingly cites Valentinus who believed that Jesus himself exercised such a high degree of bodily self-control that he ate and drank without defecating. See Clement of Alexandria, *Stromateis* 3.7.59, in *Fathers of the Church*, 85:292–93.

essentially "retune" or remake the body, transforming it into a finely calibrated engine. By fasting, the ascetic

> slowly remade his body. He turned it into an exactly calibrated instrument. Its drastic physical changes, after years of ascetic discipline, registered with satisfying precision the essential, preliminary stages of the long return of the human person, body and soul together, to an original, natural and uncorrupted state.[185]

Fasting attenuated the body's gradual dissolution, enabling the ascetic to put on a little of that bodily incorruption initiated by Christ's incarnation. The ascetic's body was slowed down by the long fasts and sleepless nights of the desert. Though the myth of Paradise weighed heavily on the rather frail bodies of the ascetics, it was nevertheless considered eminently attainable, resulting not only in a transformed mind, but an ageless body.

Indeed, Athanasius records that twenty years of solitude and fasting in the harsh desert left Antony's body lean and unchanged. Antony "was neither fat . . . nor lean from fasting . . . but was just the same as they had known him before his retirement."[186] In many respects Antony's life "seems to have stood still for a further eighty years."[187] Athanasius called for a dietary regimen that involved replacing meat with vegetables, wine with water, and gluttony with sparse meals. He could scarcely bring himself to mention "Antony" and "luxurious" food in the same sentence. "His food was bread and salt, his drink, water only. Of flesh and wine it is superfluous even to speak . . ."[188] Such advice, of course, was hardly new, and echoes earlier advice found in Porphyry's *Life of Pythagoras*.[189] One is also reminded of Daniel and his fellow exiles who, by taking only vegetables and water outshone those who enjoyed King Nebuchadnezzar's choice food and wine in both intelligence and appearance (Dan 1:6-15). There is little in the text to suggest that their enhanced appearance came from anything other than sound practices.

Though Athanasius offers little by way of specific details concerning Antony's fasting regimen, we have learned that he usually ate once daily—bread and salt—while occasionally abstaining from food for several days at a time.[190] Later on Antony planted corn and potted herbs, making his own

---

185. Brown, *Body and Society*, 223.
186. Athanasius, *Life of Antony* 14, NPNF2, 4:200.
187. Brown, *Body and Society*, 214.
188. Athanasius, *Life of Antony* 7, NPNF2, 4:198.
189. Pythagoras's occult diet of Hercules called for avoiding wine and meat. See Brakke, *Athanasius and the Politics of Asceticism*, 314.
190. Athanasius, *Life of Antony* 7-8, NPNF2, 4:197-198. It has been noted that the

bread, occasionally eating a frugal relish from palm trees.[191] Contrary to some modern notions of fasting, the practice did not involve starvation or even extended periods of complete abstinence from food. As noted earlier, Antony's exhortation to moderation applied equally to the discipline of fasting. His regime appears consistent with the advice found in the *Apophthegmata Patrum*, where the Desert Fathers discouraged prolonged periods of fasting in favor of taking a little food each day.[192] Barsanuphius of Gaza (d. 540) for instance described fasting as leaving the table with only a little less hunger and thirst than before so that fasting might not lead to a weakened body, thus hindering reflection, prayer, and self examination.[193]

The bodily benefits of fasting become more intelligible when the effects of gluttony are investigated. If fasting was thought to be a means of slowing the body down, engorging the body with food was thought to shorten one's life by bringing on premature aging. Chrysostom (347–407) believed that too much food contributed to gout, palsy, and "premature old age," among other maladies.[194] He spoke disparagingly of those who "distend their stomach[s], and blunt their senses, and sink the vessel by an overladen cargo of food . . . in some shipwreck of the body."[195] The man who lives in such a way, says Chrysostom, is "dead whilst he liveth."[196] Indeed, gluttony revealed a soul "wasted with leanness."

> If it were possible to bring the soul into view, and to behold it with our bodily eyes, that of the luxurious would seem depressed, mournful, miserable, and wasted with leanness; for the more the body grows sleek and gross, the more lean and weakly is the soul; and the more one is pampered, the more is the other hampered.[197]

---

type of bread eaten by Antony would have contained many more nutrients than the typical bread of today.

191. Athanasius, *Life of Antony* 50, NPNF2, 4:209.

192. Ware, "Way of the Ascetics," 9.

193. Barsanuphius, Letter 154, and Letter 838, in Chryssavgis, ed., *Letters from the Desert*, 91, 198 respectively. The hermit John, who came to live beside Barsanuphius, also said: "But give the body just a little less than it requires. For this is the way of the fathers [Desert Fathers]: neither to be wasteful nor to be crushed in one's discipline." Letter 212, in Chryssavgis, ed., *Letters from the Desert*, 9.

194. Chrysostom, *No One Can Harm* 8, NPNF1, 9:277. See also Musurillo, "Problem of Ascetical Fasting," 17–19.

195. Chrysostom, *No One Can Harm*, 7–8, NPNF1, 9:276–77.

196. Chrysostom, *Homilies on Timothy XIII*, NPNF1, 13:451.

197. Chrysostom, *Homilies on Timothy XIII*, NPNF1, 13:451.

The Church Fathers also recognized that such overindulgence inevitably impaired one's ability to understand Scripture. Gregory Nazianzen (330–389) did not think it possible to rightly understand Scripture apart from "keeping under the body" by fasting and submitting one's dust to the spirit "as they would do who form a just judgment of our composite nature."[198] If the Christian life allowed little room for culinary luxuries, it was only more so for the ascetic. There was no need for the perpetual dosing and constant attendance of physicians in Antony's case, who lived long by even modern standards. The life of the ascetic—and indeed all Christians—called for nothing less than a reordering of body and soul.

Reordering Body and Soul

Having briefly discussed the psychophysiological enhancements associated with the ascetic regime, it will be helpful to give a more thorough account of the relationship between the formation of body and the soul. To speak only of remaking the body by denying the needs of the body to a certain degree is to miss the larger goal of which such bodily reformation was a part, namely, the reformation of one's soul. For the desert ascetics, slowing the body down was subsumed under, though doubtless integral to, restoring the proper relationship between the body and the soul, namely, the soul's rightful rulership over the body. Both Athanasius and Antony depicted the ascetic regime as bringing the body under the influence of one's Word-guided soul, a condition that also enabled the body to assume the original state of Adam's body in paradise.

We have already seen that Antony's ascetic regime involved remaking the body in the transformation of one's soul in order that both body and soul might again assume the natural state where the soul rules over the body, echoing Athanasius's *Life of Antony*.[199] Athanasius makes this clear in his description of Antony's harsh treatment of his own body. Compelled by Jesus' admonition not to worry about one's material circumstances, he observes that Antony gave short space to the body in order that the body might once again submit fully to his soul. According to Athanasius, Antony

> used to say that it behoved a man to give all his time to his soul rather than his body, yet to grant a short space to the body

---

198. Nazianzen, *First Theological Oration* 7, NPNF2, 7:287.

199. Rubenson similarly observes that "the emphasis in the letters on original creation as rational, and on the need to return to this original rational state, to the true nature of man, is also in accordance with central notions in the *Vita*." Rubenson, *Letters*, 134.

through its necessities; but all the more earnestly to give up the whole remainder to the soul and seek its profit, that it might not be dragged down by the pleasures of the body, but, on the contrary, *the body might be in subjection to the soul.*[200]

Though fasting was an integral part of bringing the body under the soul's control, Antony also advocated making an inventory of one's thought life, so that one "may never think of what is unseemly."[201] Such exercises were not in exclusion to the body, but so that the soul might regain control over the body. For Antony concludes that such inventories enable one "to make a servant of the body and please the Lord."[202] The purpose of asceticism was not simply to suppress bodily desires solely to remake the body, but to bring the body under control of the soul.

A reordering of the body-soul relationship involves the tension of restraining the impact of the bodily desires upon the soul so that the soul might be the rightful master over the body. As David Brakke notes, "life in the desert revealed, if anything, the inextricable interdependence of body and soul."[203] Though this is certainly the case, Antony was drawn to the metaphor of servitude or enslavement used by Paul in 1 Corinthians. The metaphor of enslavement involves a tension between togetherness and distance. This distance was also evident in Antony's first letter, where the mind, under the Spirit's guidance, helps one discriminate between the body and the soul, learning how to purify them both through repentance.[204] At the same time, however, enslavement also "knit the body and soul together," even if the ascetic regime ensured that the body and soul phenomenologically kept their distance.[205] This metaphor is related to the concept of mortification, a death of sorts. Just as Athanasius understood death as complete separation of the soul from the body, so he understood ascetic death as a conceptual distancing of the soul from the body's passions through renunciation.[206] But this distancing enabled the ascetic to attend to the needs of one's soul, one's will and desires. Thus, this was no dualistic exercise. Athanasius urged those in his episcopate to fast in *both* body and soul, considering not only the

200. Athanasius, *Life of Antony* 45, *NPNF2*, 4:208, emphasis mine.
201. Athanasius, *Life of Antony* 55, *NPNF2*, 4:211.
202. Athanasius, *Life of Antony* 55, in Vivian, *Coptic Life of Antony*, 178.
203. Brown, *Body and Society*, 236.
204. Antony, Letter 1:27, in Rubenson, *Letters*, 199.
205. Brakke, *Athanasius and the Politics of Asceticism*, 241.
206. Brakke, *Athanasius and the Politics of Asceticism*, 241. Brakke also suggests that the metaphor of death "implied both the neutralization of the body's passions and the abandonment or killing of one's social self as defined by normal social and economic activities" (159).

food for the stomach, but also giving attention to the virtues (and vices) that serve as food for the soul, for good or for ill.

> Behold, my brethren, how much a fast can do, and in what manner the law commands us to fast. It is required that not only with the body should we fast, but with the soul.... For virtues and vices are the food of the soul, and it can eat either of these two meats, and incline to either of the two, according to its own will.[207]

For Athanasius there is no opposition or dichotomy between bodily fasting and the fasting of the soul. Rather, as Brakke observes, "fasting was designed to focus the soul on the divine nourishment of the virtues and the Word of God; it brought the body under the control of the soul's will."[208] Thus, the reordering of body and soul requires and even presupposes that the heart or soul be appropriately directed toward God. The "natural" state to which asceticism strives is not simply the soul in control of the body, but also the soul in communion with God.

Dallas Willard (1935–2013) has noted that fasting "reveals to us how much our peace depends upon the pleasures of eating," and how easily we "assuage the discomforts in our bodies by faithless and unwise living and attitudes."[209] Indeed, fasting "demonstrate[s] how powerful and clever our body is in getting its own way against our strongest resolves."[210] In reflecting on the Gospel of John, Willard echoes Athanasius in observing that fasting from food enables one to feast on God.

> Fasting confirms our utter dependence upon God by finding in him a source of sustenance beyond food. Through it, we learn by experience that God's word to us is a life substance, that it is not food ("bread") alone that gives life, but also the words that proceed from the mouth of God (Matt. 4:4). We learn that we too have meat to eat that the world does not know about (John 4:32, 34). Fasting unto our Lord is therefore feasting—feasting on him and on doing his will.[211]

---

207. Athanasius, *Festal Letter* 1.5, NPNF2, 4:508. The emphasis on the spiritual element in fasting is well-attested in the early church. See Musurillo, "Problem of Ascetical Fasting," 35–42; 50–54.

208. Brakke, *Athanasius and the Politics of Asceticism*, 188.

209. Willard, *Spirit of the Disciplines*, 166.

210. Willard, *Spirit of the Disciplines*, 166.

211. Willard, *Spirit of the Disciplines*, 166. See also Willard, *Divine Conspiracy*, 195–200.

Fasting involves abstaining from food so that the Christian might be equipped for God, increasingly enabled to do God's will.

When speaking of reordering the body and soul, it is not altogether inappropriate to speak again in terms of mortification as "the regaining of self-control, even the return of the object self, the body, to a person's own rational control."[212] Having already discussed the negative connotations associated with mortification of the body, Pettersen asserts that in an Athanasian sense mortification entails offering the *whole* self to the divine Logos, inviting the Word to effectively take over the self.[213] Such mortification involves a dying to one's self.

> Mortification here means a transformation of the will, a metamorphosis of one's whole attitude and a radical shifting of the very centre of the personality from the self to God. In this sense "death" to selfishness is not too strong a description.[214]

This death to selfishness is also characterized as the right reordering of body and soul, as the "reasonable dominion of the body by the soul."[215] According to Athanasius, a disciplined body is no longer a hindrance to one's soul, but becomes employable to one's soul in service to God.

> When the body is disciplined, its temptations cease to be temptations; its needs are met but not indulged; and its capacities are used in the service of God, through the guidance of the rational soul, and are not allowed to dictate and to rule the soul—which then irrationally connives with its body—to its own selfish ends.[216]

Pettersen however correctly stresses that fasting aims to bring body and soul together as one—even as the soul leads the body—through ascetic practices, concluding that the ascetic engages in a process whereby gradually she becomes fully herself.

> Slowly but surely the rational soul is graciously allowed to play its proper role towards its own body, wherein a person becomes fully himself or herself in the unity of both the body and the

---

212. Pettersen, *Athanasius and the Human Body*, 102. Pettersen also construes mortification as putting to death our rebellious acts against God.
213. Pettersen, *Athanasius and the Human Body*, 101.
214. Pettersen, *Athanasius and the Human Body*, 101.
215. Pettersen, *Athanasius and the Human Body*, 100.
216. Pettersen, *Athanasius and the Human Body*, 99.

soul, the body being animated and the soul expressing itself through its body in obedience to God.[217]

If asceticism aimed at reordering both body and soul in the transformation of the whole person, Athanasius recognized that one must begin with the body, an appropriate starting point in light of the incarnation.

Beginning with the Body

Among the Desert Fathers there was general agreement that the first step in bringing the body under control of the soul involved disciplining the body. In Antony's first letter he instructs his initiates to first begin with purifying the body before turning one's attention to the soul.

> First the body is purified by much fasting, by many vigils and prayers and by the service which makes a man to be straightened in body, cutting off from himself all the lusts of the flesh. . . . Then the Spirit that is his guide begins to open the eyes of his soul, to give to it also repentance, that it may be purified.[218]

Thus, the purification of one's soul requires that one first discipline the body, quieting its desires that wage war upon one's soul. As Derwas Chitty observed, however, the body served as instructor: "In the desert tradition, the body was allowed to become the discreet mentor of the proud soul."[219] Peter Brown has also noted that bodily self-mortification was only a *preliminary* step, where the conquering of hunger and sexual drives along with past habits allowed the ascetic to focus on his heart and his private will.[220] The ascetic

> had to learn, over the long years of life in the desert, to do nothing less than to untwist the very sinews of his private will. Fasting and heavy labor were important, in their own right, in the first years of the ascetic life, and especially for young monks in their full physical vigor.[221]

---

217. Pettersen, *Athanasius and the Human Body*, 104.
218. Chitty, *Letters of Antony*, 2.
219. Brown, *Body and Society*, 237.
220. Brown, *Body and Society*, 225.

221. Brown, *Body and Society*, 224. Bushell too acknowledges that this same principle holds among the Ethiopian monks and hermits today, whereby fasting helps bring the bodily desires under control so that the ascetic can continue on the work of plowing up one's soul or will. See Bushell, "Psychophysiological and Comparative Analysis," 558.

Once the bodily impulses are dealt with, the more difficult task of breaking up the hardened soil of one's heart could begin in the hopes of attaining that blessedness enjoyed by the prelapsarian Adam.

> Once the florid symptoms of greed and sexual longing, associated with the ascetic's past habits, had subsided, he was brought face to face with the baffling closedness of his own heart. It was to the heart, and to the strange resilience of the private will, that the great tradition of spiritual guidance associated with the Desert Fathers directed its most searching attention. In Adam's first state, the "natural" desires of the heart had been directed toward God, with bounding love and open-hearted awe in the huge delight of Paradise. It was by reason of Adam's wilfulness that these desires had become twisted into a "counter-nature."[222]

The real problem then was not Adam's stomach, but his will. Thus, the initial steps in returning the soul to its rightful place as leader of the body involved disciplining the body and quieting its effect on the soul, enabling the ascetic to untwist the tangled mess of conflicting motives and desires while simultaneously redirecting his gaze toward God. Without some measure of the former, the latter hardly seemed possible.

As we have seen, the importance of the body for refining the *whole person* can scarcely be underestimated. Antony recognized that the first step in reordering body and soul was careful attention to the body through fasting and vigils. There could be no significant purification of the soul without first attending to one's body; there could be no purification of the soul without prior purification of the body. Athanasius records that Antony's harsh treatment of his body enabled him not only to slow his body down, but also helped him conquer his soul and the demonic forces that sought to assail him. As Brown observed, "Seldom, in ancient thought, had the body been seen as more deeply implicated in the transformation of the soul; and never was it made to bear so heavy a burden."[223] If indeed the body had never been so heavily implicated in the transformation of one's soul, as Brown suggests, it has been shown that the body also reaped the benefits of having served in the soul's transformation through fasting, effectively slowing it down and affording it a measure of immunity from aging and corruption.

There are suggestions in the *Life of Antony* that the body is the direct beneficiary of a soul that is in tune with God. Athanasius observes that Antony's bodily disposition and movements reflected the state of his soul. Though he was not conspicuous by his appearance, Antony did stand out

---

222. Brown, *Body and Society*, 225.
223. Brown, *Body and Society*, 235.

for his serene manner and the purity of his soul, says Athanasius. "From his bodily movements could be perceived the condition of his soul."[224] Moreover, this visible serenity inevitably drew others to him. Other ascetics, notes David Brakke, "ran to him as if dragged by his eyes," though once again there was nothing particularly noteworthy about Antony's physical appearance.[225] Athanasius concludes, "thus Antony was recognized, for he was never disturbed, for his soul was at peace; he was never downcast, for his mind was joyous."[226] This visible serenity has been variously described as "the physical byproduct of a spiritual state," it was "human nature as it was made to be."[227] But, in a helpful summary, Brakke also reminds us, that *theōsis* would not have been possible without the prior condescension of the divine Word in the incarnation, who guides and assists Christians in the process.

> As the Word perfectly controlled his assumed body and remained untouched by its passions, he transformed the body itself, rendering it incorruptible, both morally and physically: The Word's perfect guidance divinized the flesh. Moral courage and control of the bodily passions were once again possible for human beings because they shared a "kinship of the flesh" with the Word's assumed body.[228]

Indeed, in Athanasius's portrait of Antony, we see more than just an example for Christians to imitate; in Antony we are presented with nothing less than the image of deified humanity.

There is certainly evidence of "human nature as it was made to be" in the *Life of Antony*. Athanasius reports a visible stillness in Antony's physical appearance when he first appeared before several of his followers after twenty years of solitude. Observing that Antony appeared unchanged in body over this length of time, Athanasius is able to read the state of Antony's soul from his general comportment as

> neither contracted as by grief, nor relaxed by pleasure, nor possessed by laughter or dejection, for he was not troubled when he beheld the crowd, nor overjoyed at being saluted by so many.

---

224. Athanasius, *Life of Antony* 67, NPNF2, 4:214.

225. Brakke, *Athanasius and the Politics of Asceticism*, 244, translating Athanasius, *Life of Antony*, 67.

226. Athanasius, *Life of Antony* 67, NPNF2, 4:14.

227. Brown, *Body and Society*, 224; Harmless, *Desert Christians*, 93.

228. Brakke, *Athanasius and the Politics of Asceticism*, 150.

But he was altogether even as a being guided by reason, and abiding in a natural state.[229]

Elements of Stoic thought in Athanasius's description can certainly be detected here and elsewhere, though Antony is never described as attaining a state that could be described as *apatheia*. But Athanasius's asceticism is not a flight from the transient impulses of the flesh, an *apatheia* that seeks to rise above the distractions of the body, for he rejected the common philosophical association of evil with mutability and good with the unchanging. While the exhortation to kill the passions was not an uncommon theme among the Desert Fathers, Ware rightly asks, "Cannot even the passions be redirected and used in God's service?" He avers that asceticism "can also be interpreted in more affirmative terms, as the reintegration of the body and the transformation of the passions into their true and natural condition."[230] Asceticism was not an attempt to entirely transcend the material, but involved bringing the soul in proper relation to God, enabling it to rightly govern the body, which in turn benefits by attaining a measure of incorruption that will be fully realized in the eschaton.

CONCLUSION

In this somewhat tedious study of the nature and role of the body in the asceticism of Athanasius and Antony, we have seen that bodily practices such as fasting were viewed as the primary means by which the Christian might regain a measure what was lost by Adam's sin, namely, a heightened degree of bodily incorruptibility allowing for the possibility of longer life. The asceticism espoused by Athanasius and Antony is situated within a theological framework that, while sharing surface commonalities with Platonic, Gnostic, and Stoic thought, is nevertheless distinguishable from these by an unqualified affirmation of embodiment, refusing even the idea that the body is merely an instrumental good insofar as it facilitates the reformation of one's soul. Though any ascetic regime is susceptible to abuse, Antony and Athanasius affirmed the inherent goodness of both the body and the soul as God's good creation *ex nihilo*. Their asceticism was not aimed at eliminating desires, but at redirecting one's desires under control of the Spirit, thereby restoring the soul as the rightful ruler of the body. Among the Desert

---

229. Athanasius, *Life of Antony* 14, NPNF2, 4:200. See *Life of Antony* 67, NPNF2, 4:214.

230. Ware, "Way of the Ascetics," 11, 12. Ware also notes that John Cassian adapted the tradition of *apatheia* to a Western audience, defining it as "purity of heart" (*puritas cordis*).

Fathers, fasting was recognized as a crucial first step in the reordering of one's body and soul. Only after one had effectively quieted the impulses of one's body could one most effectively deal with the more stubborn desires of the will. As a result, the body would doubly reap the benefits of fasting and by being under the benevolent governance of a well-ordered soul. In light of these findings, a few conclusions on contemporary aging attenuation are in order.

We have seen that Athanasius and the Desert Fathers believed that fasting enabled the Christian to remake his body by effectively slowing it down. Athanasius believed that an ascetic regime enabled one to put on a heightened degree of bodily incorruptibility, a fact borne out in Antony's unusually long life. Though Athanasius was largely uninterested in how specifically the body was remade and aging attenuated, such transformation was only considered possible because of Christ's incarnation, which was explanation enough. Moreover, though a heightened potential for longevity was more than an unintended consequence, enhanced longevity *per se* was hardly the desired outcome. Antony's instructions, for instance, stand in marked contrast to those of Cicero (106–43 BCE), who advised a moderate diet of just enough food and drink to help the in the battle against old age, "to fight against it as we would fight against disease."[231] As we saw in the first two chapters, echoes of such hygienic advice abound today.[232]

For Athanasius and Antony, however, the prospect of a heightened degree of bodily incorruption was a *moral* project whereby one's soul became subservient to the Spirit's guidance, forming habits and character that benefited one's body as well. The remaking of one's body by moderation in exercise and fasting was never carried out simply for the sake of longevity itself, but was infused with moral significance. The desert ascetics believed that the body was indispensable in the formation of one's soul or character; there could be no significant transformation of one's soul, no refining of the will, without also attending to the body. The ascetic who was able to quiet his body was thus better equipped to deal with issues of the heart, where, over time he was increasingly able to submit to God through prayer, reflection, and meditation on Scripture. Indeed, disciplining the body through fasting was the first step in self-transformation, where, as Brown observed, "the body was allowed to become the discreet mentor of the proud soul."[233]

---

231. Cicero, *On Old Age* 11.36, in Henderson, ed., *Cicero*, 20:45.

232. See Walford, *The 120 Year Diet*; Walford, *Beyond The 120 Year Diet*; Walford and Walford, *The Anti-Aging Plan*.

233. Brown, *Body and Society*, 237.

Fasting was integral *to*, yet subsumed *under*, the reordering of both the body and soul.

Athanasius believed that one could to some degree slow down the aging process through asceticism, even though this was not the primary goal. While both Antony and Athanasius saw asceticism as a return to Adam's prelapsarian state, neither specifically mentioned a return to antediluvian life-spans, as did Bacon and others. There may be several possible explanations for this. First, and most simply, this absence suggests that extending one's life by slowing the body down was not a matter of primary importance. This seems reasonable given that primary goal of asceticism was a proper reordering of soul and body. The real benefit enjoyed by Adam was his intimate fellowship with God, though doubtless Adam's body benefited from the intimacy of this relationship. In such a close relationship, one's life-span might even have been irrelevant. It could also be that the ascetic life entailed the kind of hardships that made longer life less attractive, even if those very practices may have enabled one to live longer. The ascetic life increased the probability of a prolonged bodily life, which would always entail a struggle against sin to some degree. Finally, the Christian hope of the resurrection may have limited any allusions to an extended life on this earth. The narrative in which the ascetic remade his earthly body was firmly rooted in the context of creation, the fall, and redemption. Both Antony and Athanasius recognized the tension between returning back to paradise and looking forward to the resurrection body, between Eden and the New Jerusalem. Antony observed that engaging in the discipline of fasting enabled the ascetic to "take on something of that other spiritual body which will be taken on at the resurrection of the just."[234] Indeed, the Holy Spirit gives the ascetic works to constrain the soul and the body so "that *both* may be purified and enter together into their inheritance."[235] Thus, a recovery of the Adamic body had a distinctly eschatological component. A return to one's natural condition was not solely a harkening back to Eden, but was also oriented towards the future resurrection.

The ascetic regime of Athanasius and Antony offers a theologically robust account of the body and its role in the formation of virtue. Their account also involved a degree of what might be called aging attenuation, though this was not the primary aim. Like Bacon's account, Athanasius and Antony were drawn by the imagery of prelapsarian Eden. Their respective approaches to the body however were very different. It could be said that

---

234. Antony, Letter 1:71, in Rubenson, *Letters*, 202.

235. Chitty, *Letters of Antony*, 2, emphasis mine. See also Athanasius, *Four Discourses* 2.21.16, NPNF2, 4:381.

if Bacon sought to regain Eden by working *against* the body, the Desert Fathers sought this return by working *with* it or even *through* it. Though Bacon viewed slowing aging as a primary good necessary to pursuing one's duties in life, Athanasius and Antony saw attenuated aging as an incarnational by-product of moral discipline. If Bacon sought to reorder the fallen world through a new practical science guided by charity, the Desert Fathers were content to reorder the fallen body and soul.

It is important to stress here that the point of making such comparisons is not to set one approach against another, much less to suggest that Athanasius's approach was more hygienic or "natural" than Bacon's and therefore preferable. As we have already observed, their approaches were not aiming at the same thing. Moreover, their theological outlook was different, even though both perspectives held that the body could effectively be remade. Though Bacon's view of fallen nature was more pessimistic than that of Athanasius and other Church Fathers in the East, he still distanced himself from Calvin and the Reformers in this regard. But considering the ascetic tradition has however given a thicker account of body, providing another lens through which to consider life extension by slowing aging with the use of technology. Here we should also note that the point of this chapter has not been to show that what is now described as "caloric restriction" or "fast-mimicking diet" was known much earlier in the Christian tradition, as if the claims of the Christian faith depended on the findings of modern science. Much less is this book about using contemporary science to demythologize these early Christian accounts of longevity as a way of either propping them up or dismissing them altogether. Calling the Desert Fathers' ascetic regime a form of "life extension" is at best an unacceptably thin reading, while using the science to either prove or disprove the Desert Fathers' understanding of remaking the body is equally misguided. Nevertheless, we will make use of this theological account in evaluating contemporary forms of slowing aging in the final chapter.

In both this chapter and the last we have been presented with two different interpretations of a return to Eden within the Christian tradition. Both Bacon and Athanasius (and Antony) situated this return within the Christian narrative of creation, fall, and redemption. Both sought to regain the conditions of life enjoyed by prelapsarian Adam, though both accounts to some degree projected their own ideals of humanity onto Adam in ways that fit their overall projects. This underscores another challenge for Bacon's program in particular, insofar as he was more heavily invested in a "literal" reading of Genesis than the Church Fathers, especially when it came to interpreting the longevity of the patriarchs (in this respect the Desert Fathers were wise to avoid excessive speculation on the nature of prelapsarian

Adam).[236] Even though both acknowledged that creation had been thrown into disorder on account of Adam's sin, in Bacon's interpretation humanity had more to lose when it came to the length of life. In addition, the rise of evolutionary theory complicates matters further, not only by posing interpretive challenges for the creation accounts (which are by no means insurmountable), but also by making it much more difficult to determine precisely *how* nature has been affected by the fall. Indeed, it is challenging enough to specify the givens of nature, though, since nature is also God's creation, such givens exist. But if, as suggested in chapter 3, Bacon's account of attenuating aging might be repaired by a more christological account of embodiment, a christological approach will also address the thorny issues of both grounding and articulating some useful norms of human existence. By giving more attention to the relationship of body and soul as revealed in Jesus Christ, we will be in a position to offer a theological critique of contemporary attempts to biomedically slow aging. Moreover, it will help us glean more fruitful insights into the behaviors and practices that flow from a disordered body and soul. Here we will be aided by the work of Karl Barth, who identifies the perfectly ordered body and soul in the *last* Adam, Jesus Christ. Taken together, the Athanasian and Barthian accounts of the incarnation will provide the theological material from which to evaluate contemporary attempts to attenuate aging.

---

236. "Literal" is deliberately placed in scare quotes to indicate how difficult this term is to define.

Chapter 5

The Last Adam and Slowing Aging

> We have sinned and grown old,
> and our Father is younger than we.
>
> —G. K. Chesterton

> Who of you by worrying can add a single hour to your life?
>
> —Luke 12:25 (NIV)

In the last chapter we considered Athanasius's anthropology, with particular reference to bodily incorruptibility and other psychophysiological enhancements attainable through ascetic practices. We saw that the primary goal of such discipline was a proper reordering of one's body and soul, which also enabled one to effectively "remake" one's body by slowing it down. Athanasius in particular offered a more theologically robust account of the body in relation to the soul, an account that might qualify Bacon's program of regaining Eden through science. We also noted however that both accounts of a return to Eden would benefit from a christological treatment to address the limitations in appealing to prelapsarian Adam. If Bacon's program can be repaired or supplemented by Athanasius's account of the body, especially concerning the relationship between the body and soul, Karl Barth's analysis of the real man Jesus will be useful in situating the body-soul relationship on more solid christological footing. After examining Barth's Christology as it relates to embodiment and longevity, we will finally be in a position to consider contemporary attempts to slow aging as part of the modern biomedical project—particularly through pharmacogenetics—which recognizes the validity of Bacon's project while also qualifying it with concerns raised by Barth's Christology. Indeed, Barth's insights regarding the real man Jesus, the second Adam, will enable us to offer a more *Christian* account of life extension by slowing aging.[1]

Barth's christological account of the human person proves instructive in relation to life extension for several reasons. First, Barth's understanding of the human being is thoroughly infused with a profound recognition of both human finitude and death. Fergus Kerr has rightly noted that "no theologian has written about the finite conditions of human existence more often or at greater length than Karl Barth."[2] Barth acknowledged his own struggle with mortality, that he would one day be buried and reduced to "a superfluous and disturbing [thing] in the land of the living."[3] Yet, Barth was also acutely aware of a proper and appropriate desire for long life in the face of such limitedness, conceding that life indeed is merely a "fragment" crying out for continuation.[4] Second, while Barth's reflections on human limitedness contain an existential component, he insisted that all attempts to make sense of death and finitude be firmly grounded in Jesus Christ as the clearest manifestation of God and God's purposes for the human creature. Indeed, he was sharply critical of any anthropology rooted in the subjectivities of human experience *in abstracto*.[5] Rather, our existence must be explained and examined in light of Jesus' existence. "The ontological determination of humanity is grounded in the fact that one man among all others is the man Jesus... Theological anthropology has no other choice in this matter."[6] Jesus is the "Archimedean point" from which true knowledge of humanity might be established;[7] any other vantage point can at best produce "the phenomena of the human."[8] Certainly, this is not a straightforward task, for there

---

1. Christology is so central in Barth's theology that he refers to Jesus as the *first* Adam and the created Adam as the *second* Adam. See Barth, CD 4/1:512–13.

2. Kerr, *Immortal Longings*, 23.

3. Barth, *Dogmatics in Outline*, 117–18. See also Barth, CD 3/4:589.

4. Barth, CD 1/2:589.

5. Barth, CD 1/1:195–98.

6. Barth, CD 3/2:132.

7. Barth, CD 1/2:117.

8. Barth, CD 3/2:136. More strongly, Barth contends that any theological anthropology not originating in a christological starting point is *"ipso facto* non-human." CD 3/2:226.

remains an indissoluble ontological difference between Jesus and ourselves, meaning that there can be no direct or formulaic moves from Christology to anthropology but only inferential ones.[9] Third, Barth's christological anthropology rejects the Cartesian dualism that underwrites so many of the practices of modern medicine.[10] He entertains no notions of the human as a composition of a mutually independent *res cogitans* and *res extensa*, but rather speaks of a particular order of soul and body whose determinative relationship is found in the real man Jesus, an order in unity that is instructive for our own limitedness. Finally, Barth writes at length regarding the tension between the appropriateness of our "allotted time" on the one hand, based on the humanity of the real man Jesus who lived in his own "restricted time" and whose resurrection revealed him as the "Lord of Time," and the legitimate desire for more life on the other, which nicely frames the deep ambiguities inherent in slowing aging.[11]

It might appear that Jesus' humanity, which serves as the foundation for our "allotted time," runs contrary to the appropriateness of our limited time, and therefore forecloses any attempt to slow aging. While, as we will see, Barth is sharply critical of an abstract desire for more life—life apart from our recognition of our divinely determined existence for fellowship with God and our fellow creatures—*this* determination of our existence poses the strongest possible theological argument for longer life, an argument that should not be dismissed too quickly. Listening to Barth here will prove useful in framing subsequent christologically informed discussions on the relationship between one's body and soul as it relates to slowing aging, building on the insights of the Desert Fathers as discussed in the last chapter.

For Barth, to be human is to be "determined by God for life with God."[12] Barth's theological anthropology rests precisely on the fact that God has determined and created humans to be God's covenant partner, to whom we owe a response of obedience, thanks, and praise. Even in our distinction from God as purely human creatures, we cannot be human without being directed to the fulfillment of our determination as being ordained as God's covenant-partner by the grace of God. Indeed, to be God's covenant-partner is to *be* human.

---

9. Barth, *CD* 3/2:54, 71, 222, 512. See Cortez, *Christological Anthropology*, 148.

10. Kerr, "Cartesianism According to Karl Barth"; Cushman, "Barth's Attack upon Cartesianism."

11. Barth, *CD* 3/2:437–511. Indeed, any meaningful consideration of our own human nature requires that "we keep to the determination of man revealed in Him when we accept man's craving for life as such." Barth, *CD* 3/2:571.

12. Barth, *CD* 3/2:203, 204.

> Even in his distinction from God, even in his pure humanity, or, as we might say, in his human nature, man cannot be man without being directed to and prepared for the fulfillment of his determination, his being in the grace of God . . . Consciously or unconsciously, he is the sign here below of what he really is as seen from above, from God.[13]

As Gerald McKenny observes, "our creaturely nature is unintelligible, in its very creatureliness, apart from its ordination to fellowship with God."[14] Human nature then has no normative significance of its own, but only when seen in the context of God's covenant of grace, in its divine determination for fellowship with God.

But this determination presents us with a problem, says Barth, as our finite creaturely nature appears to contradict this divine determination. Does not being a covenant-partner of the eternal God require an unbounded life in order to realize the growth and development required of this divinely ordained task? This is no idle question, says Barth. It is far from self-evident "that human life requires for its development, and therefore acquires and has, only this limited space."[15] To put the matter more strongly, Barth asks whether our divine determination as covenant-partners with God and our relationships with our fellow humans don't actually *demand* that life endures. To be clear, the demand for unbounded life of which Barth speaks does not stem from an "abstract desire for life" where our preferences inevitably exceed the time needed to pursue them. He readily dismisses such "abstract" longings by pointing out that "man has no right to an extension of life, no claim to more than an allotted span, merely for the sake of continuing in life."[16] To crave this is to cry for the moon; it is the craving of sinful man apart from his determination as God's covenant-partner.[17] No, the real problem is that our divine determination itself as God's covenant-partner appears to *require* life's duration rather than its limit. "What but an unlimited, permanent duration can be adequate for the fulfillment of this determination?" asks Barth.[18] Once again, life under the Word of God demands

---

13. Barth, *CD* 3/2:207. Indeed, our humanity simply "cannot, therefore, be alien and opposed to this determination." Barth, *CD* 3/2:206.

14. McKenny, "Biotechnology," 31.

15. Barth, *CD* 3/2:555. The "demand for duration," observes Barth, is "neither mistaken nor presumptuous."

16. Barth, *CD* 3/2:556.

17. Barth, *CD* 3/2:556.

18. Barth, *CD* 3/2:556–57.

duration for the fulfillment of our relationships with God and others, both vertically and horizontally.

> Is not God's Word—both as a summons to God Himself and a direction to fellow-men—the real reason why human life must regard itself as an unfathomable and inexhaustible reality? Does not God's Word provide the real reason why duration must be demanded, why there never seems to be enough time, why the allotment of a particular span is a problem? . . . How can it ever be adequately either life for God according to its promise, or life with its fellows according to its gifts and tasks? In both these directions it may and will and must endure. It has an urge for perfection; it is impatient with all limitations; it storms all barriers . . . Man as he really is, man under God and with his fellow men, cannot accept the fact that once he was not under and therefore for God, and with and therefore for his fellows, and that one day he will be so no longer.[19]

We cannot accept the fact that "the path to perfection is cut off."[20] It is because man has a life with God, says Barth, that we cannot abandon the demand that we ought to burst the limits of our temporality. In short, our life as a "gift and task from the eternal God is the cause of the discontent."[21]

Barth thus takes up desire for longer life with the utmost seriousness from the perspective of God's gracious covenant with his creatures—a covenant that is not merely applied to human beings *ad extra*, but actually establishes and indeed constitutes the human creature *as* human. And yet, in spite of the strong case he has just made against it, Barth insists that our natural, bounded life-span *is* a sign of our divine determination. Once again, Barth asserts that in the real man Jesus we learn that our creaturely determination with its boundaries is the sign of our divine determination for fellowship with God; our bearings for understanding what it means to be creatures in time must come from "the man Jesus in His time."[22] Our allotted span is based on the Word incarnate, on Jesus' own humanity as the *imago Dei* (Col 1:15), the very "repetition and reflection of God Himself."[23] If our earthly lives are determined by the gift of God's life in and through the real man Jesus, then it is proper for our lives to be bounded by a beginning and an end. "The existence of the man Jesus in time is our assurance that

19. Barth, *CD* 3/2:557.
20. Barth, *CD* 3/2:558.
21. Barth, *CD* 3/2:559.
22. Barth, *CD* 3/2:439. See also Barth, *CD* 3/2:207.
23. Barth, *CD* 3/2, 219.

time as the form of human existence is willed and created by God and given to man, and is therefore real."[24] But this Jesus has also been revealed as Lord of Time. By raising Jesus from the dead, God has freed Jesus from the limits of temporality as demonstrated in Easter Time. The very time God has assumed in Jesus is now given as a gift to human creatures.[25] Because the time every human being has, has been determined by the time God has taken on in Jesus Christ and given to humans, it is real time, but it is also allotted time, as affirmed by the embodied limitedness of the real man Jesus. Moreover, Jesus' embodied limitedness in time was necessary for Jesus to die on the cross—"infinitude and immortality would have disqualified Jesus from this."[26] But Jesus' finitude, notes Barth, also means that human mortality is proper to our existence, and should not be regarded as "intrinsically evil."

> [Given] the determination of His [Jesus'] true and natural being as man, how can we maintain that all this has nothing to do with the nature of man as created good by God? And if his dying—in virtue of what it was as His—is the sum total of the good which God has shown to the world, how can we dare to understand man's mortality as something intrinsically negative and evil?[27]

Rather, we are to welcome our allotment "with gratitude and joy."[28] We cling to Jesus Christ as our only full and perfect hope, for God is our beyond.[29] Moreover, this is significant for Christian ethics, for our limited span gives us an urgency that would otherwise be lacking were we to merely "set our hopes on deliverance from the limitation of our time, and therefore beyond, instead of on the eternal God Himself."[30] Thus, "We are right to ask for duration and perfection in our life; and to exist in this request. . . . [but] wrong if we were to conclude that we ourselves can and must achieve this duration and perfection by a power immanent in our life as such."[31]

Barth's christological account of the human creature as both finite and yet destined to everlasting fellowship with God does not appear to provide

---

24. Barth, *CD* 3/2:552.

25. Barth, *CD* 3/2:455. "It is the Lord of Time who became temporal and had time . . . It is the time which He took to Himself, thus granting it as a gift to the men of all time. It is the time which He willed to have for us in order to inaugurate and establish His covenant."

26. Barth, *CD* 3/2:630. "But He had to be able to die."

27. Barth, *CD* 3/2:630.

28. Barth, *CD* 3/2:555.

29. Barth, *CD* 3/2:632.

30. Barth, *CD* 3/2:633.

31. Barth, *CD* 3/2:566.

any definitive answer regarding the length of human life. In fact, the tension between these two divine determinations for the human creature—for unlimited duration of fellowship with God as God's co-partners in the covenant on the one hand and yet a finite allotment of time on the other—would seem to allow for the use of technology to extend human life in all but the most extreme instances, such as the pursuit of immortality itself.[32] As Gerald McKenny observes, Barth may be silent on aging-attenuation technologies so long as the human creature does not aim at immortality itself. "Not only does Barth have no direct objection to such proposals; his conception of the normative significance of human nature seems to have nothing at all to say about them, unless it is simply to issue a warning not to cross the line into actual immortality and thus eliminate one boundary of our lives."[33] Though Barth does briefly speculate that an unbounded life would lose its shape by being perpetually *in via*, and therefore vitiate our responsibility for "the perfection which fellowship with God demands," it hardly seems to follow that an extra ten years—or ten decades—would require rejecting either aspect of God's divine determination for human life as revealed by the real man Jesus.[34] Might then technology be employed to slow aging and thereby significantly extend one's life-span in order to pursue the perfection demanded of us as co-partners in God's gracious covenant? Once again, it seems that this remains a possibility.

Though it might appear as if Barth has little to say on the matter of aging-attenuating technologies, there may be other, indirect approaches. In light of the normativity of our limited span, grounded in the humanity of the real man Jesus, McKenny asks whether our involvement in such technologies can acknowledge the divine determination of our limitedness as co-partners with God's gracious covenant. "As we deliberate over these technologies, do the reasons that support them express the meaning and value of the biological life span as a natural sign of divine grace?"[35] This is not an easy question to answer. As McKenny acknowledges, it may be difficult to discern whether engaging in technologies to lengthen our span *obscures* the sign of our nature as bounded by God by "relentlessly pushing it in the direction of a life without such boundaries," or whether such technologies

---

32. See for instance Kurzweil and Grossman, *Nine Steps to Living Well Forever*; Kurzweil, *Age of Spiritual Machines*.

33. McKenny, "Biotechnology," 35.

34. McKenny, "Biotechnology," 33. See Barth, CD 3/2:561–62. "Even if it were in unlimited time, this could only mean the possibility of a constant reaching out to this perfection."

35. McKenny, "Biotechnology," 35.

might *illuminate* "the abundance of the covenant relationships which . . . prohibits us from simply resigning to our allotted span of time."[36]

Though there seems to be no definitive Christian response to the use of aging-attenuating technology, Barth's christologically determined anthropology acknowledges both a proper desire for continued existence while also insisting on the goodness of our allotted span. As we have just seen, however, this theological anthropology is not determinative one way or the other when it comes to attenuating aging. But there are still other perspectives to consider, perspectives that acknowledge the nature of embodiment that are no less christologically determined, perspectives that take the relationship between our souls and bodies into account. Indeed, if to be the soul of our body is another way of speaking of human finitude, of being in time, then Barth's account of the body-soul relationship as revealed in the real man Jesus may have something to say concerning both asceticism and longevity.[37] Instead of asking whether engaging in technologies to lengthen our span obscures the sign of our nature as bounded by God or illuminates the covenant relationship which prohibits simple resignation to our allotted span—itself a helpful, though difficult question—we may ask what, if anything, is at stake with respect to the body-soul relationship as revealed in the real man Jesus. This entails building on the anthropological insights of Athanasius and the Desert Fathers. As with his discussion on human finitude, Barth's insights on the real man Jesus, whose life is determinative for relating a Spirit-sustained soul and body in their proper order will help frame the discussion, though we may be left with still more questions that defy definitive answers.

BARTH ON ASCETICISM AND THE DYS-INTEGRATION[38] OF BODY AND SOUL

Unlike Athanasius, Barth locates the proper ordering of one's soul and body not in the primeval, prehistorical Adam, but in Jesus Christ. Barth's

---

36. McKenny, "Biotechnology," 35. McKenny also suggests that Barth could have put forth a consequentialist argument that the use of life-extending technology might undermine if not eliminate *our awareness* of our lives as bounded by God's grace, thereby tempting us to think of our lives as unbounded and making us "infinitely responsible" for the perfection demanded by our covenant determination, though McKenny finds this unconvincing given the inevitable difficulties in predicting the effects of technology on our attitudes and dispositions.

37. Barth, *CD* 3/2:521.

38. The Greek prefix "dys" is meant to draw attention to its meaning as commonly employed within medicine as "impaired," "difficult," "nonfunctional," "defective," or "disordered," meanings that the Latinized "dis" may not convey quite as forcefully, due perhaps to

discussion of the disorder of body and soul parallels Athanasius's and Antony's thought, while helpfully considering the implications of our desire for longer life. Here we consider the proper order and relationship between body and soul as found in the real man Jesus, which will serve as the basis and standard against which any disorder or dys-integration gains its intelligibility. To this end it will be instructive to point out that while Barth freely employs the biblical language of body and soul, he is not interested in providing a detailed account of the mind/body relationship, even though his work here concerns human ontology. While it may be tempting to interpret the biblical terminology of "body"—and especially "soul"—along Platonic or Aristotelian lines, "soul" for Barth primarily denotes the subjective life of the human creature, who is no less a material organism.[39] To have a soul is to have life; the soul is "the life of a particular subject."[40] This does not mean that Barth is uninterested in the mind/body problem. At times he stresses that the human being should be considered a "concrete monism," which might be read as a physicalist or materialist account of humanity, while at other times he affirms "the concrete and Christian dualism of soul and body." In fact, these two assertions occur on successive pages.[41] Nevertheless, Barth is critical of both materialism and substance dualism—particularly the latter—insofar as it undermines holistic unity of body and soul and thus diminishes the significance of embodiment as essential to being human. Once again however, these criticisms stem from our understanding of humanity as revealed in the real man Jesus as attested in Scripture.

The Body-Soul Relationship in the Real Man Jesus

For Barth, theological anthropology is primarily christological anthropology:

> In our exposition of the doctrine of man we must always look in the first instance at the nature of the man as it confronts us in the person of Jesus and only secondarily—asking and answering from this place of light—at the nature of man as that of every man and all other men.[42]

---

the profusion of English words that begin with "dis." In addition, "disintegration" might be confused with decomposition where orderliness is lost altogether, which would certainly not be correct as Barth speaks of the relationship between one's body and soul.

39. Barth, *CD* 3/2:364. See Cortez, *Christological Anthropology*, 151.
40. Barth, *CD* 3/2:374.
41. Barth, *CD* 3/2:393 and 394 respectively.
42. Barth, *CD* 3/2:46. For an earlier, similar formulation, see Barth, *Ethics*, 461.

Any attempt to understand humanity that begins with observable human phenomena apart from Jesus Christ leads to a confused and vicious circle of understanding, giving rise to a phantom man.[43] Wary of the reductionist anthropology of scientific materialism on the one hand and the uncritical appropriation of Greek dualism throughout the history of Christianity on the other, Barth put forward a "dynamic anthropology" or a "dialectical-dialogical" anthropology with respect to the body and soul.[44] To understand the relationship between body and soul, we must look to the one true man, Jesus, "the ontological determination of humanity."[45] As the one whole man, "embodied soul and besouled body," Jesus is the One by whom we judge what it means to have a soul and a body.[46] Moreover, unlike Antony and the rest of fallen humanity, there is no war or "ascetic conflict" between the body and the soul; the Spirit of God resting on *this* whole man, notes Barth, renders asceticism "superfluous."[47] In Jesus there is no opposition between the body and the soul; in Jesus this meeting of the "willing spirit" and "weak flesh" (Matt 26:41) operates in favor of the Spirit. Jesus "does not permit His body to become the enemy and conqueror of His soul; nor does it consist in the soul masquerading as the enemy or conqueror of the body." On the contrary, "we are confronted by the picture of peace between these two moments of human existence."[48]

Barth was at pains to point out that there could be no discussion of Jesus' body without speaking of his soul, and vice versa. Yet, in this order of peace there is a first and a second.

> Jesus spoke and acted and suffered in obedience and omnipotence in and not without His body, so that He was also wholly

---

43. Barth, *CD* 3/2:76. See also Barth, *CD* 3/2, 75. "No definition of human nature can meet our present need if it is merely an assertion and description of immediately accessible and knowable characteristics of the nature which man thinks he can regard as that of his fellows and therefore of man in general." It is not that Barth is opposed to what the social and hard sciences have to say about humanity, but that such findings must be critiqued from a christological vantage point which by nature involves faith assumptions. See McLean, *Humanity in the Thought of Karl Barth*, 28–29.

44. Price, *Karl Barth's Anthropology*, 9, 20–22, especially 234–44. However, Price notes that this term primarily applies to Barth's understanding of the *imago Dei* in view of the relational aspect of the Trinity.

45. Barth, *CD* 3/2:132.

46. Barth, *CD* 3/2: 327 [*KD* 3/2:394]. Barth derives this from Galatians 1:4; 2:20 where Paul asserts that Jesus gave himself for our sins, giving up both his soul (*psychē*) for us (Matt 20:28; John 10:11, 15; 1 John 3:16) and his body (*sōma*) (Luke 22:19; Heb 10:10). See *CD* 3/2, 328–31.

47. Barth, *CD* 3/2:338, also 336.

48. Barth, *CD* 3/2:338.

this body. Yet His action and passion are first, *a parte potiori*, those of His soul, and in that way and on that basis of His body. His body is used and governed by Him for the purpose of a specific and conscious speech and action and suffering. It serves Him in the execution of His purpose. It is impregnated with soul, i.e., a body filled with this consciousness; but we obviously cannot say that his soul is impregnated with body, i.e., a soul filled by the needs and desires of His bodily life. This is the distinction and inequality to be noted within the oneness and the wholeness. The fulfilment, the willing and the execution and therefore the true movement of his body occurs from above downwards, from the soul to body and not *vice versa*.[49]

This Jesus *is* God in the flesh. Jesus Christ is not God *in* man, but God *as* man, a man whose body was a medium of expression in service of his soul, or subjectivity. For Barth, any theological discussion of humanity begins with the biblical picture of this man.[50]

Humanity in Light of the Real Man Jesus

In light of Jesus' nature as attested in Scripture, the human person is likewise the soul of her organic, living body (*Leib*); the soul enlivens a material body or corpse (*Körper*), making it an organic body (*Leib*). "The organic body [*Leib*] is distinguished from the purely material body [*Körper*] by the fact that . . . it is besouled and filled and controlled by independent life."[51] Apart from this ensouling, the person would be "subjectless." Similarly, the soul is not a soul unless it has an organic body. At the same time however, Barth asserts that a human being cannot be herself without also being her body—"I cannot be myself without at the same time being my body."[52] Barth refers to this understanding of the human as "concrete reality" or "concrete monism" in an attempt to move beyond the Cartesian categories of substance. Rather, he considers the soul and body "as two moments of the indivisibly one human nature, the soul as that which quickens and the body as that which is quickened and lives."[53] Moreover, this ordering of soul and body is sustained by the Spirit of God, which grounds, constitutes, and maintains the human

---

49. Barth, *CD* 3/2:339.
50. Barth, *CD* 3/2:344.
51. Barth, *CD* 3/2:378; Krötke, "Humanity of the Human Person," 170.
52. Krötke, "Humanity of the Human Person," 170, observes that this sentence is missing in the English translation of Barth, *CD* 3/2.
53. Barth, *CD* 3/2:393, 399, 417.

creature as the soul of his body.[54] Barth concedes that speaking in terms of body and soul is still dualist in a sense, yet, so long as one holds to the premise that "man is as he has Spirit," one has what he calls a "Christian dualism of soul and body."[55] In light of the Spirit's sustaining power, Jesus' soul has preeminence over his body. This is so, says Barth, because the Spirit has a special and direct relationship to the soul and only an indirect relationship to the body. Thus, while "the soul is *a priori* the element in which the turning of God to man and the fellowship of man with God in some way take place," says Barth, "the same is to be said of the body, but only *a posteriori*."[56] Therefore, the body and soul have operations that, while not operating in exclusivity to each other, nevertheless have their proper order. Though the human person is a concrete monism, embodied soul and besouled body, there are basic operations that find their primacy in either the soul or the body, but never in exclusion of the other. Barth also describes the human creature as both a percipient and active being. As percipient beings, humans exercise both thought and awareness. Though thought is related to the soul and awareness to the body, these functions cannot be distributed exclusively to the soul or the body. Rather, the man "as soul of his *body* is empowered for awareness, and as *soul* of his body for thought."[57] Nevertheless, when considering man's act in totality, the soul is primary in both awareness and thinking.[58]

Similarly, Barth asserts that as active beings humans both desire and will. While desiring and willing can only be separated conceptually, "there is indeed a special relation of desiring to the bodily nature of man, and of willing to the soul."[59] Thus, while desire is an intrinsically bodily process that arouses likes or dislikes, "it is I who decide and determine my relation to my desiring."[60] To will is simply to make up one's mind. Therefore, as with

---

54. Barth, *CD* 3/2:393. Any abstract conception of the human without reference to the sustaining power of the Spirit can only result in the "puzzling duality" between the mortal body and the immortal soul. "So long as soul and body are spoken of as two independent and distinct substances, no real insight is possible," says Barth. *CD* 3/2, 292–93. See Anderson, "On Being Human," 186, who has identified "contingent monism" as a more appropriate term to describe both the unity of body and soul and the work of the Spirit in sustaining this unity.

55. Barth, *CD* 3/2:394.

56. Barth, *CD* 3/2:365.

57. Barth, *CD* 3/2:400. "[W]e must speak of the primacy of the soul in relation to the two functions of awareness and thinking. The soul—the soul of the body, but still the soul and not the body—is the man himself, the human subject."

58. Barth, *CD* 3/2:405.

59. Barth, *CD* 3/2:408.

60. Barth, *CD* 3/2:409.

awareness and thought, "man desires as the soul of his *body*, and wills as the *soul* of his body," though again the soul is primary in both willing and desiring.[61] Just as there can be no desiring without the soul, so too there can be no willing without the body. Since all of humankind is called and claimed by God in its totality, says Barth, one cannot understand himself in relation to God as primarily soul, or primarily as body, for these are unacceptably dualistic. Rather, the human creature must understand himself before God as a single acting subject.

> If man understands himself in his relation to God as established and ordained by God, in relation to soul and body as the two moments of his being he can in no case understand himself as a dual but only as a single subject, as soul identical with his body and as body identical with his soul.[62]

Once again, Jesus Christ—not the primordial Adam, "the great unknown who is the first parent of the race"—determines the full extent of what it means to be human. Unlike Christ, however, human creatures—as embodied souls and ensouled bodies—who are divinely determined to be God's covenant partners for fellowship with God and our fellow creatures, have incomprehensibly disrupted the proper order of body and soul through the "impossible possibility" of sin, engendering a disorder that Barth describes as *Trägheit*, or sloth. We do not however learn this disorder of body and soul from the first Adam, for Barth is deeply suspicious concerning what might be said of humankind by looking back at primordial Eden. In fact, he betrays his impatience with such reflections by declaring that "the first man was immediately the first sinner."[63] Rather, this judgment of *Trägheit* as the disordering of body and soul can only be made by looking at the last Adam, Jesus Christ.

The Sin of Sloth: *Trägheit*

Unlike Jesus who remains wholly himself as a soul in perfect leadership of his body, the human creature has experienced a disruption in the order

---

61. Barth, *CD* 3/2:416, 418.

62. Barth, *CD* 3/2:426. Barth is also critical of the Greek tendency to privilege the abstract contemplation of being both prior and in exclusion to act, asserting that "man does not exist except in his life-act [*Lebensakt*]." While he notes that the human is at every moment soul and body, there remains a decided order—"always soul first and then body, always ruling soul [*regierende Seele*] and serving body [*dienender Leib*]." Barth, *CD* 3/2:426–427 [*KD* 3/2:512].

63. Barth, *CD* 4/1:508.

between the body and soul.[64] While the soul remains the leader of the body and the acting subject, in our fallen condition we allow the impulses of the body to exercise undue influence on the soul, willing what we should not, even as the body desires what it should not. Barth calls this disorder *Trägheit*, or sloth, and describes it as a sluggishness, indolence, or inertia that results in both evil actions and culpable inactivity.[65] For reasons that will hopefully become clear, we will use the German *Trägheit* for the time being, allowing Barth to fill out its meaning below, as "sloth" is often understood today as mere "laziness," which misses its deeper spiritual elements (elements captured with an equally opaque term, acedia). In our *Trägheit* we neither trust nor love God.[66] In *Trägheit* we reject our own reality as it confronts us in Jesus Christ, refusing to have anything to do with God and the freedom promised us in the man Jesus. Barth claims that this refusal significantly affects many of our relationships—with God, with others, the relation between body and soul, and our relationship to our historical limitation in time.[67] The effect of *Trägheit* on the soul-body relationship also carries implications for our limited life-span. Barth's discussion here will help pave the way for a christologically informed discussion of life extension as part of the modern biomedical project.

Trägheit as Body and Soul Dys-integration

According to Barth, God guarantees the ordered unity of soul and body in his creatures; however, *Trägheit* disturbs and disrupts this unity, resulting in a dualism between the psychical (*geistig-seelischen*) and the physical (*leiblish-natrülichen*) moments of the human person.[68] In considering the human creature as soul of his body, says Barth, this particular form of *Trägheit* takes the form of dissipation and indiscipline (*Disziplinlosigkeit*).[69] Sin in the form of *Trägheit* means that man lets himself fall, lets himself go, lets himself be moved and pushed. By contrast, to live authentically means "to keep oneself disciplined, . . . to be what one is as a man even at the cost

---

64. Barth, *CD* 4/2:452; 460.
65. Barth, *KD* 4/2:452 [*CD* 4/2:403]. "Wir antworten jetzt: des Menschen Sünde ist des Menschen Trägheit."
66. Barth, *CD* 4/2:405.
67. Barth, *CD* 4/2:409. *Trägheit* thus takes the form of (1) stupidity, (2) inhumanity, (3) dissipation, and (4) care or anxiety respectively.
68. Barth, *KD* 4/2:474.
69. Barth, *CD* 4/2:454 [*KD* 4/2:511].

of severity against oneself."[70] However, we are vagabonds who refuse to accept and exercise discipline over ourselves, though we freely impose it on others. By our giving ourselves permissions rather than commands, the unity of the body and the soul suffers disruption and dys-integration. In man's *Trägheit*, says Barth, the body and soul

> begin to go their separate ways. His soul will no longer control his body, nor his body obey his soul. The two not only contradict one another in their mutual relationship, but also, refusing their distinct function in this relationship, contradict their own essence as the two integrated elements of human nature. If the dissipated man wills, as he does, to be without spirit, he has entered on the irresistible way on which he will finally be soulless and bodiless; the way which can lead only to death.[71]

In short, we are lazy creatures who shun and hate discipline. We take pleasure in our dys-integration by either relieving our soul of its role as ruler, guardian, and preserver of our body in pursuit of spiritual or inward life, or by releasing our body from its service to our soul, allowing it to pursue its own impulses and needs. In practice, our lives are marked by a perpetual hovering between these two possibilities, often engaging in both simultaneously, driven by the illusion that releasing the soul from its responsibility to the body or the body's servitude to the soul is the pathway to liberation. In reality however, these choices are nothing but a "twofold Docetism," a choosing of the flesh.[72] The vagabond within wants to throw off any regime that might prevent the body and soul from going their separate ways. "Is not the discipline which prevents these releases a kind of foreign rule which man does not need to accept, which—far from exercising—he can and must repudiate?"[73] This Docetic "two-step" of self-deception tempts us to define true humanity where we are simultaneously liberated from the body and free to gratify and celebrate its impulses. But if *Trägheit* enables the body and soul to "go their separate ways," it also induces a frenetic anxiety, adversely affecting our perception of time.

---

70. Barth, *CD* 4/2:454.
71. Barth, *CD* 4/2:454.
72. Barth, *CD* 4/2:459.
73. Barth, *CD* 4/2:460.

Trägheit and Our Limited Span of Life

Trägheit not only involves a dys-integration and disorder of body and soul, but also impacts our attitude towards our finitude. In short, *Trägheit* means that "our allotted duration of human life will become quite unendurable."[74] This inability to accept our own limited life-span is a "direct consequence of the destruction and disintegration of human nature, of being in the flesh."[75] As such, the dissipated man cannot accept death as the determination of human existence, and is therefore constantly seeking a flight from a unified and whole life, pursuing either an upward (idealistic) or downward (materialistic) path. Following Augustine and Aquinas, Barth observes that our desires know no limits. One way or another, all of our desires aim at infinity; temporary satisfaction only fuels more desire. Whether one pursues the "upward" path or the "downward" path, asserts Barth, "it opens up magic casements with unlimited views which give us the thrill either of solemnity or of an arrogant rejoicing."[76] However, notes Barth, any thrill afforded by these apparent openings in the face of infinity can only be a thrill of horror when set against the backdrop of our own limitedness. As such, the dissipated man seeks solace in an exclamatory *Carpe diem!*, which, in reality, is nothing more than a hollow expression of panic when faced with the closed door that he wishes to remain open indefinitely.[77] Here Barth presciently speaks of the anxiety that drives our frenetic quests for longer life:

> There is no infinite to satisfy our infinite desires. But this is something which the dissipated man, who has broken loose from the unity and totality of soul and body in which God has created him for existence in the limit of his time, cannot grasp, but must endlessly repudiate in his own endless dissatisfaction. In what he takes to be his successful hunt, he is himself the one who is hunted with terrible success by anxiety.[78]

The dissipated man of *Trägheit* whose body and soul are in a state of dys-integration is unable to grasp that in the desperate pursuit of extending his life, he is the one who is haunted and hunted.

Barth defines this last form of *Trägheit* as anxiety or "care" (*Sorge*). Care is the fear of death without God, without hope, and inevitably the source of all evil. Care also "leads no less necessarily to the disorder which we have

74. Barth, *CD* 4/2:462.
75. Barth, *CD* 4/2:462.
76. Barth, *CD* 4/2:463.
77. Barth, *CD* 4/2:463.
78. Barth, *CD* 4/2:463.

called the disintegration of the disciplined unity of man as the soul of his body."[79] In fact, "so strong is the self-contradiction into which the anxious man plunges himself in his discontent with his finitude that it is inevitable that this unity [of body and soul] should be severely jeopardized."[80] In the fear of his impending death, man cannot remain whole, and is unable to rule as a soul or serve as a body. Even though finitude is a reality of created existence as revealed in the real man Jesus, the dissipated man is gripped with fear.[81] Under the influence of *Sorge*, his soul flees to invented regions of his own making while his body reacts to this encroaching death in various forms of self-assertion, renunciation, or sickness, which only results in the further dissolution of his body and soul. According to Barth, we seek to conceal the fact of our own death either by plunging ourselves into unceasing conscientious work, attempting to make ourselves masters in things great and small, or by sinking into a law of relaxation and passivity, adopting a lifestyle that mirrors the "lilies of the field."[82]

It is certainly possible to construe the modern biomedical project of aging attenuation as "unceasing conscientious work," an assertion of the naked will over against the passive, undisciplined, aging body. Nor is it difficult to see aging attenuation as driven by a deep discontentment over one's finitude under the influence of *Sorge*, that combination of desire, anxiety, and apprehension over the gradual physiological decline that serves as a reminder that our lives are indeed limited. Moreover, *Trägheit* as the dys-integration of the body and soul and *Trägheit* as a profound discontent with one's limited life-span (*Sorge*) are mutually reinforcing. Just as the disintegration of body and soul engenders dissatisfaction with our limited span and a fear of death, so too our dissatisfaction with our finitude and fear of death lead to the disintegration of body and soul. Hence, Barth asserts that *Sorge*—"a disruption of the right relationship of man to his temporality"—is both the consequence and the cause of the disorder and disintegration of body and soul.[83] But the reality that *Sorge* suppresses, says Barth, is that Christ lives

---

79. Barth, *CD* 4/2:477 [*KD* 4/2:540]. For a further description of *Sorge*, see Barth *CD* 4/2:468, 477, especially 472.

80. Barth, *CD* 4/2:477.

81. "Rather than tolerating our own limitation with a sigh, we have every reason to take it seriously, to affirm it, to accept it, and to praise God for the fact that in it we are what we are and not something else." Barth, *CD* 3/4:568. John Webster has noted that Barth's ethic concerning our freedom in limitation in *CD* 3/4 is a lengthy argument to demonstrate "that such limitation *specifies* rather than *hems in* the creature." See Webster, *Barth's Moral Theology*, 115.

82. Barth, *CD* 4/2:470.

83. Barth, *CD* 4/2:475.

at the very frontier where our earthly time runs out; our existence in time with bodies subject to physiological decay leading to our inevitable death is set in light of the man Jesus, who because he was mortal in his humanity, affirms our finite existence as part of the good order of God.[84] This fact does not necessarily mean that we abandon all attempts for longer life, as we have seen above. But it does remind Christians that aging attenuation can certainly go wrong when we fail to acknowledge our divine determination as limited creatures with allotted time as revealed in the real man Jesus.

If, as Barth has argued, the proper order of the body-soul relationship for the human creature is one of a disciplined unity (*der disziplinierten Einheit*), a unity undermined by *Trägheit*, which he describes as indiscipline (*Disziplinlosigkeit*), then incorporating spiritual disciplines in the Christian life may offer a means by which the Christian can reorder her soul and body, which in turn places her in a better relationship to her own finitude, or allotted span. Hence, discipline or asceticism, understood as a proper reordering of body and soul, might significantly thwart our tendency towards the sin of *Trägheit*, and hence our desire to live on indefinitely on our own strength. Before considering this argument more closely, however, it will prove useful to investigate Barth's view of discipline or asceticism.

Barth on Discipline and Asceticism

Though Barth describes *Trägheit* as a lack of discipline, he generally viewed ascetic practices with ambivalence and even suspicion, though he seemed unable to dismiss them entirely. Barth readily admits that human life in its psychophysical structure involves "primitive" or "animal" impulses that must be dealt with humanely, such as hunger, the need for sex, and sleep.[85] On the other hand, those who give free rein to their impulses are "sub-animal," notes Barth, for even animals instinctively know when their needs are adequately satiated. Only humans are capable of engaging in "hypertrophies of satisfaction," to which unfettered impulses tend.[86] Echoes of St. Antony may be detected when Barth says that our primitive impulses must be viewed as "the form of a physical process guided and governed by

---

84. Barth, *CD* 4/2:468–69. See also Barth, *CD* 3/2:630–32; *CD* 3/4:592. For Barth's exposition of our limited time as preserved by God and part of his good order, see *CD* 3/3: 61–63, 84–90, 226–38. A helpful summary of the human person in limited time is offered by Krötke, "Humanity of the Human Person," 171–73. See also Webster, *Barth's Moral Theology*, 99–123.

85. Barth, *CD* 3/4:345.

86. Barth, *CD* 3/4:345.

the soul as awakened by the divine *pneuma*, and therefore in the form of freely chosen and executed decisions."[87] At the same time however, Barth concedes that "radical restrictions, renunciations, abstentions and sacrifices" are occasionally required—indeed, "may well be demanded from us by His decrees and commands"—especially when it comes to our impulses.[88] Though Barth views asceticism then in terms of impulse control for the purpose of the "higher necessities" of life, he readily recognizes a social dimension to discipline: asceticism is also for others. He thus defines asceticism (*Askese*) as

> a form of a partial or complete renunciation of the gratification of the needs in question . . . as a means of disciplining the corresponding impulses, perhaps also for the sake of the higher necessities of life, and above all for the sake of one's neighbours.[89]

Barth is quick to point out however that the Bible actually encourages one to eat and drink and live "naturally." After all, eternal life itself is represented as a great feast (Matt 22:10).[90] Moreover, he notes that Paul's command to mortify one's earthly members (Col 3:5)—a text that informed both Athanasius's and Antony's understanding of asceticism—must be understood in the context of Paul's earlier warning against false religious humility involving a harsh treatment of the body that is ineffective in restraining one's sensual appetite (Col 2:23). Aware that "a powerful ascetic can be a vessel of much greater wickedness than even the most indulgent," Barth is wary of both excessive repression and unrestrained liberality, aware the human creature can neither surrender to her impulses nor rid herself of them entirely.[91]

Later in the *Church Dogmatics*, however, Barth's stance becomes decidedly more negative. In the context of the doctrine of reconciliation, Barth considers monasticism as a futile and misguided attempt to achieve what has already been accomplished by the condescension and exaltation of the Son. Barth is critical of both the motives that animate asceticism and especially the institutions to which such practices gave birth, reserving harsher criticism for the latter.[92] Monasticism for Barth was primarily a flight from the

---

87. Barth, *CD* 3/4:345.
88. Barth, *CD* 3/4:346.
89. Barth, *CD* 3/4:346 [*KD* 3/4:393].
90. Barth, *CD* 3/4:347.
91. Barth, *CD* 3/4:348. Indeed, Barth here goes on to point out that we should not easily forget "that one may be a non-smoker, abstainer and vegetarian, and yet be called Adolf Hitler."
92. Barth, *CD* 4/2:11-12, 18. Barth first mentions asceticism in his famous

world and other people, exemplified by that "quite unfounded and radical unrest" of the anchorites who fled to the deserts of Egypt.[93] Indeed, a flight away from the things of the world into the desert need not have anything to do with Christianity: "One thing is for sure—that even in his hut or cave the hermit will never be free from the most dangerous representative of the world, i.e., himself."[94] True enough. But Barth seems to miss that this was *precisely* the point of flight: not to find solace in the barren desert as a means of escape, but to come face to face with the far bleaker landscape of one's own heart. Flight *from* the world involved traveling to a place where one could *not* escape oneself, aware of our propensity to flee from the darker realities that inform our habits, thoughts, and inclinations by immersing ourselves in the frenetic activities of daily life. While Barth is critical of anchoritic monasticism, he somewhat begrudgingly recognized those ascetics who formed into communities—coenobitic monasticism—as having more legitimacy.[95]

Even in the face of these stronger objections however, Barth acknowledges that there might be room for a certain inward retreat from the world that does not require monastic codification, and asks rhetorically whether the church or individuals might not *require* some genuine retreat: "Has there not to be (not merely a healthy but a spiritually necessary) rhythm in this matter, in which there will always be a place for ἀναχωρεῖν [*anachōrein*—ascetic withdrawal]?"[96] When pursuing this question, Barth turns from monasticism as an organized system to asceticism, which he understands here as "exercise or training for the successful attainment of a goal."[97] He acknowledges abstention from particular habits can "serve the liberation of

---

distinction between religion and revelation, assigning asceticism to the former. CD 1/2:308–9. He also draws a distinction between the original exponents and their successors, in favor of the former, as the latter invariably confused and distorted the primary issues.

93. Barth, CD 4/2:12.

94. Barth, CD 4/2:12. Barth also acknowledges that some anchorites may have fled to the desert as a protest against the worldly church, 13–14. Later however Barth considers "monasticism" whereby the Christian seeks to become a witness to the world "by holding as far aloof from it as possible, or at least from its tendencies, habits, and forms of life," an unacceptable extreme. See Barth, *Christian Life*, 197. Immediately following however, in excised typescript, Barth allows that sometimes the Christian may be called to withdraw into some form of monk-like existence in obedience to a special command in a special situation, though he elaborates no further.

95. Barth, CD 4/2:13.

96. Barth, CD 4/2:14.

97. Barth, CD 4/2:14.

man from the downward drag of sin."[98] Indeed, this "negative principle" is the reverse side of the positive principle; namely, that "this liberation itself is to serve the redemptive and exclusively necessary freedom of man for God and his fellows, for the Church and therefore for the world."[99] However, Barth remains wary of the arbitrary nature of such abstentions, noting that it is possible to refrain from certain activities while remaining unchanged in one's character.[100] Abstention from particular desires, and "the mechanical sealing off of these whole spheres," will not provide sufficient relief from our desires, and may not leave us open to the commandment of God.[101]

Though Barth remained skeptical of the various forms of monastic theology, he recognized that Christian perfection and dedication to any worthy aim should by no means be suppressed—even by an appeal to the *sola fides* by which the Christian is justified (and sanctified) in the sight of God. Better to be a monk who unceasingly battles his flesh while remaining active in spiritual and physical labor, the arts and scholarship, social work and teaching, including the monastic *opus Dei*—the adoration of God in private and communal worship. This monk "could and can positively attest something of that freedom for God and his fellows which is supposed to be the *telos* of monastic asceticism."[102] Inevitably, Barth recognizes that Christian life of freedom for God and neighbor must, to some degree, be an ascetic life:

> We have finally to ask whether there can be any Christian existence at all in Christian freedom, in that direction to the goal set for man by the grace of God, whether there can be any worship of God in Spirit and in truth or genuine service to our fellows, whether there can be any fitness for it, without an acceptance of the conflict in these spheres, without definite renunciations and abstentions, and therefore without asceticism [*Askese*]—not perhaps an asceticism in principle and subject to rule, but all the more serious on that account. This certainly seems to be an impossibility in the Gospels and according to the nature of the case, both individually and collectively. Only those who can and will sacrifice can and will serve and are free to do so.[103]

---

98. Barth, *CD* 4/2:14.
99. Barth, *CD* 4/2:14.
100. Barth, *CD* 4/2:15.
101. Barth, *CD* 4/2:15.
102. Barth, *CD* 4/2:16.
103. Barth, *CD* 4/2:16 [*KD* 4/2:15–16].

Once again, Barth's primary concern with systematic or monastic asceticism is that particular practices still leave human beings free for God and neighbor, and that such practices are never construed as means of attaining salvation, perfection, or even sanctification. Rather, the Christian must remember that such practices rest securely on the foundation of God's salvation and sanctification *already* accomplished through Jesus Christ, for *Trägheit* is essentially a denial of our being in Jesus Christ.[104] In our *Trägheit*, or sloth, we "refuse to be those we already are in Him, hesitating to make use of the Spirit in the flesh which we are given in Him."[105] The goal of asceticism is not freedom *from* desires (as if this were possible) in an attempt to gain God's favor, but freedom *for* God and the obedience that such discipleship entails, including freedom *for* one's fellow creatures. Unfortunately, Barth does not speak of asceticism explicitly with respect to the relationship between one's soul and body.[106] Certainly, even with Barth's hesitations, there is little reason to doubt that the Christian life calls for abstentions, renunciations, and hence for some form of asceticism. This has implications, as will be discussed shortly, for the formation of Christian character, including the *Trägheit* and *Sorge*, the sloth and care which hinder our obedience to Christ, engendering anxiety and dissatisfaction with our limited life-span.

In the remainder of this chapter we offer an analysis of life extension by retarding aging in light of the Christian narrative of redemption and transformation as informed by both Barth's conception of sloth and care and Athanasius's theological understanding of ascetic practice. Specifically, we will consider whether current efforts at life extension might be described as the epitome of *Sorge*, driven by fear of death, bodily decay, and dissatisfaction with one's temporal limit, which suggests that the body and soul may be in considerable disorder. Against the background of an ascetic "remaking" of the body as understood by Athanasius and Antony, subsumed as it was under the Christian quest for holiness, the contemporary search for aging retardation though genetic engineering or pharmacogenetics could be described as problematic to the degree it fails to address the sin of *Trägheit* as a phenomenological separation of body and soul. The degree to which this construal is accurate may determine the degree to which we ought to be

---

104. Barth, *CD* 4/2:517–18. See 1 Cor 6: 9–11; Col 1:21–23.

105. Barth, *CD* 4/2:452. On account of this sloth "we fail to recognize and to exist as those who we already are in and by that One."

106. It is also unclear how exactly asceticism (*Askese*) relates to discipline (*Disziplin*), though they are certainly related. Barth tends to reserve the term *asceticism* for speaking of particular abstentions while he understands the exercise of discipline as "simply the obedience that we owe to God." Barth, *CD* 4/2:461.

wary of such projects. Conversely, the fear of death and dissatisfaction with our limited span of life (*Sorge*) might also be mitigated by the "reordering" of the body and soul through the exercise of basic disciplines necessary for a Christian life of holiness before God and our neighbors.

Aging Attenuation as Sloth?

Though Barth understands *Trägheit* as sloth taking the form of *Sorge* or anxiety with respect to our temporal earthly existence, "sloth" seems a curious descriptor of the frenetic efforts underway to slow human aging. As mentioned above, we have retained the German *Trägheit* to avoid common misunderstandings concerning the word *sloth*. We are now ready however to consider "sloth" more closely. Barth observes that our sloth is frequently hidden under a veil of respectable, conscientious work. "When it is translated into conscientious work, who can possibly recognize it as a form of human sloth?"[107] Jean Bethke Elshtain has also identified a somewhat paradoxical element in sloth, noting that "busyness, strangely enough, may constitute its own version of laziness, as acquiescence in cultural forms that promote slackness of purpose as every moment of every day is gobbled up in a frenzy of activity."[108] In the Middle Ages sloth was thought to be the source of restlessness, and was often identified as acedia, one of the seven *vitia capitalia*. Joseph Pieper has noted that sloth (acedia) leaves one unable to rest before God in the "givenness" of one's own being, one's own humanness: it is a despairing refusal to be one's own self.[109] In this way sloth may take the form of frenetic activity or "conscientious work." As we have seen, Barth relates sloth to our finitude. In our sloth "we fret at the inevitable realization that our existence is limited. We would rather things were different. We try to arrest the foot which brings us constantly nearer to this frontier."[110] The conscientious work of which Barth speaks may certainly assume the form of scientific activity, particularly in our attempts to uncover the mechanisms of human aging. Extending the healthy life-span by attenuating aging might indeed be described as the latest attempt to "arrest the foot" that carries us to death by slowing, to some degree, the body's aging process. Attempts to slow human aging, whether through pharmacogenetics or genetic manipulation, could be seen as the epitome of an increasing dissatisfaction with our limited duration (at least in the affluent West), as the bitter fruit of *Trägheit*.

107. Barth, *CD* 4/2:473.
108. Elshtain, *Who Are We?*, 82.
109. Pieper, *Leisure*, 43–45. See Kierkegaard, *Sickness unto Death*, 77–104.
110. Barth, *CD* 4/2:468.

Our frenetic search for longevity might very well bear witness to our dissatisfaction with our life-spans that are as long as any time in recorded history. While this century has witnessed tremendous advances in medicine in treating and even curing diseases and disorders that have historically cut life short, this has not proven enough. As we have seen, the longevity that we seek and the ideal of health driving it will not be achieved by defeating disease, but achieving control over aging itself.

The notion that our life-span is inadequate with respect to our aspirations and desires is a common, if not universal sentiment. Christine Overall's assertion that "other things being equal, a longer life is a better one, provided that one is in a minimally good state of health," seems perfectly reasonable; her statement captures a wider dissatisfaction with our limited span, and to some degree informs our attitudes toward embodiment.[111] As one ethicist puts it, "the only concern with health is that the disposition of my body not interfere with my life plan."[112] As Gerald McKenny has observed, the body is construed as the property of one's "person" and hence the instrument of one's desires.[113] Moreover, the more one wishes to accomplish and enjoy, the more death—and our bodies—become the enemy. Our aging and disintegrating bodies remind us that our desires and aspirations will nearly always outstrip the longevity of our bodies, making an enemy of death. When death precludes the accomplishment of our goals, "when *finis* so capriciously frustrates the possibility of achieving *telos*," noted Reinhold Niebuhr, our human existence becomes filled with anxiety.[114]

Death however is not only an enemy because it forecloses future possibilities. In an age of lengthened life-spans (though only marginally so), death is increasingly associated with suffering and decline. The opening story in this book is one of many such stories. Death slowly erodes our autonomy, and ultimately our ability to pursue the things we desire. Carl Elliott depicts our perception of this decline as death's "instruments of torture," alluding to the dualistic assumptions behind such perceptions:

> [W]e have become accustomed to the idea that the tragedy of aging is physical and mental decline: the soul of a young person trapped in a debilitated, traitorous body. Often it is not Death that we fear so much as the instruments of torture that he carries

---

111. Overall, "Longevity, Identity, and Moral Character," 287.
112. Shuman, *Body of Compassion*, 83.
113. McKenny, *To Relieve the Human Condition*, 198.
114. Niebuhr, *Nature and Destiny of Man*, 2:303.

with him: the degeneration and disability, the creaking joints and aching bones, the loss of stamina and sexual attractiveness.[115]

When medical advances afford increasing control over the body, its loss becomes all the more fearful. In the face of this scenario, the concepts of human dignity and autonomy are often employed in the service of a "dignified death" as the final exercise of one's absolute right to define life's very ending. Through aging attenuation it is hoped that we might both greatly compress the period of morbidity before death and extend the healthy human life-span at the same time. There is no doubt that the same developments in medicine that have contributed to a longer, healthier life-span have also led to a longer, protracted period of decline. The price we pay for a longer life is a longer dying. We must then be careful of being overly critical of attempting to slow human aging—especially when the goal is reducing the period of morbidity which precedes it—mindful of the tension created by our divine determination to have fellowship with the eternal God and the gift of life as an allotted span as revealed in the real man Jesus.

We must still ask then whether current attempts to lengthen our allotted span by attenuating aging itself appear to stem from *Sorge*, a fear of dependency, decrepitude, and death as evidenced by our dissatisfaction over the length of life already afforded by scientific and medical advances. In light of our anxieties it appears that that the body and soul have gone their separate ways. Our seemingly insatiable capacity for new experiences asserts itself over against the disintegrating body that proves unable keep up with our desires. That the body is interpreted as the passive recipient of aging attenuating technology—whether pharmacological or genetic—in order to extend our lives may point to a dys-integration of body and soul. Indeed, to return to an earlier discussion, Barth's articulation of *Trägheit* as the phenomenological separation of body and soul may to some degree implicate the birth of modern science as a project of care or *Sorge*, an anxiety over one's finitude.

TRÄGHEIT AND THE BIRTH OF MODERN SCIENCE

Earlier we focused primarily on the work of Francis Bacon and what has become widely known as the "Baconian Project." But René Descartes (1596–1650) also played a considerable role in the development of modern science by interpreting the human being as a body (*res extensa*) and mind (*res cogitans*) that are separable, having no necessary connection. Drew

---

115. Elliott, *Better Than Well*, 276.

Leder has intriguingly argued that this separation was as much existential as it was epistemological, motivated in large part by a fear of death and decay. According to Leder, "The *Meditations* is a text inaugurated not only by a confrontation with error but with death."[116] He detects a two-pronged approach in Descartes's defense against his fear of death by which the body and soul were separated—one theological and one scientific. On the one hand, Descartes hoped to establish the existence of God and "that the human soul does not perish with the human body."[117] On the other hand, he hoped that by increasing our knowledge "we could avoid many infirmities, both of mind and body, and perhaps even the decline of old age."[118] According to Leder, Descartes's likening the body to a corpse (*Körper*) with no substantive relation with the immortal soul was a therapeutic response to the twofold threat of sickness and death:

> In proving that the body is a mechanical, mathematical entity, free of all soul attributes, he lays the groundwork for modern scientific medicine. In this way he hopes to discover the ways to indefinitely prolong embodied life. But such a life cannot go on forever. Hence, the necessity of proving the immaterial nature of the rational soul, and thereby its immortality. Body and soul, science and theology. Descartes's schema serves to combat death on all fronts.[119]

Descartes's biographical material reveals his life-long concern with death. Distress over his own aging body spoke to the encroaching reality of death, adding to the urgency of slowing down the aging process. "The fact that my hair is turning gray," noted Descartes in a letter, "warns me that I should spend all my time trying to set back the process."[120] In this same letter he revealed that he had already been at work on this for some time and hoping for success, despite insufficient experimentation. Later correspondence reveals Descartes's increasing desperation in hopes of prolonging his life by slowing aging, but having made no progress. A letter to the Dutch poet and composer Constantijn Huygens (1596–1687) underscores Descartes's anxiety born of a scientific hope for longer life:

---

116. Leder, *Absent Body*, 139.

117. Descartes, *Meditations on First Philosophy*, in *Philosophical Works*, 1:134.

118. Descartes, *Discourse on Method*, 44.

119. Leder, *Absent Body*, 140–41. See Descartes, *Meditations on First Philosophy*, in *Philosophical Works* 1:151. More recently the role of the corpse in medicine has been eloquently articulated by Jeffrey Bishop, *Anticipatory Corpse*.

120. Vrooman, *René Descartes*, 141.

> I have never taken such pains to protect my health as now, and whereas I used to think that death might rob me of thirty or forty years at most, it could not now surprise me unless it threatened my hope of living more than a hundred years.[121]

Leder convincingly shows that the primary motivation for Descartes's metaphysical and scientific investigations was the threat of sickness and his own demise.

But Leder's analysis also demonstrates that the methodological foundation upon which much of science rests is the fear of death, decline, and decay. Whatever might be said of Descartes's arguments for the immortality of the soul, the evaporation of this belief only adds urgency to the scientific quest to extend life. Indeed, science is the only option left on the table. Moreover, Leder's analysis suggests that the treatment for such fears can be carried out on the largely passive body without raising too many substantive moral questions. With the mapping of the human genome and the rapid development of new tools like CRISPR to manipulate genes with breathtaking precision, the casement has swung open, revealing attractive vistas of extended youth and death delayed. Barth might very well have attributed Descartes's project to *Sorge*, where "man makes his future his own problem."[122] Aging attenuation represents the latest "turn to the body" in an effort to combat the *Sorge* stemming from—and contributing to—the dys-integration and disorder of body and soul. The body, both methodologically and phenomenologically, is increasingly distanced from the soul. This is especially evident in contemporary antiaging research, where *Trägheit* is concealed under a flurry of care, or, in Barth's words, in "conscientious work."

THE AGING BODY IN MODERN BIOMEDICAL PROJECT

As Leder has argued, the contemporary biomedical view of the body as a corpse (*Körper*) in contrast to the lived body (*Leib*), stems in part from Descartes's attempt to separate the body and soul, a separation motivated by his fear of death and bodily disintegration. Gerald McKenny has also implicated Descartes as a key figure in initiating a process that brings mortality and disease "under the mastery of the seeing eye and the intervening hand," while also "distancing the essential person, the soul, from the body that, despite the power of medicine, is destined to decay."[123] As we have already

---

121. Vrooman, *René Descartes*, 142.
122. Barth, *CD* 4/2:476 [*KD* 4/2:538].
123. McKenny, *To Relieve the Human Condition*, 192.

seen, the search to uncover the mysteries of aging may be fittingly described as the latest form of the Baconian Project—the mitigation of disease and even death itself—inspiring awe and increasing both the fear of death and our dissatisfaction with the limits imposed from within by our degenerating bodies. But McKenny also claims that the Baconian Project not only *replaces* attitudes and practices that recognize the moral significance of the body with respect to health, susceptibility to aging, and disease, but "*is itself* a set of attitudes and practices regarding the body, and one that is pervasive in our self-formation."[124] In the first chapter we argued that contemporary scientific approaches to aging attenuation are increasingly inclined to identify aging itself as a disease, under which the body is viewed as little more than a problem or as an adversary, a stance that in many respects contrasts older hygienic methods that tended to view the body as one's ally. The body is largely described in reductionist terms—whether at the organ, cellular, or genetic level—as if the body were a functioning corpse.

Recall Dr. Kirkwood's striking description of the human body as disposable. In chapter one we observed that this assessment derives from the vantage point of our own germ cells which, unlike somatic cells, possess replicative immortality. Thus, Kirkwood recapitulates a new dualism of sorts, but one rooted firmly in the material order. As germ cells propagate, giving rise to human bodies, our very bodies eventually become disposable, and somewhat incidental to the process; they serve as "transport vehicles" for the propagation of the essential germ cells. Kirkwood candidly acknowledges that the name of his theory was prompted by comparing the human body "with disposable products like coats, cars, and washing machines."[125] In its own way Kirkwood's account of the body remains strikingly Cartesian. While there may be nothing objectionable to Kirkwood's hypothesis insofar as evolutionary biology is concerned, such accounts easily cross over into metaphysical explanations—often with little awareness that a boundary has been crossed. For instance, Robert Arking, professor of biology, reflects on the metaphysical implications of Kirkwood's "disposable soma" theory for aging under the guise of a biological explanation:

> And so we age, not because of some philosophically satisfying cosmic reason that requires our senescence and death, but simply because the body's energy allocations are such that our failure to repair ensures that there is no reason not to age. This biological conclusion may seem dark and despondent to some.

---

124. McKenny, *To Relieve the Human Condition*, 219, emphasis mine.
125. Kirkwood, *Time of Our Lives*, 68.

Who, after all, wants to believe that his or her death serves no larger purpose at all?[126]

Even a purportedly biological explanation of aging as "our failure to repair" has implications for our understanding of embodiment, as the term *failure* is readily conscripted into a scientific project. After all, failure is the stepping stone to (scientific) success. Moreover, such thin, ostensibly antimetaphysical accounts of the body inevitably carry moral implications.

When scientific accounts of the body are presented as the comprehensive story on embodiment loosed from the restrictions of broader teleological explanations, the transition from "disposable body" to the "body at our disposal" appears almost seamless. In failing to give an adequate account of what the body is *for*, the body becomes another object for which we have devised a use.[127] Within this framework, "our world, including our bodies, is now plastic, to be shaped in our image." In this respect, notes Peter Scott, "some of us, at least, are *sicut deus*."[128] Indeed, apart from the incarnation, *theōsis* can only take the form of *sicut deus*. Nevertheless, as McKenny notes, genetic advances tempt us to treat the body as increasingly subservient to the unencumbered "naked will."

> Because of the triumph of the Cartesian view, most of us view the body as a biological substratum whose characteristics are best described in physical and biochemical terms. Fixed with regard to the naked will that stands over against it, the body is nevertheless alterable by technology, which promises to bring the body under the dominion of the will.[129]

Given the common assumption in contemporary ethical discourse that acknowledges that life is good and assumes that a longer life is better, it appears perfectly reasonable to ask how one might alter one's body to fit this desire. Theologically speaking, there is little to quibble over here, since life is God's good gift to humanity. Problems occur however when we too readily suppress or dismiss questions concerning the moral force of the body, and what role, if any, the aging, finite body might play in moral formation.

We may be witnessing what Paul Ramsey called a redefinition of our understanding of sloth against the messianic positivism of molecular biology, where righteousness is supplanted by the biological *summum bonum*. Ramsey presciently asserted that "the new form of spiritual sloth will be

---

126. Arking, "Extending Human Longevity," 183.
127. O'Donovan, *Resurrection and Moral Order*, 52.
128. Scott, "Nature, Technology and the Rule of God," 275.
129. McKenny, *To Relieve the Human Condition*, 199.

not to want to be bodily perfect and genetically improved."[130] In terms of aging research, prolongevity activists have recently coined a new term embodying this sentiment—*gerontologiphobia*—a pejorative term reserved for those wary of slowing aging.[131] The desire to genetically refashion the body for longer durability suggests some degree of contempt for the body, not because it hinders an ascent to things divine (e.g., Porphyry) or spiritual activity, but because it fails to live up to our expectations and sets a limit to our unlimited desires. Since our projects, desires, and longings continually threaten to outstrip the longevity of our bodies, it is tempting to hold the body in contempt, even in acknowledging that the healthy, functioning body is a crucial prerequisite for autonomy and future flourishing. That the body is perceived as imposing unnecessary limits on one's desire for more experiences, love interests, and intellectual or artistic quests, and that the body must be genetically redesigned to allow for these expanded possibilities, indicates that the body and soul are in disorder, having already gone their separate ways; the body becomes a threat or even the enemy. Perhaps the most poignant example of this separation is found in caloric restriction mimetics, one of the most promising avenues of attenuating aging.

TRÄGHEIT AND CALORIC RESTRICTION

As we have noted, scientists are uncovering the mechanisms of aging in part by studying the effects of caloric restriction on laboratory animals in hopes of developing mimetics for human consumption. Caloric restriction serves as a particularly illuminating example of the ways aging attenuation may support the sloth that brings the disorder of body and soul. As discussed earlier, one such pathway involving the SIR2 gene first identified in yeast may one day allow scientists to replicate the aging attenuation process in humans without any significant change in one's eating habits. Indeed, the discovery of a similar gene in the family of sirtuins known as SIRT1, known to slow aging in mammals, has already yielded promising results in preventing cellular senescence in humans, as the 2019 study conducted by the Max Plank Institute for Heart and Lung Research at Stanford University has shown.[132] In light of Barth's understanding of the order of body and soul vis-à-vis the real man Jesus, we might assert that the frenetic search for aging-attenuating mechanisms represents a contemporary form of sloth.

130. Ramsey, *Fabricated Man*, 145, emphasis mine.
131. Miller, "Extending Life," 244.
132. Ianni et al., "Sirt7 Stabilizes rDNA Heterochromatin"; Paredes et al., "Epigenetic Regulator SIRT7."

Genetic alteration is not only more promising in terms of efficacy, but also threatens to undermine certain spiritual disciplines such as fasting and its role in shaping one's character while benefitting the body as well. The desire to extend one's days can be more easily realized by avoiding the conflict between one's will and one's bodily needs. Nearly twenty years ago, S. Jay Olshansky and Bruce Carnes already recognized that "the value of research on caloric restriction is not going to come from encouraging people to restrict their intake of food."[133] Others echo this sentiment and believe that the likelihood of people willingly committing to a 20 to 30 percent reduction in caloric intake on a regular basis is extremely small.[134] Indeed, Olshansky and Carnes have suggested that

> future benefits to public health from this area of [aging] research will more likely come from identifying the underlying biological mechanisms that are responsible for the effect [aging attenuation through caloric restriction], rather than encouraging the adoption of diets that almost nobody wants to follow.[135]

Twenty years later, their observations have proven accurate as the evidence for the efficacy of caloric restriction and related approaches continues to mount.

As discussed in chapter one, such insights have spawned a new field of "caloric restriction mimetics" devoted to engineering pharmaceuticals that trigger the types of gene expressions that might otherwise be produced by following caloric restriction (CR) or fast-mimicking diet (FMD).[136] As we have also seen, the discovery of the genetic mechanisms related to slowing aging have spawned several companies intent on manufacturing a pharmaceutical fix, in hopes of both treating diseases related to aging and ultimately slowing the aging process itself. Cynthia Kenyon, currently Calico's vice president of aging research, garnered fame for laboratory success in extending the life-spans of the nematode worms. When her research yielded a sixfold increase in healthy life-span, she exclaimed, "I wanted to be those worms."[137] (Jesus too speaks of a place where the worm does not die.)[138] Kenyon exclaimed, "If our company could make a pill, everyone would want it."[139] The

---

133. Olshansky and Carnes, *Quest for Immortality*, 193.
134. Casadesus et al., "Eat Less, Eat Better," 213.
135. Olshansky and Carnes, *Quest for Immortality*, 193.
136. Roth, "Caloric Restriction."
137. Boyce, "Hurry to Slow Life's Clock," 74.
138. Mark 9:48.
139. Boyce, "Hurry to Slow Life's Clock," 74.

company to which she referred, Elixir Pharmaceuticals, is now defunct, and bears witness to the enormous challenges associated with manufacturing a pill to modulate aging. Nevertheless, we have seen several promising avenues of aging attenuation, ranging from select drugs already on the market such as metformin, to the recent development of senolytics. Indeed, Richard Miller, biogerontologist at the University of Michigan who heads one of three NIH-funded labs dedicated to understanding aging, conceded that until the early 1990s the notion that one could develop a pill to slow aging was little more than "a science fiction trope." However, Miller has now recanted, and asserts that "recent research has shown that pessimism is wrong."[140] A growing consensus of scientists believe that a pill is on the horizon.[141]

The search for caloric restriction mimetics offers an insightful example of the ways in which it is possible to plunge into *Trägheit* or sloth, further dys-integrating the body and soul. Given however that the human creature is an embodied soul and an ensouled body, remaking the body to fit one's desire for longer life runs the risk of falling into sloth, possibly mitigating the body's role in the formation of one's character in the pursuit of perfection, a process which in turn may have beneficial effects for one's body.[142] In light of what we have learned from the real man Jesus, we may say that the biomedical search for attenuating aging is deficient to the degree that it fails to address the issues of *Trägheit* as a separation or dys-integration of body and soul. Indeed, it seems to exacerbate this separation. In light of the practice and goals of asceticism according to Antony and Athanasius in the previous chapter, it is reasonable to conclude that the biomedical quest for longevity effectively negates the formative role the body might otherwise play in the refining of one's soul, and fails to recognize that modifying the body to allay fears of death can never mitigate the fear that dwells in one's (embodied) soul.

TRÄGHEIT: LOSING THE BODY IN THE REFINEMENT OF ONE'S SOUL

The life of St. Antony casts current attempts to extend the human life-span into sharp relief. Certainly, there are significant differences between the ascetic and biomedical remaking of the body, apart from the more obvious

140. Taylor, "A 'Fountain of Youth' Pill?"

141. Taylor, "A 'Fountain of Youth' Pill?" "Despite concerns about the hype, scientists are hopeful of finding a way forward by relying on hard evidence. The consensus: A pill is on the horizon. It's just a matter of time—and solid research."

142. See Barth, *CD* 3/2:566.

differences of method (e.g., hygienic vs. genetic) and efficacy. As we have seen in the previous chapter, it could hardly be said that the goal of the ascetic life was a prolonged existence in the body, even though it was thought possible to attain an "idling" state. Yet, the desert ascetics' conception of embodiment was heavily implicated with a moral significance that is largely absent in contemporary cultural and scientific perspectives. No longer is the body implicated in the development of the whole person. As has been shown, the body is at best morally neutral, as the object of one's desires, or at worst the enemy, a threat to one's continued autonomous existence. If the body was once indispensable in the development of the whole person, the body has now become an object of technological control in hopes of realizing our desire for longer life, a desire that is not altogether wrong. For Antony, recognizing the body's limitedness was critical to both bodily and spiritual development, yet not in an absolute sense, for Antony looked for the resurrection body to come. Whereas Athanasius lauded Antony's longevity as an indirect *result* of his good life, those engaged in aging attenuation research tend to see greater longevity as a *prerequisite* for it. As such, caloric restriction mimetics may merely reinforce our sloth. By such efforts, the body and the soul remain dys-integrated and disordered, as the moral force of the body dissolves, divided into a myriad of genetic pathways that will one day succumb to our technological control. The sentiment that a restriction in food intake or diet—which should not be confused with fasting—will adversely affect the quality of one's life reveals that the body has little to say about the development of one's character, and merely underscores that the body and soul have already gone their separate ways.

This new "longevity asceticism" in the form of caloric restriction mimetics or the senolytic cocktail known as dastanib and quercetin (D+Q) is likely to ensure that they remain separated. This is not to say however that disciplining one's body by restricting food intake cannot also drive a wedge between the body and soul, or be pursued for reasons that have little to do with moral formation. The very public forty-four day fast by endurance artist David Blaine in 2003 who, in neo-Stylite fashion encased himself in a clear plastic cube suspended from a crane on the south bank of the River Thames, is a case in point.[143] It is only to acknowledge that the most common type of "fasting" that caloric-restriction mimetics may one day render obsolete is hygienic fasting, or dieting, where one seeks to reshape one's body through the hard effort of restricting what one eats. Caloric restriction mimetics is

---

143. One recent television program called "I Want to Look Like a High School Cheerleader Again" chronicles the intense workout routines of ten overweight women seeking to regain their cheerleader physique with the unquestioned assumption that the ideal body type is that of an indefatigably nubile seventeen-year-old girl.

attractive because it offers a potential escape from the type of regimens required to fit into particular clothes, or to enhance one's physique, or even to slow down the aging process. Such forms of dieting reveal a potential problem in one's soul, and may represent another form of the naked will over against the body, though we must be careful here, and would not wish to say that all forms of dieting stem from questionable motives. Moreover, caloric restriction mimetics may reinforce the assumption adopted by some in Corinth who mistakenly believed that "food is meant for the stomach and the stomach for food," a belief challenged by Paul, who countered with the reminder that the body is meant for the Lord, "and the Lord for the body" (1 Cor 6:13 RSV). The possibility of taking a pill to mimic the effects of caloric restriction to achieve greater longevity may simply reinforce sloth, encouraging us to live under the illusion of additional time while freeing us from exercising wise rulership over our bodies in service to the Lord, masking over what failed diets ought to reveal about our own recalcitrant wills and desires.

If caloric restriction mimetics promises (or threatens) to eliminate the need for hygienic fasting, it would also seem to mitigate against the practice of fasting for higher purposes. By taking a pill to slows one's aging while simultaneously allowing one to live under the illusion that food is only for the stomach and the stomach only for food, the pathway by which one "enters the desert" and comes face to face with the haunted regions of one's soul may effectively be sealed off. The bodily hunger that reminds us of, and creates within us a deeper hunger for God and his will, the hunger that reminds us that God has food of which the world does not know (John 4:32), that Jesus Christ himself is the bread of life (John 6:35, 48, 51), and that fasting from food enables us to feast on God (John 4:34), may one day be mitigated by a pill. The following journal excerpt reveals both the recalcitrance of the human will and the slowness of progress. Moreover, it also helps us distinguish between fasting as a spiritual discipline and dieting as a form of hygienic bodily management.

> (1) I felt it a great accomplishment to go a whole day without food. Congratulated myself on the fact that I found it so easy... (2) Began to see that the above was hardly the goal of fasting. Was helped in this by beginning to feel hunger... (3) Began to relate the food fast to other areas of my life where I was more compulsive... I did not have to have a seat on the bus to be contented, or to be cool in the summer and warm when it was cold. (4)... Reflected more on Christ's suffering and the suffering of those who are hungry and have hungry babies... (5) Six months after beginning the fast discipline, I began to see why

a two-year period has been suggested. The experience changes along the way. Hunger on fast days became acute, and the temptation to eat stronger. For the first time I was using the day to find God's will for my life. Began to think about what it meant to surrender one's life. (6) I now know that prayer and fasting must be intricately bound together. There is no other way and yet that way is not yet combined in me.[144]

These diary excerpts reveal that the experience of hunger can serve as a powerful impetus to the refinement of one's will. As Dietrich Bonhoeffer (1906–1945) noted, "fasting helps to discipline the self-indulgent and slothful will which is so reluctant to serve the Lord, and it helps to humiliate and chasten the flesh."[145]

Having suggested however that caloric restriction mimetics might bypass the need for hygienic discipline, it must be conceded that caloric restriction need not preclude the discipline of fasting for the spiritual purposes. Indeed, one must grant this possibility, though it might be difficult to envision reasons for doing both. For in this particular scenario the wisdom gained by reflecting on one's allotted time on earth—a reflection in which one is aided by the reminder of one's very aging and disintegrating body—appears diminished. As will be shown shortly, this was integral to Antony's asceticism. Barth too understood that recognizing one's bodily limits, or recognizing one's allotted time, was an essential element in carrying one's cross. He speaks of the cross that the Christian must bear in sanctification, where one affirms and indeed loves life as a gift from God, warding off pain and death when appropriate. At the same time however the Christian must be able to say "Yes" to pain, suffering, and death, "because his sanctification in fellowship with Jesus Christ . . . ultimately includes the fact that he has to see and feel and experience the limit of his existence—even of his Christian existence engaged in sanctification—as the limit of his human and creaturely life, which leads necessarily to death, and proclaiming it, and finally involving it."[146] The Christian is not to seek or induce death, says Barth, but rather affirm life as this frontier approaches. The Christian will affirm both life and death for Jesus' sake. "He will accept the fact that this limit or frontier is set, and that he has to note it. He will take up his cross."[147] For Barth, our cross includes death and the sickness and aging that accompany it, not

---

144. Foster, *Celebration of Discipline*, 72–73. See also O'Connor, *Search for Silence*, 103–4.
145. Bonhoeffer, *Cost of Discipleship*, 169.
146. Barth, *CD* 4/2:602–3.
147. Barth, *CD* 4/2:603.

solely according to the laws of nature, but according to our fellowship with Christ, who "endured that that limit should be set for Him in the negation of His life."[148] By Christ's resurrection and defeat of death, the Christian need only fear the Lord. Thus, caloric restriction mimetics may jeopardize the process of sanctification to the extent that the Christian fails to recognize her own creaturely limitedness, which is ultimately affirmed by Jesus' limitedness. Recognizing and understanding what might be learned from our bodily limits becomes increasingly important as advances in molecular and evolutionary biology promise to bring the body increasingly under our control. Though there is much more to be learned about the body at the cellular, molecular, and genetic levels, in other respects the body has nothing more to teach us.

TRÄGHEIT: TREATING THE BODY TO CURE THE SOUL; MUST BACON BE ABANDONED?

While both Bacon and Athanasius envisioned a return to prelapsarian paradise, they offered two very different paths. Bacon sought bodily incorruptibility through increasing knowledge for the "reinvesting, in great part, of man to the sovereignty and power . . . which he had in his first state of creation." Athanasius, on the other hand, believed that bodily incorruptibility was the result of a rightly ordered body-soul relationship that one appropriated on account of the One who took on human flesh and defeated death and corruption.[149] What might this study of Bacon, Barth, and the Desert Fathers have to say to those presently engaged in the "Baconian Project" of aging-attenuation science? Athanasius and Barth might argue that no increase in control over the body, no amount of knowledge gained of its functioning, no amount of attention focused on genetically or pharmacologically remaking the body for greater longevity will resolve the problem of *Sorge* in one's soul. By such attempts science continually reenacts the "turn to the body" by which Adam forfeited his intimate fellowship with God, resulting in the fear of death and a potentially shortened life span.

On the other hand, Bacon reminds us that creation is in some disorder on account of Adam's sin. Despite all of the challenges of appealing to the first Adam as normative for human existence, Bacon recognized that a longer life on this earth could indeed be put to good use in relieving humanity's estate. Moreover, he also recognized that nature, operating in accordance with God's laws, also placed some limits on our projects. And yet, since

---

148. Barth, *CD* 4/2:603, 611.
149. Bacon, *Valerius Terminus* 1, *WFB*, 3:222.

Bacon referred primarily to the first Adam instead of the last Adam, he found himself unable to articulate these limits in any detail. Rather, they must be empirically discovered. Though with Barth we can say that aging itself is not a disease, but a part of our divinely-determined creatureliness as revealed in the real man Jesus, it seems a stretch to label Bacon's hopes to slow aging merely as "biomedical enhancement," much less a project animated by *Sorge*. Though Bacon's project would benefit from further qualification by Barth's analysis of the *last* Adam, it seems hasty to reject it altogether.

We should also resist a false dichotomy that relegates science and medicine to the care of the body and religion to the care of the soul. We must to some degree acknowledge that the fear and anxiety of our finite span cannot be adequately dealt with apart from accepting the very limitedness of our bodies and our allotted span. For Antony and the eremitic ascetics, remaking the body was subsumed under the larger goal of transforming one's soul, even as such practices attenuated aging. On the other hand, the modern biomedical project—or "Baconian Project"—seems bent on transcending the very bodily limits that are beneficial for instructing one's soul. For in the Baconian narrative, the declining and disintegrating body is perceived as a threat—an enemy—so that one's body and soul are in a sense, dys-integrated. But if indeed *Sorge*, or "care," both contributes to and results from the separation of body and soul, it has been shown that the resolution of this anxiety only occurs through practices that involve a reintegration of body and soul, practices that begin by allowing the body to "become the discreet mentor of the proud soul."[150] The Desert Fathers remind us that the process of refining one's will and desires requires attending to the body as well, specifically, by limiting, to some degree, its everyday needs. This suggests that the degree to which science discovers how to genetically remake the body for more efficient metabolism, heightened durability, and greater longevity, reflects the degree to which this project potentially undermines the body's role in mentoring the soul. If, in the desert ascetics, the body was heavily invested in the transformation of the soul—even as the body itself was "remade," and slowed down—there is little evidence to suggest that body today under our Cartesian gaze carries any such weight. Moreover, given that the dissatisfaction with one's temporal span stems not simply from one's aging body, but also reflects a disorder of one's soul, pursuing practices that reorder the body and soul might help mitigate this fear, the very means advocated by Athanasius and employed by Antony.

---

150. Brown, *Body and Society*, 237.

ASCETICISM AND ITS ROLE IN COUNTERING *TRÄGHEIT* AND *SORGE*

Insofar as sloth and care lead to anxiety over one's limited existence which contribute to, and result from, a separation of body and soul—are also characterized as a lack of discipline, ascetic practices informed by a Christian narrative may help reintegrate and reorder the body and soul, allaying the fear, anxiety (*Trägheit*), and care (*Sorge*) borne out by their separation. The goal of such reordering as understood by Athanasius and Antony was that the body might become subservient to one's Word-guided soul, so that the whole person—ensouled body and embodied soul—might become a medium of incarnate expression. The real man Jesus exemplified this perfect ordering, living his life in perfect obedience to God as an embodied soul perfectly ruling his ensouled body. Thus, a form of Christian asceticism that minimally involves fasting, meditation, and prayer, may offer the means by which the body and soul are reintegrated and reordered, thereby mitigating the fear of death and limitedness that have allowed the body and soul to go their separate ways. Recall that Athanasius argued that the death and resurrection of Christ enabled the Christian to defeat the fear of death, the very fear that originated in Adam's turn towards the body.[151] With Christ's defeat of death through his crucifixion and resurrection however, our own death is no longer something that ought to inspire an unwarranted level of fear. Though we are by nature afraid of death and the disintegration of the body, says Athanasius, "there is this most startling fact, that he who has put on the faith of the Cross despises even what is naturally fearful, and for Christ's sake is not afraid of death."[152] The evidence that this is already the case, says Athanasius, is borne out by those Christian martyrs who willingly face death for the sake of Christ.[153] "We fast meditating on death, that we may be able to live," says Athanasius, "hastening to announce the sign of victory over death."[154] Hence, Athanasius drew a connection between discipline, and despising death, as evidenced by the early Christian martyrs. As David Brakke observes,

> Thanks to the Word's victory on the cross, the monk's consideration of death can increase his moral effort instead of making

---

151. Ellen Charry has addressed this in *By the Renewing of Your Minds*, ch. 4, "Defeating the Fear of Death: Athanasius of Alexandria."

152. Athanasius, *On the Incarnation* 28.2, NPNF2, 4:51. See also Athanasius, *On the Incarnation* 27.1, 28.4–6, NPNF2, 4:50, 51 respectively.

153. Athanasius, *On the Incarnation* 27.3–4, NPNF2, 4:51; Pettersen, *Athanasius*, 97.

154. Athanasius, Letter 5.4, NPNF2, 4:519.

him fearful and morally disordered.... [T]he monk can replace the disorienting fear of death with an attitude toward death that results in moral courage and an intensified life of virtue.[155]

For Antony too, "the soul's anxiety about death lies at the root of the human inability to lead a virtuous life."[156]

Once again, Athanasius expressed this point most forcefully in the *Life of Antony*. For Antony the very *brevity* of life served as a motivating factor as he daily "increased in his discipline," a brevity further punctuated by the promise of eternity. As noted earlier, Athanasius observes that Antony spent much time in his cell fixing his desires on heaven and continually "pondering over the shortness of man's life."[157] Antony knew that a new body awaited him at the resurrection, one that was not only free from the deleterious effects of aging, but a body that would no longer be implicated in the struggle against sin. Hence, he advocated reflecting on the words of Paul in 1 Corinthians 15:31 (RSV)—"I die every day," living "as though under the daily expectation of death," in order that sin might be avoided, a recurring theme in the *Life of Antony*.[158] Similarly, in reflecting on Psalm 90, he noted that the span of our lives is short when "measured by the ages to come." Whether then "we live full fourscore years, or even a hundred in the discipline, . . . we shall reign for ever and ever . . . having put off the body which is corrupt, we shall receive it incorrupt."[159]

For Athanasius asceticism was firmly rooted in the reality that the body decays and eventually dies, for this reflects the good order of God by whom our limited existence is sustained. But it also reflects the victory over death won by Christ, whereby a limited degree of incorruptibility might be regained on this earth, though it pales in comparison to the absolute bodily incorruptibility to be received in the resurrection. Under these considerations, the length of one's own life is subsumed under the desire to do God's will and answer his call. Barth also recognized the benefit of a *meditatio futurae vitae*, where one's absolute will for life "may perhaps in many ways be weakened, broken, relativised and finally destroyed."[160] While the Des-

---

155. Brakke, *Athanasius*, 223.

156. Brakke, *Athanasius*, 222.

157. Athanasius, *Life of Antony* 45, NPNF2, 4:208. Antony did struggle with the fact that some lived longer than others. The *Apophthegmata Patrum* records that Antony wondered why God allowed some to die young, while others "drag on to extreme old age." See Ward, ed., *Sayings of the Desert Fathers*, 2.

158. Athanasius, *Life of Antony* 19, NPNF2, 4:201. See *Life of Antony* 89, 91, NPNF2, 4:219, 220 respectively.

159. Athanasius, *Life of Antony* 16, NPNF2, 4:200.

160. Barth, *CD* 3/4:342.

ert Fathers did not consider the desire for long life as necessarily bad, they generally attributed the fear of protracted bodily decline and a dependence on others to avarice. According to Evagrius Ponticus (345/6–399), "avarice suggests to the mind a lengthy old age, inability to perform manual labor . . . sickness that will visit us, [and] . . . the great shame that comes from accepting the necessities of life from others."[161] It is precisely this scenario of a prolonged senescence—a "lengthy old age" where one must accept "the necessities of life from others"—that animates the scientific search to gain control over the way we age, for the threat our aging bodies pose to our independence is in many respects no less fearsome than the specter of death.

At the same time, however, we must be careful in criticizing autonomy too harshly. It is perhaps better to speak of freedom. Douglas Burton-Christie asserts that the Desert Fathers practiced discipline to mitigate care and attain the freedom that enabled one to serve others, issues which were so critical for Barth.[162] Indeed, while Barth asserted that *Sorge* puts one in *bondage* to the future, Burton-Christie describes the *freedom* attained through discipline:

> The *telos* of the monks' life in the desert was freedom: freedom from anxiety about the future; freedom from the tyranny of haunting memories of the past; freedom from an attachment to the ego which precluded intimacy with others and with God. They hoped also that this freedom would express itself in a positive sense: freedom to love others; freedom to enjoy the presence of God; freedom to live in the innocence of a new paradise.[163]

Freedom is much richer than autonomy. For the Christian ascetic, the freedom from anxiety over the future enabled him to be free for others. We are reminded once again however that no degree of success in slowing aging can secure our freedom from the fear of decay and death that can only come from reordering the body and soul in recognition of the limitedness of the body, a limitedness confirmed as good and proper by the very man Jesus Christ who, as an embodied soul and ensouled body conquered death, gave us our allotted spans as a gift.

Through the disciplines of prayer and fasting, Antony was able to conquer his fear of death that may have otherwise hindered his service to God. The goal of this process, informed by Scripture and permeated with

---

161. Evagrius, *Praktikos* 9, 17.

162. Recall that the second form of *Trägheit* was characterized as man's inhumanity whereby his relationship to his fellow creatures is damaged.

163. Burton-Christie, *Word in the Desert*, 222. The heading of the section from which this quote was taken is entitled "Freedom from Care."

God's will for one's life, involved restoring the soul as the rightful leader of the body, to be offered in service to God as a "sacramental body." When one's soul has been transformed by first submitting to the body, concern over the length of one's life is somewhat relativized, even as one recognizes that fasting offers the possibility of remaking the body for greater longevity on this earth. Thus, the Christian who first comes under the tutelage of the body may no longer find the prospect of an extended life-span alluring. The Apostle Paul expressed this in his letter to the Philippians: "to live is Christ and to die is gain." Paul could hardly conceive of his life-span in terms of years, but rather in terms of God's tasks, hopeful in the knowledge that "Christ will be exalted in my body, whether by life or by death" (Phil 1:20–21 NIV).[164] Once again however, it is important to be reminded that it is not necessarily wrong to want a longer life, as long life is indeed a good gift to be used in fellowship with and service to God. Moreover, suggesting that the spiritual discipline of fasting might enable one to mitigate the fear of death and decay, effectively relativizing the significance of one's life-span—even as it enhances the body and the possibility of living longer—by no means precludes the use of medicine to treat and cure diseases which would otherwise cut one's life short.[165]

One must also acknowledge that it is possible to have one's life extended by the successful treatment or cure of an illness or disease, and yet desire such things for the wrong reason—out of a fear of decay, decline, and the potential loss of autonomy, because one has things left to accomplish—reasons that reveal life itself is one's ethical lord.[166] By God's grace, healing is made possible through the use of medicine and technology, even though the extra time allotted might very well be put to selfish ends (2 Kgs 20, Luke 17:12–18). It is equally important to recognize that bodily decay and illness can themselves serve as moral projects. McKenny notes that the suffering that occurs from the decay of one's own body can be used "for meditation on sin and the need for grace, and many of the disciplines."[167] This echoes the thoughts of Barsanuphius of Gaza (d. 540), who asserted that "illness is greater than discipline, and is reckoned as a substitute for

---

164. See Acts 20:24 (NIV), where Paul considers his life "worth nothing to me," asking only that he be allowed to "finish the race" and "complete the task the Lord Jesus has given me."

165. The methods utilized of course must be scrutinized by a Christian understanding of the human creature in light of the creation, fall, and reconciliation enacted by Jesus Christ.

166. Barth, *CD* 3/4:326.

167. McKenny, *To Relieve the Human Condition*, 221.

ascetic behavior."[168] Though there are strong theological warrants for the use of medicine to effect healing, we should also recognize that we run the risk of distancing phenomenologically speaking, the body from the soul.

To suggest however that fasting is a preferable alternative to genetic manipulation for greater longevity fails to recognize that fasting was subsumed under the larger moral project of sanctification that reorients the soul and body to their proper order, even as it was crucially integral to this process. In a similar vein, to simply observe that the Desert Fathers recognized a link between fasting and aging well before it was "discovered" by modern science is to miss the point entirely. Nor should we succumb to the temptation to demythologize the mystery of the incarnation and its effect on human nature by holding Athanasius's narrative accountable to the one propagated by modern biomedical science, rewriting it in terms of genetics. Still less is this an argument to pursue life extension through the supposedly more "natural" means of fasting, wary that pharmacogenetics or caloric restriction mimetics will undermine some essentialist conception of humanity or undermine our appreciation for the "givenness" of things. Nevertheless, it is clear that these competing visions of longevity are situated within radically different narratives with considerably divergent notions of what it means to flourish as embodied creatures. For the modern biomedical project or "Baconian Project" is fuelled by the notion that our bodies are at best morally neutral and at worst the enemy, and should therefore be fully subject to our desire to be free from its limitations. From this perspective, our aging bodies serve as a reminder of our finitude and dependency, and as such become the objects of technological control. More positively, we may say that the Christian who integrates the discipline of fasting into her life as an aid to prayer and *meditatio scripturarum* in the transformation of one's character may indeed slow down the aging of her body, even as the length of her life takes on less importance, thereby becoming a relative, not an absolute good. Scripture bears ample witness to the significance of fasting for the Israelites as God's people—in various forms and for various reasons—that is in no way marginalized in the New Testament.[169] In Antony, however, fasting appears taken to an extreme. Yet, contrary to Athanasius's presentation

---

168. Barsanuphius, Letter 78, in Chryssavgis, ed., *Letters from the Desert*, 80. Moreover, the ascetic rule concerning fasting is essentially useless when the body is unwell. See Barsanuphius, Letter 23, in Chryssavgis, ed., *Letters from the Desert*, 66.

169. Scripture records various modes of fasting, from complete abstinence (Esth 4:16; Acts 9:9), to avoiding certain kinds of food (Dan 1:12–15, 10:3). Moreover, there were several reasons for fasting, including the corporate fast on the day of atonement (Lev 23:27), and national emergencies (2 Chr 20:1–4, Esth 4:16, Joel 2:15). Jesus of course assumed that his disciples would fast (Matt 6:16; 9:15).

of Antony as a model for all to follow, the ascetic life neither demanded a virtuoso performance of heroic proportions, nor did it require a flight to the desert in search of an extended solitude. Indeed, as Barth recognized, these Christian practices in the struggle to holiness are not always to be carried out in isolation, and become deficient if they are always separated from the communities of faith.

Athanasius's *Festal Letters* are replete with exhortations indicating that prayer and fasting were to be a normal part of every Christian's life, and practiced with increased vigor during particular times of the year, especially the forty days preceding Easter.[170] David Brakke observes that Athanasius's promulgation of the ascetic lifestyle did not exempt ordinary Christians from practicing spiritual disciplines, much less Bishops in his episcopate. Athanasius encouraged the newly elected Bishop Dracontius to fast and lead by example: "For it is possible for you also as a bishop to hunger and thirst as Paul did. . . in order that thus fasting after his example you may feast others with your words, and while thirsting for lack of drink, water others by teaching."[171] The difference between the ordinary and advanced Christian was one of degree, and not fundamentally different in character.[172] Indeed, other early church documents such as the *Didache* reveal that fasting was important for *all* believers.[173]

Recent scholarship has also revealed that the lines between the city and the desert, between isolation and living in a community, between those advanced in the ascetic life and those less so, are considerably blurred.[174] Though the average Christian in Alexandria was expected to fast as part of the Christian life, none were required to live the life of a hermit. Even Antony served and ministered to others who sought him out. Derwas Chitty's

170. Athanasius, Letter 6.11–12 and Letter 19.8–9, *NPNF2*, 4:522–23, 547–48 respectively. See Brakke, *Athanasius*, 183.

171. Athanasius, Letter to Dracontius 9, *NPNF2*, 4:560

172. Brakke, *Athanasius*, 181. See Pettersen, *Athanasius*, 100. "It is most noteworthy that practicing the higher form of Christian life is not limited to those who withdraw from society; it may be embraced within society."

173. Schaff, ed., *Didache* 3.3, 164. See also Schaff, ed., *Didache* 8.1, 187–88.

174. Regarding the anachronistic distinction between anchoritic and coenobitic monasticism, see Goehring, *Ascetics, Society, and the Desert*, chapters 1–3. On page 21 he asserts that the ascetic life—whether practiced alone or with like-minded individuals—constitutes a withdrawal from certain social patterns of life, and need not entail a physical separation from the community. See also Brown, "Rise and Function of the Holy Man," 353–76, where he amends his earlier article, "Rise and Function of the Holy Man in Late Antiquity." Brown admits that his concept of the holy man was incorrect in asserting that he had to be different than everyone else, and that his holy man was essentially "flattened" by emphasizing the holy man's translocation over his transformation.

seminal work entitled *The Desert a City*, borrows a phrase from the *Life of Antony*, who effectively colonized the desert with monks.[175] Paul Ramsey (1913–1988), a pioneer of Christian bioethics, has also alluded to the ascetic nature of the Christian life with respect to fasting.

> Through infused temperance, however, a Christian moderates his bodily appetites, . . . for the sake of his unqualifiedly enthusiastic love for God. To the degree that the human soul is loyally subject to God and perfectly obedient, a proportionately greater emphasis will, as a consequence, be placed upon subjecting the body to the soul. Thus, by infusion of moral virtue, a Christian is shifted slightly to the ascetic extreme, though he still engages in the moderate satisfaction of desire.[176]

This description of the Christian life serves as an apt summary of Athanasius's position.

There are of course dangers to fasting. We must be mindful of John Howard Yoder's "positive doctrine of human fallibility."[177] Indeed, it is clear that fasting can stem from suspect or conflicting motives, including an inadequate or disparaging view of one's body. Intentions and motives are rarely, if ever, singular in nature and notoriously difficult to discern. John Cassian (360–435) acknowledged that it was easy for the beginner in fasting to become prideful, or to derive enjoyment from the transformation of their bodies into a slimmer physique.[178] Carl Elliott has shown how a remade body through the practice of discipline can in turn shape one's character for the worse, drawing on Sam Fussell's autobiographical account of his transformation from a skinny, pale, timid, bookish intellectual into an enormous, steroid-enhanced world-class body builder.[179] In remaking his body, Fussell gradually realized that he had become the person he once so greatly feared and despised; he had become a bully himself.[180] Fussell's account illustrates not only how difficult it is to discern the outcome(s) of our actions, but particularly how physiological regimes stemming from not entirely unwarranted motives can be harmful to one's body *and* one's soul.

175. See Athanasius, *Life of Antony* 14, *NPNF2*, 4:200.
176. Ramsey, *Basic Christian Ethics*, 228.
177. Yoder, *Priestly Kingdom*, 5.
178. Cassian, *Institutes of the Cœnobia* 12.13, *NPNF2*, 11:278.
179. Elliott, *Better Than Well*, 35ff, commenting on Fussell, *Muscle*. Elliot's interest in Fussell's account concerns the language Fussell employs in describing his own self-transformation, which ranges from becoming his authentic self to bodybuilding as self-invention.
180. Fussell, *Muscle*, 68.

Fasting can also be a serious problem with those who struggle with a healthy body image. Ellen Driscoll notes that girls and women in particular are *encouraged* to be uncomfortable with their untransformed bodies, uncritically adopting "the rhetoric of fitness [that] requires that we be unremittingly vigilant and penitent in liberating our bodies from fat and from the shame of our histories."[181] Joan Jacobs Brumberg has observed a gradual shift in American adolescent girls' perceptions of their own bodies over the last century, noting that language and locus of self-improvement has shifted from one's *character* to one's *body*, though both could be described as moral projects.[182] Indeed, it has been suggested that becoming thin is the new religion of our culture. "Slimming has become the national religion in America, and slenderness the measure of one's moral caliber."[183] There is also a more pernicious form of extreme fasting closely related to the disorders of anorexia nervosa and bulimia nervosa, which are largely understood as ways of using food by starving oneself to mitigate tension, anger, and anxiety, and to gain a sense of control.[184] Several have identified similar behavioral patterns between contemporary eating disorders and the fasting regimens of Catherine of Siena (1347–1380), Teresa of Avila (1515–1582), and other medieval mystics.[185] In her work *Holy Fast and Holy Feast*, Caroline Walker Bynum has noted the complex relationship between food and spirituality for medieval women mystics who often fasted to near starvation throughout the week so that they might enjoy a mystical union with Christ by feasting on Christ in the eucharist.[186]

181. Driscoll, "Hunger, Representation, and the Female Body," 96.

182. Brumberg, *Body Project*. See also Brumberg, *Fasting Girls*; Bruch, *Golden Cage*.

183. Ellmann, *Hunger Artists*, 5. Ellmann argues that fasting can also be imposed for numerous reasons, from war, making a political statement, famine, psychosis, to disease, dieting, or piety.

184. J. P. Feighner's criteria for these disorders are numerous, including onset before the age of twenty-five, a lack of appetite accompanied by at least a 25 percent loss in original body weight, an implacable attitude toward eating that may include enjoyment in losing weight with overt manifestations that refusing food is very pleasurable, and no known physical illnesses or psychiatric disorders. For a fuller description, see Bell, *Holy Anorexia*, 2–3. This eating disorder was first identified in the nineteenth century by Charles Lasègue, "De l'anorexie hystérique," though the terminology was first employed by Sir William Gull (1816–1890). See Hepworth, *Social Construction of Anorexia Nervosa*. The term *bulimia*, "ravenous hunger," was first used by M. Boskind-Lodhal and Gerald Russell working in the Royal Free Hospital in London in 1977.

185. See Reineke, "This is My Body." See also Bell, *Holy Anorexia*; Lelwica, *Starving for Salvation*; Vandereycken and Van Deth, *From Fasting Saints to Anorexic Girls*.

186. Bynum, *Holy Fast and Holy Feast*. Bynum suggests that 23 percent of those women canonized as saints between 1000 and 1700 died from asceticism, while 53 percent considered illness as central to their sanctity.

Others have identified clear parallels between these mystic saints and contemporary anorectics. Gail Corrington, for instance, sees historical and psychological continuities between anorexic women and the mystic saints in that both view fasting as a form of self-control, including the search for identity and autonomy.[187] Though there are commonalities between anorexic fasting and "holy fasting," the causes and influences in both eras are exceedingly complex. While Rudolph Bell asserts that "whether anorexia is holy or nervous depends on the culture in which a young woman strives to gain control of her life," Caroline Walker Bynum maintains that there is a clear distinction between choosing to renounce food and an inability to eat.[188] Bynum rightly warns against identifying these phenomena as identical, given that in both cases such behavior "is learned from a culture that has complex and long-standing traditions about women, about bodies, and about food," including exactly what kind of behaviors are in need of a "cure."[189] Thus, for those already struggling with an eating disorder, it may very well be that *eating well and often* becomes a form of spiritual discipline, where one learns to give up some element of control in learning to affirm one's body as God's temple.[190] Given then the difficulty in discerning the motives of fasting and the potential abuses to which fasting may be put, it must be said that fasting is not a discipline that all Christians must follow, at least to the degree or regularity of the Desert Fathers or medieval spiritual mystics. But if such disciplines are integral to the Christian life, they are best situated within the communal practices of baptism and the eucharist.

FASTING AND THE BODY OF CHRIST: BAPTISM AND THE EUCHARIST

It has been well noted that the most important practices regarding food for the early Christians were fasting and the eucharist.[191] Since the third century, fasting and abstinence have become extensive corporate practices

---

187. Corrington, "Anorexia, Asceticism, and Autonomy." See also Bell, *Holy Anorexia*, 17.

188. Bell, *Holy Anorexia*, 20; Bynum, *Holy Fast*, 198. See also Reineke, "This is My Body," 254.

189. Bell, *Holy Anorexia*, 20.

190. After I presented a paper on fasting as a spiritual discipline, a young woman who was being treated for anorexia nervosa asked whether she should engage in fasting as a spiritual discipline. My response, however inadequate, reflects what is written here.

191. Bynum, *Holy Fast*, 31, 33, 250.

among Christians.[192] Bynum reminds us that fasting connects Eden and the cross:

> Fasting was most basically something that brought Christians together—in gratitude for God's gift of the harvest; in obedience to God's command of abstinence, violated in the Garden of Eden but fulfilled on the cross; in charity toward the neighbors who would benefit from alms; and in foretaste of union with the saints in heaven.[193]

Fasting was intimately bound up with the body of Christ. A meal deliberately forsaken could be given to those in need. In this manner, "Christ is fed, . . . for what one denied to oneself in fast was given to Christ's own body, his Church."[194] If by fasting we are able to feed Christ, we are also constituted as the people of God by dying and being raised with Christ, and by feasting on Christ, through baptism and the eucharist.

The early church maintained a relationship between the discipline of fasting and baptism. In addition to the various fasts outlined in the *Didache*, both baptizers and catechumens were commanded to fast two days prior to the event.[195] Baptism is "deadly work."[196] It reminds Christians that we are baptized into the death of Jesus Christ, having been buried with him, reminding us of the inevitability of death and of our identity in the one who willingly succumbed to it for our sake (Rom 6:3). The catechumen's submersion under water and temporary disappearance from witnesses reminded observers that they too shall one day be lowered out of sight from those standing around their grave. The resurfacing of the catechumen attests equally to Christ's resurrection (Rom 6), pointing to his new life in Christ. Baptism reinforces the centrality of the resurrection, the very resurrection toward which, Athanasius asserted, fasting pointed. In this way, notes Therese Lysaught, baptism "frees us from the power illness and death threaten to exert over our lives," a power that might also guard against the temptation to rely on modern science to slow aging that threatens to separate the body and soul.[197]

If baptism reminds us of Christ's death and resurrection, the eucharist focuses more specifically on Christ's sacrifice, though it too has an eschatological component. In the eucharist the community not only engages in

---

192. Bynum, *Holy Fast*, 38.
193. Bynum, *Holy Fast*, 39.
194. Bynum, *Holy Fast*, 33–34.
195. Schaff, ed., *Didache* 7.4, 187.
196. Willimon, *Service of God*, 95.
197. Lysaught, "Becoming One Body," 275. See also Lysaught, "Memory, Funerals, and the Communion of Saints."

a life-shaping remembering, *anamnēsis*, but simultaneously proclaims his death until he comes again (Matt 26:29, 1 Cor 11:26). It is an act of committal, notes Carole Bailey Stoneking, and, like baptism, is also "deadly work."

> Jesus commits himself into God's hands. Likewise, Christian participation in the Lord's Supper is an act of committal. It is deadly work. Receiving the cup of Christ is deadly work because it forms our lives not in terms of what we will do with them, but what God will do with our lives, in our living and our dying. Receiving the cup of Christ is deadly work because it forms us into a people ready to die for what we believe.[198]

The eucharist is closely related to the goals of fasting put forward by Athanasius and Antony. The battles fought in the desert were to align one's will with God's, so that the body might serve as an instrument of God's activity on earth. The discipline of fasting as practiced by Antony involved making the body subject to his Word-guided will. Fasting and the eucharist enable the Christian to bring the body into submission of one's will, through the act of recommitting one's life to the one who fully entrusted his life to God. Fasting reminds the Christian that the body is not solely the instrument of one's unexamined desires, but the instrument of righteousness (Rom 6:13).

In tearing and crumbling the loaf and reciting the words of Jesus, "This is my body given for you," and "This cup is the new covenant in my blood, which is poured out for you" (Luke 22:19, 20 NIV), the Christian is reminded of Christ's body that he freely offered up to God, yielding to death so that he might defeat death. The eucharist also has the potential to expose our pretensions that our lives will somehow outlast those of others, reminding us that faith in the good of biomedical advances is always tenuous at best. The eucharist makes it difficult to reconcile our mysterious participation in Christ's body and blood with dreams of longer life through the project of slowing aging, for it reminds us that we are claimed by the one who for our sake surrendered his life—body and soul—to God, the one who also bids us to come and die.[199] The eucharist reminds us that we are not to be overly concerned with living, but with learning to die for the right thing.[200] Insofar as "the fear of aging, suffering, and dying so characteristic of our therapeutic culture is indicative of our refusal to die in Christ," fasting and the eucharist enable the Christian to foster what Alan Lewis has termed an

---

198. Stoneking, "Receiving Communion," 379–80.
199. Bonhoeffer, *Cost of Discipleship*, 89.
200. Hauerwas, *Suffering Presence*, 92.

"Easter Saturday identity," a life lived in conformity with the self-sacrifice of Christ, a life increasingly free from *Sorge*:[201]

> Theirs is a willingness—which may have little or nothing to do with martyrdom or the physical laying down of life for others, though that can never be excluded—to lead risky, unprotected, costly lives, open to others and committed to self-expenditure on their behalf. This they attempt in conscious but unambitious imitation—though never emulation, continuation, or displacement—of the life, and supremely the death, of Jesus.[202]

The eucharist reminds the Christian that she only finds life in taking up the cross to follow Jesus, a life that, paradoxically, can only be received by losing it for the sake of the one who freely gave his life for the sake of the world (Matt 10:38–39). While it is right to celebrate victories against aging, disease, and death as demonstrations of God's kingdom coming, such victories are relativized by Jesus' victory over the grave. Jesus' death and resurrection serve as a reminder that while death is indeed an enemy, it is a defeated enemy (1 Cor 15:54). The eucharist also reminds the Christian that fasting must be regularly broken by feasting, which proleptically points to the great banquet where people from all nations will gather together at the Lord's table.

The community of believers who gather around the Lord's table also provides a context for evaluating the potential impact life extension might have on a community of faith. Just as Paul chastised those who undermined the community by abusing the communal meal by feasting in the presence of the hungry (1 Cor 11:20–22), the church may one day be faced with a new inequality between those who age slowly and those who do not or cannot. Even though aging-attenuation technology is not yet available for humans, we should consider how such technologies might impact unity among believers. In this respect the eucharist might once again remind Christians of the dangers in relying on the promises of technology rather than the promises of Christ, though these need not be mutually exclusive. Even should one be spiritually mature enough to pursue the genetic or pharmacological option (as difficult as this may be to envision), might it not be better to forego such technology for the sake of the "weaker" brother in order to maintain unity?[203]

---

201. Meador and Henson, "Growing Old in a Therapeutic Culture," 110.

202. Lewis, *Between Cross and Resurrection*, 454.

203. See 1 Corinthians 8. "Weaker" is in scare quotes lest we too readily assume that the weaker brother or sister has a troubled conscience over the use of aging-attenuation technology.

CONCLUSION

In this chapter we considered slowing aging as part of the modern biomedical or Baconian Project with particular reference to Barth's christological anthropology. We saw that while Barth's understanding of our divine determination as co-partners of God's covenant seems to demand that our lives continue on indefinitely, it is nevertheless good for us to be limited creatures in time as revealed in the real man Jesus. However, while Barth's affirmation of our limited span as determined by Jesus' humanity forecloses the possibility of earthly immortality, it leaves open the question of using aging-attenuating technology to significantly extend life. By examining more closely the implications of Jesus' finite humanity as embodied soul and ensouled body, we were able to draw some tentative conclusions concerning our attitude to the length of life. In particular, I drew on Barth's conception of *Trägheit*, "sloth," and *Sorge*, "care," understood as the dys-integration of body and soul that often manifests itself as anxiety over one's limited lifespan in terms of frenetic activity over manufacturing more time. As such, I argued that life extension efforts as part of the modern biomedical project is a contemporary expression of the *Trägheit* and *Sorge* that stem from and contribute to the phenomenological and methodological dys-integration of the body and soul, with caloric restriction mimetics as a poignant example of this phenomenon. In particular, we have seen how the doctrine of life extension as narrated by this project fails to recognize the moral significance of the body, especially as it relates to the formation of one's soul or character. We have also considered the role of asceticism in addressing the conceptual distance between the body and the soul, arguing that reappropriating the ancient Christian practice of fasting is one way of reordering the body and soul, bringing them into christological alignment, as a way to combat the anxiety over our limited span engendered by *Trägheit* and *Sorge*, even as such fasting might also attenuate the aging process and extend the span of life. I have also argued that fasting is a corporate discipline—and not merely for the spiritual elite—set within the broader context of baptism and the eucharist, and therefore meant to serve the body of Christ.

Finally, though Barth's analysis has exposed potentially dangerous spiritual elements in pursuing aging attenuation within the context of the modern biomedical project, we have noted that it may not completely foreclose the possibility of lengthening life (which can only be an *a posteriori* judgment) by such means. This means that to some degree Bacon's account of slowing aging through inductive science—though deficient with respect to the moral force of embodiment—may not be entirely without warrant. And yet, as we have learned from Barth's account of humanity in light of the real man Jesus, any use of biotechnology towards these ends—especially caloric restriction mimetics—is not without risk, as it may threaten our pursuit of the proper order of body and soul, and thus our ability to faithfully follow the one who has become one of us that we might be like him.

Conclusion

We have examined the modern biomedical quest for longevity within the Christian narrative that recognizes both the significance of the body as part of God's good creation and as integral to the practices by which one's soul is transformed into the image of Christ. Though the quest for longer life is littered with the wreckage of failed attempts—whether through alchemy, geographical explorations, or hygiene—and generally disastrous results, modern medicine has discovered promising avenues to slow down aging in hopes of extending the healthy human life-span. Along the way we observed that the more deeply science has probed into the body the more aging itself has come to be seen as a disease. But the more aging is treated as a disease, the more the aging body tends to be seen as an enemy rather than an ally. The body has come to be seen as the object of one's will and desires, leaving a conceptual space between one's body and one's soul, a space in which *Trägheit* and *Sorge* are allowed to flourish.

We have also seen however that the modern biomedical project of aging attenuation has a long and complicated relationship with theology. Indeed, the modern biomedical project is often referred to as the "Baconian Project" in recognition of Francis Bacon's call for a new scientific methodology aimed at "relieving man's estate," a project that was inscribed within the Christian narrative and interpreted as a return to Eden. Bacon's contributions to modern medicine came however at the expense of his Puritan heritage and its close association with a Calvinism that emphasized both the total depravity of humankind and the inscrutable sovereignty of God, who ultimately determines the length of one's life (and not nature). Though Bacon remained within the Reformed tradition with its recognition that the created order has been adversely affected on account of Adam's sin, his theology was more amenable than other Reformed accounts to the redemption of creation, including our human bodies, construing the *imago Dei* primarily in terms of sovereignty and control. Following in the long tradition of interpreting the Genesis accounts "literally," Bacon believed that by regaining man's forfeited sovereignty and control over nature, it was possible to live as long as Methuselah, if not longer. But we concluded that Bacon's theological anthropology was ill-formed, as his heavy reliance on prelapsarian Adam readily accommodated Bacon's vision of the modern scientist in God's service in overcoming the effects of the fall, remaking creation as God had originally intended it. In short, Bacon was able to project his vision onto this prelapsarian Adam with little resistance. As such, we argued that Bacon's theological anthropology was in need of some theological repair.

By drawing on the rich supply of resources within the Christian tradition, the Church Father Athanasius, and the modern theologian Karl Barth in particular, we offered a theological critique of the modern biomedical project of life extension, which also addressed the anthropological shortcomings of Bacon's approach. Athanasius presented an alternative account of a return to Eden, affording the body the theological attention missing in Bacon. Athanasius believed that one could "remake" one's body through the spiritual discipline of fasting, a process that enabled the body to return to its idling state, effectively slowing the aging process. For Athanasius, the desert ascetic St. Antony, who lived over 100 years, represented a contemporary example of prelapsarian Adam. The primary aim of fasting however was not simply to remake the body, but to *reorder* it by bringing it once again under the benevolent direction and tutelage of one's Word-guided soul. The primary aim of fasting was one of moral formation, which, when joined with other disciplines like prayer and meditation, enabled one to overcome the dys-integration of body and soul occasioned by sin. According to Athanasius, the body inevitably reaps the benefits of the soul rightly turned toward God; namely, its decay slows. Though Athanasius's account of Adam, mediated through the life of St. Anthony, attends more closely to the spiritual life of Adam in relating the divine Word to embodiment and aging, we have argued that Athanasius's theological anthropology can be further refined by reflecting not only on the Word, but the Word made flesh (John 1).

With the help of Barth's theological anthropology and his treatment of the *last* Adam, we found a christological ground for normative claims concerning the goodness of finitude and a limited life-span as evidenced in the real man Jesus. Though Barth asks why the length of human life should *not* be limited in light of our divine determination as partners in God's covenant of grace, he concludes that Jesus' humanity—his embodied finitude—is determinative of ours, and that our allotted span is a sign of God's grace. Barth says nothing however about the proper *length* of one's life, but only *that* life be limited as determined by the real man Jesus, leaving open the question concerning the use of biotechnology to live longer. We considered one way of addressing this open question by returning to the relationship between the body and soul as it relates to longevity. For Barth, the proper relationship between the body and soul has been revealed in Jesus, whose existence as a perfectly ordered embodied soul and ensouled body is determinative for human existence. Though Barth's description of the proper body and soul echoes that of Athanasius, he goes further by identifying how their disorder impacts our existence, specifically in relation to our limitedness.

Barth identified the disorder and dys-integration of body and soul as *Trägheit* or the sin of sloth. In sloth the body and soul "go their separate ways," leaving one fearful and anxious (*Sorge*) over one's finite life-span and encroaching death. Insofar as the modern biomedical project reflects this anxiety over our limited span, it can be theologically construed as a project of care or anxiety (*Sorge*), an exercise that is both driven by, and leads to a further separation of the body from the soul. Therefore, we concluded that use of biomedical technology—caloric restriction mimetics in particular—runs the risk of significantly minimizing the body's role in moral formation by tempting us to treat our bodies merely as the objects of our desires. Moreover, the use of such technology toward remaking the body to slow aging and gain time may do little to assuage the anxiety in one's soul. Finally, insofar as Barth has characterized *Trägheit* as a separation of body and soul stemming from a lack of discipline, we have argued that the Christian practice of fasting may be beneficial in effectively reordering the body and soul to their proper order as revealed in the real man Jesus, counteracting the fear of death, even as such practices slow one's aging.

While Barth's analysis does not entirely prohibit the use of biotechnological developments—even caloric restriction mimetics—it nevertheless raises substantial questions concerning our view of embodiment as well as our trust in our good future as secured by God. At the same time, however, it seems that Bacon's program of alleviating suffering and expanding our power over creation cannot be entirely dismissed, even though, as we have argued, it requires christological repair. Though in a sense Bacon leaves the body behind in his account insofar as it is viewed as the object of instrumental knowledge, we have seen that Barth's theological anthropology in its reference to the real man Jesus has not entirely closed off longer life through biotechnology. Hence, it seems that an irresolvable tension remains between accepting aging as proper to our creaturely design on the one hand,

and seeking longer life by slowing it down on the other, a tension reflected in the core doctrines of the Christian faith—the full divinity and full humanity of Christ; that we are finite creatures on the one hand yet made for eternal fellowship with God on the other; that *enduring* suffering may be no less redemptive than *alleviating* it. From a Christian perspective, it seems that aging itself remains deeply ambiguous.

Even when we acknowledge the theological goodness of human finitude—whether we appeal to the first Adam or the last—it is not entirely clear why we should not try to slow down aging, especially as we aim at assuaging the diseases common to aging. In the meantime, however, we do well to continue in the disciplines of prayer, fasting, and meditation of Scripture in the larger context of communities of faith where baptism and the eucharist regularly remind us what life is for and to whom we ultimately belong. By faithfully attending to these practices we may become the kinds of people who, as embodied souls and ensouled bodies, develop the character to accommodate longer lives. On the other hand, for some these two propositions—engaging in Christian practices and using biotechnology to extend life by slowing aging—are simply irreconcilable. Indeed, we have suggested that Christians who engage in such disciplines might no longer be all that concerned about extending one's life by slowing aging. And yet, if life—even with its brokenness, heartache, and sorrow—is a good gift of God, there seems something proper about wanting just a little bit more. Perhaps the best question is whether the use of such biotechnology will help or hinder our pursuit of Jesus, who bids us to take up our crosses and follow (Matt 16:24)—whether indeed this biotechnology helps or hinders our learning to die for the right kinds of things.

Bibliography

Abbott, Alison. "Trial Hints at Age-Clock Reversal." *Nature* 573 (2019) 173.
Achenbaum, Wilbert A. *Crossing Frontiers: Gerontology Emerges as a Science.* Cambridge: Cambridge University Press, 1995.
———. *Old Age in the New Land: The American Experience Since 1790.* Baltimore: Johns Hopkins University Press, 1978.
———. "Old Age in the United States: 1790 to the Present." PhD diss., University of Michigan, 1976.
———. *Older Americans, Vital Communities: A Bold Vision for Societal Aging.* Baltimore: Johns Hopkins University Press, 2007.
Adam, David. "What If Aging Were A Disease?" *MIT Technology Review*, September/October 2019, 14–18.
Adams, William. *Light at Eventide: A Book of Support and Comfort for the Aged.* Edited by John S. Holme. New York: Harper, 1871.
Albertson, David, and Cabell King, eds. *Without Nature? A New Condition for Theology.* New York: Fordham University Press, 2010.
Alcott, William. *The Laws of Health, or, Sequel to The House I Live In.* Boston: J. P. Jewett, 1860.
Alexander, Brian. *Rapture: How Biotech Became the New Religion.* New York: Basic, 2003.
Allard, Michel, et al. *Jeanne Calment: From Van Gogh's Time to Ours, 122 Extraordinary Years.* New York: W. H. Freeman, 1998.
Allen, Diogenes. "Epilogue: Extended Life, Eternal Life: A Christian Perspective." In *The Fountain of Youth: Cultural, Scientific, and Ethical Perspectives on a Biomedical Goal*, edited by Stephen G. Post and Robert H. Binstock, 387–96. Oxford: Oxford University Press, 2004.
Allolio, Bruno, and W. Arlt. "DHEA Treatment: Myth or Reality?" *Trends in Endocrinology and Metabolism* 13 (2002) 288–94.
Alzheimer's Association. "2011 Alzheimer's Disease Facts and Figures." *Alzheimers & Dementia: The Journal of the Alzheimer's Association* 7 (2011) 1–68.
Ambrose. *De Paradiso.* In *The Fathers of the Church: A New Translation.* Edited by Sister M. Josephine Brennan et al. Vol. 42, *Hexameron, Paradise, and Cain and Abel*. Translated by John J. Savage. Washington, DC: Catholic University of America Press, 1961.
American Heart Association. "Living Longer is Important, But Those Years Need to Be Healthy Ones." January 29, 2020, https://www.eurekalert.org/pub_releases/2020-01/aha-lli012420.php.
Ames, Bruce N., et al. "Oxidants, Antioxidants, and the Degenerative Diseases of Aging." *Proceedings of the National Academy of Science, USA* 90 (1993) 7915–22.

Anatolios, Khaled. *Athanasius: The Coherence of His Thought*. London: Routledge, 1998.
Anderson, Ray S. "On Being Human: The Spiritual Saga of a Creaturely Soul." In *Whatever Happened to the Soul? Scientific and Theological Portraits of Human Nature*, edited by Warren S. Brown et al., 175–94. Minneapolis: Fortress, 1998.
———. *Theology, Death and Dying*. Oxford: Basil Blackwell, 1986.
Anson, Peter F. *The Call of the Desert*. London: SPCK, 1964.
Aquinas, Thomas. *Commentary on Aristotle's De Anima*. Translated by Kenelm Foster and Silvester Humphries. Notre Dame, IN: Dumb Ox, 1951.
———. *Summa Contra Gentiles*. 4 vols. Translated by Anton C. Pegis et al. London: University of Notre Dame Press, 1955–1957.
———. *Summa Theologica*. 5 vols. Translated by Fathers of the English Dominican Province. Notre Dame, IN: Ave Maria, 1981.
Ariès, Philippe. *The Hour of Our Death*. Translated by Helen Weaver. London: Penguin, 1977.
———. *Western Attitudes Towards Death: From the Middle Ages to the Present*. Translated by Patricia M. Ranum. Baltimore: Johns Hopkins University Press, 1974.
Aristotle. *The Complete Works of Aristotle: The Revised Oxford Translation*. Edited by Jonathan Barnes. 2 vols. Princeton, NJ: Princeton University Press, 1984.
———. *Generation of Animals*. Translated by A. L. Peck. Cambridge, MA: Harvard University Press, 1953.
———. *Nicomachean Ethics*. Translated and edited by Roger Crisp. Cambridge: Cambridge University Press, 2000.
———. *Physics*. Translated by R. P. Hardie and R. K. Gaye. In *The Complete Works of Aristotle: The Revised Oxford Translation*. Edited by Jonathan Barnes, vol. 1. Princeton, NJ: Princeton University Press, 1984.
Arking, Robert. *The Biology of Aging: Observations and Principles*. 3rd ed. Oxford: Oxford University Press, 2006.
———. "Extending Human Longevity: A Biological Probability." In *The Fountain of Youth: Cultural, Scientific, and Ethical Perspectives on a Biomedical Goal*, edited by Stephen G. Post and Robert H. Binstock, 177–200. Oxford: Oxford University Press, 2004.
Aronson, Louise. *Elderhood: Redefining Aging, Transforming Medicine, Reimagining Life*. New York: Bloomsbury, 2019.
Arrison, Sonia. *100 Plus: How the Coming Age of Longevity Will Change Everything, from Careers and Relationships to Family and Faith*. New York: Basic, 2011.
Asprey, David. *Superhuman: The Bulletproof Plan to Age Backward and Maybe Even Live Forever*. New York: HarperCollins 2019.
Athanasius. *Ad Adelphium*. In *Nicene and Post-Nicene Fathers*, Second Series. Edited by Philip Schaff and Henry Wace. Vol. 4, *St. Athanasius: Select Works and Letters*. Peabody, MA: Hendrickson, 1996.
———. *Ad Dracontium*. In *Nicene and Post-Nicene Fathers*, Second Series. Edited by Philip Schaff and Henry Wace. Vol. 4, *St. Athanasius: Select Works and Letters*. Peabody, MA: Hendrickson, 1996.
———. *Against the Heathen*. In *Nicene and Post-Nicene Fathers*, Second Series. Edited by Philip Schaff and Henry Wace. Vol. 4, *St. Athanasius: Select Works and Letters*. Peabody, MA: Hendrickson, 1996.

---. *Festal Letters*. In *Nicene and Post-Nicene Fathers*, Second Series. Edited by Philip Schaff and Henry Wace. Vol. 4, *St. Athanasius: Select Works and Letters*. Peabody, MA: Hendrickson, 1996.

---. *Four Discourses against the Arians*. In *Nicene and Post-Nicene Fathers*, Second Series. Edited by Philip Schaff and Henry Wace. Vol. 4, *St. Athanasius: Select Works and Letters*. Peabody, MA: Hendrickson, 1996.

---. *Letters of Athanasius*. In *Nicene and Post-Nicene Fathers*, Second Series. Edited by Philip Schaff and Henry Wace. Vol. 4, *St. Athanasius: Select Works and Letters*. Peabody, MA: Hendrickson, 1996.

---. *Life of Antony*. In *Nicene and Post-Nicene Fathers*, Second Series. Edited by Philip Schaff and Henry Wace. Vol. 4, *St. Athanasius: Select Works and Letters*. Peabody, MA: Hendrickson, 1996.

---. *On the Incarnation of the Word*. In *NPNF*, Second Series, ed. Philip Schaff and Henry Wace. Vol. 4, *St. Athanasius: Select Works and Letters*. Peabody, MA: Hendrickson, 1996.

Attridge, Harold W., and George W. MacRae, trans. "The Gospel of Truth (I,3 and XII,2)." In *The Nag Hammadi Library in English*, edited by James M. Robinson, rev. ed., 38–51. New York: HarperCollins, 1991.

Augustine. *The City of God Against the Pagans*. Edited and Translated by R. W. Dyson. Cambridge: Cambridge University Press, 1998.

---. *On the Morals of the Manicheans*. In *Nicene and Post-Nicene Fathers*, First Series. Edited by Philip Schaff and Henry Wace. Vol. 4, Augustin: The Writings Against the Manichaens, and Against the Donatists. Peabody, MA: Hendrickson, 1996.

Austad, Steven N. "Adding Years to Life: Current Knowledge and Future Prospects." Washington, DC: The President's Council on Bioethics, 2002. https://bioethics archive.georgetown.edu/pcbe/transcripts/deco2/session1.html.

---. *Why We Age: What Science Is Discovering About the Body's Journey through Life*. New York: John Wiley, 1997.

Bacon, Francis. *The Oxford Francis Bacon*. Edited by Graham Rees and Lisa Jardine. Vol. 6, *Philosophical Studies*, translated by Graham Rees and Michael Edwards. Oxford: Clarendon, 1996.

---. *The Works of Francis Bacon: Baron of Verulam, Viscount St. Alban, and Lord High Chancellor of England*. 14 vols. Edited by James Spedding, et al. London: Longman, 1857–1874.

Bacon, Roger. *The Cure of Old Age, and Preservation of Youth*. Translated by Richard Browne. London: Printed for Tho. Flesher and Edward Evets, 1683.

---. *Fratris Rogeri Bacon De retardatione accidentium senectutis, cum aliis opusculis de rebus medicinalibus*. Edited by A. G. Little and E. Withington. Oxford: British Society of Franciscan Studies, 1928.

---. *The Opus Majus of Roger Bacon*. 2 vols. Translated by Robert Belle Burke. London: Humphrey Milford, University of Oxford Press, 1928.

---. *Roger Bacon's Letter Concerning the Marvelous Power of Art and of Nature and Concerning the Nullity of Magic*. Translated by Tenney L. Davis. Easton, PA: Chemical, 1923.

Bagnall, Roger, and Bruce Frier. *The Demography of Roman Egypt*. Cambridge: Cambridge University Press, 1994.

Bailey, Ronald. "Forever Young: The New Scientific Search for Immortality." *Reason Magazine*, August 2002. http://reason.com/0208/fe.rb.forever.shtml.

———. "Intimations of Immortality, Part I." *Reason Magazine*, March 7, 1999. http://reason.com/opeds/rb030700.shtml.
———. "Intimations of Immortality, Part II." *Reason Magazine*, March, 6, 1999. http://reason.com/opeds/rb030600.shtml.
Baillie, John. *And the Life Everlasting*. London: Oxford University Press, 1934.
———. *Natural Science and the Spiritual Life*. London: Oxford University Press, 1951.
Baillie, John, et al., eds. *Western Asceticism*. Translated by Owen Chadwick. London: SCM, 1958.
Ballenger, Jesse F. *Self, Senility, and Alzheimer's in Modern America: A History*. Baltimore: Johns Hopkins University Press, 2006.
Banks, Dwayne A., and Michael Fossel. "Telomeres, Cancer, and Aging: Altering the Human Life Span." *Journal of the American Medical Association* 278 (1997) 1345-48.
Banner, Michael. *Christian Ethics and Contemporary Moral Problems*. Cambridge: Cambridge University Press, 1999.
Barash, David P. *Aging: An Exploration*. Seattle: University of Washington Press, 1983.
Barger, Jamie L., et al. "The Retardation of Aging by Caloric Restriction: Its Significance in the Transgenic Era." *Experimental Gerontology* 38 (2003) 1343-51.
Barnes, Albert. *Practical Sermons: Designed for Vacant Congregations and Families*. Philadelphia: H. Perkins and Purves, 1841.
Barr, James. *The Garden of Eden and the Hope of Immortality*. London: SCM, 1992.
Barsanuphius and John. *Letters from the Desert: A Selection of Questions and Responses*. Translated by John Chryssavgis. Yonkers, NY: St. Vladimir's, 2003.
Barth, Karl. *The Christian Life: Church Dogmatics IV,4, Lecture Fragments*. Translated by Geoffrey W. Bromiley. Edinburgh: T. & T. Clark, 1981.
———. *Church Dogmatics*. 4 vols, 14 parts. Edited by G. W. Bromiley and T. F. Torrance. Edinburgh: T. & T. Clark, 1956-1977.
———. *Deliverance to the Captives*. Translated by Marguerite Wieser. London: SCM, 1961.
———. *Die kirchliche Dogmatik*. Vol. III, *Die Lehre von der Schöpfung*, pt. 2. Zurich: Evangelischer Verlag AG, 1948.
———. *Die kirchliche Dogmatik*. Vol. III, *Die Lehre von der Schöpfung*, pt. 4. Zurich: Evangelischer Verlag AG, 1951.
———. *Die kirchliche Dogmatik*. Vol. IV, *Die Lehre von der Versöhnung*, pt. 2. Zurich: Evangelischer Verlag AG, 1955.
———. *Dogmatics in Outline*. Translated by G. T. Thomson. London: SCM, 1956.
———. *Ethics*. Edited by Dietrich Braun. Translated by G. W. Bromiley. Edinburgh: T. & T. Clark, 1981.
———. *The Humanity of God*. Translated by John Newton Thomas and Thomas Weiser. Atlanta: John Knox, 1960.
Bartke, Andrzej, et al. "Extending the Lifespan of Long-lived Mice." *Nature* 414 (2001) 412.
Barzilai, Nir, et al. "Metformin as a Tool to Target Aging." *Cell Metabolism* 23 (2016) 1060-65.
Bauman, Zygmunt. *The Individualized Society*. Cambridge, UK: Polity, 2002.
———. *Mortality, Immortality and Other Life Strategies*. Cambridge, UK: Polity, 1992.
Baur, Ferdinand C. *Die christliche Gnosis, oder, die christliche Religions-philosophie in ihrer geschichtlichen Entwiklung*. Tübingen: C. F. Osiander, 1835.
Beard, George Miller. *Legal Responsibility in Old Age*. New York: Russells, 1874.

———. "On the Decline of the Moral Faculties in Old Age." Unpublished lecture to the Long Island Historical Society, New York, 1840. http://resource.nlm.nih.gov/101162285.
Becker, Carl L. *The Heavenly City of the Eighteenth-Century Philosophers*. New Haven, CT: Yale University Press, 1932.
Becker, Ernst. *The Denial of Death*. New York: Free, 1973.
BeDuhn, Jason David. *The Manichaean Body: In Discipline and Ritual*. Baltimore: Johns Hopkins University Press, 2000.
Beecher, Henry Ward. *Beecher: Christian Philosopher, Pulpit Orator, Patriot and Philanthropist: A Volume of Representative Selections from the Sermons, Lectures, Prayers, and Letters of Henry Ward Beecher*. Edited by Thomas W. Hanford. Chicago: Donohue, Henneberry, 1888.
———. *Forty-Eight Sermons: Preached Previous to 1867*. 4th ed. 2 vols. London: R. D. Dickinson, 1890.
———. *Sermons by Henry Ward Beecher, Plymouth Church, Brooklyn*. 2 vols. New York: Harper and Brothers, 1868–1869.
———. *Sermons in Plymouth Church, Brooklyn*. Edited by T. J. Ellin Wood. New York: Fords, Howard, and Hulbert, 1882.
Beeke, Joel R. *The Quest for Full Assurance: The Legacy of Calvin and His Successors*. Edinburgh: Banner of Truth Trust, 1999.
Bell, Rudolph. *Holy Anorexia*. Chicago: University of Chicago Press, 1985.
Benecke, Mark. *The Dream of Eternal Life: Biomedicine, Aging and Immortality*. Translated by Rachel Rubenstein. New York: Columbia University Press, 2002.
Bercovici, Jeff. "How Peter Thiel Is Trying to Save the World." *Inc.*, July/August 2015. www.inc.com/magazine/201507/jeff-bercovici/can-peter-thiel-save-the-world.html.
Bernard, Claude. *An Introduction to the Study of Experimental Medicine*. Translated by H. C. Greene. New York: Dover, 1957.
Bernarducci, Marc P., and N. J. Owens. "Is There a Fountain of Youth? A Review of Current Life Extension Strategies." *Pharmocotherapy* 16 (1996) 183–200.
Beth, Evert W. "Critical Epochs in the Development of the Theory of Science." *British Journal for the Philosophy of Science* 1 (950) 27–42.
Birch, Bruce C., and Larry L. Rasmussen. *Bible and Ethics in the Christian Life*. Rev. ed. Minneapolis: Augsburg, 1989.
Bishop, Jeffrey P. *The Anticipatory Corpse: Medicine, Power, and the Care of the Dying*. Notre Dame, IN: University of Notre Dame Press, 2011.
Bitto, Alessandro, et al., "Transient Rapamycin Treatment Can Increase Lifespan and Healthspan in Middle-Aged Mice." *eLife* 5 (2016). https://doi:10.7554/eLife.16351.
Blackburn, Elizabeth. "New Health Program Promises to Slow Down Your Aging Processes and Prevent Chronic Disease." *Canada News Wire (CNW)*. http://www.newswire.ca/en/story/1160837/new-health-program-promises-to-slow-down-your-aging-processes-and-prevent-chronic-diseases-nobel-laureate-shares-telomere-link-in-toronto-may-15-16.
Blackburn, Elizabeth, and Elissa Epel. *The Telomere Effect: A Revolutionary Approach to Living Younger, Healthier, Longer*. New York: Grand Central, 2017.
Blackford, Russell. "Life Extension and Its Enemies." *Quadrant* 43 (1999) 58–63.
Blagosklonny, Mikhail V. "From Rapalogs to Anti-Aging Formula." *Oncotarget* 8 (2017) 35492–507.

———. "Koschei the Immortal and Anti-Aging Drugs." *Cell Death and Disease* 5 (2014) e1552. https://doi.org/10.1038/cddis.2014.520.

Blaikie, Andrew. *Ageing and Popular Culture*. Cambridge: Cambridge University Press, 1999.

Bloom, David E., and David Canning. "The Health and Wealth of Nations." *Science* 287 (2000) 1207–9.

Bloss, Tim A., et al. "Suppression of CED-3-Independent Apoptosis Through Mitochondrial βNAC in *Caenorhabditis elegans*." *Nature* 424 (2003) 1066–1071.

Blumenthal, Herman T. "The Aging/Disease Dichotomy: True or False?" *Journal of Gerontology: Medical Sciences* 58A (2003) M138–45.

———. "Milestone or Genomania? The Relevance of the Human Genome Project to Biological Aging and the Age-Related Diseases. *Journal of Gerontology: Medical Sciences* 56A (2001) M529–37.

Bodkin, Noni L., et al. "Long Term Dietary Restriction in Older-Aged Rhesus Monkeys: Effects of Insulin Resistance." *Journal of Gerontology Biological Science* 50A (1995) B142–47.

Bodnar, Andrea G., et al. "Extension of Life-Span by Introduction of Telomerase into Normal Human Cells." *Science* 279 (1998) 349–52.

Bonhoeffer, Dietrich. *The Cost of Discipleship*. Translated by R. H. Fuller and Irmgard Booth. 1st Touchstone ed. New York: Simon & Schuster, 1995.

Boorse, Christopher. "On the Distinction between Illness and Disease." *Philosophy and Public Affairs* 5 (1975) 49–68.

Boyce, Nell. "In a Hurry to Slow Life's Clock." *U.S. News and World Report*, December 29, 2003, 74–75.

Bozeman, Theodore Dwight. *Protestants in an Age of Science: The Baconian Ideal and Antebellum American Religious Thought*. Chapel Hill, NC: University of North Carolina Press, 1977.

Braaten, Carl E., and Robert W. Jenson, eds. *Union with Christ: The New Finnish Interpretation of Luther*. Grand Rapids: Eerdmans, 1998.

Brady, Catherine. *Elizabeth Blackburn and the Story of Telomeres: Deciphering the Ends of DNA*. Cambridge, MA: MIT Press, 2007.

Brague, Rémi. *Curing Mad Truths: Medieval Wisdom for the Modern* Age. Notre Dame, IN: University of Notre Dame Press, 2019.

Brakke, David. *Athanasius and the Politics of Asceticism*. Oxford: Clarendon, 1995.

Brane, Andrew C., and Trygve O. Tollefsbol. "Targeting Telomeres and Telomerase: Studies in Aging and Disease Utilizing CRISPR/Cas9 Technology." *Cells* 8 (2019) 186.

Briggs, John Channing. "Bacon's Science and Religion." In *The Cambridge Companion to Bacon*, edited by Markku Peltonen, 172–99. Cambridge: Cambridge University Press, 1996.

Brock, Brian. *Christian Ethics in a Technological Age*. Grand Rapids: Eerdmans, 2010.

Bromiley, Geoffrey W. *An Introduction to the Theology of Karl Barth*. Grand Rapids: Eerdmans, 1979.

Brown, Peter R. L. *The Body and Society: Men, Women, and Sexual Renunciation in Early Christianity*. New York: Columbia University Press, 1988.

———. "The Rise and Function of the Holy Man in Late Antiquity, 1971–1997." *Journal of Early Christian Studies* 6 (1998) 353–76.

---. "The Rise and Function of the Holy Man in Late Antiquity." *Journal of Roman Studies* 61 (1971) 80-101.

---. *The World of Late Antiquity: From Marcus Aurelius to Muhammad*. London: Thames and Hudson, 1971.

Brown, Warren S., Nancey Murphy, and H. Newton Malony, eds. *Whatever Happened to the Soul? Scientific and Theological Portraits of Human Nature*. Minneapolis: Fortress, 1998.

Browne, Richard. "To the Reader." In *The Cure of Old Age, and Preservation of Youth*, by Roger Bacon. London: Printed for Tho. Flesher and Edward Evets, 1683.

Bruch, Hilde. *Eating Disorders*. London: Routledge and Kegan Paul, 1973.

---. *The Golden Cage: The Enigma of Anorexia Nervosa*. First Harvard University Press Paperback ed. Cambridge, MA: Harvard University Press, 2001.

Brumberg, Joan Jacobs. *The Body Project: An Intimate History of American Girls*. New York: Random House, 1997.

---. *Fasting Girls: The History of Anorexia Nervosa*. Newbury Park, CA: Vintage, 2000.

Buckley, Jorunn J. "Tools and Tasks—Elchasaite and Manichaean Purification Rituals." *Journal of Religion* 66 (1986) 99-113.

Burghardt, Walter J. "Aging, Suffering and Dying: A Christian Perspective." In *Aging*, edited by Lisa Sowle Cahill and Dietmar Meith, 65-71. London: SCM, 1991.

Burton-Christie, Douglas. *The Word in the Desert: Scripture and the Quest for Holiness in Early Christian Monasticism*. Oxford: Oxford University Press, 1993.

Bushell, William C. "Psychophysiological and Comparative Analysis of Ascetico-Meditational Discipline: Toward a New Theory of Asceticism." In *Asceticism*, edited by Vincent L. Wimbush and Richard Valantasis, 553-75. Oxford: Oxford University Press, 1995.

Butler, Robert N. "Is There an Anti-aging Medicine?" *Generations: The Journal of the Western Gerontological Society* 25 (2001-2002) 63-65.

Butler, Robert N., et al. "Anti-aging Medicine: What Makes It Different from Geriatrics?" *Geriatrics* 55 (2000) 36-43.

Bynum, Caroline W. "Fast, Feast, and Flesh: The Religious Significance of Food to Medieval Women." *Representations* 11 (1985) 1-25.

---. *Holy Fast and Holy Feast: The Religious Significance of Food to Medieval Women*. Berkeley, CA: University of California Press, 1987.

Cahill, Lisa Sowle. "'Embodiment' and Moral Critique: A Christian Social Perspective." In *On Moral Medicine: Theological Perspectives in Medical Ethics*, edited by Steven E. Lammers and Allen Verhey, 2d ed., 401-2. Grand Rapids: Eerdmans, 1998.

Cahill, Lisa Sowle, and Dietmar Meith, eds. *Aging*. London: SCM, 1991.

Calhoun, Richard B. *In Search of the New Old: Redefining Old Age in America, 1945-1970*. New York: Elsevier, 1978.

Callahan, Daniel. "Aging and the Goals of Medicine." *Hastings Center Report* 24 (1994) 39-41.

---. "Aging and the Life Cycle: A Moral Norm?" In *A World Growing Old: The Coming Health Care Challenges*, edited by Daniel Callahan et al., 20-27. Washington, DC: Georgetown University Press, 1995.

---. *False Hopes: Why America's Quest for Perfect Health Is a Recipe for Failure*. New York: Simon & Schuster, 1998.

———. *Setting Limits: Medical Goals in an Aging Society*. New York: Simon & Schuster, 1987.

———. *The Troubled Dream of Life: Living With Mortality*. New York: Simon & Schuster, 1993.

———. *What Price Better Health? Hazards of the Research Imperative*. Berkeley, CA: University of California Press, 2003.

Callahan, Daniel, and Eva Topinkova. "Is Aging a Preventable or Curable Disease?" *Drugs and Aging* 13 (1998) 93–98.

Calvin, John. *A Commentarie of John Calvine, upon the First Booke of Moses Called Genesis*. Translated by Thomas Tymme. London, 1578.

———. *Commentaries on the First Book of Moses Called Genesis*. 2 vols. Translated by John King. Edinburgh: Calvin Translation Society, 1847–1860.

———. *Institutes of the Christian Religion*. 2 vols. Edited by John T. McNeill. Translated by Ford Lewis Battles. Philadelphia: Westminster, 1960.

Caplan, Arthur L. "An Unnatural Process: Why It Is Not Inherently Wrong to Seek a Cure for Aging." In *The Fountain of Youth: Cultural, Scientific, and Ethical Perspectives on a Biomedical Goal*, edited by Stephen G. Post and Robert H. Binstock, 271–85. Oxford: Oxford University Press, 2004.

———. "The 'Unnaturalness' of Aging—A Sickness Unto Death?" In *Concepts of Health and Disease: Interdisciplinary Perspectives*, edited by Arthur L. Caplan et al., 725–37. London: Addison-Wesley, 1981.

Carper, Jean. *Stop Aging Now! The Ultimate Plan for Staying Young and Reversing the Aging Process*. San Francisco: Harper Collins, 1995.

Carrick, Paul. *Medical Ethics in Antiquity*. Dordrecht: D. Reidel, 1985.

Casadesus, Gemma, et al. "Eat Less, Eat Better, and Live Longer: Does It Work and Is It Worth It? The Role of Diet in Aging and Disease." In *The Fountain of Youth: Cultural, Scientific, and Ethical Perspectives on a Biomedical Goal*, edited by Stephen G. Post and Robert H. Binstock, 201–27. Oxford: Oxford University Press, 2004.

Cassel, Christine. "Ethics and the Future of Aging Research: Promises and Problems." *Generations: The Journal of the Western Gerontological Society* 16 (1992) 61–65.

Cassian, John. *Institutes of the Cœnobia*. In *Nicene and Post-Nicene Fathers*, Second Series. Edited by Philip Schaff and Henry Wace. Vol. 11, *Sulpitius Servus, Vincent of Lerins, John Cassian*, ed. Edgar C. S. Gibson. Peabody, MA: Hendrickson, 1996.

Cesario, Thomas C., and Daniel Hollander. "Life Span Extension by Means Other Than Control of Disease." In *Life Span Extension: Consequences and Open Questions*, edited by Frederick C. Ludwig, 43–54. New York: Springer, 1991.

Cetron, Marvin, and O. Davies. *Cheating Death: The Promise and the Future Impact of Trying to Live Forever*. New York: St. Martin's, 1998.

Chapman, Audrey R. "Ethical Implications of Prolonged Lives." *Theology Today* 60 (2004) 479–96.

———. "The Social and Justice Implications of Extending the Human Lifespan." In *The Fountain of Youth: Cultural, Scientific, and Ethical Perspectives on a Biomedical Goal*, edited by Stephen G. Post and Robert H. Binstock, 340–61. Oxford: Oxford University Press, 2004.

Charcot, Jean M. *Clinical Lectures on the Diseases of Old Age*. Translated by Leigh H. Hunt. New York: William Wood, 1881.

Charry, Ellen T. *By the Renewing of Your Minds: The Pastoral Function of Christian Doctrine*. Oxford: Oxford University Press, 1997.

———. "The End of Satisfaction." *Theology Today* 59 (2002) 1–5.
Cheng, Chia-Wei, et al. "Prolonged Fasting Reduces IGF-1/PKA to Promote Hematopoietic-Stem-Cell-Based Regeneration and Reverse Immunosuppression." *Cell Stem Cell* 14 (2014) 810–23.
———, et al. "Fasting-Mimicking Diet Induces Pancreatic Lineage Reprogramming to Promote Ngn3-Driven-b-cell Regeneration." *Cell* 168 (2017) 1–14.
Chernyak, Leon, and Alfred L. Tauber. "The Idea of Immunity: Metchnikoff's Metaphysics and Science." *Journal of the History of Biology* 23 (1990) 187–249.
Chesterton, G. K. *Orthodoxy*. Garden City: Doubleday, 1959.
Chitty, Derwas J. *The Desert a City: An Introduction to the Study of Egyptian and Palestinian Monasticism under the Christian Empire*. Oxford: Basil Blackwell, 1966.
———. *The Letters of St. Antony the Great*. Oxford: SLG, 1975.
Choron, Jacques. *Death and Western Thought*. New York: Collier, 1963.
Christensen, Michael J., and Jeffrey A. Wittung, eds. *Partakers of the Divine Nature: The History and Development of Deification in the Christian Traditions*. Grand Rapids: Baker Academic, 2007.
Chrysostom. *Homilies on Timothy*. In *Nicene and Post-Nicene Fathers*, First Series. Edited by Philip Schaff and Henry Wace. Vol. 13, *Chrysostom: Homilies on Galatians, Ephesians, Philippians, Colossians, Thessalonians, Timothy, Titus and Philemon*. Peabody, MA: Hendrickson, 1996.
———. *A Treatise to Prove That No One Can Harm the Man Who Does Not Injure Himself*. In *Nicene and Post-Nicene Fathers*, First Series. Edited by Philip Schaff and Henry Wace. Vol. 9, *Chrysostom: On the Priesthood, Ascetic Treatises, Select Homilies and Letters, Homilies on the Statutes*. Peabody, MA: Hendrickson, 1996.
Chryssavgis, John, ed. *Letters from the Desert: Barsanuphius and John*. Crestwood, NY: St. Vladimir's Seminary Press, 2003.
Chudacoff, Howard P. *How Old Are You? Age Consciousness in American Culture*. Princeton, NJ: Princeton University Press, 1989.
Cicero, Marcus Tullis. *On Old Age*. In *Cicero*, edited by Jeffrey Henderson. Vol. 20, *De Senectute, De Amicitia, De Divinatione*. Translated by W. A. Falconer. Cambridge, MA: Harvard University Press, 1923.
Clark, Elizabeth A. "New Perspectives on the Origenist Controversy: Human Embodiment and Ascetic Strategies." *Church History* 59 (1990) 145–62.
Clark, Stephen R. L. *How to Live Forever: Science Fiction and Philosophy*. London: Routledge, 1995.
Clark, William R. *A Means to an End: The Biological Basis of Aging and Death*. New York: Oxford University Press, 1999.
Clement of Alexandria. *On Spiritual Perfection (Stromateis, III)*. In *Alexandrian Christianity: Select Translations of Clement and Origen*. Edited by Henry Chadwick. Translated by John E. L. Oulton. London: SCM, 1954.
———. *Stromateis*. In *The Fathers of the Church: A New Translation*. Edited by Sister M. Josephine Brennan, Hermilgild Dressler, Thomas P. Halton, Robert P. Russell, and William R. Tongue. Vol. 85, *Clement of Alexandria: Stromateis Books One to Three*, edited by John Ferguson. Washington, DC: Catholic University of America Press, 1991.
Cohen, Haim Y., et al. "Calorie Restriction Promotes Mammalian Cell Survival by Inducing the SIRT1 Deacetylase." *Science* 305 (2004) 390–92.
Cole, Thomas R. "Aging in American Culture." *Tikkun* 17 (2002) 50–51.

———. *The Journey of Life: A Cultural History of Aging in America*. Cambridge: Cambridge University Press, 1992.

Cole, Thomas R., and Barbara Thompson. Introduction to "Anti-aging: Are You For It Or Against It?" *Generations: The Journal of the Western Gerontological Society* 25 (2001–2002) 6–8.

Comfort, Alex. *The Biology of Senescence*. 3rd ed. New York: Elsevier, 1979.

Conniff, Richard. "The Hunger Gains: Extreme Caloric Restriction Diet Shows Anti-Aging Results." *Scientific American*, February 16, 2017, https://www.scientificamerican.com/article/the-hunger-gains-extreme-calorie-restriction-diet-shows-anti-aging-results/.

Conradie, Ernst M. "Resurrection, Finitude, and Ecology." In *Resurrection: Theological and Scientific Assessments*, edited by Ted Peters et al., 277–96. Grand Rapids: Eerdmans, 2002.

Cooper, John M., and D. S. Hutchinson, eds. *Plato: Complete Works*. Indianapolis: Hackett, 1997.

Cooper, John W. *Body and Soul, and Life Everlasting*. Grand Rapids: Eerdmans, 1989.

Cornaro, Luigi. *Discourses on the Temperate Life*. In *The Art of Living Long*, translated and edited by William F. Butler, 3–54. Milwaukee: W. F. Butler, 1903.

———. *Sure and Certain Methods of Attaining a Long and Healthful Life: With Means of Correcting a Bad Constitution, &c.* 3rd ed. Translated by W. Jones and A. B. Dublin: Printed for Richard Gunne, 1740.

Corrington, Gail. "Anorexia, Asceticism, and Autonomy: Self-Control as Liberation and Transcendence." *Journal of Feminist Studies in Religion* 2 (1986) 51–61.

Cortez, Marc. *Christological Anthropology in Historical Perspective: Ancient and Contemporary Approaches to Theological Anthropology*. Grand Rapids: Zondervan, 2016.

Cottingham, John, ed. *The Cambridge Companion to Descartes*. Cambridge: Cambridge University Press, 1992.

Creighton, Gilbert. "When Did a Man in the Renaissance Grow Old?" *Studies in the Renaissance* 14 (1967) 7–32.

Crichton-Browne, James. "The Prevention of Senility and a Sanitary Outlook." In *The "Fixed Period" Controversy*, edited by Gerald J. Gruman, 1–68. New York: Arno, 1979.

Crossley, Ronald C. "Aging with God: Old Age and New Theology." *Church and Society* 89 (1999) 9–19.

Crowley, Christopher, and Henry S. Lodge. *Younger Next Year: Live Strong, Fit, and Sexy—Until 80 and Beyond*. Reprint ed. New York: Workman, 2007.

Cullmann, Oscar. *Immortality of the Soul or Resurrection of the Dead? The Witness of the New Testament*. New York: Macmillian, 1958.

Cushman, Robert E. "Barth's Attack upon Cartesianism and the Future of Theology." *The Journal of Religion* 36 (1956) 207–23.

Dally, Ann. *Fantasy Surgery, 1880–1930: With Special Reference to Sir William Arbuthnot Lane*. Amsterdam: Editions Rodopi B. V., 1996.

Daly, Todd T. W. "Chasing Methuselah: Transhumanism and Christian *Theosis* in Critical Perspective." In *Transhumanism and Transcendence*, edited by Ronald Cole-Turner, 131–44. Washington, DC: Georgetown University Press, 2011.

———. "Life-Extension in Transhumanist and Christian Perspectives: Consonance and Conflict." *Journal of Evolution and Technology* 14 (2005) 69–87.

Darwin, Charles. *On the Origin of the Species: A Facsimile of the First Edition*. New York: Atheneum, 1967 [1859].

Das, Abhirup, et al. "Impairment of an Endothelial NAD+-H2S Signaling Network Is a Reversible Cause of Vascular Aging." *Cell* 173 (2018) 74–89.

Davidson, Noah, et al. "A Single Combination Gene Therapy Treats Multiple Age-Related Diseases." *Proceedings of the National Academy of Sciences of the United States of America* 116 (2019) 23505–11.

Davis, John K. *New Methuselahs: The Ethics of Life Extension*. Cambridge, MA: MIT Press, 2018.

de Cabo, Rafael, and Mark P. Mattson. "Effects of Intermittent Fasting on Health, Aging, and Disease." *The New England Journal of Medicine* 381 (2019) 2541–51.

de Condorcet, Jean-Antoine-Nicholas de Caritat. *Sketch for a Historical Picture of the Progress of the Human Mind*. Translated by June Barraclough. London: Weidenfeld and Nicolson, 1955.

de Grey, Aubrey, D. N. J., et al. "Anti-aging Technology and Pseudoscience." *Science* 296 (2002) 656a.

———, et al. "Is Human Aging Still Mysterious Enough to Be Left Only to Scientists?" *Bioessays* 24 (2002) 667–76.

———, et al. "Time to Talk SENS: Critiquing the Immutability of Human Aging." *Annals of the New York Academy of Science* 959 (2002) 452–62.

Deane-Drummond, Celia, ed. *Brave New World? Theology, Ethics, and the Human Genome*. London: T. & T. Clark, 2003.

Deane-Drummond, Celia, et al., eds. *Re-ordering Nature: Theology, Society and the New Genetics*. London: T. & T. Clark International, 2003.

Deeken, Alfons. *Growing Old, and How to Cope with It*. New York: Paulist, 1972.

Descartes, René. *Description of the Human Body*. In *Œuvres de Descartes*, edited by Charles Adam and Paul Tannery. Vol. 11, *Le Monde: Description du corps humain: Passions de l'âme: Anatomica Varia*. Paris: L. Cerf., 1909.

———. *Discourse on the Method for Guiding One's Reason and Searching for Truth in the Sciences*. In *René Descartes: Discourse on Method and Related Writings*, translated by Desmond M. Clarke. London: Penguin, 1999.

———. *Meditations on the First Philosophy in which the Existence of God and the Distinction between the Mind and the Body Are Demonstrated*. In *The Philosophical Works of Descartes*. Translated by Elizabeth S. Haldane and G. R. T. Ross. Vol. 1. Cambridge: Cambridge University Press, 1912.

———. *Philosophical Letters*. Translated and edited by Anthony Kenny. Oxford: Clarendon, 1970.

Di Francesco, Andrea, et al. "A Time to Fast." *Science* 362 (2019) 770–75.

Donne, John. *The Complete Poetry and Selected Prose of John Donne*. Edited by Charles M. Coffin. New York: Random House, 1952.

———. "Death's Duel." In *Devotions Upon Emergent Occasions and Death's Duel*, by John Donne and Izaak Walton, 153–77. New York: Vintage, 1999.

Donnelly, John. "Eschatological Enquiry." In *Language, Metaphysics, and Death*, edited by John Donnelly, 2d ed., 302–19. New York: Fordham University Press, 1994.

Dörries, Hermann. "Die Vita Antonii als Geschichtsquelle." *Nachrichten der Akademie der Wissenschaften in Göttingen* 14. Göttingen: Vandenhoeck & Ruprecht, 1949.

Drexler, Eric K. "Long Life in an Open World." In *Engines of Creation*. Garden City: Anchor/Doubleday, 1986.

Driscoll, Ellen. "Hunger, Representation, and the Female Body: An Analysis of Intersecting Themes in Feminist Studies in Religion and the Psychology of Women." *Journal of Feminist Studies in Religion* 13 (1997) 91–104.

Edgar, Brian. "A New Immortality?" *Evangelical Review of Theology* 23 (1999) 363–82.

Edwards, Jonathan. *A Humble Inquiry into the Rules of the Word of God, Concerning the Qualifications Requisite to a Compleat Standing and Full Communion in the Visible Christian Church*. Boston: S. Kneeland in Queenstreet, 1749.

Elbere, Ilze, et al. "Significantly Altered Peripheral Blood Cell DNA Methylation Profile as a Result of Immediate Effect of Metformin Use in Healthy Individuals." *Clinical Epigenetics* 10 (2018). https://doi.org/10.1186/s13148-018-0593-x.

Elliott, Carl. *Better Than Well: American Medicine Meets the American Dream*. New York: W. W. Norton, 2003.

Ellmann, Maud. *The Hunger Artists: Starving, Writing, and Imprisonment*. Cambridge, MA: Harvard University Press, 1993.

Elshtain, Jean Bethke. *Who Are We? Critical Reflections and Hopeful Possibilities*. Grand Rapids: Eerdmans, 2000.

Emerson, Ralph Waldo. *The Complete Works of Ralph Waldo Emerson*. Vol. 11, *Miscellanies*, edited by Edward W. Emerson. Boston: Houghton-Mifflin, 1903–1904.

Emmons, Nathanael. *The Works of Nathanael Emmons, D.D., Third Pastor of the Church in Franklin, Mass*. 6 vols. Edited by Jacob Ide. Boston: Congregational Board of Publication, 1860–1863.

Engelhardt, H. Tristram, Jr. "Genetic Enhancement and Theosis: Two Models of Therapy." *Christian Bioethics* 5 (1999) 197–99.

Epel, Elissa, et al. "Can Meditation Slow Rate of Cellular Aging? Cognitive Stress, Mindfulness, and Telomeres." *Annals of the New York Academy of Sciences* 1172 (2009) 34–53.

Epictetus. *The Discourses as Reported by Arrian, the Manual, and Fragments*. 2 vols. Edited by W. A. Oldfather. London: William Heinemann, 1925–1926.

Esposito, John L. *The Obsolete Self: Philosophical Dimensions of Aging*. Berkeley, CA: University of California Press, 1987.

Evagrius, Ponticus. *The Prakiktos: Chapters on Prayer*. Translated by John Eudes Bamberger. Kalamazoo: Cistercian, 1981.

Evans, Gillian R., ed. *The First Christian Theologians: An Introduction to the Theology in the Early Church*. Oxford: Blackwell, 2004.

Ewbank, Jonathan J., et al. "Structural and Functional Conservation of the *Caenorhabditis elegans* Timing Gene Clk-1." *Science* 275 (1997) 980–83.

Fahy, Gregory M., et al. "Reversal of Epigenetic Aging and Immunosenescent Trends in Humans." *Aging Cell* 18 (2019). https://doi.org/10.1111/acel.13028.

Fairweather, Ian C. M., and J. I. H. McDonald. *The Quest for Christian Ethics: An Inquiry into Ethics and Christian Ethics*. Edinburgh: Handsel, 1984.

Faulkner, Robert. *Francis Bacon and the Project of Progress*. Lanham, MD: Rowman and Littlefield, 1993.

Federal Interagency Forum on Aging-Related Statistics. *Older Americans 2010: Key Indicators of Well-Being*. Washington, DC: U.S. Government Printing Office, 2016.

Feher, Michel, ed. *Fragments for a History of the Human Body*. Part 1. New York: Zone, 1989.

Feifel, Eugene. "Pao-p'u tzu nei-p'ien." *Monumenta Serica* 6 (1941) 113–211.

Feinberg, John. S. "A Theological Basis for Genetic Intervention." In *Genetic Ethics: Do the Ends Justify the Genes?*, edited by John F. Kilner et al., 183–92. Grand Rapids: Eerdmans, 1997.

Feldman, Fred. *Confrontations with the Reaper: A Philosophical Study of the Nature and Value of Death*. New York: Oxford University Press, 1992.

Ferbeyre, Gerardo, and Scott W. Lowe. "The Price of Tumor Suppression?" *Nature* 415 (2002) 26–27.

Feuerbach, Ludwig. *The Essence of Christianity*. Translated by George Elliot. Amherst, NY: Prometheus, 1989.

Finch, Caleb R. *The Biology of Human Longevity: Inflammation, Nutrition, and Aging in the Evolution of Lifespans*. Waltham, MA: Academic, 2007.

———. *Longevity, Senescence, and the Genome*. Chicago: University of Chicago Press, 1990.

Finch, Caleb E., and Edward L. Schneider, eds. *Handbook of the Biology of Aging*. 2d ed. New York: Van Nostrand Reinhold, 1985.

Finlan, Stephan, and Vladimir Kharlamov, eds. *Theōsis: Deification in Christian Theology*. Eugene, OR: Pickwick, 2006.

Finney, Charles G. *Lectures on Systematic Theology*. 2 Vols. Oberlin, OH: James M. Fitch, 1847.

———. *Sermons on Important Subjects*. New York: J. S. Taylor, 1836.

Fischer, David H. *Growing Old in America*. Oxford: Oxford University Press, 1977.

Fossel, Michael. *Reversing Human Aging*. New York: William Morrow, 1996.

———. *The Telomerase Revolution: The Enzyme that Holds the Key to Human Aging and Will Lead to Longer, Healthier Lives*. Dallas: Benbella, 2015.

Foster, Michael B. "The Christian Doctrine of Creation and the Rise of Modern Natural Science." *Mind* 43 (1934) 446–68.

———. *Mystery and Philosophy*. London: SCM, 1957.

———. "Some Remarks on the Relations of Science and Religion." *The Christian News-Letter* 299, supplement (1947) 5–16.

Foster, Richard J. *Celebration of Discipline: The Path to Spiritual Growth*. Rev. ed. London: Hodder and Stoughton, 1989.

Fowler, Orson S. *Practical Phrenology*. New York: O. S. and L. N. Fowler, 1847.

Franklin, Benjamin. *The Works of Benjamin Franklin: Including the Private As Well As the Official and Scientific Correspondence Together with the Unmutilated and Correct Version of the Autobiography*. Vol. 8, *Letters and Misc. Writings, 1779–1781*, edited by John Bigelow. New York: G. P. Putnam's Sons, Knickerbocker, 1904.

Fransquet, Peter D., et al. "The Epigenitic Clock as a Predictor of Disease and Mortality Risk: A Systematic Review and Meta-Analysis." *Clinical Epigenetics* 11 (2019). https://doi.org/10.1186/s13148-109-0656-7.

Friedman, David B., and T. E. Johnson. "A Mutation in the Age-1 Gene in *Caenorhabditis elegans* Lengthens Life and Reduces Hermaphrodite Fertility." *Genetics* 118 (1988) 75–86.

Fries, Heinrich. "Myth." In *Encyclopedia of Theology: The Concise* Sacramentum Mundi, edited by Karl Rahner. London: Burnes & Oats, 1975.

Fries, James F. "Aging, Natural Death and Compression of Morbidity." *New England Journal of Medicine* 303 (1980) 130–35.

———. "An Introduction to the Compression of Morbidity." *Gerontologica Perspecta* 1 (1987) 5–8.

Frolkis, Vladimir V., ed. *Aging and Life-Prolonging Processes*. Translated by Nicholas Bobrov. New York: Springer-Verlag Wien, 1982.

Frolkis, Vladimir V., and K. K. Muradian. *Life Span Prolongation*. Boca Raton, FL: CRC, 1991.

Fukuyama, Francis. *Our Posthuman Future: Consequences of the Biotechnology Revolution*. New York: Farrar, Straus and Giroux, 2002.

Funkenstein, Amos. *Theology and the Scientific Imagination: From the Middle Ages to the Seventeenth Century*. Princeton: Princeton University Press, 1986.

Fussell, Samuel W. *Muscle: Confessions of an Unlikely Body Builder*. New York: Avon, 1991.

Gabbatt, Adam. "Is Silicon Valley's Quest for Immortality a Fate Worse Than Death?" *The Guardian*, February 23, 2019. https://www.theguardian.com/technology/2019/feb/22/silicon-valley-immortality-blood-infusion-gene-therapy.

Gaukroger, Stephen. *Francis Bacon and the Transformation of Early-Modern Philosophy*. Cambridge: Cambridge University Press, 2004.

Gavrilov, Leonid A. "Pieces of the Puzzle: An Interview with Leonid A. Gavrilov." *Journal of Anti-Aging Medicine* 5 (2002) 255–63.

Gay, Craig M. *The Way of the (Modern) World: Or, Why It's Tempting to Live As If God Doesn't Exist*. Grand Rapids: Eerdmans, 1998.

Gemelli, Benedino. "The History of Life and Death: A 'Spiritual' History from Invisible Matter to Prolongation of Life." Translated by Richard Matthews, *Early Science and Medicine* 17 (2012) 134–57.

Gems, David. "Is More Life Always Better? The New Biology of Aging and the Meaning of Life." *Hasting Center Report* 33 (2003) 31–39.

Gerson, Lloyd P. *The Cambridge Companion to Plotinus*. Cambridge: Cambridge University Press, 1996.

Gilson, Étienne. *God and Philosophy*. 2d ed. New Haven, CT: Yale University Press, 2002.

Glannon, Walter. "Extending the Human Lifespan." *Journal of Medicine and Philosophy* 27 (2002) 339–54.

———. "Identity, Prudential Concern, and Extended Lives." *Bioethics* 16 (2002) 266–83.

———. *Genes and Future People: Philosophical Issues in Human Genetics*. Boulder, CO: Westview, 2001.

———. "Reply to Harris." *Bioethics* 16 (2002) 292–97.

Godwin, William. *Enquiry Concerning Political Justice, and Its Influence on Morals and Happiness*. 2 vols. 3rd ed. Edited by F. E. L. Priestley. Toronto: University of Toronto Press, 1946.

Goehring, James E. *Ascetics, Society, and the Desert: Studies in Early Egyptian Monasticism*. Harrisburg, PA: Trinity, 1999.

Gompertz, Benjamin. "On the Nature of the Function Expressive of the Law of Human Mortality and on a New Mode of Determining Life Contingencies." *Philosophical Transactions of the Royal Society of London* 115 (1825) 513–85.

Gordon, Siamon. "Elie Metchnikoff: Father of Natural Immunity." *European Journal of Immunology* 38 (2008) 3257–64.

Gosden, Roger G. *Cheating Time: Science, Sex, and Aging*. New York: W. H. Freeman, 1996.

Graham, Sylvester. *A Lecture to Young Men on Chastity*. Boston: Light and Stearns, 1834.

———. *Lectures on the Science of Human Life, Containing Three Lectures—Eighth, the Organs and their Uses; Thirteenth, Man's Physical Nature and the Structure of His Teeth; Fourteenth, the Dietetic Character of Man*. Battle Creek, MI: The Office of The Health Reformer, 1872.

Grant, Robert M. *Gnosticism: An Anthology*. London: Collins, 1961.

———. *Gnosticism and Early Christianity*. New York: Columbia University Press, 1959.

Grant, Robert M., and D. N. Freedman, eds. *The Secret Sayings of Jesus*. Garden City, NY: Doubleday, 1960.

Green, Robert M., trans. *A Translation of Galen's Hygiene: De Sanitate Tuenda*. Springfield, IL: Charles C. Thomas, 1951.

Greer, Rowan A. "Special Gift and Special Burden: Views of Old Age in the Early Church." In *Growing Old in Christ*, edited by Stanley Hauerwas et al., 19–37. Grand Rapids: Eerdmans, 2003.

Gregg, Robert C., ed. *Athanasius: The Life of Antony and the Letter to Marcellinius*. London: SPCK, 1980.

Gregory of Nyssa. *On the Making of Man*. In *Nicene and Post-Nicene Fathers*, Second Series. Edited by Philip Schaff and Henry Wace. Vol. 5, *Select Writings and Letters of Gregory, Bishop of Nyssa*. Peabody, MA: Hendrickson, 1996.

Greider Carol W., and Elizabeth H. Blackburn. "Identification of a Specific Telomere Terminal Transferase Activity in *Tetrahymena* Extracts." *Cell* 43 (1985) 405–13.

Gruman, Gerald J. "C. A. Stephens—A Pioneer of American Gerontology." *Geriatrics* 14 (1959) 332–36.

———. "C. A. Stephens—Popular Author and Prophet of Gerontology." *New England Journal of Medicine* 254 (1956) 658–60.

———. *The "Fixed Period" Controversy*. New York: Arno, 1979.

———. "A History of Ideas about the Prolongation of Life: The Evolution of Prolongevity Hypotheses to 1800." In *Transactions of the American Philosophical Society* 56 (1966) 1–102.

Grumett, David, and Rachael Muers. *Theology on the Menu: Asceticism, Meat and Christian Diet*. London, Routledge, 2010.

Guarente, Leonard P. *Ageless Quest: One Scientist's Search for Genes That Prolong Youth*. Cold Spring Harbor: Cold Spring Harbor Laboratory, 2003.

———. "Forestalling the Great Beyond with the Help of Sir2." *The Scientist* 18, April 26, 2004, http://www.the-scientist.com/2004/4/26/34/1.

Guarante, Leonard P., and C. Kenyon. "Genetic Pathways That Regulate Ageing in Model Organisms." *Nature* 408 (2000) 255–62.

Gull, William W. "Apepsia Hysterica, Anorexia Nervosa." *Transactions of the Clinical Society* 7 (1874) 22–24.

Gustafson, James M. *Ethics from a Theocentric Perspective*. Vol. 2, *Ethics and Theology*. Chicago: University of Chicago Press, 1984.

Haber, Carole. "Anti-Aging: Why Now? A Historical Framework for Understanding the Contemporary Enthusiasm." *Generations: The Journal of the Western Gerontological Society* 25 (2001–2002) 9–14.

———. *Beyond Sixty-Five: The Dilemma of Old Age in America's Past*. 2d ed. Cambridge: Cambridge University Press, 1985.

Haber, Carole, and Brian Gratton, eds. *Old Age and the Search for Security: An American Social History.* Bloomington, IN: Indiana University Press, 1993.

Hackler, Chris. "Troubling Implications of Doubling the Human Life Span." *Generations: The Journal of the Western Gerontological Society* 25 (2001–2002) 15–19.

Hahn, William C., et al. "Inhibition of Telomerase Limits the Growth of Human Cancer Cells." *Nature Medicine* 5 (1999) 1164–70.

Hall, Stephen S. "Is an Anti-Aging Drug around the Corner?" *MIT Technology Review*, September/October 2019, 22–23.

———. *Merchants of Immortality: Chasing the Dream of Human Life Extension.* Boston: Houghton-Mifflin, 2003.

Hankinson, R. J. "Philosophy of Science." In *The Cambridge Companion to Aristotle*, edited by Jonathan Barnes, 109–39. Cambridge: Cambridge University Press, 1995.

Hanson, Mark. "An Open Letter to Leon Kass on Genetics." *Dialog: A Journal of Theology* 43 (2004) 125–28.

Harley, Calvin B., et al. "A Natural Product Telomerase Activator as Part of a Health Maintenance Program." *Rejuvenation Research* 14 (2011) 45–56.

Harman, Denham. "Aging: Overview." *Annals of the New York Academy of Science* 928 (2001) 1–21.

———. "The Aging Process." *Proceedings of the National Academy of Sciences of the USA* 78 (1981) 7123–28.

———. "Aging: A Theory Based on Free Radical and Radiation Chemistry." *Journal of Gerontology* 11 (1956) 298–300.

———. "Free Radical Theory of Aging: Consequences of Mitochondrial Aging." *Age* (1983) 86–94.

Harman, Denham, et al., eds. *Towards Prolongation of the Healthy Lifespan: Practical Approaches to Intervention.* New York: New York Academy of Sciences, 1998.

Harmless, William, SJ. *Desert Christians: An Introduction to the Literature of Early Monasticism.* Oxford: Oxford University Press, 2004.

Harnack, Adolf von. *History of Dogma: Complete in Seven Volumes Bound as Four.* Vol. 1. Translated by Neil Buchanan. New York: Dover, 1961.

Harrington, John, et al. *The School of Salernum: Regimen Sanitatis Salernitanum.* New York: Paul B. Hoeber, 1920.

Harris, John. *Clones, Genes, and Immortality.* Oxford: Oxford University Press, 1998.

———. "Intimations of Immortality." *Science* 288 (2000) 59.

———. "A Response to Walter Glannon." *Bioethics* 16 (2002) 284–91.

Harris, John, and Søren Holm. "Extending the Human Lifespan and the Precautionary Paradox." *Journal of Medicine and Philosophy* 27 (2002) 355–68.

Harrison, David E., et al. "Rapamycin Fed Late in Life Extends the Lifespan in Genetically Heterogeneous Mice." *Nature* 460 (2009) 392–95.

Harrison, Peter. *The Bible, Protestantism, and the Rise of Modern Science.* Cambridge: Cambridge University Press, 1998.

———. *The Fall of Man and the Foundations of Science.* Cambridge: Cambridge University Press, 2007.

Hart, R. W., and A. Turturro. "Theories of Aging." In *Review of Biological Research in Aging*, vol. 1, edited by M. Rothstein, 5–18. New York: Alan R. Liss, 1983.

Hauerwas, Stanley. *Naming the Silences: God, Medicine, and the Problem of Suffering.* Grand Rapids: Eerdmans, 1990.

———. *Suffering Presence: Theological Reflections on Medicine, the Mentally Handicapped, and the Church*. Notre Dame, IN: University of Notre Dame Press, 1984.

Hauerwas, Stanley, et al., eds. *Growing Old In Christ*. Grand Rapids: Eerdmans, 2003.

Hauerwas, Stanley, and Samuel Wells, eds. *The Blackwell Companion to Christian Ethics*. Oxford: Blackwell, 2004.

Hauerwas, Stanley, and Samuel Wells. "The Gift of the Church and the Gifts God Gives It." In *The Blackwell Companion to Christian Ethics*, edited by Stanley Hauerwas and Samuel Wells, 13–27. Oxford: Blackwell, 2004.

Hayasaki, Erika. "The Mouse That Died of Young Age." *MIT Technology Review*, September/October 2019, 24–29.

Haycock, David B. *Mortal Coil: A Short History of Living Longer*. New Haven, CT: Yale University Press, 2008.

Hayflick, Leonard. "Anti-Aging Medicine: Hype, Hope, and Reality." *Generations: The Journal of the Western Gerontological Society* 25 (2001–2002) 20–26.

———. "The Future of Aging." *Nature* 408 (2000) 267–69.

———. *How and Why We Age*. New York: Ballantine, 1994.

———. "Theories of Biological Aging." *Experimental Gerontology* 20 (1985) 145–49.

———, and P. Moorhead. "The Serial Cultivation of Human Diploid Strains." *Experimental Cell Research* 25 (1961) 585–621.

Henry, John. *Knowledge is Power: How Magic, the Government, and Apocalyptic Vision Inspired Francis Bacon to Create Modern Science*. London: Icon, 2002.

Hepworth, Julie. *The Social Construction of Anorexia Nervosa*. London: Sage, 1999.

Hess, Beth B., and Elizabeth W. Markson, eds. *Growing Old in America*. 4th ed. New Brunswick: Transaction, 1991.

Hewitt, Glenn A. *Regeneration and Morality: A Study of Charles Finney, Charles Hodge, John W. Nevin, and Horace Bushnell*. Brooklyn, NY: Carlson, 1991.

Hippocrates. *Hippocrates*. Vol. 4, *The Nature of Man*, translated by W. H. S. Jones and E. T. Withington. London: William Heinemann, 1931.

Holden, Constance. "The Quest to Reverse Time's Toll." *Science* 295 (2002) 1032–33.

Holstein, Martha B. "A Feminist Perspective on Anti-Aging." *Generations: The Journal of the Western Gerontological Society* 25 (2001–2002) 38–43.

Honda, Yoko, and Shuji Honda. "Oxidative Stress and Life Span Determination in the Nematode *Caenorhabditis elegans*." *Annals of the New York Academy of Science* 959 (2002) 466–74.

Howitz, Konrad T., et al. "Small Molecule Activators of Sirtuins Extend *Saccharomyces cerevisiae* Lifespan." *Nature* 424 (2003) 191–96.

Hung, Ko. *Alchemy, Medicine, Religion in the China of 320 A.D.: The 'Nei p'ien of Ko Hung (Pao p'u tzu)*. Translated by James R. Ware. Cambridge, MA: MIT Press, 1966.

Ianni, Alessandro, et al. "Sirt7 Stabilizes rDNA Heterochromatin Through Recruitment of DNMT1 and Sirt1." *Biochemical and Biophysical Research Communications* 492 (2017) 434–40.

Ignatius of Antioch. *The Epistle of Ignatius to the Ephesians*. In *Ante-Nicene Fathers: The Writings of the Fathers Down to A.D. 325*, ed. Alexander Roberts, James Donaldson, and A. Cleveland Coxe. Vol. 1, *The Apostolic Fathers, Justin Martyr, Irenaeus*. Peabody, MA: Hendrickson, 1996.

Illich, Ivan. "The Political Uses of Natural Death." In *Death Inside Out: The Hasting Center Report*, edited by Peter Steinfels and Robert M. Veatch, 25–42. New York: Harper and Row, 1974.

Ingram, Donald K. "Is Aging Measurable?" In *Life Span Extension: Consequences and Open Questions*, edited by Frédérick C. Ludwig, 18–42. New York: Springer, 1991.

Irenaeus. *Against Heresies*. In *Ante-Nicene Fathers*, eds. Alexander Roberts, James Donaldson, and A. Cleveland Cox. Vol. 1, *The Apostolic Fathers, Justin Martyr, Irenaeus*. Peabody, MA: Hendrickson, 1996.

Isaacson, Betsy. "Silicon Valley Is Trying to Make Humans Immortal—And Finding Some Success." *Newsweek*, March 5, 2015. www.newsweek.com/2015/03/13/silicon-valley-trying-make-humans-immortal-and-finding-some-success-311402.html.

Jacobs, Alan. "Leon Kass and the Genesis of Wisdom." *First Things* 134 (2003) 30–35.

Jacobs, Tonya L., et al. "Intensive Meditation Training, Immune Cell Telomerase Activity, and Psychological Mediators." *Psychoneuroendocrinology* 36 (2011) 664–81.

Jacobus, Mary, et al., eds. *Body/Politics: Women and the Discourses of Science*. New York: Routledge, 1990.

James, Michael. "167 or Not, Indian Uses His Fists to Break Up Press Conference." *New York Times*, September 28, 1956.

Jamieson, Anne, et al., eds. *Critical Approaches to Ageing and Later Life*. Philadelphia: Open University Press, 1997.

Jantzen, Grace M. "Do We Need Immortality?" *Modern Theology* 1(1984) 33–44.

Jaskelioff, Mariela, et al. "Telomerase Reactivation Reverses Tissue Degeneration in Aged Telomerase-Deficient Mice." *Nature* 469 (2011) 102–6.

Jazwinski, S. Michal. "Longevity, Genes, and Aging." *Science* 273 (1996) 54–59.

Jean-Nesmy, Claude. "The Perspective of Senescence and Death: An Opportunity for Man to Mature." In *Life Span Extension: Consequences and Open Questions*, edited by Frédérick C. Ludwig, 146–153. New York: Springer, 1991.

Jeeves, Malcom A., ed. *From Cells to Souls—and Beyond: Changing Portraits of Human Nature*. Grand Rapids: Eerdmans, 2004.

Jerome. *Saint Jerome's Hebrew Questions on Genesis*. Translated by C. T. R. Hayward. Oxford: Clarendon, 1995.

Joad, C. E. M. *The Recovery of Belief: A Restatement of Christian Philosophy*. London: Faber and Faber, 1952.

John of Shmūn. *An Encomium on Saint Antony*. In *The Life of Antony: The Coptic Life and the Greek Life*, translated by Tim Vivian and Apostolos N. Athanassakis, 1–36. Kalamazoo: Cistercian, 2003.

Johnson, Malcom Lewis, ed. *The Cambridge Handbook of Age and Ageing*. Cambridge: Cambridge University Press, 2005.

Johnson, Thomas E. "Genetic Influences on Aging." *Experimental Gerontology* 32 (1997) 11–22.

———. "Increased Life-Span of *age-1* Mutant in *Caenorhabditis elegans* and Lower Gompertz Rate of Aging." *Science* 249 (1990) 908–12.

Jonas, Hans. "The Burden and Blessing of Mortality." *Hastings Center Report* 22 (1992) 34–40.

———. *The Gnostic Religion: The Message of the Alien God and the Beginnings of Christianity*. 2d ed. London: Routledge, 1963.

———. "Immortality and the Modern Temper." *Harvard Theological Review* 55 (1962) 1–20.

———. "Technology, Ethics, and Biogenetic Art: Observations on the New Role of Man as Creator." *Communio* 12 (1985) 92–107.
Jones, Richard F. *Ancients and Moderns: A Study of the Rise of the Scientific Movement in Seventeenth-Century England.* 2d ed. St. Louis: Washington University Press, 1961.
Jonsen, Albert R. *A Short History of Medical Ethics.* Oxford: Oxford University Press, 2000.
Juengst, Eric T., et al. "Biogerontology, 'Anti-aging Medicine,' and the Challenges of Human Enhancement." *Hasting Center Report* 33 (2003) 21–30.
Juniper, D. F. *Man against Mortality, or Seven Essays on the Engineering of Man's Divinity.* New York: Charles Scribner's Sons, 1974.
Justice, Jamie N., et al. "Senolytics in Idiopathic Pulmonary Fibrosis: Results from a First-in-Human, Open-Label, Pilot Study." *EBioMedicine* 40 (2019) 554–63.
Juvin, Hervé. *The Coming of the Body.* Translated by John Howe. London: Verso, 2010.
Kaeberlein, Matt. "How Healthy is the Healthspan Concept?" *Geroscience* 40 (2018) 361–64.
———, et al. "The *SIR2/3/4* Complex and *SIR2* Alone Promote Longevity in *Saccharomyces cerevisiae* by Two Different Mechanisms." *Genes Development* 13 (1999) 2570–80.
Kammerer, Paul. *Rejuvenation and the Prolongation of Human Efficiency Experiences with the Steinach-Operation on Man and Animals.* London: Methuen, 1924.
Kannengiesser, Charles. "Antony, Athanasius, Evagrius: The Egyptian Fate of Origenism." *Coptic Church Review* 16 (1995) 3–8.
———. "Athanasius of Alexandria and the Ascetic Movement of His Time." In *Asceticism*, edited by Vincent L. Wimbush and Richard Valantasis, 479–92. Oxford: Oxford University Press, 1998.
Kapahi, Pankaj, et al. "Regulation of Lifespan in *Drosophila* by Modulation of Genes in the TOR Signaling Pathway." *Current Biology* 14 (2004) 885–90.
Kart, Cary S., and Barbara Bolling Manard. *Aging in America: Readings in Social Gerontology.* 2d ed. Sherman Oaks, CA: Alfred, 1981.
Kass, Leon R. "Ageless Bodies, Happy Souls: Biotechnology and the Pursuit of Perfection." *The New Atlantis: A Journal of Technology and Society* (2003) 9–28, http://www.thenewatlantis.com/archive/1/kassprint.htm.
———. "The Case for Mortality." *The American Scholar* 52 (1983) 173–191.
———. "L'Chaim and Its Limits: Why Not Immortality?" *First Things* 113 (2001) 17–24.
———. *Life, Liberty and the Defense of Dignity: The Challenge for Bioethics.* San Francisco: Encounter, 2002.
———. *Toward A More Natural Science: Biology and Human Affairs.* New York: Free, 1985.
Kassner, Enid, and Robert W. Bectel. *Midlife and Older Americans with Disabilities: Who Gets Help? A Chartbook.* Washington, DC: AARP Public Policy Institute, 1998.
Katz, Stephen. *Disciplining Old Age: The Formation of Gerontological Knowledge.* Charlottesville: University Press of Virginia, 1996.
———. "Growing Older Without Aging? Positive Aging, Anti-Ageism, and Anti-Aging." *Generations: The Journal of the Western Gerontological Society* 25 (2001–2002) 27–32.
Kelly, J. N. D. *Early Christian Doctrines.* 2d ed. London: Adam and Charles Black, 1960.
Kennedy, Brian K., and Juniper K. Pennypacker. "Aging Interventions Get Human." *Oncotarget* 6 (2015) 590–91.

Kenyon, Cynthia, et al. "A *C. elegans* Mutant That Lives Twice as Long as Wild Type." *Nature* 399 (1993) 362–66.
Kerr, Fergus. "Cartesianism According to Karl Barth." *New Blackfriars* 77 (1996) 358–68.
———. *Immortal Longings: Versions of Transcending Humanity*. London: SPCK, 1997.
Kett, Joseph F. "Decline and Fall." *Reviews in American History* 21 (1993) 309–313.
Kierkegaard, Søren A. *The Sickness unto Death: A Christian Psychological Exposition for Upbuilding and Awakening*. Translated and edited by Howard V. Hong and Edna H. Hong. Princeton: Princeton University Press, 1980.
Kimble, Melvin, and Susan H. McFadden, eds. *Aging, Spirituality, and Religion: A Handbook*. 2 vols. Minneapolis: Fortress, 1995–2003.
King, Charles W. *The Gnostics and Their Remains: Ancient and Mediaeval*. 2d ed. London: D. Nutt, 1887.
Kirk, Kenneth E. *The Vision of God: The Christian Doctrine of the Summum Bonum*. 2d ed. New York: Harper Torchbooks, 1932.
Kirkland, James L., and Tamara Tchkonia. "Aging, Cell Senescence, and Chronic Disease: Emerging Therapeutic Strategies." *Journal of the American Medical Association* 320 (2018) 1319–20.
———, et al. "The Clinical Potential of Senolytic Drugs." *Journal of the American Geriatrics Society* 65 (2017) 2297–301.
Kirkwood, Thomas B. L. "The Genetics of Old Age." In *A Companion to Genethics*, edited by Justine Burley and John Harris, 43–50. Malden, MA: Blackwell, 2004.
———. *Time of Our Lives: The Science of Human Aging*. Oxford: Oxford University Press, 1999.
Klatz, Ronald. "Anti-Aging Medicine: Resounding, Independent Support for Expansion of an Innovative Medical Specialty." *Generations: The Journal of the Western Gerontological Society* 25 (2001–2002) 59–62.
Klein, Bruce J., ed. *The Scientific Conquest of Death: Essays on Infinite Lifespans*. Buenos Aires: Libros en Red, 2004.
Krötke, Wolf. "The Humanity of the Human Person in Karl Barth's Anthropology." Translated by Philip G. Ziegler. In *The Cambridge Companion to Karl Barth*, edited by John Webster, 159–76. Cambridge: Cambridge University Press, 2000.
Kübler-Ross, Elisabeth. *On Death and Dying*. New York. Collier, 1969.
Kurtzman, Joel, and Phillip Gordon. *No More Dying: The Conquest of Aging and the Extension of Human Life*. Los Angeles: J. P. Tarcher, 1976.
Kurzweil, Ray. *The Age of Spiritual Machines: When Computers Exceed Human Intelligence*. New York: Penguin, 2000.
Kurzweil, Ray, and Terry Grossman. *Nine Steps to Living Well Forever*. New York: Rodale, 2009.
Lakowski, Bernard, and S. Hekimi. "Determination of Lifespan in *Caenorhabditis elegans* by Four Clock Genes." *Science* 272 (1996) 1010–13.
Lammers, Steven E., and Allen Verhey, eds. *On Moral Medicine: Theological Perspectives in Medical Ethics*. 2d ed. Grand Rapids: Eerdmans, 1998.
Lane, Mark A., et al. "The Serious Search for an Anti-Aging Pill." *Scientific American* 287 (2002) 24–29.
———, et al. "Caloric Restriction and Aging in Primates: Relevance to Humans and Possible CR Mimetics." *Microscopy Research and Technique* 59 (2002) 335–38.
Laplante, Mathieu, and D. M. Sabatini. "mTOR Signaling in Growth Control and Disease." *Cell* 149 (2012) 274–93.

Larchet, Jean-Claude. *Theology of the Body*. Translated by Michael Donley. Yonkers, NY: St. Vladimir's Seminary Press, 2016.
Larsen, Pamela L., et al. "Genes That Regulate Both Development and Longevity in *Caenohrabditis elegans*." *Genetics* 139 (1995) 1567–83.
Lasch, Christopher. "Aging in a Culture Without a Future." *The Hastings Center Report* (1977) 42–44.
Lasègue, Charles. "De l'anorexie hystérique." *Archives générales de médecine* 21 (1873) 385–403.
Leder, Drew. *The Absent Body*. Chicago: University of Chicago Press, 1992.
Leder, Drew, ed. *The Body in Medical Thought and Practice*. Dordrecht: Kluwer Academic, 1992.
Lee, Cheol-Koo, et al. "Gene Expression Profile of Aging and Its Retardation by Caloric Restriction." *Science* 285 (1999) 1390–93.
Lee, Newton, ed. *The Transhumanism Handbook*. Cham, Switzerland: Springer Nature Switzerland, 2019.
Lee, Shin-Hae, et al. "Sirtuin Signaling in Cellular Senescence and Aging." *BMB Reports* 52 (2019) 24–34.
Lelwica, Michelle Mary. *Starving for Salvation: The Spiritual Dimensions of Eating Problems among American Girls and Women*. New ed. Oxford: Oxford University Press, 2002.
Lepore, Jill. *The Mansion of Happiness: A History of Life and Death*. New York: Alfred A. Knopf, 2012.
Lewis, Alan E. *Between Cross and Resurrection: A Theology of Holy Saturday*. Grand Rapids: Eerdmans, 2001.
Leyser, Conrad. *Authority and Asceticism from Augustine to Gregory*. New York: Oxford University Press, 2000.
Liao, Chen-Yu, et al. "Genetic Variation in the Murine Lifespan Response to Dietary Restriction: From Life Extension to Life Shortening." *Cell* 9 (2010) 92–95.
Lin, Su-Ju, et al. "Requirement of NAD and SIR2 for Life-Span Extension by Calorie Restriction in *Saccharomyces cerevisiae*." *Science* 289 (2000) 2126–28.
Longo, Valter D. *The Longevity Diet: Discover the New Science Behind Stem Cell Activation and Regeneration to Slow Aging, Fight Disease, and Optimize Weight*. New York: Avery, 2018.
Longo, Valter D., and Salvatore Cortellino. "Enhancing Stem Cell Transplantation with 'Nutri-technology.'" *Cell Stem Cell* 19 (2016) 681–82.
Losee, John. *A Historical Introduction to the Philosophy of Science*. 4th ed. Oxford: Oxford University Press, 2001.
Louth, Andrew. *The Origins of the Christian Mystical Tradition: From Plato to Denys*. Oxford: Clarendon, 1981.
Luckinbill, Leo S., et al. "Selection for Delayed Senescence in *Drosophila melanogaster*." *Evolution* 38 (1984) 996–1003.
Ludwig, Frédérick, C. ed. *Life Span Extension: Consequences and Open Questions*. New York: Springer, 1991.
Luther, Martin. *The Babylonian Captivity of the Church*. In *Three Treatises: From the American Edition of* Luther's Works. Philadelphia: Fortress, 1970.
Lysaught, M. Therese. "Becoming One Body: Health Care and Cloning." In *The Blackwell Companion to Christian Ethics*, edited by Stanley Hauerwas and Samuel Wells, 263–75. Oxford: Blackwell, 2004.

———. "Memory, Funerals, and the Communion of Saints: Growing Old and Practices of Remembering." In *Growing Old in Christ*, edited by Stanley Hauerwas et al., 267–301. Grand Rapids: Eerdmans, 2003.

MacIntyre, Alasdair. *After Virtue: A Study in Moral Theory*. 2d ed. London: Gerald Duckworth, 1985.

Malthus, Thomas Robert. *An Essay on the Principle of Population, as it Affects the Future Improvement of Society, with Remarks on the Speculations of Mr. Godwin, M. Condorcet, and other Writers*. London: Printed for J. Johnson, 1798.

Mannick, Joan B., et al. "mTOR Inhibition Improves Immune Function in the Elderly." *Science Translational Medicine* 6 (2014). https://doi: 10.1126/scitranslmed.3009892.

Martin, George M., et al. "Genetic Analysis of Ageing: Role of Oxidative Damage and Environmental Stresses." *Nature Genetics* 13 (1996) 25–34.

Masoro, Edward J. "Caloric Restriction and Aging: An Update." *Experimental Gerontology* 35 (2000) 299–305.

Mather, Cotton. *Parentator: Memoirs of the Remarkable in the Life and Death of the Ever-Memorable Dr. Increase Mather, Who Expired August 23, 1723*. Boston: B. Green, 1724.

Mather, Increase. *Pray for the Rising Generation: Or a Sermon Wherein Godly Parents Are Encouraged to Pray and Believe for Their Children*. Boston: John Foster, 1678.

———. *Two Discourses Shewing I. That the LORD'S Ears are open to the Prayers of the Righteous, II. The Dignity and Duty of Aged Servants of the LORD*. Boston: Printed by B. Green for Daniel Henchmen, 1716.

Matthews, Steven. *Theology and Science in the Thought of Francis Bacon*. Hampshire, UK: Ashgate, 2008.

Mattison, Julie A., et al. "Caloric Restriction Improves Health and Survival of Rhesus Monkeys." *Nature Communications* (2017). https://doi:10.1038/ncomms14063.

———, et al. "Resveratrol Prevents High Fat/Sucrose Diet-Induced Central Arterial Wall and Stiffening in Non-Human Primates." *Cell Metabolism* 20 (2014) 183–90.

May, William F. "The Sacral Power of Death in Contemporary Experience." In *Perspectives on Death*, edited by L. O. Mills, 168–96. New York: Abingdon, 1969.

McCay, Clive M., and M. F. Crowell "Prolonging the Life Span." *Scientific Monthly* 39 (1934) 405–14.

McKenny, Gerald P. "Bioethics, the Body, and the Legacy of Bacon." In *On Moral Medicine: Theological Perspectives in Medical Ethics*, edited by Steven E. Lammers and Allen Verhey, 2d ed., 308–23. Grand Rapids: Eerdmans, 1998.

———. "Biotechnology and the Normative Significance of Human Nature: A Contribution from Theological Anthropology." *Studies in Christian Ethics* 26 (2013) 18–36.

———. "Gene Therapy: Ethics, Religious Perspectives." In *Encyclopedia of Ethical, Legal and Policy Issues in Bioethnology*, edited by T. H. Murray and M. J. Mehlman, vol. 1, 300–311. New York: John Wiley, 2000.

———. "Religion and Gene Therapy: The End of One Debate, the Beginning of Another." In *A Companion to Genethics*, edited by Justine Burley and John Harris, 287–301. Malden, MA: Blackwell, 2004.

———. "Religion, Biotechnology and the Integrity of Nature: A Critical Examination." In *Claiming Power over Life: Religion and Biotechnology Policy*, edited by Mark J. Hanson, 169–91. Washington, DC: Georgetown University Press, 2001.

———. "Technologies of Desire: Theology, Ethics, and the Enhancement of Human Traits." *Theology Today* 59 (2000) 90–103.
———. *To Relieve the Human Condition: Bioethics, Technology, and the Body.* Albany, NY: State University of New York Press, 1997.
McKnight, Scot. *Fasting.* Nashville: Thomas Nelson, 2009.
McKnight, Stephen A. *The Religious Foundations of Francis Bacon's Thought.* Columbia, MO: University of Missouri Press, 2006.
McLean, Stuart D. *Humanity in the Thought of Karl Barth.* Edinburgh: T. & T. Clark, 1981.
Meador, Keith, and Shaun Henson. "Growing Old in a Therapeutic Culture." In *Growing Old in Christ*, edited by Stanley Hauerwas et al., 90–111. Grand Rapids: Eerdmans, 2003.
Medvedev, Zhores A. "An Attempt at a Rational Classification of Theories of Ageing." *Biological Reviews and Biological Proceedings of the Cambridge Philosophical Society* 65 (1990) 375–98.
———. "The Structural Basis of Aging." In *Life Span Extension: Consequences and Open Questions*, edited by Frédérick C. Ludwig, 9–17. New York: Springer, 1991.
Meilaender, Gilbert C. *Bioethics: A Primer for Christians.* Grand Rapids: Eerdmans, 1996.
———. *Body, Soul, and Bioethics.* Notre Dame, IN: University of Notre Dame Press, 1995.
———. *Should We Live Forever? The Ethical Ambiguities of Aging.* Grand Rapids: Eerdmans, 2013.
———. "*Terra es animata:* On Having a Life." In *On Moral Medicine: Theological Perspectives in Medical Ethics*, edited by Steven E. Lammers and Allen Verhey, 2d ed., 390–400. Grand Rapids: Eerdmans, 1998.
———. "Why Remember?" *First Things* 135 (2003) 20–24.
Melov, Simon, et al. "Extension of Life-span With Superoxide Dismutase/Catalase Mimetics." *Science* 289 (2000) 1567–69.
Meredith, Anthony. "Asceticism—Christian and Greek." *Journal of Theological Studies* 27 (1976) 313–32.
Messer, Neil. *Flourishing: Health, Disease, and Bioethics in Theological Perspective.* Grand Rapids: Eerdmans, 2013.
Metchnikoff, Élie. *The Nature of Man: Studies in Optimistic Philosophy.* Translated by P. Chalmers Mitchell. London: Putnam, 1904.
———. *The Prolongation of Life: Optimistic Studies.* Rev. ed. London: William Heinemann, 1910.
Metchnikoff, Olga. *Life of Elie Metchnikoff.* London: Constable, 1921.
Meyers, Carol. *Discovering Eve: Ancient Israelite Women in Context.* New York: Oxford University Press, 1988.
Midgley, Mary. *Science as Salvation: A Modern Myth and Its Meaning.* London: Routledge, 1992.
Miles, Margaret R. *Plotinus on Body and Beauty: Society, Philosophy, and Religion in Third-Century Rome.* Oxford: Blackwell, 1999.
Miller, Perry. *The New England Mind: From Colony to Province.* Boston: Beacon, 1953.
———. *The New England Mind: The Seventeenth Century.* Cambridge, MA: Harvard University Press, 1967.
Miller, Philip Lee, and Monica Reinagel. *The Life Extension Revolution: The New Science of Growing Older Without Aging.* New York: Bantam, 2005.
Miller, Richard A. "Extending Life: Scientific Prospects and Political Obstacles." In *The Fountain of Youth: Cultural, Scientific, and Ethical Perspectives on a Biomedical*

Goal, edited by Stephen G. Post and Robert H. Binstock, 228–48. Oxford: Oxford University Press, 2004.

Miller-McLemore, Bonnie J. *Death, Sin and the Moral Life: Contemporary Cultural Interpretations of Death*. Atlanta: Scholars, 1988.

———. "The Sting of Death." *Theology Today* 45 (1989) 415–26.

Mills, Liston O. *Perspectives on Death*. Nashville: Abingdon, 1969.

Minois, Georges. *History of Old Age: From Antiquity to the Renaissance*. Translated by Sarah Hanbury Tenison. Chicago: University of Chicago Press, 1989.

Mitchell, C. Ben. "The Quest for Immortality." In *Aging, Death, and the Quest for Immortality*, edited by C. Ben Mitchell et al., 153–62. Grand Rapids: Eerdmans, 2004.

Mitford, Jessica. *The American Way of Death*. Harmondsworth: Penguin, 1963.

Mobbs, Charles V., et al. "Neuroendrocrine and Pharmacological Manipulations to Assess How Caloric Restriction Increases Life Span." *Journal of Gerontology: Biological Sciences and Medical Sciences* 56A, special issue (2001) 34–44.

Monroe, Rachel. "The Guru's Dilemma." *Men's Health*, January/February 2019, 108–11.

Moody, Harold R. *Aging: Concepts and Controversies*. Thousand Oaks, CA: Pine Forge, 2002.

———. "The Meaning of Old Age: Scenarios for the Future." In *A World Growing Old: The Coming Health Care Challenges*, edited by D. Callahan et al., 9–19. Washington, DC: Georgetown University Press, 1995.

———. "Who's Afraid of Life Extension?" *Generations: The Journal of the Western Gerontological Society* 25 (2001–2002) 33–37.

Moon, Maggie. *The Telomere Diet and Cookbook: A Scientific Approach to Slow Your Genetic Aging and Live a Longer, Healthier Life*. Berkeley, CA: Ulysses, 2019.

Moore, Thomas J. *Life Span: Who Lives Longer—and Why*. New York: Simon & Schuster, 1993.

More, Max, and Natasha-Vita More, eds. *The Transhumanist Reader: Classical and Contemporary Essays on the Science, Technology, and Philosophy of the Human Future*. West Sussex, UK: Wiley-Blackwell, 2013.

Morgan, Edmund S. *The Puritan Family: Religion and Domestic Relations in Seventeenth-century New England*. 2d ed. New York: Harper and Row, 1966.

Muntersbjorn, Madeline M. "Francis Bacon's Philosophy of Science: *Machina intellectus* and *Forma indita*." *Philosophy of Science* 70 (2003) 1137–48.

Murphy, Coleen T., et al. "Genes That Act Downstream of DAF-16 to Influence the Lifespan of *Caenorhabditis elegans*." *Nature* 424 (2003) 277–83.

Murphy, Kevin, and Robert Topel. "The Value of Health and Longevity." *Journal of Political Economy* 114 (2006) 871–904.

Murphy, Timothy F. "A Cure for Aging?" *The Journal of Medicine and Philosophy* 11 (1986) 237–55.

Musurillo, Herbert. "The Problem of Ascetical Fasting in the Greek Patristic Writers." *Traditio* 12 (1956) 1–64.

Nashiro, Kaoru, et al. "Brain Structure and Function Associated with Younger Adults in Growth Hormone Receptor-Deficient Humans." *Journal of Neuroscience* 37 (2007) 1696–1707.

Nassif, Bradley. *Bringing Jesus to the Desert*. Grand Rapids: Zondervan, 2011.

National Institutes of Health. "Senolytic Drugs Reverse Damage Caused by Senescent Cells in Mice." July 9, 2018. https://www.nih.gov/news-events/news-releases/senolytic-drugs-reverse-damage-caused-senescent-cells-mice.

Nazianzen, Gregory. *Orations*. In *Nicene and Post-Nicene Fathers*, Second Series. Edited by Philip Schaff and Henry Wace. Vol. 7, *Cyril of Jerusalem, Gregory Nazianzen*. Peabody, MA: Hendrickson, 1996.

Niebuhr, H. Richard. *The Responsible Self: An Essay in Christian Moral Philosophy*. San Francisco: Harper and Row, 1963.

Niebuhr, Reinhold. *The Nature and Destiny of Man: A Christian Interpretation*. 2 vols. London: Nisbet, 1943.

Noll, Mark A. *America's God: From Jonathan Edwards to Abraham Lincoln*. Oxford: Oxford University Press, 2002.

Nouwen, Henri J. M., and Walter J. Gaffney. *Aging: The Fulfillment of Life*. Garden City, NY: Image, 1976.

Ocampo, Ambeth R., et al. "In Vivo Amelioration of Age-Associated Hallmarks by Partial Reprogramming." *Cell* 167 (2016) 1719–33.

O'Connor, Elizabeth. *Search for Silence*. Waco, TX: Word, 1971.

O'Donovan. Oliver. *Begotten Or Made?* Oxford: Oxford University Press, 1984.

———. *Church in Crisis: The Gay Controversy and the Anglican Communion*. Eugene, OR: Cascade, 2008.

———. "Keeping Body and Soul Together." In *On Moral Medicine: Theological Perspectives in Medical Ethics*, edited by Steven E. Lammers and Allen Verhey, 2d ed., 223–38. Grand Rapids: Eerdmans, 1998.

———. *Resurrection and Moral Order: An Outline for Evangelical Ethics*. 2d ed. Grand Rapids: Eerdmans, 1994.

———. *Self, World, and Time: Ethics as Theology*. Vol. 1. Grand Rapids: Eerdmans, 2013.

O'Meara, Dominic J. *Plotinus: An Introduction to the Enneads*. Oxford: Clarendon, 1993.

Olshansky, S. Jay. "Practical Limits to Life Expectancy in France." In *Longevity: To the Limit and Beyond*, edited by Jean-Marine Robine, James W. Vaupel, and Michael Bernard Jeune, 1–10. Berlin, NY: Springer, 1997.

———. "Session 2: Duration of Life: Is There a Biological Warranty Period?" The President's Council on Bioethics. December 12, 2002. https://bioethicsarchive.georgetown.edu/pcbe/transcripts/dec02/session2.html.

———. "A Wrinkle in Time: A Modest Proposal to Slow Aging and Extend Healthy Life." *Slate Magazine*, November 12, 2010, http://www.slate.com/id/2274468/pagenum/all/#p.2.

———, et al. "In Pursuit of the Longevity Dividend: What Should We Be Doing to Prepare for the Unprecedented Aging of Humanity?" *The Scientist* 20, March 2006, 28–33.

Olshansky, S. Jay., and Bruce A. Carnes. "No Truth to the Fountain of Youth." *Scientific American* 286 (2002) 78–81.

———. *The Quest for Immortality: Science at the Frontiers of Aging*. New York: W. W. Norton, 2001.

———, et al. "In Search of Methuselah: Estimating the Upper Limits to Human Longevity." *Science* 250 (1990) 634–40.

Orr, William C., and R. C. Sohal. "Extension of Life-Span by Overexpression of Superoxide Dismutase and Catalase in *Drosophila melanogaster*." *Science* 263 (1994) 1128–30.

Osler, William. "The Fixed Period." In *The "Fixed Period" Controversy*, edited by Gerald J. Gruman, 373–93. New York: Arno, 1979.

Ossewaarde, Marlies E., et al. "Age at Menopause, Cause-specific Mortality and Total Life Expectancy." *Epidemiology* 16 (2005) 556–62.
Overall, Christine. *Aging, Death, and Human Longevity: A Philosophical Inquiry.* Berkeley, CA: University of California Press, 2003.
———. "Longevity, Identity, and Moral Character: A Feminist Approach." In *The Fountain of Youth: Cultural, Scientific, and Ethical Perspectives on a Biomedical Goal*, edited by Stephen G. Post and Robert H. Binstock, 286–303. Oxford: Oxford University Press, 2004.
Packard, Francis R., and F. H. Garrison, eds. *The School of Salernum: Regimen sanitatis Salernitanum.* Translated by John Harrington. New York: Hoeber, 1920.
Pagels, Elaine. *The Gnostic Gospels.* New York: Random House, 1979.
Paracelsus. *A Treatise Concerning Long Life.* In *Paracelsus His Dispensatory and Chirurgery: The Dispensatory Contains the Choicest of His Physical Remedies. And All That Can Be Desired of His Chirurgery, You Have in the Treatises of Wounds, Ulcers, and Aposthumes. Faithfully Englished, by W. D.*, 369–407. London: Printed by T. M. for Philip Chetwind, 1656.
Paredes, Silvana, et al. "The Epigenetic Regulator SIRT7 Guards Against Mammalian Cellular Senescence Induced by Ribosomal DNA Instability." *Journal of Clinical Chemistry* 293 (2018) 11242–50.
Park, Ed. *The Telomere Miracle: Scientific to Fight Disease, Feel Great, and Turn Back the Clock on Aging.* Carlsbad, CA: Hay House, 2018.
Park, Sang-Kyu, and Tomas A. Prolla. "Lessons Learned from Gene Expression Profile Studies of Aging and Caloric Restriction." *Ageing Research Review* 4 (2005) 55–65.
Partridge, Linda, and D. Gems. "Mechanisms of Ageing: Public or Private?" *Nature Reviews Genetics* 3 (2002) 165–75.
Partridge, Linda, and N. H. Barton. "Optimality, Mutation and the Evolution of Aging." *Nature* 62 (March 1993) 305–11.
Paterson, Timothy H. "On the Role of Christianity in the Political Philosophy of Francis Bacon." *Polity* 19 (1987) 419–42.
Pearson, Birger A. *Ancient Gnosticism: Traditions and Literature.* Minneapolis: Fortress, 2007.
Peltonen, Markku, ed. *The Cambridge Companion to Bacon.* Cambridge: Cambridge University Press, 1996.
———. "Introduction." In *The Cambridge Companion to Bacon*, edited by Markku Peltonen, 1–24. Cambridge: Cambridge University Press, 1996.
Pepper, William. *The Medical Side of Benjamin Franklin.* Philadelphia: W. J. Campbell, 1911.
Perls, Thomas T., et al. "The Genetics of Exceptional Human Longevity." *Journal of the American Geriatrics Society* 50 (2002) 359–68.
Perry, Daniel. "The Rise of the Gero-Techs." *Genetic Engineering News* 20 (2000) 57–58.
Pettersen, Alvyn. *Athanasius.* London: Geoffrey Chapman, 1995.
———. *Athanasius and the Human Body.* Bristol: Bristol, 1990.
———. "Athanasius' Presentation of Antony of the Desert's Admiration for His Body." *Studia Patristica* 21 (1987) 438–47.
Picard, Frédéric, et al. "Sirt1 Promotes Fat Mobilization in White Adipocytes by Repressing PPAR-γ." *Nature* 429 (2004) 771–76.
Pieper, Joseph. *Leisure: The Basis of Culture.* Translated by Alexander Dru. San Francisco: Ignatius, 2009.

Piore, Adam. "I Tried the Starvation Diet So You Wouldn't Have To." *MIT Technology Review*, September/October 2019, 64–69.
Plantinga, Alvin. *Where the Conflict Really Lies: Science, Religion, and Naturalism*. Oxford: Oxford University Press, 2011.
Plato. *Cratylus*. In *Plato: Complete Works*, edited by John M. Cooper and D. S. Hutchinson. Indianapolis: Hackett, 1997.
———. *Euthyphro, Apology, Crito, Phaedo, Phaedrus*. Edited by Harold North Fowler. Cambridge, MA: Harvard University Press, 1966.
———. *Laws*. In *Plato: Complete Works*, edited by John M. Cooper and D. S. Hutchinson. Indianapolis: Hackett, 1997.
———. *Lysis, Symposium, Gorgias*. Edited by W. R. M. Lamb. Cambridge, MA: Harvard University Press, 1967.
———. *Plato: The Republic*. Edited by G. R. F. Ferrari. Translated by Tom Griffith. Cambridge: Cambridge University Press, 2000.
———. *Sophist*. In *Plato: Complete Works*, edited by John M. Cooper and D. S. Hutchinson. Indianapolis: Hackett, 1997.
———. *Theatetus*. In *Plato: Complete Works*, edited by John M. Cooper and D. S. Hutchinson. Indianapolis: Hackett, 1997.
———. *Timaeus, Critias, Cleitophon, Menexenus, Epistles*. Edited by G. P. Goold. Translated by R. G. Bury. Cambridge, MA: Harvard University Press, 1966.
Plotinus. *Plotinus*. 7 vols. Edited by T. E. Page. Translated by A. H. Armstrong. Cambridge, MA: Harvard University Press, 1966–1988.
Poehlman, Eric T., et al. "Caloric Restriction Mimetics: Physical Activity and Body Composition Changes." *Journal of Gerontology: Biological Sciences and Medical Sciences* 56A (2001) 45–54.
Posner, Richard A. *Aging and Old Age*. Chicago: University of Chicago Press, 1995.
Post, Stephen G. "Decelerated Aging: Should I Drink from a Fountain of Youth?" In *The Fountain of Youth: Cultural, Scientific, and Ethical Perspectives on a Biomedical Goal*, edited by Stephen G. Post and Robert H. Binstock, 72–93. Oxford: Oxford University Press, 2004.
Post, Stephen G., and Robert H. Binstock, eds. *The Fountain of Youth: Cultural, Scientific, and Ethical Perspectives on a Biomedical Goal*. Oxford: Oxford University Press, 2004.
Post, Stephen G., and Robert H. Binstock. "Introduction." In *The Fountain of Youth: Cultural, Scientific, and Ethical Perspectives on a Biomedical Goal*, edited by Stephen G. Post and Robert H. Binstock, 1–8. Oxford: Oxford University Press, 2004.
The President's Council on Bioethics. *Beyond Therapy: Biotechnology and the Pursuit of Happiness*. Washington, DC, 2003.
———. *Taking Care: Ethical Caregiving in Our Aging Society*. Washington, DC, 2005.
Price, Daniel J. *Karl Barth's Anthropology in Light of Modern Thought*. Grand Rapids: Eerdmans, 2002.
Puccetti, Roland. "The Conquest of Death." In *Language, Metaphysics, and Death*, edited by John Donnelly, 163–175. New York: Fordham University Press, 1978.
Raghu, Ganesh, et al. "Idiopathic Pulmonary Fibrosis in US Medicare Beneficiaries Aged 65 Years and Older: Incidence, Prevalence, and Survival, 2001–11." *Lancet Respiratory Medicine* 2 (2014) 566–72.
Ramsey, Paul. *Basic Christian Ethics*. London: SCM, 1950.

———. *Fabricated Man: The Ethics of Genetic Control*. New Haven, CT: Yale University Press, 1970.

Rattan, Suresh. "Gene Therapy for Ageing: Mission Impossible?" *European Journal of the Genetics Society* 3 (1997) 27–29.

———. "Gerontogenes: Real or Virtual?" *The Federation of American Societies for Experimental Biology Journal* 9 (1995) 284–86.

———. "The Quest for Immortality." *Biogerontology* 3 (2002) 191–2.

Rattan, Suresh, and Ripudaman Singh. "Progress and Prospects: Gene Therapy in Aging." *Gene Therapy* 16 (2008) 3–9.

Reade, William Winwood. *The Martyrdom of Man*. London: Trübner, 1872.

Reed, Esther D. *The Genesis of Ethics: On the Authority of God as the Origin of Christian Ethics*. London: Dartmon, Longman and Todd, 2000.

Rees, Graham. "Introduction." In *The Oxford Francis Bacon*, edited by Graham Rees and Lisa Jardine, vol. 6, *Philosophical Studies*, xvii–cxvi. Oxford: Clarendon, 1996.

Regalado, Antonio. "The Immortality Faith," *MIT Technology Review*, September/October 2019, 70–75.

———. "Is This the Anti-Aging Pill We've All Been Waiting For?" *MIT Technology Review*, March, 28, 2017. https://www.technologyreview.com/s/603997/is-this-the-anti-aging-pill-weve-all-been-waiting-for/.

Regnault, Lucien. *The Day-to-Day Life of the Desert Fathers in Fourth-Century Egypt*. Translated by Étienne Poirier, Jr. Petersham, MA: St. Bede's, 1999.

Reineke, Martha Jane. "This is My Body: Reflections on Abjection, Anorexia, and Medieval Women Mystics." *Journal of the American Academy of Religion* 58 (1990) 245–65.

Reiss, Michael J. "'And in the World to Come, Life Everlasting.'" In *Brave New World? Theology, Ethics, and the Human Genome*, edited by Celia Deane-Drummond, 49–67. London: T. & T. Clark, 2003.

Renan, Ernest. *The Life of Jesus*. London: J. M. Dent, 1834.

Rist, John M. "Plotinus on Matter and Evil." *Phronesis* 6 (1961) 154–66.

———. *Plotinus: The Road to Reality*. Cambridge: Cambridge University Press, 1967.

Ritschl, Albrecht. *The Christian Doctrine of Justification and Reconciliation: The Positive Development of the Doctrine*. Translated by H. R. Mackintosh and A. B. Macaulay. Edinburgh: T. & T. Clark, 1900.

Robine, Jean-Marine, et al., eds. *Longevity: To the Limit and Beyond*. Berlin, NY: Springer, 1997.

Robinson, James M., ed. *The Nag Hammadi Library in English*. Rev. ed. New York: HarperCollins, 1990.

Rodgers, Joseph T., et al. "Nutrient Control of Glucose Homeostasis through a Complex of PGC-1a and SIRT1." *Nature* 434 (2005) 113–18.

Rose, Michael R. "Aging as a Target for Genetic Engineering." In *Engineering the Human Germline*, edited by Gregory Stock and John Campbell, 49–56. New York: Oxford University Press, 2000.

———. *Evolutionary Biology of Aging*. Oxford: Oxford University Press, 1994.

———. "Laboratory Evolution of Postponed Senescence in *Drosophila melanogaster*." *Evolution* 38 (1984) 1004–10.

———. *The Long Tomorrow: How Advances in Evolutionary Biology Can Help Us to Postpone Aging*. New York: Oxford University Press, 2005.

Rossi, Paolo. *Francis Bacon: From Magic to Science*. Translated by Sacha Rabinovich. London: Routledge & Kegan Paul, 1968.
Roth, George S. "Caloric Restriction and Caloric Restriction Mimetics: Current Status and Promise for the Future." *Journal of the American Geriatrics Society* 53 (2005) s280–83.
Roth, George S., et al. "Biomarkers of Caloric Restriction May Predict Longevity in Humans." *Science* 297 (2002) 811.
Roth, Leon. *Descartes' Discourse on Method*. Oxford: Clarendon, 1937.
Rubenson, Samuel. "Christian Asceticism and the Emergence of the Monastic Tradition." In *Asceticism*, edited by Vincent L. Wimbush and Richard Valantasis, 49–57. Oxford: Oxford University Press, 1998.
———. *The Letters of St. Antony: Monasticism and the Making of a Saint*. Minneapolis: Fortress, 1995.
Russell, Gerald F. M. "Bulimia Nervosa: An Ominous Variant of Anorexia Nervosa." *Psychological Medicine* 9 (1979) 429–48.
———. "Thoughts on the 25th Anniversary of Bulimia Nervosa." *European Eating Disorders Review* 12 (2004) 139–52.
Russell, Norman. *The Doctrine of Deification in the Greek Patristic Tradition*. Oxford: Oxford University Press, 2004.
———. *Fellow Workers with God: Orthodox Thinking on Theosis*. Crestwood, NY: St. Vladimir's Seminary Press, 2009.
Sabom, Stephen W. "The Gnostic World of Anorexia Nervosa." *Journal of Psychology and Theology* 13 (1985) 243–54.
Saigol, Lina. "Companies Race to Find the Key to Eternal Life." *MarketWatch*, August 19, 2019. https://www.marketwatch.com/story/companies-race-to-find-the-key-to-eternal-life-2019-08-19.
Saint Ephrem the Syrian. *Hymns on Paradise*. Translated by Sebastian Brock. Crestwood, NY: St. Vladimir's Seminary Press, 1990.
Salk Institute. "Turning Back Time: Salk Scientists Reverse Signs of Aging," December 15, 2016. https://www.salk.edu/news-release/turning-back-time-salk-scientists-reverse-signs-aging/.
Sample, Ian. "Harvard Scientists Reverse the Ageing Process in Mice—Now for Humans." *The Guardian*, November 28, 2010. https://www.theguardian.com/science/2010/nov/28/scientists-reverse-ageing-mice-humans.
Sandars, Nancy K., trans. *The Epic of Gilgamesh: An English Version with an Introduction*. Rev. ed. London: Penguin, 1972.
Savage, Neil. "Growing Up: Scientists Seeking to Reverse or Stall the Effects of Ageing Are Trying to Make the Leap from Laboratory Research to Human Trials." *Nature* 552 (2017) S58.
Sayers, Dorothy. *Letters to a Diminished Church: Passionate Arguments for the Relevance of Christian Doctrine*. Nashville: Thomas Nelson, 2004.
Schäfer, Daniel. "'That Senescence Itself is an Illness': A Transitional Concept of Age and Ageing in the Eighteenth Century." *Medical History* 46 (2002) 525–48.
Schaff, Philip, ed. and trans. *The Oldest Church Manual Called the Teaching of the Twelve Apostles, The Didache and Kindred Documents in the Original*. Edinburgh, T. & T. Clark, 1885.

Schmidt, Peter. *The Conquest of Old Age: Methods to Effect Rejuvenation and to Increase Functional Activity*. Translated by Eden Paul and Cedar Paul. New York: E. P. Dutton, 1931.

Schneider, Edward L., and J. D. Reed. "Life Extension." *New England Journal of Medicine* 312 (1985) 1159–68.

Scott, Peter. "Nature, Technology and the Rule of God: (En)countering the Disgracing of Nature." In *Re-Ordering Nature: Theology, Society and the New Genetics*, edited by Celia Deane-Drummond et al., 275–92. London: T. & T. Clark, 2003.

Sengoopta, Chandak. "'Dr. Steinach Coming to Make Old Young!': Sex Glands, Vasectomy and the Quest for Rejuvenation in the Roaring Twenties." *Endeavour* 27 (2003) 122–26.

Shaw, Teresa M. *The Burden of the Flesh: Fasting and Sexuality in Early Christianity*. Minneapolis: Fortress, 1998.

Shostak, Stanley. *Becoming Immortal: Combining Cloning and Stem-Cell Therapy*. Albany, NY: State University of New York Press, 2002.

Shuman, Joel James. *The Body of Compassion: Ethics, Medicine, and the Church*. Boulder, CO: Westview, 1999.

———. "The Last Gift: The Elderly, the Church, and the Gift of a Good Death." In *Growing Old with Christ*, edited by Stanley Hauerwas et al., 151–66. Grand Rapids: Eerdmans, 2003.

Shuman, Joel James, and Keith G. Meador. *Heal Thyself: Spirituality, Medicine, and the Distortion of Christianity*. Oxford: Oxford University Press, 2003.

Shuster, Marguerite. *The Fall and Sin: What We Have Become as Sinners*. Grand Rapids: Eerdmans, 2004.

Sifferlin, Alexandra. "Is an Anti-Aging Pill on the Horizon?" *Time*, February 26, 2018.

Sinclair, David A., and Matthew D. LaPlante. *Lifespan: Why We Age—and Why We Don't Have To*. New York: Atria, 2019.

Singer, Peter. "Research into Aging: Should It be Guided by the Interests of Present Individuals, Future Individuals, or the Species?" In *Life Span Extension: Consequences and Open Questions*, edited by Frédérick C. Ludwig, 132–45. New York: Springer, 1991.

Song, Robert. *Human Genetics: Fabricating the Future*. Ethics and Theology. London: Darton, Longman and Todd, 2002.

———. "The Human Genome Project as a Soteriological Project." In *Brave New World? Theology, Ethics, and the Human Genome*, edited by Celia Deane-Drummond, 164–84. London: T. & T. Clark, 2003.

Sophocles. *Sophocles*, vol. 1, *Oedipus the King, Oedipus at Colonus, Antigone*. Translated by Francis Storr. London: William Heinemann, 1924.

South, Robert. *Sermons Preached upon Several Occasions of Robert South*. Oxford, 1679.

Spaulding, Carol C., et al. "The Accumulation of Non-replicative, Non-functional Senescent T Cells with Age is Avoided in Calorically Restricted Mice by an Enhancement of T Cell Apoptosis." *Mechanisms of Aging and Development* 93 (1997) 25–33.

Speakman, John R., and C. Hambly. "Starving for Life: What Animal Studies Can and Cannot Tell Us about the Use of Caloric Restriction to Prolong Human Lifespan." *Journal of Nutrition* 137 (2007) 1078–86.

Stannard, David E. *The Puritan Way of Death: A Study in Religion, Culture, and Social Change*. New York: Oxford University Press, 1977.

Stephens, C. A. *Immortal Life: How It Will Be Achieved.* Norway Lake, ME: The Laboratory at Norway Lake, 1920.
———. *Long Life: The Occasional Review of an Investigation of the Intimate Causes of Old Age and Organic Death, with a Design to Their Alleviation and Removal.* Norway Lake, ME: The Laboratory at Norway Lake, 1896.
———. *Natural Salvation: The Message of Science Outlining the First Principles of Immortal Life on the Earth.* Norway Lake, ME: The Laboratory at Norway Lake, 1905.
———. *Salvation by Science: Immortal Life on Earth from the Growth of Knowledge and the Development of the Human Brain.* Norway Lake, ME: The Laboratory at Norway Lake, 1913.
———. *When Life Was Young at the Old Farm in Maine.* Norway Lake, ME: The Old Squire's Bookstore, 1912.
Stipp, David. "Researchers Seek Key to Anti-aging in Calorie Cutback." *Wall Street Journal,* October 30, 2006.
———. *The Youth Pill: Scientists at the Brink of an Anti-aging Revolution.* New York: Current, 2010.
Stock, Gregory. *Redesigning Humans: Our Inevitable Genetic Future.* New York: Houghton Mifflin, 2002.
Stone, Eliab. *A Discourse Delivered at Reading, North Parish, May 19, 1811, In Which Warnings of Death are Considered as Excitements to Review Life.* Boston: Watson and Bangs, 1811.
Stoneking, Carole Bailey. "Modernity: The Social Construction of Aging." In *Growing Old with Christ,* edited by Stanley Hauerwas et al., 63–89. Grand Rapids: Eerdmans, 2003.
———. "Receiving Communion: Euthanasia, Suicide, and Letting Die." In *The Blackwell Companion to Christian Ethics,* edited by Stanley Hauerwas and Samuel Wells, 375–87. Oxford: Blackwell, 2004.
Swift, Jonathan. *Gulliver's Travels.* Edited by Paul Turner. Oxford: Oxford University Press, 1998.
Taylor, Charles. *Sources of the Self: The Making of the Modern Identity.* Cambridge, MA: Harvard University Press, 1989.
Taylor, Marisa. "A 'Fountain of Youth' Pill? Sure, If You're a Mouse." *Kaiser Health News,* February 11, 2019, https://khn.org/news/a-fountain-of-youth-pill-sure-if-youre-a-mouse/.
Tazearslan, Cagdas, et al. "Impaired IGF1R Signaling in Cells Expressing Longevity-Associated Human IGF1R Alleles." *Aging Cell* 10 (2011) 551–54.
Terence. *Terence.* Vol. 2, *Phormio, The Mother-in-Law, The Brothers.* Edited and translated by John Barsby. Cambridge, MA: Harvard University Press, 2001.
Tessore, Dag. *Fasting.* Hyde Park, NY: New City, 2007.
Thane, Pat, ed. *A History of Old Age.* Los Angeles: Getty, 2005.
Thoma, Helmut. *Anorexia Nervosa.* Translated by Gillian Brydone. New York: International Universities Press, 1967.
Tian, Xiao, et al. "SIRT6 Is Responsible for More Efficient DNA Double-Strand Break Repair in Long-Lived Species." *Cell* 177 (2019) 622–38.
Tolstoy, Leo. *Father Sergius.* In *Tolstoy: Master and Man and Other Stories.* Translated by Paul Foote. Harmondsworth: Penguin, 1977.
Torrance, T. F. *Calvin's Doctrine of Man.* London: Lutterworth, 1949.

———. *The Ground and Grammar of Theology: Consonance between Theology and Science*. Edinburgh: T. & T. Clark, 1980.
———. *Karl Barth: Biblical and Evangelical Theologian*. Edinburgh: T. & T. Clark, 1990.
———. *Theological Science*. London: Oxford University Press, 1969.
———. *Theology in Reconstruction*. Grand Rapids: Eerdmans, 1965.
Tovey, George V. "Toward a New Understanding of Francis Bacon's Reform of Philosophy." *The Philosophical Review* 61 (1952) 568–74.
Troyansky, David G. *Old Age in the Old Regime: Image and Experience in Eighteenth Century France*. Ithaca, NY: Cornell University Press, 1989.
Tucker, L. A. "Physical Activity and Telomere Length in U.S. Men and Women: An NHANES Investigation." *Preventative Medicine* 100 (2017) 145–51.
Tyner, Stuart D., et al. "p53 Mutant Mice That Display Early Aging-associated Phenotypes." *Nature* 415 (2002) 45–53.
University of Texas Health Science Center at San Antonio. "First-in-Human Trial of Senolytic Drugs Encouraging: Small Pilot Study Points to Feasibility of Larger Trials in Age-Related Diseases." *ScienceDaily*, January 7, 2019. www.sciencedaily.com/releases/2019/01/190107112944.htm.
Urbach, Peter. *Francis Bacon's Philosophy of Science: An Account and a Reappraisal*. Chicago: Open Court, 1987.
Urfer, Silvan, et al. "A Randomized Controlled Trial to Establish Effects of Short-Term Rapamycin Treatment in 24 Middle-Aged Companion Dogs." *GeroScience* 39 (2017) 117–27.
Vandereycken, Walter, and Ron Van Deth. *From Fasting Saints to Anorexic Girls: A History of Self-Starvation*. New York: New York University Press, 1994.
Veach, Robert M., ed. *Life Span: Values and Life-Extending Technologies*. San Francisco: Harper and Row, 1979.
Vellai, Tibor, et al. "Influence of TOR Kinase on Lifespan in *C. elegans*." *Nature* 426 (2003) 620.
Verani, Salim S., et al. "Heart Disease and Stroke Statistics—2020 Update." *Circulation* 141 (2020). https://www.ahajournals.org/doi/10.1161/CIR.0000000000000757
Verhey, Allen. *The Christian Art of Dying: Learning from Jesus*. Grand Rapids: Eerdmans, 2011.
———. *Nature and Altering It*. Grand Rapids: Eerdmans, 2010.
———. *Reading the Bible in the Strange World of Medicine*. Grand Rapids: Eerdmans, 2003.
Viereck, George Sylvester. *Glimpses of the Great*. New York: Macaulay, 1930.
Viereck, George Sylvester. [George F. Corners, *pseud.*] *Rejuvenation: How Steinach Makes People Young*. New York: Thomas Seltzer, 1923.
Virgil. *The Aeneid*. In *Virgil's Works: The Aeneid, Eclogues, Georgics*. Translated by J. W. MacKail. New York: Random House, 1950.
Vitousek, Kelly M. "The Case for Semi-Starvation." *European Eating Disorders Review* 12 (2004) 275–78.
Vivan, Tim. *The Coptic Life of Antony by Saint Athanasius of Alexandria*. Translated by Tim Vivian, *Coptic Church Review* 15 (1994) 98–128.
Vivian, Tim, and Apostolos N. Athanassakis, eds. *The Life of Antony: The Coptic and the Greek Life*. Kalamazoo, MI: Cistercian, 2003.
Vrooman, Jack Rochford. *René Descartes: A Biography*. New York: G. P. Putnam's Sons, 1970.

Wade, Nicholas. "A Pill to Extend Life? Don't Dismiss the Notion Too Quickly." *New York Times*, September 22, 2000. https://www.nytimes.com/2000/09/22/us/a-pill-to-extend-life-don-t-dismiss-the-notion-too-quickly.html.

———. "Ecuadorean Villagers May Hold Secret to Longevity." *New York Times*, February 16, 2011. https://www.nytimes.com/2011/02/17/science/17longevity.html.

Waldrop, Charles T. *Karl Barth's Christology: Its Basic Alexandrian Character*. New York: Mouton, 1984.

Walford, Roy L. *Beyond the 120 Year Diet: How to Double Your Vital Years*. New York: Four Walls Eight Windows, 2000.

———. *Maximum Life Span*. New York: W. W. Norton, 1983.

———. *The 120 Year Diet: How to Double Your Vital Years*. New York: Simon and Schuster, 1987.

Walford, Roy L., et al. "Caloric Restriction in Biosphere 2: Alterations is Physiologic, Hematologic, Hormonal, and Biochemical Parameters in Humans Restricted for a Two-Year Period." *The Journals of Gerontology, Series A* 57 (2002) B211–24.

Walford, Roy L., and Lisa Walford. *The Anti-Aging Plan: The Nutrient-Rich, Low-Calorie Way of Eating for a Longer Life—the Only Diet Scientifically Proven to Extend Your Healthy Years*. 10th ed. New York: Marlowe, 2005.

Wallace, Karl R. *Francis Bacon on the Nature of Man*. Urbana, IL: University of Illinois Press, 1967.

Wang, Chen-Pin, et al. "Differential Effects of Metformin on Age Related Comorbidities in Older Men with Type 2 Diabetes." *Journal of Diabetes and Its Complications* 31 (2017) 679–86.

Ward, Benedicta, ed. *The Sayings of the Desert Fathers [Apophthegmata Patrum]: The Alphabetical Collection*. Translated by Benedicta Ward. Rev. ed. Kalamazoo, MI: Cistercian, 1984.

Ware, Kallistos. "The Way of the Ascetics: Negative or Affirmative?" In *Asceticism*, edited by Vincent L. Wimbush and Richard Valantasis, 3–15. Oxford: Oxford University Press, 1998.

Warner, Hubert R., and R. J. Hodes. "Hype, Hope, and Reality: Telomere Length, Telomerase, and Aging." *Generations: The Journal of the Western Gerontological Society* 24 (2001–2) 48–53.

Warthin, Alfred S. *Old Age, the Major Involution: The Physiology and Pathology of the Aging Process*. New York: P. B. Hoeber, 1930.

Weber, Max. *The Protestant Ethic and the Spirit of Capitalism*. Translated by Talcott Parsons. London: George Allen and Unwin, 1930.

Webster, Charles. *The Great Instauration: Science, Medicine and Reform, 1626–1660*. London: Duckworth, 197.

Webster, John, ed. *Barth's Ethics of Reconciliation*. Cambridge: Cambridge University Press, 1995.

———. *Barth's Moral Theology: Human Action in Barth's Thought*. Grand Rapids: Eerdmans, 1998.

———. *The Cambridge Companion to Karl Barth*. Cambridge: Cambridge University Press, 2000.

Weddle, David L. *The Law as Gospel: Revival and Reform in the Theology of Charles G. Finney*. London: Scarecrow, 1985.

———, and Richard Valantasis, eds. *Asceticism*. Oxford: Oxford University Press, 1995.

Wei, Min, et al. "Fast-Mimicking Diet and Markers/Risk Factors for Aging, Diabetes, Cancer, and Cardio Vascular Disease." *Science Translational Medicine* 9 (2017). https://doi:10.1126/scitranslmed.eaai8700.

Weinberger, Jerry. *Science, Faith, and Politics: Francis Bacon and the Utopian Roots of the Modern Age*. Ithaca, NY: Cornell University Press, 1985.

Weindruch, Richard, et al. "Caloric Restriction Mimetics: Metabolic Interventions." *Journal of Gerontology: Biological Sciences and Medical Sciences* 56A, special issue (2001) 20–33.

Weindruch, Richard, and R. Walford. *The Retardation of Aging and Disease by Dietary Restriction*. Springfield, IL: Charles C. Thomas, 1988.

Weismann, August. *Essays upon Heredity and Kindred Biological Problems*. Oxford: Clarendon, 1891.

West, Michael D. *The Immortal Cell: One Scientist's Quest to Solve the Mystery of Human Aging*. New York: Doubleday, 2003.

White, Howard. *Peace among the Willows: The Political Philosophy of Francis Bacon*. The Hague: Martinus Nijhoff, 1968.

Whitney, Charles. "Francis Bacon's Instauratio: Dominion of, and over Humanity." *Journal of the History of Ideas* 50 (1989) 371–90.

Whorton, James C. *Crusaders for Fitness: The History of American Health Reformers*. Princeton: Princeton University Press, 1982.

Wick, Georg. "'Anti-aging' Medicine: Does It Exist? A Critical Discussion of 'Anti-aging Health Products.'" *Experimental Gerontology* 37 (2002) 1137–40.

Wickens, Andrew P. *The Causes of Aging*. Amsterdam: Harwood Academic, 1998.

Wilde, Oscar. *The Picture of Dorian Gray*. New York: Barnes and Noble Classics, 1995.

Wilkinson, John. *The Bible and Healing: A Medical and Theological Commentary*. Grand Rapids: Eerdmans, 1998.

Willard, Dallas. *The Divine Conspiracy. Rediscovering Our Hidden Life in God*. San Francisco: Harper Collins, 1996.

———. *The Spirit of the Disciplines: Understanding How God Changes Lives*. San Francisco: HarperCollins, 1988.

Willey, Basil. *The Seventeenth Century Background: Studies in the Thought of the Age in Relation to Poetry and Religion*. London: Chatto, 1949.

Williams, George C. "Pleiotropy, Natural Selection and the Evolution of Senescence." *Evolution* 11 (1957) 398–411.

Willimon, William H. *The Service of God: How Worship and Ethics are Related*. Nashville: Abington, 1983.

Willmes, Diana M., et al. "The Longevity Gene INDY (*I'm Not Dead Yet*) in Metabolic Control: Potential as Pharmacological Target." *Pharmacology and Therapeutics* 185 (2018) 1–11. https://doi.org/10.1016/j.pharmthera.2017.10.003.

Wilmoth, John R. "The Future of Human Longevity: A Demographer's Perspective." *Science* 280 (1998) 395–97.

Wilson, Robert McLachlan. *The Gnostic Problem: A Study of the Relations between Hellenistic Judaism and the Gnostic Heresy*. London: A. R. Mowbray, 1958.

Wimbush, Vincent L., ed. *Ascetic Behavior in Greco-Roman Antiquity: A Sourcebook*. Minneapolis: Fortress, 1990.

Wright, Willmer C., ed. *Julian: Orations 6–8, Letters to Themistius, To the Senate and the People of Athens, To a Priest, The Caesars, Misopogon*. Cambridge, MA: Harvard University Press, 1913.

Xu, Jiaquan, et al. "Mortality in the United States, 2018." NCHS Data Brief no. 355 (Hyattsville, MD: National Center for Health Statistics, 2020).

Xu, Ming, et al. "Senolytics Improve Physical Function and Increase Lifespan in Old Age." *Nature Medicine* 24 (2018) 1246–56.

———. "Transplanted Senescent Cells Induce an Osteoarthritis-Like Condition in Mice." *The Journals of Gerontology: Series A, Biological Sciences and Medical Sciences* 72 (2017) 780–85.

Yamaza, Haruyoshi, et al. "Life Span Extension by Caloric Restriction: An Aspect of Energy Metabolism. *Microscopy Research and Technique* 59 (2002) 325–30.

Yang, Jiwei, et al. "Human Endothelial Cell Life Extension by Telomerase Expression." *Journal of Biological Chemistry* 374 (1999) 26141–48.

Yoder, John Howard. *The Priestly Kingdom*. Notre Dame, IN: University of Notre Dame Press, 1984.

Young, Amos. *Designer Evolution: A Transhumanist Manifesto*. Amherst, NY: Prometheus, 2005.

Yousefzadeh, Matthew J., et al. "Fisetin is a Senotherapeutic That Extends Health and Lifespan." *Ebiomedicine* 36 (2018) 18–28.

Yu, Byung P., ed. *Modulation of Aging Processes by Dietary Restriction*. Boca Raton, FL: CRC, 1994.

Zagorin, Perez. *Francis Bacon*. Princeton: Princeton University Press, 1998.

Zhu, Yi, et al. "The Achilles' Heel of Senescent Cells: From Transcriptome to Senolytic Drugs." *Aging Cell* 14 (2014) 644–58.

Zizioulas, John. *Communion and Otherness: Further Studies in Personhood and the Church*. Edited by Paul McPartlan. London: T. & T. Clark, 2006.

Zumstein, Louis A., and Victoria Lundblad. "Telomeres: Has Cancer's Achilles' Heel Been Exposed?" *Nature Medicine* 5 (1999) 1129–30.

Subject Index

Abode of the Blest, 21
acedia, 217, 226
Adam, vi, vii, xii, 16–17, 23, 26, 87, 88,
    93, 98, 101, 110, 124–30, 131,
    142, 146, 149, 150, 153–155,
    158–60, 162–65, 169–71, 186–
    89, 192, 197, 199, 201–5, 211,
    216, 239–41, 255–56, 258
AgeX Therapeutics, 9, 68
aging (ageing), ix, xi–xii, 2, 4–18, 20–
    21, 23, 25–27, 29–32, 34–37,
    39–40, 42–85, 87–103, 105,
    107–115, 126–27, 132, 134–35,
    137–38, 140–44, 146–150, 152–
    58, 160, 165, 167, 177, 180, 183,
    191, 197, 200–207, 209–11,
    213, 215, 217–21, 223, 225–43,
    245, 247, 249–53, 255–58
aging, as disease, ix, 11–12, 16, 21, 36, 39,
    69–77, 134, 141, 231, 240, 255
aging, humoral theory, 29, 39, 138
aging attenuation, 4, 8–9, 11–15,
    17–18, 21, 23, 25–26, 34–35,
    39–40, 42, 44, 46–48, 50, 52–
    53, 57–60, 62, 65, 67–69, 72,
    74–77, 96, 110, 112, 114, 132,
    135, 137, 140–42, 146–150,
    152–54, 156–57, 183, 190–92,
    197, 200–206, 210–11, 220–21,
    226, 228–31, 233–37, 240, 243,
    245, 250–53, 255–58

alchemy, 14, 25–29, 30–32, 76, 79, 138,
    140–41, 255
Alcor Life Extension Foundation, 67
Alcott, William P., 92–95, 97, 100
Alzheimer's Disease, 5–6, 10, 50,
    56–57, 60–61, 99
Ambrose, Saint, 124, 165
anachōrein, 223
anamnēsis, 251
anchorite, 136, 223, 246
Anderson, Ray S., 7, 215
Anderson, Rozalyn, 58
angels, 150
Anorexia Nervosa, 58, 248–49
anthropology, 107, 180, 205–6, 213
anthropology, Christian, ix
anthropology, Christological, xi, 15,
    17, 206, 211–13, 254
anthropology, dualistic, 33
anthropology, Gnostic, 172
anthropology, theological, 17, 24, 33,
    95–96, 158–65, 204–6, 211–13,
    256–57
anti-aging, xi, 8–11, 14–15, 34, 47, 56,
    58–59, 61–62, 64–66, 68–70,
    74, 200, 230
Antony, Saint, xii, 17, 136, 139,
    157–58, 164–71, 173, 181–93,
    196–202, 212–13, 221–22, 225,
    235–36, 238, 240–43, 245–47,
    251, 256

anxiety, 33, 217–20, 225–29, 240–43, 248, 253, 257
apatheia. See Stoicism.
Apophthegmata Patrum, 169, 191, 242
apoptosis. *See* death, cellular.
aqua vitae, 27
Aquinas, Thomas. *See* Thomas Aquinas.
Arianism, 161–62, 164, 186
Aristotle (Aristotelian), 27, 29, 31–32, 71, 115–20, 119, 122, 128, 138, 147, 212
Arking, Robert, 45, 231–32
ars moriendi, 81
asceticism, 17, 33, 41, 107, 137, 157–58, 164–70, 172–73, 175, 180, 183–190, 192–202, 204, 211, 213, 221–25, 235–36, 238, 240–43, 245–48, 253, 256
askēsis. See asceticism.
Asprey, David, 67
Athanasius, Saint, xii, 17–18, 154–55, 157–71, 173, 181–202, 203–4, 211–12, 222, 225, 235–36, 239–42, 245–47, 250–51, 256–57
Atherton, Gertrude, 35
Augustine, Saint, 22, 92, 124, 127, 133, 139, 149, 173, 219
autarkic system, 188
autophagy, 56, 60
avarice, 243
Avicenna, 31, 138

Bacon, Francis, xii, 16, 18, 27–28, 31, 33, 112–15, 117–24, 127–57, 165, 201–5, 228, 239–40, 253, 255–57
Bacon, Roger, 26–27, 30–32, 34, 71
Baconian Project, 114, 141–46, 151–52, 154, 156, 228, 231, 239–40, 245, 253, 255
bacteria, 37–38, 40, 59, 100, 108
bacteriology, 30, 37, 108
baptism, 18, 163–64, 249–51, 253, 258
Barnes, Albert, 92
Barsanuphius of Gaza, 191, 244–45

Barth, Karl, xii, 17–18, 203–26, 228, 238–40, 242–44, 246, 253, 256–57
Bartke, Andrzej, 8, 48
Barzilai, Nir, 61
Basis Supplement, 68
Beard, George Miller, 99, 101–2
Beecher, Henry Ward, 96–97, 100
Bell, Rudolph, 248–49
biology, 40, 42, 44–45, 57, 61, 68, 71–73, 111
biology, cellular, 39
biology, evolutionary, 4, 36, 45, 73–76, 231, 239
biology, molecular, 47, 232
biology, synthetic, 111
Bishop Dracontius, 246
Blackburn, Elizabeth, 51–52
Blaine, David, 236
blue zones, 22
body, xi–xii, 7, 15–21, 24–28, 29, 33, 36–50, 52, 54–57, 60, 67, 69–74, 76–77, 79–80, 83–90, 93–95, 98–102, 106–8, 111, 120, 124, 126–27, 130, 132, 135–36, 138–39, 143, 146–47, 149–206, 211–22, 225–45, 247–51, 253–58
body, remade, 190, 200–202, 240, 247
body, and soul, xii, 17–18, 159, 164, 167, 169–70, 173–74, 181–82, 190, 192–97, 200–204, 206, 211–221, 225–26, 228–30, 233–36, 240–43, 250–53, 256–57
Bolen, Joseph, 61
Bonhoeffer, Dietrich, 238, 251
book of nature, 122–23, 131, 137, 141
Boyle, Robert, 26
brain, 41, 53, 60, 67, 74, 95, 99, 102–103, 130
Brakke, David, 159–60, 163, 165, 186, 188, 190, 193–94, 198, 241, 242, 246
Brin, Sergey, 67
Brock, Brian, 73
Brown-Séquard, Charles-Édouard, 34

SUBJECT INDEX 297

Brown, Peter, 182, 188–90, 193, 196–98, 200, 240, 246
Browne, Richard, 71, 73
Brumberg, Joan Jacob, 248
Bulimia Nervosa, 178
Bunyan, John, 91
Burnet, Thomas, 28
Burton-Christie, Douglas, 243
Bushell, William C., 183, 196
busyness, 226
Bynum, Caroline Walker, 248–50

Caenorhabditis elegans. See nematode.
Calico, 67–68, 234
Callahan, Daniel, 12
Calment, Jeanne Louise, 3–4
caloric restriction (CR), 18, 47, 49, 53–56, 58–62, 64, 202, 233–39, 245, 253–54, 257
Calvin, John, 88–90, 96, 115, 124–30, 133–34, 150, 202
Calvinism, 16, 79–82, 87, 89–90, 94, 96, 110, 112–15, 124, 130, 154, 255
cancer, 2, 4–5, 10, 45, 47–48, 50, 52–53, 55–59, 61, 66, 88, 94
Carnes, Bruce A., 12, 39, 43–44, 47, 52, 234
Carrel, Alexis, 35
Cassian, John, 199, 247
Catherine of Siena, 248
causes, 133, 136, 145, 146
cause, efficient, 115–16, 120–22, 131, 141
cause, final, 115–17, 119–22, 141–142, 148, 169, 224, 227, 243
cause, formal, 115–21, 128, 141, 148
cause, material, 115–22, 131, 141
cell (cellular), 8, 15, 35, 39–57, 59–68, 72–73, 103, 110, 148, 231, 233, 239
cell, germ, 43–44, 51, 231
cell, senescent, 45–46, 60–64
cell, somatic, 39, 43, 45, 51, 62, 231
cell, stem, 49, 57, 67–68, 148
cell, zombie, 62, 67
charity, 123, 135, 145, 150, 152, 202, 250

Chitty, Derwas J., 188, 196, 246
Christology, xi, 15, 17, 170, 203–6, 209, 211–13, 217, 253, 256–57
Chrysostom, Saint, 124, 191
Church, George, 68
Cicero, Marcus Tullius, 200
Clement of Alexandria, 182, 189
Clement, James, 66–67
coenobite, 224, 246
Cole, Thomas R., 15–16, 79–83, 89–93, 95–96, 98–101, 108–111
Condorcet, Nicholas de, 32–34, 169
Consequentialism, 13–14, 73, 211
Cornaro, Luigi, 28–32, 144
Corrington, Gail, 249
cosmogony, 171, 173
creation *ex nihilo*, 117, 158, 161, 164, 182, 185, 199
Crichton-Browne, James, 100–101
CRISPR/Cas-9, 53, 230
cryonic preservation, 32

daimonia, 174
Dally, Ann, 107–8
Daniel, 105, 130, 134, 190
Darwin, Charles, 33–34, 36–40, 73–75, 77
Dastanib and Quercetin (D+Q), 63–64, 66, 236
Davidsohn, Noah, 68
death, xii, 3, 4–5, 7–11, 13–16, 20–21, 23–25, 28–30, 33, 35, 38–43, 48, 57, 63, 67, 69–71, 74, 77–93, 95–96, 98, 100–115, 123, 125–29, 132–34, 138–39, 149–150, 153, 158–61, 165–66, 168, 193, 195, 205, 209, 218–21, 225–32, 235, 238–39, 241–44, 250–52, 257
death, cellular, 46, 49, 51–52, 60, 62
Decalogue, 93
defecto boni, 127
deification. See *theōsis*.
Demiurge, 171–72, 174, 176
demythologization, 22, 114, 169, 202, 245
DePinho, Ronald, 53
depression, 52, 61, 108

Descartes, René, 33, 121–22, 206, 214, 228–32, 240
desert, 137, 157, 165–67, 169, 189–90, 192–93, 196, 200, 223, 236–37, 240, 243, 246–47, 251, 256
deus, sive natura, 89, 117–18
diabetes, 4–6, 48, 50, 56–57, 61–65, 109
Didache, 246, 250
diet, 6, 9, 22, 25, 27–28, 30–31, 37, 51–58, 63, 93–94, 136, 140, 144, 190, 200, 234, 236–238, 248
diet, fast-mimicking, 49, 54–57, 202, 234
diet, high-fat, 63
diet, longevity, 55–57, 73
diet, low-fat, 22
diet, near starvation, 53
diet, pescatarian, 56
diet, telomerase, 51–52
diet, vegetarian, 92, 172, 185, 190
diet, 120 Year, 144, 200
disease, 4–7, 9–12, 14, 16, 19, 21, 25–26, 28, 30–31, 33, 36–37, 39, 43, 47–48, 50, 52–53, 55–57, 59–64, 66, 68–72, 74–77, 80, 87, 90, 93, 95, 98–99, 106–7, 109, 112, 123, 126, 129, 132, 134, 136–37, 141, 143, 145, 148, 150, 153–54, 157, 171, 200, 227, 230–31, 234, 240, 244, 248, 252, 255, 258
disease, and aging. *See* aging, as disease.
disease, heart. *See* heart disease.
disposable soma, 43–45, 73, 231
DNA methylation, 61, 64–65
docetism, 218
donum superadditum, 127
Dorotheus of Gaza, 183
Driscoll, Ellen, 248
Drosophila melanogaster. *See* fruit fly.
dualism, 33, 80, 90, 107, 110, 171–72, 193, 206, 212–13, 215–17, 227, 231
dwarfism. *See* Laron syndrome.

Ebionite, 106
Eden, xii, 16–18, 22–23, 26–27, 31, 34–35, 103–4, 110, 112, 115, 123–24, 131, 134, 137, 150, 153–54, 156–58, 171, 188–89, 201–2, 204, 216, 250, 255–56
Edwards, Jonathan, 90
Edwards, Tristan, 68
Egypt, 157, 165, 189, 223
election, 88, 90–91, 96
Elixir Pharmaceuticals, 9, 235
elixir vitae, xii
Elliott, Carl, 227–28, 247
Ellison, Larry, 67–68
Elshtain, Jean Bethke, 226
Elysium, 9, 68
embryogenesis, 55, 57
Emerson, Ralph Waldo, 71
Emmons, Nathanael, 82–90, 94, 111, 115, 134
endocrinology, 34, 36
energia, 179
enhancement, 192, 204, 240
Ephrem, Saint, vi
Epicurus, 119
epigenetic clocks, 8, 64–65
Epimenides, 144
eschatology, 102, 135, 164, 201, 250
ethics, ix, 11, 116
ethics, Christian, xi, xiii, 73, 164, 209, 212, 247
ethics, medical, 71, 92
ethics, theological, xi, 15
Ethiopia(n), 140, 183, 196
Eucharist, 18, 163, 183, 248–53, 258
Eve, 23, 35, 93, 124–25, 129, 142, 146, 149, 158, 160, 164–65, 188, 189
evolution, 4, 7, 34, 36–38, 42, 44–45, 55, 57, 73–76, 102–3, 108, 203, 231, 239
exercise, 24, 28, 52, 55, 65, 72, 79, 93–94, 166, 175, 200
existentialism, 16, 80–82, 89, 102, 110–11, 205, 229

fasting, xii, 11, 17–18, 54–58, 130, 136, 157, 164–67, 170, 173, 183–84,

SUBJECT INDEX

186–97, 199–201, 234, 236–38, 241, 243–53, 256–58
fasting, intermittent, 58–59, 64
fasting, mimicking diet. *See* diet, fast-mimicking.
fat, 22, 56, 62–63, 138, 166, 190, 194, 248, 250, 252
Fathers, Church, 112, 139, 189, 192, 202, 256
Fathers, Desert, 183–84, 189, 191, 196–97, 199–200, 202, 206, 211, 239–40, 242–43, 245, 249
finis, 227
Finney, Charles Grandison, 90–92
Fischer, David Hackett, 80
fisetin, 66–67
Fossel, Michael, 45, 47–48, 51–52
Franklin, Benjamin, 19, 32
Freud, Sigmund, 35
fruit fly, 9, 44, 47, 50, 59, 62
Fussell, Sam, 247

Gaffney, Walter J., 70
Galen, 29, 31–32, 71
Galileo, 117
gene, 8–9, 22, 43–44, 46, 48–53, 55–56, 59, 68–69, 72, 147, 230, 233–234
Genesis, 22–23, 31–32, 36, 75, 85, 110, 115, 123–25, 130–31, 139–40, 149, 151, 171, 202, 256
genetic, genetics, 8–9, 15, 20, 36, 39, 42, 44–46, 48–49, 52, 54, 65, 68, 72, 76, 110, 225, 228, 231–34, 236, 245, 252
genetic intervention/manipulation, 8–9, 12, 47, 49, 54, 68, 79, 147–48, 225–26, 228, 230, 233–35, 239, 240, 245
genome, 20, 47, 64, 76, 230
geriatrics, 9, 110
geriatrics, geriatric medicine, 110
geriatrics, geriatric society, 63
Geron Corporation, 44, 53
gerontogenes, 19, 48
gerontologiphobia, 233

gerontologist, gerontology, 4, 7–8, 10, 37, 40, 43, 45–48, 55, 58, 110, 141, 235
Gilgamesh, 15, 20–21, 23, 47, 76
glaucoma, 49
gluttony, 169, 173–74, 184, 190–91
gnōsis, 171
Gnosticism, gnostic, 42, 168, 171–74, 180, 183–84, 199
Godwin, William, 32–34
Golgotha, 150
Graham, Sylvester, 92
Greally, John, 65
Great Awakening, 90
Greider, Carol, 51
growth hormone, 48–49, 56, 64
Gruman, Gerald J., 21–27, 29–33, 40, 141
Guarente, Leonard, 48–49, 68, 69
Guevara-Aguirre, Jamie, 48, 56

Haeckel, Ernst, 40
hagiography, 157, 169
Harrison, Peter, 114, 124, 127–29
Hayflick, Leonard, 45, 47, 51–52, 54, 62, 72
Hayflick Limit, 47, 51–52, 62
healthspan, 6, 9, 55, 57
heart disease, 5, 6, 10, 50, 55, 60
Heaven, 24, 27, 31, 33, 41, 80–81, 96, 102–04, 106, 116–17, 122, 126, 131, 135, 161–62, 174, 242, 250
hedonism, 11, 172
Herodicus, 144
Hesiod, 23
Hippocrates, 31
Holy Spirit, 130, 163, 169–70, 184, 193, 196, 199, 200–201, 211, 213–15, 224–25
Horvath, Steve, 8, 64
hsein, 24
Hufeland, Christopher, 30
humanism, 11, 95
hunger, 22, 58, 109, 125, 143, 183, 191, 196, 221, 237–38, 246, 248
Hutchinson-Gilford Progeria Syndrome, 46
Hutter, Jakob, 36

SUBJECT INDEX

Huygens, Constantijn, 229
hygiene, 5–6, 22, 26–33, 37–40, 53, 58, 71–72, 76, 79, 88–89, 91–92, 95, 96, 100–101, 110, 141, 200, 202, 231, 236–38, 255
hypostasis, hypostases, 171, 176, 178

Ignatius of Antioch, 127–28
imago Dei, 158, 208, 213, 256
immortality, 7, 8, 10, 12, 19–20, 23–25, 107, 108–9, 127–28, 131, 149, 159, 162, 209–10, 229, 230
immortality, earthly, scientific, 26–32, 41, 43, 47, 67, 78, 103–106, 113, 116, 124, 132, 139, 234, 253
immortality, replicative, 231
immunology, 36, 108
immunosenescence, 60–61
incarnation, 17, 107, 150–52, 158, 160–65, 185–88, 190, 196, 198, 200, 202–3, 232, 241, 245
Irenaeus of Lyon, Saint, 129, 131
Isaac of Cellia, 183
Isaiah, 94, 105
Itskov, Dmitry, 67

Jerome, Saint, 124, 139
Joad, C. E. M., 151
John of Shmūn, 156
John, Apostle, 84, 131
Joseph of Panephō, 183
Julian, 178
Juvenescence, 9, 68

Kammerer, Paul, 36
Kellogg, Harvey, 92
Kenyon, Cynthia, 48, 69, 234
Kerr, Fergus, 205–06
Kirkland, James L., 63, 66–67
Kirkwood, Tom, 12, 37, 43–45, 46, 51, 54, 73, 231
koinōnia, 179
Körper, 214, 229–30

Lamarckism, 33
Land of Yima, 22
Laron syndrome, 48, 56
Leder, Drew, 229–30

legend, 4, 19–22, 37, 46–47, 76, 79
legend, fountain, 141
legend, hyperborean, 21, 22
Leib, 214, 216, 230
Lent, 189
Lepore, Jill, 71, 78, 95–96
Lewis, Alan E., 251–252
Lewis, C. S., 151
libertinism, 172
Life Biosciences, 68
lifespan, xi, 4–5, 8–11, 16, 22–23, 26, 28, 30, 37, 40, 46–51, 53–56, 59–67, 70–71, 73–74, 85–86, 89, 91–92, 107–108, 117, 128, 132, 134, 139, 149, 201, 207–11, 217, 219–21, 225–28, 234–35, 239, 240, 242–44, 253, 255–57
Logos. See Word, Logos.
longevity, xi–xii, 4–5, 7–11, 15–17, 20–22, 25–28, 30–31, 33–34, 37–39, 44, 46–49, 51, 53–59, 62, 64, 67–69, 72–73, 76, 80, 87–88, 92–95, 97–98, 100–101, 107, 110, 112, 128, 134, 136, 139–41, 144–45, 150, 154, 157–58, 165, 200, 202, 205, 211, 227, 232–33, 235–37, 239–40, 244–45, 255, 257
Longo, Walter, 55–57, 72, 73
Lord's Supper. See Eucharist.
Luther, Martin, 26, 123–24, 129, 150–51
Lysaught, M. Therese, 250

Maillard reaction, 54
Malthus, Thomas, 34
Mani, 172
Manichaeism, 172–74, 183
Mannick, Joan, 60–61
marriage, 173, 186
martyrs, martyrdom, 74, 241, 252
masturbation, 95
materialism, 212–13
materialism, vitalist, 40
Mather, Increase, 78, 81
Max Plank Institute, 50, 233
McCay, Clive, 53

McKenny, Gerald P., 111, 114, 142–43, 148, 152, 153–54, 207, 210–11, 227, 230–32, 244
Medawar, Peter, 42–43, 45
meditation, 24, 33, 52, 67, 96, 121, 125, 173, 200, 241, 244, 256, 258
meditation, on scripture (*meditatio scripturarum*), 245
meditation, on the end of life (*meditatio futurae vitae*), 242
menopause, 44
metaphysics, 116, 120–21
Metchnikoff, Élie, 37–41, 73–74, 100, 101, 107–10, 137
metformin, 61, 64–66, 235
Methuselah, 22, 26, 28, 44, 86, 89, 94, 134, 139, 149, 256
Methuselah Foundation, 9
Methuselahs, new, 13
Mezentius, 138
mice, 8–9, 47–50, 52–54, 56, 58–60, 62–66, 68
Miles, Margaret, 178, 181
millennialism, 130, 131
Miller, Richard, 58
mimetics, caloric restriction (CR), 57–59, 233–39, 245, 253–54, 257
mimetics, exercise, 50
mitochondria, 40, 61
monasticism, monastic, 137, 222–25
monasticism, coenobitic, 224, 246
monkey, 35, 54, 57–58
morbidity, 54, 63
morbidity, compressed, 9–11, 57, 69, 228
mortification, 183–85, 189, 193, 195–96
Moses, 85, 139, 168
Musi, Nicholas, 64
myth, 7, 20, 22–23, 36, 43, 47, 74–77, 110, 190

nanotechnology, 148
natural philosophy, 115, 117, 119, 148
natural selection. *See* evolution.
Nazianzen, Saint Gregory, 192
nematode, 8, 47–48, 59, 234

Neoplatonism, 117, 138, 159, 181–182, 184
New Jerusalem, 201
Newton, Isaac, 26
nicotinamide adenine dinucleotide (NAD), 50
nicotinamide mononucleotide (NMN), 65
Niebuhr, H. Richard, xi, 15
Niebuhr, Reinhold, 227
nous, 159, 176, 182
Nouwen, Henri, 70
Novartis Pharmaceuticals, 60–61
nutritechnology, 55
nutrition, 41–42, 53, 55–58

O'Donovan, Oliver, 15, 144, 232
Olshansky, S. Jay, 5, 7, 10–12, 39, 43–44, 47, 52, 59, 234
Oracle, 67
Origen of Alexandria, Saint, 124, 126, 159, 182, 185
Original Sin. *See* sin, Original.
orthobiosis, 38, 73
Osler, William, 99–102, 109
osteoarthritis, 62
osteonecrosis, 18
osteoporosis, 50, 63
Overall, Christine, 227

Page, Larry, 67
Pantheism, 23–24, 117
Paracelsus, 25–27, 31, 138
Parkinson's disease, 5, 60
Parr, Thomas, 30
Pasteur Institute, 107, 110, 137
patriarchs, 28, 85–86, 100, 128, 139–40, 154, 168, 202
Paul the Hermit, 136, 139
Paul, Apostle, 18, 33, 41, 123, 170, 183–184, 193, 213, 222, 237, 242, 244, 246, 252
Pelagian(ism), 98
penance, 81, 136
Pereira, Javier, 22
Pettersen, Alvyn, 163, 182–184, 186–88, 195–96, 241
phagocytes, 108

phagocytosis, 108
pharmacogenetics, 4, 205, 225–26, 245
physics, 115, 119–21
Pieper, Joseph, 226
piety, 84–85, 87–88, 90, 98, 137, 167, 248
Piore, Adam, 58
Plato, 116, 119, 121, 144, 159, 163, 168, 171, 173–77, 179, 181–83, 199, 212
Pliny the Elder, 22
Plotinus, 171, 176–82, 184
pneuma, 171–72
pneumatics, 222
Ponticus, Evagrius, 243
Porphyry, 178, 180–81, 190, 233
prayer, xii, 24–25, 81, 83, 87–88, 136–37, 157, 164, 166–67, 170, 173, 184, 191, 196, 200, 238, 241, 243, 245–46, 256, 258
predestination, 88, 90, 104
President's Council on Bioethics, 5–6, 9
progeria, 46
ProLon, 56–58
prolongevity, 16, 20, 24–25, 67, 101, 233
Prometheus, 23, 110, 139
providence, special, 83, 87, 111, 122, 133–134, 142
providence, general, 133
psychē, 159, 213
pulmonary fibrosis, 46, 63
PureTech, 61, 68
Puritan, 80–82, 90–91, 112, 115, 129–31, 133–35, 149–50, 255

quinta essentia, 27, 71

Ramsey, Paul, 232–33, 247
Ranchin, François, 36
rapamycin, 59–61, 66–67
rapamycin, rapalogs, 60, 66
rationality, 125–28
rationality, Adam's, 129, 158
rationality, common sense, 90
rationality, practical, 114
rats, 53–54
Reformation, 117–118, 122, 124, 127, 151, 153

Rejuvenate Bio, 9, 68
reprobation, 88, 91–92
res cogitans, 206, 228
res extensa, 206, 228
resTORbio, 61
resurrection, 16, 29, 41, 85, 104, 106–7, 144, 150, 158, 163, 165, 168, 170, 184, 187, 201, 206, 232, 236, 239, 241–42, 250, 252
resveratrol, 62, 65
righteous, righteousness, 84, 87, 90, 93, 95, 125–26, 232, 251
Robert, Leslie, 58
Romanticism, 80, 92, 96–98
Rose, Michael, 44
Rubenson, Samuel, 169–170, 182–85, 187, 192–93, 201
Russell, Norman, 163–64, 248

Salk Institute, 49
salvation, 84, 99, 103, 117, 151, 161, 163, 225, 248
salvation, by works, 29, 87
salvation, gnostic, 171–76, 183
salvation, hygienic, 90–91
salvation, natural, 33, 40–42, 77, 102–7
salvation, scientific, 102–7
Second Great Awakening, 90, 93
secularization, 114
sēma, 174
senescence, 28, 36, 44–46, 50–51, 60–61, 62–64, 66, 72, 231, 233, 243
senolytic, senolytics, 62–67, 235–36
sexual act, 43, 93, 96, 172–74, 189
sexual desire, urge, 33, 41, 93, 174, 177, 196–97, 221
sexual reproduction, 39, 42–43, 59
Shakespeare, 100–101
sickness, 70–71, 86–87, 90, 93, 96, 135, 220, 226, 229–30, 238, 243
sicut deus, 232
Simeon, 87
Simeon Stylites, 136
sin, 32, 90, 92, 95–97, 104–7, 111, 114, 126, 129–130, 133, 135, 140, 146, 149–50, 156, 158–62, 187–88, 196, 201, 204, 207,

SUBJECT INDEX

213, 216–17, 221, 224–25, 242, 244, 256–257
sin, Adam's, 87–88, 126, 128, 131, 146, 149–150, 159, 163, 189, 199, 203, 239, 255
sin, Original, 26, 87, 90, 96, 98, 111, 126, 131, 149
Sinclair, David, 49–50, 56, 61, 64–66, 68–72
sirtuins, 49–50, 65–66, 233
sloth, 17, 95, 139, 216–17, 225–26, 232–33, 235–38, 241, 253, 257
Socrates, 175, 181
sōma, 43, 159, 174, 178, 213
somatic cells. *See* cell, somatic.
Sophocles, 23
Sorge, 219–220, 225–226, 228, 230, 239–41, 243, 252–53, 255, 257
soul, xii, 17–18, 34, 41, 82, 85, 93, 103–4, 107, 111, 116, 125–27, 138, 151–52, 154, 156–57, 159, 164, 166–84, 186–206, 211–22, 225–30, 233, 235–37, 239–45, 247, 250–51, 253–58
South, Robert, 129
starvation, 53, 55, 58, 185, 191, 248
Steinach, Eugen, 34–36
Stephens, Charles Asbury, 39–42, 101–10
Stoicism, 25, 89, 179–180, 199
Stone, Eliab, 81, 93
Stoneking, Carole Bailey, 14, 251
Stone, Eliab, 81, 93
Streptomyces hygroscopicus, 59
stress, 23–24, 50, 59
stress, chronic, 52
stress, oxidative, 54
suffering, 11, 76, 79–80, 93–95, 98, 111–12, 114, 119, 123, 135, 141–43, 148, 172, 214, 227, 237–38, 234, 251, 257–58
suicide, 108

tao, Taoism, 23–25, 28, 144
teleology, ix, 116, 144
telomerase, 47, 51–53
telomere, 44–45, 47–48, 51–53, 66

telos. *See* cause, final.
Temple, Sir William, 30
Teresa of Avila, 248
theology, 7, 15–16, 79–80, 82, 85, 91–93, 110–12, 114–15, 117–18, 121–22, 128, 130–31, 133–34, 137, 148, 151, 205, 220–21, 224, 229, 255–56
theoria, 115
theōsis, 150–51, 161, 163–64, 188, 198, 232
theotokos, 162
therapy, 5, 11, 54, 68
therapy, somatic, 12
therapy, telomere, 47, 51, 53, 66
Thiel, Peter, 67–68
Thomas Aquinas, 127–28, 219
thymus, 8, 64
Tír na nÓg, 21, 43
Tolstoy, Leo, 185
Torrance, T. F., 110, 117, 118, 121, 122, 126, 145
Trägheit, 216–21, 225–26, 228, 230, 235, 241, 243, 253, 255, 257
transhumanism, 10, 67, 74, 107

vaccine, 30, 60
Verhey, Allen, 75, 114, 143, 152
vice, 167, 179–80, 194
Viereck, George Sylvester, 35
Virgil, 138
voluntarism, 32, 76, 86, 88–89, 91, 134
Voronoff, Serge, 35

Walford, Roy, 55, 58, 144, 200
Ware, Kallistos, 183, 185–86, 188, 191, 199
Water of Paradise, 137
Weismann, August, 39–40, 42, 45
Werner's Syndrome, 46
West, Michael, 44
Whitefield, George, 90
Willard, Dallas, 194
Williams, George C., 43
Word, divine, 15, 158, 160–64, 185, 192, 194–95, 198, 207–8, 241, 251, 256
Word, Logos, 162–163, 187, 195

yeast, 49, 233
Yamanaka factor, 49

Yamanaka, Shinya, 49
Yeats, William Butler, 35
Yoder, John Howard, 247

Scripture Index

Genesis
1:26–28	118, 124
1:26–27	149
1:27	186
1:28–30	114, 148, 151, 153
1:31	186
2:17	110, 125, 139, 160
3	87, 88, 117, 125, 145
3:19	130, 139
3:22b	23
3:22–24	149
5–11	117

Exodus
20:12	93

Leviticus
23:27	245n169

Deuteronomy
34:7	168

2 Kings
20	244

2 Chronicles
20:1–4	245n169

Esther
4:16	245n169

Psalms
19:1	122
55:23	97
90	85, 242
90:10	139
102:24	87

Proverbs
25:2	122n48

Ecclesiastes
12:1–7	20
12:1	1

Isaiah
65:20	94

Daniel
1:12–15	245n169
10:3	245n169
12:4	130n134

Joel

2:15	245n169

Wisdom of Solomon

6:21	128

Matthew

4:4	194
6:16	245n169
6:25	39
9:12	71
9:15	245n169
10:38–39	252
16:24	258
17:20	123n51
19:14	121
19:21	165
20:28	213n46
22:10	222
26:29	251
26:41	213

Mark

2:17	71
9:48	234n138
10:14	121

Luke

2:29	88
2:36–37	131n94
5:21	71
12:25	204
17:12–18	244
18:16–17	121
22:19	213n46, 251
22:20	251

John

1	256
1:1	162
4:32	194, 237
4:34	194, 237
6:35	237
6:48	237
6:51	237
10:11	213n46
10:15	213n46
11:21	83

Acts

9:9	245n169
20:24	244n164

Romans

5:12–21	87, 149
6	250
6:3	250
6:13	251

1 Corinthians

2:14	125
6:9–11	225n104
6:13	237
8	252n203
8:1	123n51
9:27	33, 183
9:27a	170
11:20–22	252
11:26	251
15:31	242
15:45–57	149
15:53	41
15:54	252

Galatians

1:4	213n46
2:20	213n46
5:19	126n71

Philippians

1:20–21	244
1:21	18

Colossians

1:15	208
1:21–23	225n104
3:5	184n155, 222
2:23	222

Hebrews

10:10   213n46

2 Peter

1:3–4   150
1:4   161, 165

1 John

3:16   213n46
5:21   121